Time Out

Boston

timeoutboston.com

Time Out Guides Ltd
Universal House
251 Tottenham Court Road
London W1T 7AB
United Kingdom
Tel: +44 (0)20 7813 3000
Fax: +44 (0)20 7813 6001
Email: guides@timeout.com
www.timeout.com

Published by Time Out Guides Ltd, a wholly owned subsidiary of Time Out Group Ltd.
Time Out and the Time Out logo are trademarks of Time Out Group Ltd.

© **Time Out Group Ltd 2011**
Previous editions 1999, 2001, 2004, 2007.

10 9 8 7 6 5 4 3 2 1

This edition first published in Great Britain in 2011 by Ebury Publishing.
A Random House Group Company
20 Vauxhall Bridge Road, London SW1V 2SA

Random House Australia Pty Ltd 20 Alfred Street, Milsons Point, Sydney, New South Wales 2061, Australia

Random House New Zealand Ltd 18 Poland Road, Glenfield, Auckland 10, New Zealand

Random House South Africa (Pty) Ltd Isle of Houghton, Corner Boundary Road & Carse O'Gowrie, Houghton 2198, South Africa

Random House UK Limited Reg. No. 954009

Distributed in the US and Latin America by Publishers Group West (1-510-809-3700)
Distributed in Canada by Publishers Group Canada (1-800-747-8147)

For further distribution details, see www.timeout.com.

ISBN: 978-1-84670-188-7

A CIP catalogue record for this book is available from the British Library.

Printed and bound by Firmengruppe APPL, aprinta druck, Wemding, Germany.

The Random House Group Limited supports The Forest Stewardship Council (FSC), the leading international forest certification organisation. All our titles that are printed on Greenpeace approved FSC certified paper carry the FSC logo. Our paper procurement policy can be found at http://www.rbooks.co.uk/environment.

Time Out carbon-offsets its flights with Trees for Cities (www.treesforcities.org).

Contents

Introduction

Perhaps no other city in the United States offers such a palpable combination of new and old as Boston. Reminders of colonial America – from graveyards to Revolutionary landmarks – stand in the shadows of skyscrapers, just as old-money bankers and college students researching cutting-edge technologies wait together in line at a donut shop. History buffs and art aficionados, sports fans and aspiring writers add to the complexity of a city so often described as 'manageable'.

Boston has seen waves of immigration spanning centuries, and though residents hail from increasingly divergent origins, they tend to become fiercely loyal to New England. The city is also home to a substantial gay and lesbian community, ranking in the top five in the United States. While this diversity can breed localized prejudices and create municipal hurdles, especially in a town where housing prices make it difficult to survive for new residents, it also makes Boston a great place for visitors.

Boston is a city of superlatives: it has the best universities; it's the best walking city; it has the best-preserved examples of Victorian architecture in the US. Perhaps it's the burden of comparison with New York, or the long history of many of the city's institutions, but the pride Bostonians feel for their hometown is evident in everything from their fanaticism for the Red Sox to the caliber of the contemporary and fine arts museums to the glorious sprinkling of parkland dubbed the Emerald Necklace. All of these provide rewarding opportunities for just about any visitor's itinerary.

When coming to the Hub – as residents love to call it – you should be ready to explore. Hidden alleyways in Beacon Hill reveal beautiful red brick row houses and mansions, while specialty grocery stores tucked away on North End side streets provide the raw materials for the perfect picnic. Bustling restaurants in Chinatown and intimate music venues in Cambridge are just waiting to be discovered. And you could spend hours – or days – perusing the shops of Back Bay and idling about the cafés and bistros of the South End. There's no formula for the quintessential trip to Boston; the best advice is to put on some comfortable shoes and pick a couple of destinations – but leave plenty of time to get sidetracked along the way. *Matthew Killorin, Author*

Boston in Brief

IN CONTEXT
The history of Boston is the history of the US. From the first colonial settlements to the key sites and primary players of the Revolutionary War, Boston offers an account of early America in a way no other city can. That history is still very alive today – an urban blend of old and new that is visible not only in the city's Federalist architecture and 19th-century green spaces, but in the personalities of its residents.
▶ *For more, see pp13-40.*

SIGHTS
They don't call Boston 'America's Walking City' for nothing. While manageable in size, Boston has enough diverse neighborhoods and historical points of interest, museums and parks to offer something for everyone. From quaint original shops housed in Victorian buildings to the yard of the most prestigious university in America, Boston is meant to be absorbed on foot.
▶ *For more, see pp41-93.*

CONSUME
Lately, the Hub has come into its own when it comes to food – and Bostonians also know a thing or two about drink. Innovative chefs are infusing the dining scene with a globe-spanning menu drawing on regional ingredients but preserving the seafood classics. And from old Irish haunts and craft breweries to modern hotel bars focusing on fresh cocktail creativity, Boston has a great mix of pubs and bars.
▶ *For more, see pp95-176.*

ARTS & ENTERTAINMENT
Rock clubs, museums, arthouse cinemas and temples dedicated to the 'big four' sports teams make Boston a rich cultural destination. You can find a decent rock band playing any night of the week, or watch a military re-enactment or a burlesque performance of *The Nutcracker*. And that's not to forget the home of the Red Sox: many consider Fenway Park the most important landmark in town.
▶ *For more, see pp177-230.*

ESCAPES & EXCURSIONS
From colonial outposts to scenic coastal landscapes, there are plenty of rewarding sights and activities outside of Boston. You can go whale-watching, sunbathe on a Cape Cod beach or picnic in a sculpture park. And it's a short drive to places where you can relive the American War of Independence, from the taverns where battles were planned to the battlefields where the first shots were fired.
▶ *For more, see pp231-248.*

Boston in 48 Hours

Day 1 On the Trail of History (and Sea Life)

9AM Boston is so full of spots rich with historical significance that, even if you're not a Revolutionary War buff, you may as well embrace the opportunity to see the cradle of American independence. Start by downloading a map of the two-mile **Freedom Trail** (*see p49* **Trail Blazers**) and setting off at your own pace. If you don't want to spend all day looking at Boston Tea Party relics, focus on the four major sites in the North End.

NOON Like most people who visit the **North End** (*see p68*), you can just follow your nose to find a great place for lunch in the city's Italian neighborhood. Try the **Daily Catch** (*see p128*) for casual seafood Italian style or pick out some cured meats, olives, cheese and bread from one of the *salumerias* around Hanover and Salem Streets, then head over to the **Rose Kennedy Greenway** (*see p76*) for an impromptu picnic.

1PM If you prefer your seafood still living, walk along the waterfront to the **New England Aquarium** (*see p75*), a modernist building housing a giant cylindrical fish tank with everything from sea turtles to sharks swimming inside. Alternatively, you can hop aboard one of their whale-watching charters.

4PM If your Freedom Trail excursion hasn't taken you there already, visit the 19th-century **Quincy Market** (*see p48*) and colonial **Faneuil Hall** (*see p47*), where you can shop for souvenirs or watch the street performers.

6PM Walk back up along the harbor to the Congress Street Bridge, where you can see the original location of the **Boston Tea Party** (*see p78*). Carrying on, you'll reach local celebrity chef Barbara Lynch's new restaurant and bar complex. Grab a spot on the waiting list at the casual Italian luncheonette **Sportello** (*see p132*); afterwards (or while you're waiting), head down to **Drink** (*see p149*), the subterranean home to Boston's best cocktail mixologists.

NAVIGATING THE CITY

Boston's compact city centre and many path-lined green spaces make travel on foot the preferred mode of transportation. Though the weather in New England can be fickle, grab your map anyway and cut through the cobblestone streets to absorb the city's charm and heritage.

Keep in mind, though, that the appellation 'America's Walking City' is often thought of more as a deterrent to driving than an invitation to walk. For drivers, the streets are labyrinthine, traffic a nightmare and parking exorbitantly priced or non-existent. So why bother?

Taxis are plentiful and reasonably priced, there are tour buses and harbor cruises, and the 'T' – the subway system run by the MBTA – is more regular, safe and reliable than locals may lead you to believe. Buy a CharlieCard loaded with a LinkPass for $15 to get unlimited travel on all local bus, subway and inner-harbor ferry trips for a week. Just remember: the

Day 2 The fine art of shopping – and sport

7AM Take an early walk along the red brick and cobblestone pavements past Colonial-era homes in **Beacon Hill** (*see p52* **Walk**) as the city wakes up, then join the locals for breakfast at the **Paramount** (*see p119*). Part greasy spoon, part trendy hotspot, it's cheap and the portions will set you up for the day.

10AM Start walking off breakfast by crossing through the **Public Garden** (*see p43*), where you can take a swan boat ride in warmer weather. Beginning at Arlington Street, window-shop along **Newbury Street** (*see p61*); the posh boutiques give way to more affordable shops as you carry along. Or head south to the area around **Copley Square** (*see p59*), where you'll find malls at **Copley Place** (*see p158*) and the **Prudential Center** (*see p60*). The latter's observation deck gives a stunning panorama of the city.

1PM By now, you'll probably be ravenous. At **Jasper White's Summer Shack** (*see p190*), local celebrity chef White puts his own spin on an old-fashioned New England clambake.

2.30PM It's time for a fine-art fix. Head past the **Christian Science Plaza** (*see p62*) and admire its immense reflecting pool or stop to see the unique **Mapparium** (*see p63* **Profile**), en route to the **Museum of Fine Arts** (*see p65*) with its new Art of the Americas wing. Or stroll a little further to the bijou **Isabella Stewart Gardner Museum** (*see p64*).

5.30PM If all that culture has made you thirsty, cut through the **Back Bay Fens** (*see p62*) to sample America's pastime at the **Baseball Tavern** (*see p145*) or craft brews at **Boston Beer Works** (*see p146*). If there's a baseball game on, they may be packed. If they are – or if you prefer cocktails – drop into the fashionable **Foundation Lounge** (*see p146*) instead.

7PM For dinner, head to nearby **Eastern Standard** (*see p120*), an American take on the brasserie. Or hop in a taxi to sample one of the South End's trendy bistros (*see p124*).

subway shuts down at 12.30am. For more on transport and guided tours, *see p250*.

PACKAGE DEALS

If you have the stamina, a **Go Boston Card** (www.gobostoncard.com) can be the best value for your sightseeing money. Starting at $50 for one day ($165 for a week – though there's often an online discount) the card offers free entry to more than 70 attractions, from harbor cruises to museums, in Boston and beyond the city. Just remember that the clock starts ticking once you hit your first attraction; to get your money's worth, you'll need a full itinerary. The company's **Explorer Pass** may be a better alternative: you can visit three attractions in a 30-day period for $45. The competing **Boston CityPass** (www.citypass.com/boston) offers five top attractions for $46 and is valid for nine days. With any of these, it's worth comparing what the individual attractions cost – it may work out cheaper.

Boston in Profile

DOWNTOWN

From bustling **Quincy Market** to the serene **Public Garden**, Downtown is the centerpiece of most visitors' itineraries, and many historical walks start and end here. You can visit centuries-old graveyards – the final resting places of many revolutionaries – just as easily as finding souvenir T-shirts and trinkets. Along its fringes, Chinatown and the Theater District provide plenty of options for an evening's entertainment.
► *For more, see pp43-50.*

BEACON HILL & THE WEST END

Beacon Hill has historically been home to some of Boston's most prominent families, and things haven't changed much since the founding of the city. Well-preserved red brick streets yield scenic alleyways filled with antique dealers and fantastic restaurants. The **West End** is home to a number of new hotels – handy for the Museum of Science and TD Garden arena.
► *For more, see pp51-57.*

BACK BAY & THE SOUTH END

Less than 200 years ago, **Back Bay** was a swampland destined to be filled in and eventually built up to include some of the city's most important addresses, poshest shops and finest art museums. The **South End**'s adoption by the city's gay community heralded its rise as one of Boston's happening neighborhoods, filling up with trendy bistros and chic boutiques.
► *For more, see pp58-67.*

THE NORTH END & CHARLESTOWN

Boston's Italian neighborhood, the **North End** teems with great restaurants, bakeries and cafés. The brick alleyways, old men chatting over espresso and colorful parks provide plenty of visual distraction for an afternoon stroll. Across the river in **Charlestown**, the city's historic naval heritage is on display.
► *For more, see pp68-74.*

THE WATERFRONT

Some of the newest development in Boston is in the emerging neighborhoods along the Waterfront, beyond the swathe of Boston's new linear park, the **Rose Kennedy Greenway**. Restaurants and bars are sprouting up around the **Fort Point District**, while the Institute of Contemporary Art is the big draw in the adjacent **Seaport District**.
► *For more, see pp75-79.*

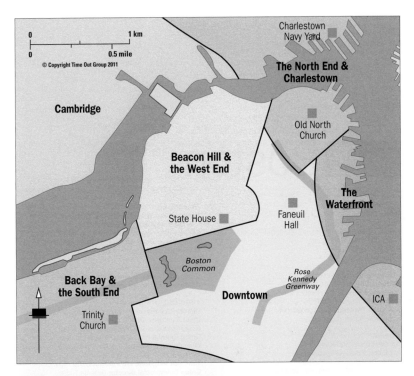

CAMBRIDGE

Harvard University has come to be synonymous with Cambridge, however a trip across the Charles River also means discovering some of the best cafés and rock clubs in Greater Boston. So though visitors may come for the iconic campus, they stay for a meal, a drink or even just a stroll through the colorful streets.
▶ *For more, see pp80-87.*

OTHER NEIGHBORHOODS

The shops and restaurants of **Somerville**'s Davis Square and **Jamaica Plain**'s Centre Street reflect the young, green-minded residents living in these areas, while **Roxbury** and **Dorchester** offer the best examples of the cuisine, art and history of Boston's African-American and Caribbean cultures.
▶ *For more, see pp88-93.*

Time Out Boston

Editorial
Editor John Shandy Watson
Author Matthew Killorin
Listings Editors Jessie Rogers, Time Out Boston;
  Adwoa Gyimah-Brempong
Proofreader John Pym
Indexer Lucy Nathan

Managing Director Peter Fiennes
Editorial Director Ruth Jarvis
Business Manager Dan Allen
Editorial Manager Holly Pick
Assistant Management Accountant
  Ija Krasnikova

Design
Art Director Scott Moore
Art Editor Pinelope Kourmouzoglou
Senior Designer Kei Ishimaru
Group Commercial Designer Jodi Sher

Picture Desk
Picture Editor Jael Marschner
Acting Deputy Picture Editor Liz Leahy
Picture Desk Assistant/Researcher Ben Rowe

Advertising
New Business & Commercial Director Mark Phillips
International Advertising Manager Kasimir Berger
International Sales Executive Charlie Sokol
Advertising Sales (Boston) Rachel Almquist,
  Time Out Boston

Marketing
Sales & Marketing Director, North America
  & Latin America Lisa Levinson
Senior Publishing Brand Manager Luthfa Begum
Group Commercial Art Director Anthony Huggins
Marketing Co-ordinator Alana Benton

Production
Group Production Manager Brendan McKeown
Production Controller Katie Mulhern

Time Out Group
Director & Founder Tony Elliott
Chief Executive Officer David King
Group Financial Director Paul Rakkar
Group General Manager/Director Nichola Coulthard
Time Out Communications Ltd MD David Pepper
Time Out International Ltd MD Cathy Runciman
Time Out Magazine Ltd Publisher/MD Mark Elliott
Group Commercial Director Graeme Tottle
Group IT Director Simon Chappell

The Editor would like to thank Androulla Harris and all contributors to previous editions of *Time Out Boston*, whose work forms the basis for parts of this book.

Maps john@jsgraphics.co.uk.

Cover Photography by Photolibrary.com
Photography by Elan Fleisher, except pages 9 (bottom), 70, 131, 133, 134, 135, 153, 155, 162, 166, 168, 172, 214, 215 Sara Skolnick; page 14 Time & Life Pictures/Getty Images; page 18 Getty Images; pages 21, 65 (right) © Museum of Fine Arts, Boston; page 25 Cecil Stoughton/The White House via AmericanPhotoArchive.com; page 63 Mark Thayer, The Mary Baker Eddy Library; page 77 Sakini; page 87 Rob Greig; page 121 Justin Ide; page 178 Susan Cole Kelley, page 181 Linda Skurchak, page 182 Paul Robicheau; page 194 Roxana Perdue; page 196 Marshall/Out of the Blue Gallery; page 201 Lynette Molnar; page 203 Chuck Anzalone; page 225 Michael Lutch; page 228 Caleb Cole; page 241 (top) Patrick O'Connor; page 241 (bottom) Douglas Mason.

The following images were supplied by the featured establishments/artists: pages 4, 31, 37, 179, 193, 211, 229, 230.

About the Guide

GETTING AROUND

The back of the book contains street maps of Boston, as well as overview maps of the city and its surroundings. The maps start on page 269; on them are marked the locations of hotels (❶), restaurants and cafés (❶), and pubs and bars (❶). The majority of businesses listed in this guide are located in the areas we've mapped; the grid-square references in the listings refer to these maps.

THE ESSENTIALS

For practical information, including visas, disabled access, emergency numbers, lost property, useful websites and local transport, please see the Directory. It begins on page 249.

THE LISTINGS

Addresses, phone numbers, websites, transport information, hours and prices are all included in our listings, as are selected other facilities. All were checked and correct at press time. However, business owners can alter their arrangements at any time, and fluctuating economic conditions can cause prices to change rapidly.

The very best venues in the city, the must-sees and must-dos in every category, have been marked with a red star (★). In the Sights chapters, we've also marked venues with free admission with a `FREE` symbol.

PHONE NUMBERS

The area codes for Boston are 617 and 857. To call within Boston you need to dial the full ten-digit number as listed in this guide (dropping the 1 unless you are calling from outside the area or from a cell phone).

From outside the US, dial your country's international access code (00 from the UK) or a plus symbol, followed by the number as listed in this guide; here, the initial '1' serves as the US country code. So, to reach the ICA, dial +1-617 478 3100. For more on phones, including information on calling abroad from the US and details of local mobile-phone access, see p258.

FEEDBACK

We welcome feedback on this guide, both on the venues we've included and on any other locations that you'd like to see featured in future editions. Please email us at guides@timeout.com.

Time Out Guides

Founded in 1968, Time Out has grown from humble beginnings into the leading resource for anyone wanting to know what's happening in the world's greatest cities. Alongside our influential weeklies in London, New York and Chicago, we publish more than 20 magazines in cities as varied as Beijing and Beirut; a range of travel books, with the City Guides now joined by the newer Shortlist series; and an information-packed website. Time Out Guides remains proudly independent, still owned by Tony Elliott four decades after he launched *Time Out London*.

Written by local experts and illustrated with original photography, our books too retain their independence. No business has been featured because it has advertised, and all restaurants and bars are visited and reviewed anonymously.

ABOUT THE TEAM

Matthew Killorin has covered the city of Boston for more than five years, writing and editing for the *Boston Herald* online and most recently serving as City Editor/Bureau Chief for *Boston Metro*.

Born and raised in Boston, Jessie Rogers is the editor of www.timeoutboston.com, the where-to-go, what-to-do site for locals, covering arts, entertainment, restaurants, shopping and more.

World Class

Perfect places to stay, eat and explore.

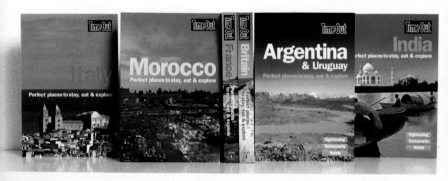

In Context

Ray and Maria Stata Center. *See p40.*

History

From Puritan settlement to
superpower – it all started here.

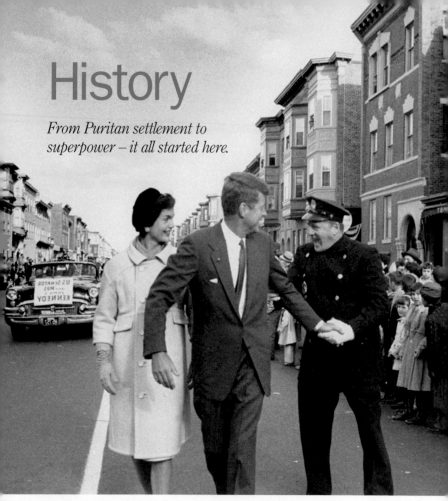

Visitors from across the USA and beyond come to Boston to see the sites that begot America: Faneuil Hall, the 'Cradle of Liberty' turned gift shop; the hallowed Revolutionary battleground of Charlestown; and the Old State House, where the Declaration of Independence was first read to the public in 1776.

A city with a strong political thrust, Boston has fostered influential leaders since America's inception, from John Adams to John F Kennedy. It has been central in scientific development and technological innovation, from Alexander Graham Bell's telephone to the world's first computer, which was built at the Massachusetts Institute of Technology (MIT). As a dominant force in academia (Harvard was the first seat of higher education in the country), the area is known for cultivating future visionaries, rulers and thinkers.

PILGRIMS' PROGRESS

Although the Boston area wasn't 'settled' until the arrival of the Puritans in the 17th century, the region had human occupants as far back as 7,500 BC. The area was heavily populated with Native Americans by 1497, when John Cabot's explorations in search of the Northwest Passage to the Orient led him to claim Massachusetts for King Henry VII of England. Just over a quarter of a century later, in 1524, Giovanni Verrazano claimed the same land for Francis I of France, thus setting up more than 200 years of squabbling over what had become known as the New World. Word of this 'paradise' reached John Brewster, leader of a strict religious sect known as the Puritans. Facing persecution in England, he began an effort to establish a Puritan colony in America. And so it was that the *Mayflower*, filled with 102 passengers, set sail in September 1620 bound for 'some place about the Hudson River.' It landed nowhere near the Hudson, actually, anchoring instead, after 65 days at sea, at the tip of Cape Cod, near what is now Provincetown. Finding the area too wild for their new town, the Puritans moved on, crossing the bay and ultimately establishing their colony on a protected stretch of sandy beach close to several cornfields maintained by local tribes. They called it Plymouth.

Utopia it surely wasn't. Winters were brutal here, and the Pilgrims had little understanding of the land, the kinds of crops that would grow here and what native vegetation was edible. They also brought diseases with them that wrought devastation on their population and on the Native American tribes. Nearly half of the Pilgrims died of pneumonia and smallpox that first winter. But in the spring local tribes taught them how to plant corn, dig clams and fish for cod. By harvest time, the settlers were sufficiently established to host a three-day feast – celebrated today as Thanksgiving.

Once things were running more smoothly on the new shores, word spread back to England about the Puritans' settlement. Within the next decade, 1,000 more settlers had arrived. They established Salem, on the north shore of Massachusetts Bay. These new settlers would ultimately form the foundation for what is now Boston. Choosing as their leader John Winthrop, many of them migrated south from Salem to the area now known as Charlestown. This didn't last, however, as the lack of fresh water forced them to relocate to a neighboring peninsula, known to the natives as Shawmut. Winthrop's settlers bought the narrow 440-acre peninsula from a hermit bachelor and renamed it Tremontaine after its three surrounding hills. They soon changed their minds and renamed it again. This time they called it Boston, after the Lincolnshire town from which many of them had originally come. As the capital of the Massachusetts Bay Colony, it quickly became the centre of activity.

STRUGGLING SETTLERS

By 1636, there were some 12,000 colonists, primarily Puritans, spread between the townships of Plymouth, Salem and Boston, with new settlements springing up almost monthly. By 1640, the population of Boston alone was 1,200. In fact, the lack of qualified ministers to keep up with the growing population led Puritan elders to establish America's first training college, which they later named after a young minister, John Harvard, who died and left the college his library. Colonists found Massachusetts curiously easy to settle and rather empty of the anticipated hostile Indians. The fact was, epidemics of smallpox, pneumonia and influenza brought over by early explorers and settlers had decimated the once-robust native population.

Relations with the remaining tribes rapidly deteriorated. The fundamental Puritan notion of a righteous life leading to the accumulation of wealth clashed with native beliefs that it was impossible to own the land. Unlike the French to the north, who converted native populations to Catholicism, the Puritans took a rather more aggressive tack. They attempted to rid Christianity of the heathen devil by burning out the Indians' settlements and appropriating their land. The Algonquin nation, under the leadership of Chief Metacomet (known to colonists as King Philip), retaliated in

1675 by raiding several outlying English settlements. But it was all in vain. Metacomet was betrayed by one of his own warriors the following year and gruesomely executed.

The Indians were not the sole targets of Puritan intolerance. Quakers and Baptists arriving in the colonies were sometimes prevented from leaving their ships; those who practiced their faith publicly were hanged for heresy. Such religious paranoia ultimately led to the witch trials of Charlestown (1648), Boston (1665) and – most infamously – Salem (1692), where 100 colonists were imprisoned and 19 were hanged in a mass hysteria that became known as the Salem witch trials.

'THE SACRED COD'

By 1700, Boston had grown into the third-largest port of the burgeoning British Empire. Some of the Puritans grew extremely wealthy, thanks primarily to the export of dried cod to the Caribbean and the Mediterranean. (To this day, a carved pine cod – known as 'the Sacred Cod' – hangs above the entrance to the House of Representatives in the State House, pointing towards the party in power.) Some got very rich in a notorious triangular shipping trade where sugar cane was harvested by slaves in the West Indies and then shipped to Boston to be distilled into rum. The Puritans shipped most of the rum to West Africa where it was traded for more slaves who were, in turn, delivered to the Caribbean sugar plantations.

One of the by-products of the city's rum production was molasses (Boston was the largest American producer of the stuff until the early 20th century). Another, more important, consequence was the introduction of slavery to American soil. By 1705, there were more than 400 black slaves – and a small number of free blacks – living in Boston.

At about the same time, England was mired in a serious financial crisis. The crown had incurred enormous expenses during its lengthy (and inconclusive) wars with France. As some of the battles were fought in New England, and as the colonists were virtually voiceless in Parliament, it established the Revenue Act of 1764, which placed heavy duties on silk, sugar and wine from the West Indies. The colonists were irate and began the first of a series of boycotts of the imports involved.

DEATH AND TAXES

Ignoring their protest, Parliament enacted another set of taxes a year later. The Stamp Act required a heavy duty to be paid on all commercial and legal documents printed in the colonies, including newspapers. This was viewed by the colonists as an attempt to remove what little voice they had through the freedom of the press. Again they fumed. Again they felt no sympathy from England. Again they boycotted, but this time, with more force. They branded their protest with the tagline 'No taxation without representation' on the grounds that they had no voice in government in England. They were heard, and the Stamp Act was hastily repealed a year later, but the British still attempted to keep their rebellious cousins in line. They next imposed the Townshend Acts of 1767 – a litany of levies on imported lead, glass, paint, paper and tea.

Britain's attempts to pull political rank enraged the colonists, especially those in Boston. Governmental meeting houses such as Faneuil Hall, the Old South Meeting House and the Old State House became hotbeds for revolutionary plotting. Rebels such as Samuel Adams, Daniel Webster, Paul Revere and James Otis gathered secretly to discuss the benefits of splintering off from the British Empire. Prodded by growing public outcry, civil unrest grew so clamorous it carried across the Atlantic and back to the monarch. To quiet the rumblings, George III reluctantly sent troops overseas in 1768, but military occupation in the colonies created more problems than it solved.

Lieutenant General Thomas Gage, commander-in-chief of British forces in the colonies, was faced with a near-impossible situation. Perhaps understandably, he hated Boston and its inhabitants. 'I wish this cursed place was burned,' he wrote in 1770. 'America is a mere bully, from one end to the other, and the Bostonians by far the greatest bullies.'

IN CONTEXT

Profile Samuel Adams

The brewer who came to tea.

Walk into any Boston pub and you'll see him behind the bar: **Samuel Adams**, the patron saint of Boston beer. Nearly three centuries ago, Adams played a key role in the Revolution and was a signatory of the Declaration of Independence. But since Samuel Adams Boston Lager came on the scene in 1984, Adams has become better known for his place in the brewing industry. So who was the man who gave his name to the brew?

Born in 1722, Adams grew up in Quincy (*see p93*). He entered Harvard and after receiving a Master's degree, inherited his father's brewery in 1748. Meanwhile, he became increasingly active in politics, sermonizing at town hall meetings and obtaining city offices such as Clerk of the Market and Tax Collector.

But in 1764, the brewery closed due to fiscal mismanagement, and Adams began to devote himself to politics full time. He regularly decried Britain in public forums and penned insurgent manifestos denouncing the Crown's control. When Britain imposed the Revenue Act in 1764 (a tariff on imported sugar, rum, and certain wines), Adams drafted the colonies' angry response, a deed that led him to being elected to the Massachusetts General Court. Then in 1770, after British troops fired into a crowd of rioting civilians, killing five, Adams dubbed the event the 'Boston

Massacre', painting the casualties as martyrs.

Adams was also a major force behind the Boston Tea Party. In 1773, the British repealed the Townshend Acts, a tax on imported lead, glass, paint, paper and tea. But as an insult to the tea-loving colonists, Parliament continued to tax tea under the new Tea Act and brought in an Asian company selling tea cheaply, hoping to put colonial tea merchants out of business. On 16 December, Adams and a group of protesters ran aboard a major tea shipment and threw 342 crates of tea into Boston Harbor. This act sparked the American Revolutionary War.

When the first Continental Congress was held the following year, Adams was the Massachusetts representative. From 1789 to 1794 he was governor of Massachusetts. He died in 1803 aged 81, and today rests in the Granary Burying Ground (*see p44*).

AN INSPIRED BREW For visits to the modern-day incarnation of the **Samuel Adams Brewery**, *see p91.*

But it was the British who looked like bullies when, on 5 March 1770, a group of unarmed anti-royalists sparred with English soldiers in front of the Old State House. The Redcoats were antagonized – the gathered assemblage was heckling and throwing things at them. No matter, the Brits came out looking like the bad guys, because during the fray the British troops opened fire. Five colonists were fatally shot, including Crispus Attucks, an African-American slave-turned-martyr who is considered the first casualty of the American Revolution. The colonists were outraged over the attack, and impassioned insurgent Sam Adams dubbed the incident the 'Boston Massacre'. The shooting became a rallying cry for those who supported plans for a revolution.

TEA PARTY POLITICS

Word of the incident quickly spread throughout the colonies, causing King George III to fear (and rightly so) that this bloodshed might be the match that would light the powder keg. To avert such an outcome, the king quickly abolished the Townshend Acts – all except for its provisions on tea, which would continue to be taxed under the Tea Act of 1773. This was a little jab from the king to his subjects as George III knew it was the most popular beverage in America. Instead of easing the mood of revolt, the move added fuel to the flames and the colonists continued to plot and to boycott.

With the situation growing heated – and with the East India Company (Britain's chief exporter of tea) teetering on the brink of bankruptcy, Parliament attempted to rescue the Asian tea-sellers by exempting them from paying taxes. So while the colonists had to shell out import taxes on tea, the East India Company didn't have to pay tariffs, so it could undercut the prices of local tea merchants and flood the colonial markets. No such luck: every American port slammed shut to English tea ships – except Boston. The state's British governor, Thomas Hutchinson, stuck to the party line, ignoring the incensed citizens, and insisting that all ships could dock in Boston Harbor until the other ports accepted the tea.

The rebels hit back. On the night of 16 December 1773, a group of 60 men, calling themselves the 'Sons of Liberty', disguised themselves as Mohawk Indians (then seen as a symbol of freedom in the New World), stormed the blockaded ships and dumped 342 chests of tea into the harbor. This defiant act, known as the Boston Tea Party, electrified the colonies.

In September the following year, the first Continental Congress for Independence convened in Philadelphia. Massachusetts sent prominent delegates such as John Adams, John Hancock and Sam Adams to represent it and to help in the writing of the country's manifestos. At the same time, throughout the colonies, local militia began training for a fight.

THE BATTLE FOR INDEPENDENCE

The first shots of the revolution were fired in Lexington, Massachusetts, on 19 April 1775. British garrisons lodged in Boston heard about an arms store located in the nearby township of Concord. When the Redcoats left Boston to seize the Concord stockpiles on the night of 18 April, rebels Paul Revere and William Dawes set out on horseback to warn the local militia that the British troops were on their way. Paul Revere's ride became one of the most famous acts of the War of Independence – immortalized in Henry Wadsworth Longfellow's 1861 poem (*see p20* **Artisans of the Revolution**). The message was sent, the British marched forth and early the next morning the world's David and Goliath came to blows. The first shot of the battle, called by the rebels the 'shot heard round the world', rang out on Lexington Green where around 70 Minutemen – an elite force of local militia members – crouched waiting to ambush 700 Redcoats. The king's men quickly smothered the skirmish, killing eight rebels, and the war was underway. By then, King George was no longer reluctant to go to war. He is said to have told his counselors: 'I am glad that blows will decide it.'

IN CONTEXT

It was to be a lengthy, bitter fight, marked by heroism on the part of the outgunned, outmanned rebels, and rugged determination on the part of the British. The Americans were led by military leaders who knew only too well that their troops were fighting more with heart than skill. The colonists were plagued by a shortage of ammunition and weaponry. In the first full-scale battle of the revolution, two months after the shots at Lexington, General Israel Putnam is said to have ordered his American troops, 'Don't one of you fire until you see the whites of their eyes.' Part of the reason Putnam gave the order was to prevent the troops from wasting scarce ammunition.

That famous command came during the gory battle of Charlestown, which started on 17 June 1775, when the British attacked a group of colonists who had fortified themselves at the top of Breed's Hill. (This battle was later mistakenly identified

Artisans of the Revolution

Famous as a 'Son of Liberty', Paul Revere was also a silversmith.

*Listen, my children, and you shall hear
Of the midnight ride of Paul Revere...*

On 18 April 1775, Boston silversmith **Paul Revere** rode to Lexington, Massachusetts, to warn patriot leaders Samuel Adams and John Hancock, and households en route, of an imminent British attack. The likely targets: the arrest of Adams and Hancock or the seizure of munitions in nearby Concord. Nearly a century later, distressed by the slavery crisis and impending civil war, America's pre-eminent poet Henry Wadsworth Longfellow published 'Paul Revere's Ride' in the *Atlantic Monthly* in 1861. Revere became the personification of the Revolutionary ideals of liberty and unity that Americans had seemingly forgotten. He also became a national folk hero.

Born in Boston's North End in 1735, Revere learned the silversmith's trade from his father, a French Huguenot immigrant who anglicized his name from Apollos Rivoire to Paul Revere. The silversmith was both a laborer who made shoe buckles for artisans and an artist who designed elegant rococo-style tea sets for merchants. Paul Revere moved between the worlds of artisans and gentlemen. In 1760, he became a member of St Andrew's Lodge of Freemasons. Freemasonry, originating in the medieval

stoneworkers' guilds, reinforced ties to the artisans who dominated his lodge.

During the Stamp Act Crisis in 1765, Revere became a 'Son of Liberty'. He and his fellow rebels believed the Stamp Act was unconstitutional because colonists weren't represented in Parliament. Revere and brother artisans and Freemasons such as Gibbons Bouve, a housewright, Adam Colson, a leather-dresser, and Thomas Crafts Jr, a painter and japanner, would be critical actors in Boston's Revolutionary resistance.

Revere's position and skills allowed him to play many roles: trusted courier, engraver of inflammatory political cartoons, and protester. As an engraver, he often adapted ideas from British publications. Using vivid images and dramatic language, he depicted colonial resistance to the Stamp Act, the Townshend Act, and the presence of British troops in Boston that resulted in the Boston Massacre. In *A View of the Year 1765*, his review of the Stamp Act crisis, Boston and the united colonies protect Lady Liberty from a dragon wearing the Scottish bonnet of Lord Bute, often considered the instigator of Britain's unpopular revenue measures.

On 16 December 1773, Boston patriots took direct action against the Tea Act by destroying 342 chests of as the battle of Bunker Hill, which was, in fact, the next mound over.) Having learned from their mistakes earlier in the war, the unflinching colonists waged a tactically masterful fight: British casualties were more than double that of the Minutemen – more than 1,000 Redcoats were killed compared to 440 rebels. Unfortunately for the Americans, the fight was so heated that they exhausted their ammunition supplies. The Redcoats won that battle, but reports of the bravery of the American troops helped to inspire the spirit of insurrection throughout the colonies.

A NEW NATION

Meanwhile, in Philadelphia, the Second Continental Congress was establishing a new government. Using as an excuse the fact that King George III had not replied

tea. Revere and several members of St Andrew's Lodge were participants in the Boston Tea Party. The next day, he began his career as messenger of the Revolution by carrying the news to New York.

His legendary April 1775 ride to Lexington was the culmination of months of spying on British troops by Revere and other rebels. On 15 April, they observed preparations for an expedition. The following day, patriot leader Dr Joseph Warren ordered Revere to Lexington to alert Samuel Adams and John Hancock. Word was forwarded to Concord to hide the munitions.

Concerned that the British Army would arrest messengers leaving Boston for Lexington, Revere arranged the hanging of lantern signals from the Old North Church Steeple ('One,

if by land, and two, if by sea'). The signals were not to Revere, as Longfellow wrote, but to patriots across the Charles River in Charlestown who sent a back-up messenger.

On 18 April, when the British marched, Dr Warren ordered Revere and William Dawes to Lexington by different routes. After delivering their news to Adams and Hancock, they decided to continue to Concord. Halfway there, they and Dr Samuel Prescott, a third rider encountered on the road, were intercepted by British soldiers. Dawes and Prescott escaped. Held at gunpoint, Revere brazenly lied that he had alarmed the countryside and there would be 500 colonials at Lexington (in reality, around 70). They released him in Lexington, where he witnessed the first shots of the Revolutionary War.

When he died in Boston on 10 May 1818, aged 83, his contemporaries celebrated Revere's Revolutionary service as well as his accomplishments after the war: Grand Master of the Massachusetts Grand Lodge of Freemasons and founder of America's first successful copper-rolling mill. As an obituary writer observed: 'His country found him one of her most zealous and active of her sons.'
● *Jayne E Triber, author of* A True Republican: The Life of Paul Revere *(University of Massachusetts Press).*

IN CONTEXT

'The valor of the rebels in Boston ultimately resulted in the penning of the Declaration of Independence.'

to a petition for redress of grievances sent by the First Continental Congress, the second Congress gradually took on the responsibilities of a national government. In June 1775, the group established a continental army and currency. By the end of July of that year it had also created a post office for the 'United Colonies'.

In August 1775, England issued another proclamation, this one declaring (a bit belatedly) that the colonies were 'engaged in open and avowed rebellion'. Later that year, Parliament passed the American Prohibitory Act, which declared that all American vessels and cargoes were the property of the Crown.

It all finally reached a crescendo in Philadelphia on 7 June 1776. On that date, the Congress heard Richard Henry Lee of Virginia read a resolution that began: 'Resolved: That these United Colonies are, and of right ought to be, free and independent states, that they are absolved from all allegiance to the British Crown, and that all political connection between them and the state of Great Britain is, and ought to be, totally dissolved.'

The valor (or treachery, depending on your perspective) of the rebels in Boston ultimately resulted in the penning of the Declaration of Independence. The document, still considered one of the world's great governmental manifestos, has been taught in political science classes ever since. Its introductory paragraph is blunt and unapologetic and tells the story of how America viewed its strength in comparison to England's: 'When in the course of human events, it becomes necessary for one people to dissolve the political bands which have connected them with another… a decent respect to the opinions of mankind requires that they should declare the causes which impel them to the separation. We hold these Truths to be self-evident, that all men are created equal; that they are endowed by their Creator with certain unalienable rights, that among these are Life, Liberty and the pursuit of Happiness.'

On 4 July 1776, in Philadelphia, John Hancock of Boston signed his name to the document with a flourish. His is the largest signature by far – he is said to have written large enough that George III could read it without spectacles. Even today in America a 'John Hancock' is an expression for someone's signature.

INDUSTRY AND IMMIGRATION

At that point, of course, the war was still far from over: the fight would last for another five years. But while much of it was fought in New England, there were no more battles in Boston. When America finally did achieve its independence in 1781, Massachusetts was one of the original 13 states constituting the fledgling United States of America.

As might be expected, when it was all over, the war relegated the US to England's doghouse and trade was cut off. The loss of the English market caused Boston's status as a major port to suffer. The US economy continued to sputter until Boston embraced whaling and Far East trade; eventually, when the demand for fishing clippers grew, Boston's shipyards – especially Nantucket, New Bedford and Salem – grew into some of the largest in the world. Other Boston inventions that helped the economy were Eli Whitney's cotton gin, Charles Goodyear's vulcanized rubber, Elias Howe's sewing machine and Alexander Graham Bell's telephone.

As the city's wealth and power grew, so did its immigrant population. In the 19th century, shiploads of immigrants were turning up on its shores looking for a better life.

IN CONTEXT

The Irish arrived in 1845, escaping the potato famine; they were followed by tens of thousands of European immigrants seeking financial opportunity and religious freedom. By 1860, it was estimated that more than 60 per cent of Boston's population had been born elsewhere in the world.

Boston's skinny peninsula could hardly accommodate such an enormous influx of new citizens, so resourceful denizens looked to the fetid swamps of Back Bay. To make the bogs livable, two of Boston's three hills were leveled and several feet were shaved off the top of Beacon Hill. But the real work of filling in the marshy Back Bay didn't begin until the mid 1850s, when 3,500 loads of gravel a day were railed in and dumped into the muck. It took 40 years to complete the project – the largest engineering feat of its day. The result was 450 more acres of land, which doubled the city's size.

THE ATHENS OF AMERICA

'Their hotels are bad. Their pumpkin pies are delicious. Their poetry is not so good,' Edgar Allan Poe once wrote about Bostonians. And Poe was indeed correct. For a while, Boston's poetry wasn't so good. But it wasn't just the city's stanzas that lacked finesse; it was the entire notion of crafted aesthetics that escaped the community's inhabitants. Why had the arts been so neglected? In essence, Massachusetts housed many Puritans, who didn't consider the arts to be a godly practice. As for the other early colonists, many were preoccupied with gaining independence. 'I must study politics and war so that my sons may have liberty to study mathematics and philosophy in order to give their children a right to study painting, poetry, music, architecture,' wrote future US President John Adams to his wife Abigail in 1780.

IN CONTEXT

Name That Town

Boston by any other name.

Visitors may be puzzled by Boston's many monikers, but they all have logical origins. The Native Americans called it **Shawmut**, or 'unclaimed land'. When John Winthrop and his fellow Puritans defied the Indians by claiming it after all, they promptly renamed it **Tremontaine** (three mountains) after the three local hills that dominated the place. In no time, though, the homesick settlers had re-dubbed their village **Boston** after the Lincolnshire village from which most of them had come. A torrent of other names soon followed, all of which have stuck around for centuries.

Take, for instance, **Beantown**. In the 18th century, Boston was fairly awash with molasses, a by-product of rum production. Because of its cheap cost and plenitude, the syrup was frequently used by colonial housewives to sweeten ordinary foods. A favorite food of the day was beans that had been stewed in the sugary stuff for hours. Travelers dubbed the town Beantown, after this ubiquitous dish.

In the early 1800s, Boston became America's undisputed capital of culture. It's little wonder, then, that the city became known as the **Athens of America**.

Later in the 19th century, the writer Oliver Wendell Holmes gave the city the title that Bostonians love the most. In his popular 1858 essay *The Autocrat of the Breakfast Table*, he described Boston's State House as the 'hub of the Solar System'. In no time, Bostonians had extended the concept, calling their city the hub of the universe – and **the Hub** remains Boston's most widely used nickname today.

Luckily, economic prosperity in the 19th century was to beget a cultural awakening. When the well-heeled 'First Families of Boston', dubbed 'Brahmins' by writer Oliver Wendell Holmes, began to travel abroad, they realized just how unenlightened their city was. It didn't take the wealthy population long to rectify the situation. In the short span between the 1840s and 1880s, Boston gained a music hall, a magnificent public library, a museum of natural history, a museum of fine arts and a symphony orchestra. These new arts showcases, coupled with the talent they attracted, earned the city the sobriquet 'the Athens of America'.

Athens was also the birthplace of the Olympics, and Boston was one of the first American cities to take sports seriously. In 1897, the first Boston Marathon ran from the nearby town of Hopkinton to Back Bay. Soon afterwards, the newly invented game of baseball swung into the city. Boston's first professional team was called the Somersets, but the name only lasted one season. In 1903, Boston's new team, the Pilgrims, hosted the Pittsburgh Pirates at the World Series; by the time Fenway Park opened in 1912, the Pilgrims were renamed the Red Sox. Six years later the Red Sox won Boston's fifth World Series in 17 years – it would be the last time Boston would win a championship until 2004.

BREAKING THE CHAINS

Talk about being misunderstood: when Bostonian Wendell Phillips joined the Massachusetts Anti-Slavery Society, his Yankee family wanted to send him to a sanitarium. Fortunately, he withstood their persecution and eventually became one of abolitionism's most revered voices.

Phillips was swayed to anti-slavery when, at the age of 24, he witnessed a lynch mob drag reputed abolitionist William Lloyd Garrison half-naked through the streets. But such savage bigotry was less common in Massachusetts than anywhere else in the country.

In 1800, Boston was home to the oldest and largest population of free black people in America (a full five per cent of its then total population of 25,000), and the black community already had its heroes: Crispus Attucks was a martyr of the Boston Massacre, Peter Salem a hero of Bunker Hill. Although the black population hadn't yet been granted suffrage, they were allowed to earn wages as servants, street cleaners, shipbuilders, blacksmiths and barbers. They could also meet freely, worship as they pleased and educate themselves. The first African Meeting House in America was built on Beacon Hill in 1806, and the first black school, Abiel Smith, in 1834.

Hence, it wasn't surprising that, as tensions over slavery mounted between the North and South, Boston became the centre of the abolition movement. The New England Anti-Slavery Society was founded in 1832, and prominent blacks such as Frederick Douglass, William Nell and Maria Miller Stuart began condemning slavery publicly with the support of wealthy white people. Lewis and Harriet Hayden's house at 66 Phillips Street became a station on the Underground Railroad (a network of abolitionists whose members smuggled slaves from the South to freedom in the North). When the Civil War broke out, the first free black regiment of the Union Army – the 54th Regiment of Massachusetts – was organized on Beacon Hill, trained in Jamaica Plain and sent to battle in the Carolinas. All of those soldiers died in war. Their story was largely forgotten for the better part of a century. It gained attention only in recent years – it is commemorated by a sculpture in the Boston Common and was explored in the 1989 film *Glory*.

IRISH INFLUENCE

It might be hard to believe in these days of pubs shipped over brick by brick from Dublin, but Boston didn't always ooze unconditional love for the Irish. When the potato famine of the mid 19th century first sent over 100,000 people from Ireland to Boston, the reported life expectancy of an Irish immigrant living in Boston was

IN CONTEXT

Curse of the Clan

The tumultuous history of the Kennedys.

The closest thing America has had to a 'royal family', the Kennedys came from humble beginnings. Patrick J Kennedy was an immigrant from southern Ireland who set up Boston's only Irish-owned bank. His son Joseph (born 1888) attended Harvard, married Rose, daughter of popular Boston mayor John 'Honey Fitz' Fitzgerald, and made millions in boat building, the stock market, the movie industry and Prohibition-era bootlegging, later serving as ambassador to Great Britain. But after resigning from the position and losing his first-born in World War II, Joseph devoted himself to the political futures of sons John, Robert and Edward.

John had all the makings of a president. A Harvard graduate, he became a decorated war hero, a Pulitzer Prize winner and a three-term US Senator. In 1960, he beat Richard Nixon to become the 35th US president. He was a popular leader whose picture-perfect children and beautiful young wife led the media to nickname his government 'Camelot'. But everyone knows what happened next. The Kennedy clan's reversal of fortune began in 1963, when John was shot dead during a Dallas parade. Five years later, younger brother Robert, attorney general during JFK's presidency, fell to an assassin in his own bid for America's highest office. Youngest son Edward 'Ted' Kennedy also had White House aspirations, but a car accident in Martha's Vineyard in 1969, which killed his passenger (a young female campaign worker), damaged his

reputation, and haunted his presidential bid in 1980.

The bad luck didn't stop there. In 1991, Ted's nephew William was indicted for rape, but later acquitted. In 1984, Robert's third son David, who'd battled drug addiction since the age of 13, died from a cocaine overdose at the age of 28. in 1997, his fourth son Michael slammed into a tree while playing football on skis and died. And in 1999, dashing media darling John F Kennedy Jr was in a plane crash and died with his wife Carolyn Bessette Kennedy.

After close to a century, the family's influence appears to be dwindling. Ted, who was the second most senior member of the Senate, died of brain cancer in August 2009. His son Patrick is a US Representative from Rhode Island, but has announced that he does not intend running for re-election. Joseph's granddaughter Maria, however, is married to the Governor of California, Arnold Schwarzenegger. Joseph must be rolling in his grave: Arnie is a Republican.

IN CONTEXT

> *'Holding true to his crooked ways, Curley spent much of his last term as mayor in a federal penitentiary, charged with mail fraud.'*

14 years. In this traditionally Brahmin city, blatant discrimination was common. Job postings often bore the clause 'No Irish Need Apply'.

After generations of political struggle, though, prejudices began to subside as the city's Irish political machine fought its way into power. The election of the first Irish-Catholic mayor of Boston, Hugh O'Brien, started to chip away at racial biases – so much so, that eventually Irish leaders couldn't lose a race.

'Boss' James Michael Curley was perhaps the finest example of this relative invincibility. Curley was nicknamed the Purple Shamrock – and as the moniker suggests, he was a colorful character. Curley served as congressman, governor and mayor, and over a checkered 40-year career he bought votes, got re-elected to the position of alderman while in the clink and allegedly acquired the mayoral office after threatening to expose the incumbent, John 'Honey Fitz' Fitzgerald (JFK's maternal grandfather; *see p25* **Curse of the clan**), for having a mistress. And holding true to his crooked ways, Curley spent much of his fourth and last term as mayor in a federal penitentiary, charged with mail fraud.

20TH-CENTURY BLUES
By the late 1940s, Boston had lost its major port status to the West Coast and its manufacturing to the South. What's more, it became the only major US city in the post-World War II baby boom to see a decline in population (plummeting from 800,000 to 560,000). Both the city's middle and upper classes migrated to the suburbs, and its infrastructure went with them. With downtown crime on the rise and student demonstrations blocking the streets, tourism suffered, and the city entered an economic crisis. By the mid 1960s, Boston had officially become one of the worst places to live in America.

Panicked by Boston's decline, city officials attempted to hit the brakes. Under Mayor John Hynes and the newly established Boston Redevelopment Authority (BRA), they began a 'clean up' of the city's problem areas. The 1960s saw the completion of three massive building projects with controversial results. The Prudential Tower rose out of Back Bay's abandoned Boston & Maine railyards. The West End, Boston's only ethnically mixed neighborhood, was razed to make way for a modern apartment complex called Charles River Park. Seedy Scollay Square, home to Boston's then few gay bars and jazz joints, was leveled to make way for the new Government Center. They called it urban renewal. But, basically, much of the city's character was systematically erased in the name of progress.

However inept, though, these first efforts at regeneration did have their positive side. Organizations such as the Beacon Hill Historical Society were established to protect other neighborhoods from suffering the fate of the West End. Public outcry caused subsequent developers to be attentive to architectural and historical significance. Today, the city maintains many of its most important historical buildings despite the ravages of the planners and developers of the 1960s and '70s.

RACE RIOTS
In the midst of financial chaos, Boston then entered an emotional and moral morass. The city's 1970s race riots are notorious to this day. Possibly the most striking image from those days was shot on City Hall Plaza, when a white student tried to spear a

IN CONTEXT

black passer-by with a flagpole bearing an American flag. Presages of such bigotry began in 1974, when federal judge Arthur Garrity Jr ordered the city to desegregate its public school system. Before the ruling, proximity had dictated school assignment, so poor children (often racial minorities) went to school with other poor children – and received a poor education. The court saw this as a violation of civil rights and forced an end to the practice. It ordered a racial integration policy designed to give each school a ratio of black to white children that reflected Boston's overall population.

That September, under heavy police security, the Board of Education began busing white students into black neighborhoods and black students into white neighborhoods. Huge riots flared up. Crowds of angry white parents and children filled the streets. Rocks were thrown at the black students. Bedlam ensued – most particularly in Irish South Boston and largely black Roxbury. While the violence exposed Boston's ugly underbelly to the nation, critics of busing – future Mayor of Boston Ray Flynn, President Gerald Ford, state politician William Bulger – argued fervently that this fight concerned other issues than racism. Many believed Boston's ethnic ghettos had evolved into close-knit neighborhoods – both blacks and whites feared losing their hard-earned sense of community. The court disagreed.

Finally, in 1999, precisely 25 years after the racial integration program began, the Boston School Committee voted to stop using racial quotas for school placement, saying it would never achieve its goal of making the schools truly equal. The ending was anti-climactic, nobody emerged a winner. And in the eyes of many, Boston will always be associated with those scenes of racial intolerance and hatred.

CHANGING SCENES

In the 1970s, city officials courted the emerging high-tech industry aggressively and, by the mid 1980s, Boston had reinvented itself once again. 'The Massachusetts Miracle' – as the media touted Boston's resuscitated economy – was due largely to the leadership of mayors such as Kevin White and Ray Flynn. Within the last couple of decades, Boston has become a popular location for the headquarters of national corporations. Around the turn of the century Boston also underwent a major facelift. The city's Central Artery, a six-lane elevated freeway jutting through downtown, was one of the most congested highways in the country as well as a blight on the cityscape. And so in the early '80s, local planners outlined the Big Dig, one of the largest, most technically complicated engineering projects ever undertaken in the United States. Construction began in 1991, giving birth to the Ted Williams Tunnel, a long underground stretch dedicated to one of Boston's most revered athletes; a new Boston landmark, the Leonard P Zakim Bunker Hill Bridge, the widest cable-stayed suspension bridge in the world; and a linear park, the Rose Kennedy Greenway (*see p30* **Going Green**). Now neighborhoods once cut off by the expressway are being reintegrated and waterfront development continues – the jewel in the crown is the Institute of Contemporary Arts (*see p79*), the city's first new art museum in almost a century.

Boston continues to make national history and produce influential political figures. Governor Michael Dukakis ran for President in 1988, but was defeated by George Bush Sr; in November 2004, Beacon Hill resident and Massachusetts Senator John Kerry lost by a famously narrow margin to his son. Yet another Massachusetts man, former governor Mitt Romney, a devout Mormon, was a Republican candidate in the 2008 primaries. The Boston area has also been at the centre of the fight for gay and lesbian rights. In May 2004, after a ruling by the Massachusetts Supreme Judicial Court, America's first legally recognized same-sex wedding took place in Cambridge. A proposed constitutional amendment to overturn the court's ruling was defeated by state Legislature in summer 2007, preserving the sanctity of same-sex marriage in Massachusetts. (For more on Boston's gay and lesbian past, *see p201* **A Colorful History**.)

IN CONTEXT

Boston Today

Moving forward – while harking back.

TEXT: MATTHEW KILLORIN

Cities are often described as living, breathing entities with a pulse and a personality. But while Boston is known as the intellectual hub of the United States, perhaps no other American city is as much of a head case.

Historical reverence, coupled with modern ambition, makes Boston a destination rich in character – and also in contradictions. From colonial artifacts to institutions of higher learning, Boston offers an unparalleled view of the past and the future, but this vista is qualified by financial concerns over maintenance, as state and city budgets shrivel and crucial social and municipal programs are severed.

Trail-blazing ideas – in spheres as disparate as equality and technology – first found their footing in Boston, but the city is also known as a bastion of old-school politics and provincial prejudice. Bostonians love to toss blame and take credit: the city's 21 neighborhoods are seemingly united only in their love for the Red Sox.

However, as with most human beings, it is its complexities that have made Boston the nuanced, interesting and thoroughly modern city it is today.

Matthew Killorin is a freelance writer living in Boston. He is also a graduate student in the Writing and Publishing program at Emerson College.

THE CHANGING FACE OF BOSTON

Although Boston has a rich history of immigration and diversity, it has long been divided along racial lines. However, the demographics are shifting in many neighborhoods as the high cost of living has redefined this historical demarcation. While the recent economic meltdown has cooled off housing prices, Boston is still one of the most expensive cities in the US. Rising prices in the 2000s forced many out of their homes and spurred a tidal wave of gentrification that threatened the cultural makeup of the city; at the same time, however, a chunk of the white population left the city altogether, and areas such as Roslindale and East Boston have seen their non-white populations skyrocket by approximately 40 per cent in the last 20 years.

Physically, the biggest change to the Boston landscape is the completion of the Big Dig, the largest, and perhaps most problematic, single public works project in US history. The Central Artery/Tunnel project, as it is formally known, replaced the unseemly elevated highway that had split the city in two with a series of underground tunnels. Even before completion, the project's price tag had ballooned from an estimated $2.6 billion to over $14.6 billion. However late, over-budget and marred by problems the Big Dig was, it did provide Boston with a much-needed facelift, knitting together the city, creating quicker airport access, adding new bridges and parks – notably the Rose Kennedy Greenway (*see p30* **Going Green**) – and opening the door for a new wave of development.

POLITICS AS USUAL

'Sports, politics and revenge' is the tripartite adage famously describing Boston's favorite pastimes. Politics (and elements of the other two) reaches a pinnacle in Beacon Hill, home to the State House. This is where the US first strived towards universal health-care access after the Massachusetts reform bill of 2006 was enacted into law. It's also near where the Supreme Court of Massachusetts ruled it unconstitutional to permit only heterosexual couples to marry in the landmark trial of Goodridge vs Department of Public Health. However, corruption, greed and nepotism are also traditions under the State House's great gold dome, and the antics of lawmakers over the last few years have confirmed that old habits die hard.

Soon after taking office in 2004, former Speaker of the House of Representatives Salvatore F DiMasi sponsored the universal health-care bill and worked tirelessly with business and public leaders to make the dream of health insurance for every man, woman and child in Massachusetts a reality. It seemed like a great victory: shortly after the bill was signed into law in April 2006, the Bay State reduced the number of uninsured adults by nearly half. But it was far from an unqualified success: the influx of patients resulted in long waiting lists and put a strain on primary health-care facilities. Some feared it would force the state into bankruptcy. However, the model became a forerunner to Barack Obama's controversial universal health insurance legislation, which finally became law in 2010 after a venomous and divisive national debate.

DiMasi's political career, however, came to an ignominious end in January 2009; after being indicted on fraud, he resigned, then faced further charges of extortion linked to a sweetheart deal involving state technology contracts with private firms. DiMasi, who has pleaded not guilty to all charges, is the third consecutive Speaker of the House to step down amid charges of corruption or legal violation. He isn't the only recent politician to join the long history of alleged shady dealings in Massachusetts. Former state Senator Dianne Wilkerson pleaded guilty in June 2010 to accepting bribes from undercover FBI operatives totaling $23,500 and was allegedly caught on camera cramming a portion of the cash under her shirt and into her bra at a restaurant in the Beacon Hill area.

ALL ALONG THE WATERFRONT

After the late 1990s dot-com boom retracted and the financial services industry spiraled into freefall as a result of the Great Recession, Boston's top-heavy real estate bubble finally burst. Those who hadn't already been pushed out of the market faced foreclosure or were too weary or broke to reinvest. Development slowed to a trickle and 'For Sale' signs lingered on front lawns. But while many other cities were proclaiming that the end was nigh, a spark of life has been seen in the Waterfront area of Boston.

Spurred by the clean-up of Boston Harbor, the completion of a massive new convention centre in 2004 and the relocation of the ICA (*see p79*) in 2006, Mayor Thomas Menino has been pushing to create an 'Innovation District' here, which will be part of the largest development project in Boston's history: a $3 billion new neighborhood called Seaport Square. The live/work community for information technology, clean technology and bio-technology start-ups – converting 23 acres

Going Green

An urban freeway becomes a string of parks.

On 12 April 2005, a group of politicians and civic leaders gathered at an ugly stretch of land and tossed some ceremonial earth on to the ground. 'We're now ready to fully reclaim this area for the people of Boston,' declared Matthew Amorello, who was then the state's Turnpike Authority chairman. Significant progress had already been made: the ground was once home to the Central Artery, the elevated expressway that was torn down in the biggest highway project in US history, the massively over-budget Big Dig.

Opened in 1959, the six-lane highway had sliced through the heart of Boston. To clear its path, more than 1,000 buildings were flattened and 20,000 residents displaced; for decades the streams of traffic disconnected some neighborhoods from the rest of the city. So when the time finally came to tear it down, the city was eager to use the land for the civic good. Although some people argued it should be filled with new buildings, the final plan called for green space – a place where Bostonians could gather and relax, and a welcoming bridge between once-divided areas. The 27-acre ribbon of parks was to be called the **Rose Kennedy Greenway** (www.rosekennedygreenway.org).

Massachusetts' long-time senator, the late Ted Kennedy (1932-2009), was present at that groundbreaking ceremony, beaming. The project had been named after his mother, who grew up in the nearby North End, and the parks were slated for completion in the autumn of 2006, a year and a half away. However, when that date rolled around, nothing was ready – like many major construction projects in Boston, it had got tied up in debate and financial problems. Millions of dollars once dedicated to the project were spent on other things, and the city squabbled over what features the parks should contain.

Today the Greenway offers a much-appreciated respite for tourists and residents in the heart of Boston. Throughout the summer, children can be seen playing in the water park dividing the North End and Quincy Market. Farmers markets and public gardens are sparks of interest for those wishing to walk from one end of Boston to the other. At night, the *Light Blades* sculpture makes for an appealing landmark, a good place to meet up with friends before hitting the nightclubs in the area. The city also introduced free Wi-Fi in the park during the summer of 2010. However, while there are a few art installations along the mile-long stretch that makes up the Greenway, large chunks are still bereft of the originally envisioned ambitious projects.

The crux of the problem is funding, especially during a time of fiscal austerity. Donations from the private sector are down. The state has cut funds for maintenance and development by more than a quarter for 2011. The city is bickering with business owners along the Greenway, stating that they of parking lots into 20 city blocks – would also build on the momentum of the condos, restaurants and nightlife venues that have sprouted up over the last decade and further integrate what had been artists' lofts and factory buildings with the rest of the city.

This isn't the first time Menino has pushed hard to develop the area, and, despite political and financial backing, many obstacles remain. While the iconic department store Louis has moved in and Fort Point has become a bustling appendage of the Barbara Lynch empire, with two new restaurants and an upscale bar, the district needs street-level retail and other businesses, and not just of the sort that caters to the luxury condo set at Fan Pier, if it is to succeed.

Rose Kennedy Greenway.

should cough up more cash because their land is worth three times more as a result of its construction, while others, such as Mayor Thomas Menino, are leery that developing a consortium for business interests will give the private sector undue influence over the park's future. The salaries at the nonprofit Rose Kennedy Greenway Conservancy, which runs the ribbon of green spaces, are being called exorbitant in the media. Meanwhile, the head of the conservancy, dismayed by levels of state support, believes that outside revenue streams are the only way to sustain it.

While the Greenway is one in a long line of Boston's endangered species due to the turn the economy has taken over the past few years, ostensibly it's still a beautiful park and a welcome feature to any urban landscape. The lofty plans conceived before the economic downswing – museums replete with floating glass walls, parks richly reflective of the cultural community that surrounds them and enough art installations to potentially impede foot traffic – have yet to materialize. But visitors and residents without such high expectations can still find a pleasant spot for a picnic, some farm-fresh produce or an enjoyable way to cool down on a hot day – ignoring the patches of burnt grass here and there.

PUMPING THE ECONOMY'S TIRES

At the same time, Boston is looking at other innovative and sustainable ways of rebounding from the recession and retaining its best and brightest residents. One attempt to change for the better can be seen in the grassroots movement to improve Boston's reputation as the worst cycling city in America. The municipal authorities have created designated lanes for bikes on some of the city's most congested streets, named a 'Bike Czar' and are even considering a bike-share program. Small gains like these certainly have a positive impact on quality of life in Boston, but they don't solve the larger questions as the city and state legislatures try to get back in the black.

Which programs and initiatives will be cut or scaled back due to lack of funds? What further compromises need to be made to account for the fiscal shortfall? And where will new money come from – taxes or other sources? Some feel the pressure from these issues may cause overzealous development to occur, leading to another slump like the one after the dot-com boom. Others believe the new industries eyed by lawmakers and developers will introduce new revenue streams and stave off the looming taxes and cuts.

One particularly contentious solution being considered invokes Lady Luck. All three branches of government have signaled a desire to introduce casinos into the Bay State. Despite failing to reach an 11th-hour compromise on the subject at the end of the most recent legislative session, the gambling debate is far from going away. As Beacon Hill lawmakers argue the merits of introducing resort-style casinos and slot machines into this once puritanical outpost, which only legalized tattoo parlors and the sale of alcohol on Sundays within the last decade, many question the long-term repercussions versus the short-term gains of such a plan. Gambling in Boston and Massachusetts could breed addiction and siphon money from local businesses, forcing layoffs from other economic sectors – from retail to restaurants – that outnumber the new jobs introduced at the casinos; or it could be the solution to the revenue problems that are forcing cuts and scale-backs.

With the short-term boost from federal stimulus dollars fading, Boston must consider these questions as it figures out how to sustain progress while maintaining its cultural and economic makeup. Can a city, so important to the historical fabric of its country and so instrumental to its future, learn from yesterday's blunders? And is it smart enough to sidestep the pitfalls of tomorrow?

IN CONTEXT

The T.

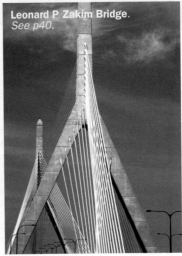

Leonard P Zakim Bridge.
See p40.

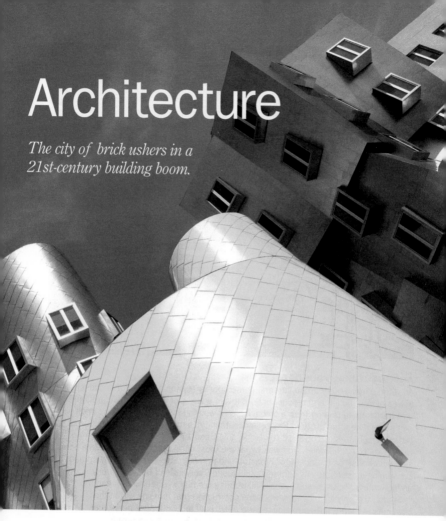

Architecture

*The city of brick ushers in a
21st-century building boom.*

Although Boston's cityscape is commonly associated
with red-brick rowhouses and the glistening State House
dome, its collection of provocative buildings is growing.
New high rises in the Financial District, and development
on the South Boston waterfront and the broad swathe of
land cleared when the old elevated highway came down
as part of the Big Dig are challenging the city's image of
itself. Whether these projects express Boston's continuing
vitality or display a willingness to deface historic treasures
in the name of 'progress' is an issue that is hotly debated.
(Pick up a copy of Jane Holtz Kay's *Lost Boston* for an
exasperating tour through the places that have fallen
to the wrecking ball.)

Flour & Grain Exchange Building.
See p38.

Harrison Gray Otis House.

ARCHITECTURAL FOUNDATIONS

As with so many other urban centers, contemporary Boston grew out of successive waves of destruction and reconstruction. It was a string of massive conflagrations that transformed Boston from a colonial city of wooden structures to one of brick and stone. Fires had plagued Boston since its initial settlement – the city suffered devastating blazes in 1653, 1676, 1679, 1711 and 1761. It was the Great Fire of November 1872, however, that was by far the most catastrophic. It started in a hoop skirt warehouse on the corner of Kingston and Summer Streets and rapidly spread, consuming most of the city center. Consequently, very little of Boston's early architecture still exists, and virtually all of Boston's hub was rebuilt in masonry.

In fact, the only 17th-century wooden construction that remains within the city limits is the **Paul Revere House** (*see p69*), built in 1680. After periods as a flophouse, souvenir shop, cigar factory and grocery store, it was saved from destruction by one of Revere's descendants and restored to its original two-story frame. Today, the house is a National Historic Landmark and museum.

Next to Revere's house is the **Pierce/Hichborn House** (*see p69*), a three-story brick structure built in 1711 for glazier Moses Pierce and later owned by Revere's cousin, shipbuilder Nathaniel Hichborn. Although the Pierce/Hichborn House was constructed only 30 years after its neighbor, there is a stark contrast between the two: picturesque Tudor gives way to orderly Georgian; clapboard to brick; diamond to gridded panes; a cramped winding staircase to one that is perfectly straight. The Pierce/Hichborn House was restored in the 1950s, and four of its rooms are open for tours.

The **Old State House** (*see p48*) is another remnant of Boston's Georgian past. Designed and constructed in 1713, this small building served as the colonial governor's offices – hence the lion and unicorn ornamentation on the façade. It was then used as a public meeting place until the Revolution, when

'The State House occupies a commanding spot on top of Beacon Hill, and its gleaming gold dome can be seen for miles.'

it became the headquarters of the British Army. Topped with a richly ornamented steeple, the three-story brick building, dwarfed by the surrounding downtown skyscrapers, now houses the Bostonian Society's museum – and, oddly, the entrance to the State Street T station.

BULFINCH'S BLUEPRINT

Though he was never formally trained, Charles Bulfinch (1763-1844) was America's first notable architect. Born into a wealthy Boston family, Bulfinch traveled extensively in England and Europe, and developed an affinity for the Greek Revival style of architecture that was fashionable at the time. Inspired, he returned to America and began designing his friends' houses for free. This led to public commissions such as the new **State House** (*see p51)* and the remodeling of **Faneuil Hall** (*see p48).*

Bulfinch is best known for the development of the Federal style – an Americanization of the Georgian Greek Revival style – and his crowning glory outside Massachusetts is the US Capitol building in Washington, DC. Typical of this genre is the austere, three-story brick **Harrison Gray Otis House** (*see p56)*, one of three houses Bulfinch designed for a close friend. Completed in 1796, the flat-faced building, now the Otis House Museum, is a masterpiece of symmetry and proportion. Rooms contain false doors to maintain balance, intricately carved fireplaces and garish color schemes – all typical of the period. Though the brick building nearly crumbled in the early 1900s, it was rescued in 1916 by the Society for the Preservation of New England Antiquities and painstakingly restored to its original state. Most of the rooms are now open to the public.

When the Otis family had settled into their home, there was little in the way of neighbors to block the view from its windows to the new State House – also designed by Bulfinch. Considered one of his best works, the State House occupies a commanding spot on top of Beacon Hill, and its gleaming gold dome can be seen for miles. Completed in 1798, it has a red-brick façade supporting white Corinthian columns flanked by tall arched windows. In 1895, the yellow-brick Brigham Annex was added to the rear, while white marble wings were added in 1917. The dome was originally clad in white wood shingles, but in 1802 Paul Revere recovered the curvature with copper sheeting and painted it grey. In 1872, as the nation's wealth grew, a coating of 23-carat gold leaf was applied. Except when it was painted grey during World War II for fear of Axis bombers, the dome has retained its glistening place on the Boston skyline.

Today, Beacon Hill is considerably more populated. Its tightly packed rowhouses reveal the extent of Bulfinch's impact, which stretched beyond his own designs. His influence can be spotted in the brick and granite detailing, green wooden doors topped with fanlights, wrought-iron grillwork and gracious bay windows that form an undulating wall along the neighborhood's narrow sloping streets. The preponderance of black shutters you see today are a 19th-century afterthought.

NEW GROUND

As the city expanded, the surrounding tidal marsh was filled in, the soft ground shored up, and new neighborhoods were built. First to spring up was the bourgeois South End, with its red brick and bay windows. Its architecture reflects Beacon Hill's Federal traditions, and many of the side streets are modeled after Bulfinch's beloved English squares. (Two wonderfully preserved examples which

IN CONTEXT

A Fine Addition to the MFA

Foster & Partners add a bold new wing to the Museum of Fine Arts.

After five years and $345 million, the Art of the Americas collection and the Ruth and Carl J Shapiro Courtyard of the **Museum of Fine Arts** (*see p65*) officially opened in 2010. The design, by famed London-based architects Foster & Partners, increases the MFA's total square footage by nearly 30 per cent. Known for their landmark glass and steel buildings and for artfully synthesizing pre-existing structures with new designs, Foster & Partners won the coveted Stirling Prize in 1998 for the American Air Museum (part of the Imperial War Museum Duxford) and again in 2004 for 30 St Mary Axe (aka the Gherkin) in the City of London.

The **Art of the Americas wing** comprises a central unit built of glass, and two glass and granite pavilions decorating the north and south faces. The stone comes from the same Deer Island quarry in Maine used by the museum's original architect, Guy Lowell (1870-1927), to create the original 1909 Beaux-Arts structure; the glass has a glaze developed and crafted by Seele in Germany specifically for the museum. Gustafson Guthrie Nichol's design for the landscaping of the MFA's campus incorporates more than 50 trees and 1,000 holly bushes, inspired by Frederick Law Olmsted's Back Bay Fens (*see p62*).

The new wing showcases what is being called the most extensive array of art from the Americas housed in one museum, and includes works from North, Central and South America that date back as far as 3,000 years ago. The wing is on four floors, with displays moving chronologically upwards. With the new wing's 121,307-square-feet to play with, the MFA aims to show commonalities in contemporaneous but geographically distant art on an unprecedented scale. Bold design elements, state-of-the-art lighting and other technological elements will enhance the viewing experience.

The wing includes 53 galleries, nine period rooms, four Behind the Scenes galleries and a 150-seat auditorium for concerts and lectures. The aesthetic elements range from imported wallpaper dating back hundreds of years in the period rooms to richly painted walls and pristine floors to counteract the natural light coming in through the windows. The columns of sunlight, for instance, flanking Thomas Sully's 1819 masterpiece, *The Passage of the Delaware* and Paul Revere's gaze of satisfaction as he contemplates his *Sons of Liberty* bowl

are worth a visit are Union Park and Rutland Square.) The South End townhouses, however, are noticeably larger than those on Beacon Hill – their high ceilings, soaring windows and mansard roofs speak of a 19th-century preoccupation with slenderness and verticality.

Back Bay, on the other hand, takes most of its architectural cues from France's Second Empire. A fetid swamp along the Charles River in the 1850s, the Back Bay was painstakingly filled with stone and soil in the 1860s to create new land for an expanding population. This is where much of Boston's upper class moved when Beacon Hill became crowded with immigrant families. The area favors Parisian avenues over English squares, and the house façades tend towards marble and sandstone rather than red brick.

Both public and private buildings are studded with embellishments. The **Ames-Webster House** (306 Dartmouth Street), for example, sports an elaborate porte cochère that kept the ladies dry as they descended from their carriages.

– which is encased in glass just steps from the famous John Singleton Copley painting from 1768 – are no accidents.

Perhaps the architectural high point, the **Shapiro Courtyard** – which soars 63 feet high – is 12,184-square-feet of open space encased by 504 panes of glass and thousands of feet of steel framing. The floating tiers of a central staircase rise from the Finnish granite floor and are framed by French limestone. The courtyard is a café and a meeting place and a venue for special events. It serves as a grand entranceway to the new wing and helps visitors get a sense of bearing while navigating the immense building. Design and architectural critics are touting the courtyard as the newest addition to Boston's growing list of must-sees.

In addition to the new construction, the MFA took the opportunity to refurbished the original structure. The Fenway entrance has been opened back up and the Huntington entrance has been renovated, recreating Lowell's original vision of a strong north/south axis. The completed renovations will be the first addition to the MFA since IM Pei's West Wing was introduced in 1981.

The **Burrage Mansion** (314 Commonwealth Avenue) is a neo-Gothic confection modeled on the Vanderbilt mansion in Newport, itself based on the Château de Chenonceau in the Loire Valley.

Throughout the Victorian era, the city embraced ostentation. The favored styles of the time were Italian Renaissance, neo-Gothic and neo-Romanesque. An area then known as Art Square was one of the first parcels of land set aside in Back Bay purely to showcase the city's fledgling cultural institutions. Later renamed Copley Square, it housed imposing examples of institutional architecture, such as the Museum of Fine Arts (later relocated to make way for the Fairmont Copley Plaza), the Museum of Natural History (recently vacated by the posh Louis Boston department store) and the magnificent **Boston Public Library** (*see p60*).

The library design by Charles McKim (1847-1909) is usually attributed to the Italian Renaissance style, though he claimed its ornate stone façade was equally inspired by a library in Paris, a temple in Rimini and the Marshall Fields department

'Richardson's Trinity Church is often cited as one of the most influential works of architecture in America.'

store in Chicago. The library was not an easy project, only completed after ten years of construction in 1895. The lobby doors were designed by Daniel Chester French (the artist who also created the statue of Abraham Lincoln in the Washington, DC memorial to the assassinated president, as well as the statue of John Harvard on the university campus in Cambridge). McKim didn't spare any expense when it came to the library's interior, commissioning murals by John Singer Sargent and Pierre Puvis de Chavannes, and sculptures by Saint-Gaudens.

While the new wing of the library (designed in 1972 by Philip Johnson; *see p39*) is seen as an uninspired attempt to strip down and reinterpret historic forms, McKim's original is worth a visit. Its grand staircase, vaulted reading room and enchanting cloistered garden have all been meticulously restored.

GRAND DESIGNS

Henry Hobson Richardson (1838-86) is considered one of the great American architects, his libraries, train stations and courthouses giving form to new institutions in a country on the threshold of modernity. A dozen Boston suburbs are graced by his buildings, but his masterpiece, **Trinity Church** (*see p60*), as well as the lovely **First Baptist Church** (*see p61*), are in Back Bay. A student of the Ecole des Beaux-Arts in Paris, Richardson was influenced by the heavy masonry, deep arches and elemental composition of 11th-century Romanesque architecture. The First Baptist Church, completed in 1871, is a characteristically asymmetrical composition, with a tall bell tower encircled at the top with a bas-relief by Frédéric Auguste Bartholdi, best known as the sculptor of the Statue of Liberty.

Commissioned in 1872, Richardson's Trinity Church opened in 1877 and cost almost four times the original budget. It seems it was worth the expense, as it is often cited as one of the most influential works of architecture in America. Like most of Richardson's buildings, Trinity is built with multicolored stone walls, round arches and heavy ornamental flourishes that are rooted in history but show his inventive spirit and keen eye for composition. Stained-glass windows and other decorative elements in the interior are the work of some of the most talented artists of the day. Although the church is so solid it appears to grow out of bedrock, it actually rests on 4,502 wooden pilings driven deep into the Back Bay landfill.

Richardson's influence can be seen in a number of buildings around town, including the **New Old South Church** (645 Boylston Street, at Copley Square) and the flamboyant **Flour & Grain Exchange Building** (177 Milk Street, near Quincy Market). His academic buildings at Harvard (**Sever** and **Austen Halls**; *see p82)* and suburban libraries (the **Crane Memorial Library** in Quincy is among the best) are architectural gems that all merit a visit.

URBAN OASES

The desire to develop Boston's green spaces was spurred by the development of New York's Central Park in the 1850s. Its renowned landscape architect Frederick Law Olmsted (1822-1903) was hired by Boston's Metropolitan Parks Commission to design a five-mile-long corridor of continuous parkland, called the 'Emerald Necklace'. **Franklin Park, Arnold Arboretum, Jamaica Park, Olmsted Park, Riverway** and the **Back Bay Fens** are connected to each other and – through the green swathe in the

IN CONTEXT

center of Commonwealth Avenue – to the Public Garden and the Common. The **Charles River Esplanade**, although conceived by Olmsted, wasn't developed until the 1930s. After the MBTA extended the Orange Line to the South End, the **Southwest Corridor Park** was designed as a 'new strand' of the Necklace in the 1980s.

A bleak irony shrouds the epilogue to Olmsted's career: he also refurbished the grounds of McLean Hospital in Belmont – the sanatorium where he was to spend his final days.

HIGHS AND LOWS

Boston's first skyscraper came in 1915, with a 30-story tower inexplicably stuck on top of the neo-classical Customs House. Shortly thereafter came the Depression, and aside from a number of art deco buildings from the late 1920s and '30s (such as the **Batterymarch** at 60 Batterymarch Street and the **John W McCormack Post Office and Courthouse** at 5 Post Office Square), few new buildings were built until the 1960s, when a new round of demolition and construction began in the name of urban renewal.

The **Prudential Center**, a bland, cheese grater of a tower, is widely considered to be among Boston's ugliest structures. Built in 1965, it grew out of the former site of the Boston & Albany railyards, with other towers rising around it. Its raised plazas, isolated from pedestrians, have been knit back into the streetscape with new retail and residential developments – although the glitzy **111 Huntington Street**, with its theme-park spaceship top, makes the subtlety of the original tower look almost appealing.

Not long afterwards, most of the old West End's red brick rowhouses, by then in disrepair, were replaced by a forest of apartment towers in a suburban-style park. Scollay Square – which in its respectable days was where Alexander Graham Bell invented the telephone, and, later, where debauchees flocked to drink, dance and visit brothels – was razed to make space for the vast expanse of **Government Center** and **City Hall Plaza**.

The respected architect IM Pei designed the masterplan for Government Center, which paved red-brick over acres of now prime urban real estate and reduced 22 city streets to six. Architects Kallmann, McKinnell and Knowles designed City Hall itself, and Walter Gropius's Architects Collaborative created the adjacent **JFK Buildings**. City Hall was among America's most acclaimed works of architecture when it was completed in 1968, but its intimidating scale and isolation from its context have left it an object of scorn for most Bostonians. Plans to reinvent the plaza, renovate the building, or tear it down and sell the land to developers pop up from time to time. Despite all the complaints, the transformation of neighboring **Quincy Market** (*see p48*) from decaying warehouse district to successful urban marketplace – and of Boston itself into a thriving metropolis – was sparked, at least in part, by this reinvestment in the city's downtown.

DRAMATIC DEVELOPMENT

The 1970s and '80s saw a new generation of skyscrapers sprout up against the historic backdrop of brick and stone. One of the best is still IM Pei and Partners' 62-story **John Hancock Tower** in Copley Square. Its slender profile, mirrored glass reflecting Trinity Church and angular shape recognizing the shifting street grid at the edge of Back Bay connect it to its context, using a contemporary architectural language. Although instantly more popular than the Prudential Center with most Bostonians, the Hancock did not escape controversy. While it was still under construction in 1973, a flaw in the glazing caused the windows to pop out and crash into the streets below. Every one of its 10,344 panes had to be replaced – first with plywood, and finally with newly engineered glass.

The 1980s saw the emergence of so-called 'post-modernism', which reinterpreted historic forms in new, often exaggerated structures. Philip Johnson's grotesquely ornamented **500 Boylston Street** and his **International Place** (on Atlantic Avenue), plastered top to bottom with what appears to be Palladian-window wallpaper, typify the genre. Newer high-rises, such as Gary Handel's **Ritz-Carlton Towers** on Tremont Street by the Common, use modern forms and materials and thoughtful detailing to reflect the scale and pedestrian orientation of traditional Boston buildings.

Today, the cycle of renewal continues. The elevated highway that ripped through the city in the 1950s has finally been buried in the $15 billion Big Dig, leaving a broad swathe of land for parks and public buildings, along with a renewed connection between downtown and the waterfront. The tall masts and slender cables of the **Leonard P Zakim Bridge** to Charlestown anchor one end of the **Rose Kennedy Greenway** (see p30 **Going Green**).

On the harbor, Boston is slowly converting what was a post-industrial wasteland into a thriving waterfront district. Rafael Viñoly's huge but elegant **Boston Convention and Exhibition Center**, a superb new **Institute of Contemporary Art** (see p79) and a number of mediocre office buildings have already gone up.

BUILDING THE FUTURE

Bostonians can be a touch provincial about architecture, often preferring watered-down replicas of the old and familiar to something new and different. Nevertheless, the conurbation does have some impressive modern architecture – albeit across the river in Cambridge.

The Massachusetts Institute of Technology (MIT) has spent decades commissioning ground-breaking works from the world's great architects. Its campus, beside the Charles River near Kendall Square, is studded with some of the most innovative designs in the country.

In 1949, **Baker House** (362 Memorial Drive) opened its doors; one of only two works in the country by iconic Finnish architect Alvar Aalto. The six-story student dorm is distinguished by its curvilinear plan, which gives 80 per cent of its rooms views of the Charles, and the cascading stairs at the back.

In 1955, the **Kresge Auditorium** (48 Massachusetts Avenue), the brainchild of another Finnish master, Eero Saarinen, was unveiled. Kresge has an outer shell that is exactly one eighth of a sphere, balanced on delicately intersecting arches, filled in with glass, below. Saarinen's small chapel next door is a revelation, lit by rippling sunlight reflected off its own moat.

The MIT campus also features several works by alumnus IM Pei, including the 1984 **Wiesner Building** (20 Ames Street) and the 1959 **Green Tower** (near the center of the campus) which, at 277 feet, is the tallest building in Cambridge.

The most recent additions to the MIT landscape are among the most stunning. The institute enlisted the services of Frank Gehry, best known for his Guggenheim Museum in Bilbao, to create the **Ray and Maria Stata Center** (32 Vassar Street) – a colliding series of sculptural towers and canopies held together by webs of glass. The complex features a 'Toon Town' color scheme in the interior and canted brick walls that come crashing down through the skylights.

No architectural pilgrimage to MIT is complete without a visit to **Simmons Hall** (243 Vassar Street), a ten-story dormitory designed by innovative New York architect Steven Holl. The exterior is wrapped in gridded aluminum with a dozen tiny square windows for each bedroom and large amoeba-shaped openings at lounges that snake up through the building. A cross between a cave dwelling and a spaceship, it's called home by the kids who are busy inventing the future.

The area's other colleges offer further exemplary works of modern architecture, suggesting that tradition and innovation can go hand in hand. Josep Lluís Sert's buildings lining the river at Boston University, Le Corbusier's **Carpenter Center** at Harvard and Rafael Moneo's **Davis Museum** at Wellesley provide the kind of challenging forms and spaces that keep greater Boston on the cutting edge – despite occasional protests from some of its citizens.

Sights

Public Garden. *See p43.*

Downtown

The historic heart, and business brain, of the city.

Downtown is the best place in Boston for people-watching: find a bench and a take-away lunch for a break between **Freedom Trail** tours and visits to historic landmarks, and watch the street performers and passers-by. Or, for quieter companionship, visit one of America's earliest cemeteries.

The sprawling **Boston Common** and the more formal **Public Garden** form the city's central green space. By contrast, **Faneuil Hall** and **Quincy Market** are among its most-visited landmarks, replete with shops flogging kitschy gifts, and eateries catering to tourists. A trip through **Chinatown** is a great way to spend an afternoon tantalizing your senses.

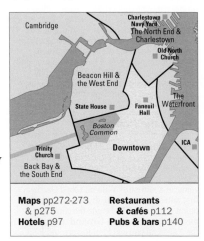

Maps pp272-273	Restaurants
& p275	& cafés p112
Hotels p97	Pubs & bars p140

BOSTON COMMON & THE PUBLIC GARDEN

Arlington, Downtown Crossing, Park St or State T.

America's oldest public park, the 48-acre **Boston Common** marks the beginning of the Freedom Trail (*see p49* **Trail Blazers**). It's also the sprawling anchor of the Emerald Necklace, a string of semi-connected green spaces designed by Frederick Law Olmsted that stretch seven miles across the city (*see p64* **Inside Track**).

Established in 1634, the Common was originally a grazing pasture for cattle, and later became a military training ground. British Redcoats also made camp here before heading north-west to Lexington and Concord in 1775. Interestingly, this leafy park had no trees at all to begin with, except one giant specimen that served as a central meeting place for the Puritans who'd settled here (until 1817, the 'Great Elm' was also used for public hangings, including that of 'witch' Ann Hibbens in 1656). The tree eventually fell victim to a series of ferocious storms that blew through the area in the mid 19th century, but by then the Common's use as a rallying point was an unshakeable tradition.

Today, watched over by the imposing gold-domed **Massachusetts State House** on Beacon Hill (*see p55*), it remains an arena for public gatherings, sunbathing in summer and ice-skating on the Frog Pond in winter. Massive protests against the Vietnam War were staged here in the 1960s; Pope John Paul II said Mass to nearly half a million people on its lawns in 1979, and more recently it's been the site of raucous marijuana legalization rallies.

Just across Charles Street from the Boston Common is the lovely 25-acre **Public Garden**. Much younger than the Common, it was only established in 1837, and was cultivated on filled-in salt marshes. As America's first public botanical garden, it was a showcase for the then-burgeoning greenhouse technology. In warmer months, its orderly English-style flowerbeds explode with color, and numerous rare species of tree flourish in its green and pleasant acres.

The Public Garden is also home to a wide array of statuary. The most striking example, which stands opposite the footbridge over the Lagoon in the centre of the park, is the commanding bronze statue of America's first president, General George Washington, astride his horse. It's an impressively detailed, true-to-life representation of equine anatomy – although the sharp-eyed may spot that the steed is mysteriously missing its tongue. Late-night pranksters also delight in stealing the general's sword as a souvenir, keeping statue sword-makers in steady business.

Several other monuments pay tribute to war heroes and statesmen, but the Garden's most humble statue is also the most charming. A bronze tribute to Robert McCloskey's classic children's book *Make Way for Ducklings*, which is set in the park, depicts a waddling mother duck followed by eight fluffy offspring. Also featured in the book are the famous **Swan Boats** (*photo p47*), which have glided gracefully on the Public Garden Lagoon, powered by pedals and pulleys, since 1877. They operate from mid April to mid September; a 15-minute ride costs $2.75 ($1.25 reductions).

Around the Common

At the north-east corner of Boston Common, across Park Street from the entrance to the T station, is the tall and austere **Park Street Church**. Its primary claim to fame is as the venue of abolitionist William Lloyd Garrison's first anti-slavery speech, thundered from the pulpit on 4 July 1829. Beside the church is the **Granary Burying Ground**, where lie the American patriots Paul Revere and John Hancock. Across the road, on Hamilton Place, stands the **Orpheum Theatre** (*see p207*), a refurbished music hall from 1852 that features ornate moldings and proscenium seating. It's played host to everything from the world première of Tchaikovsky's First Piano Concerto (1875) to concerts by the Clash and Willie Nelson.

Heading up Tremont Street, pause to gaze up at the Gothic Revival **Tremont Temple** (no.88, between Bosworth and School Streets). Built in 1894, the Baptist church looks like a Venetian palace transported to downtown

Boston; Charles Dickens and Abraham Lincoln both spoke here. On the corner of School Street is the **King's Chapel & Burying Ground**, Boston's oldest cemetery. The chapel itself, the first Anglican church in the city, was mandated by King James II, who wanted to ensure a proper foothold for the Church of England in the new colonies. School Street is so named because it was the site of the nation's first public school, **Boston Latin**, founded in 1635. Illustrious pupils included Benjamin Franklin (whose statue stands outside), John Hancock and Samuel Adams; today, the space is occupied by the 19th-century Old City Hall, now a restaurant.

At the corner of Washington and School Streets is the building known as the **Old Corner Bookstore**. Recently vacated by a jewelry store, it was the premises of several 19th-century booksellers. Literary lights such as Emerson, Dickinson, Hawthorne, Longfellow, Beecher Stowe and Dickens all passed through its doors, and works published here include *Walden*, *The Scarlet Letter* and *The Song of Hiawatha*. Across the street and a block to the south is the **Old South Meeting House**, once the largest building in colonial Boston and a sparring ground for anti-British debate before the Revolution. Between the two lies the **Boston Irish Famine Memorial**, designed by Robert Shure and unveiled in 1998 to commemorate the great famine's 150th anniversary. Although some dismiss it as a bathetic cliché – one statue depicts a family, gaunt and kneeling, imploring the heavens for sustenance, while another shows the same family, this time well fed, striding triumphantly and purposefully into the New World – in a city as indelibly marked by Irish immigration as Boston, it's at least worth acknowledging.

FREE Granary Burying Ground

At Tremont & Bromfield Streets (1-617 523 3383, www.cityofboston.gov). Park St T. **Open** 9am-4pm daily. **Admission** free.

So named because the adjacent Park Street Church was built on the site of a pre-Revolution storehouse for grain and supplies, the Granary Burying Ground is the third oldest graveyard in Boston, established in 1660. In addition to Paul Revere and John Hancock, famous figures buried here include Samuel Adams, Peter Faneuil (the Huguenot merchant who built the market and revolutionary meeting place Faneuil Hall; *see p47*), Benjamin Franklin's parents, Samuel Sewall (famous as the only Salem Witch Trial magistrate later to admit that he was wrong) and the victims of the Boston Massacre (*see p19*). Note the two gravestones for Revere – the obvious one is a more recent and elaborate pillar, but beside it is a tiny, ancient headstone that says only 'Revere's Tomb'.

Six Feet Under

Explore Boston's buried history.

With half a dozen 17th-century burial grounds in the city alone – not to mention cemeteries in the suburbs and surrounding areas – Boston is the final resting place for a diverse mix of famous folk, from revolutionary heroes to literary lions and former presidents.

The battered gravestones of the **Granary Burying Ground** (*see left*) bear the famous names of Declaration of Independence signatories John Hancock and Samuel Adams. Also interred here is Paul Revere, whose 'midnight ride' alerted the militia men in Lexington and Concord that the Redcoats were on their way in 1775. But perhaps the most intriguing plot belongs to Elizabeth Foster, who is widely thought to be the Mother Goose of nursery rhyme renown.

Further afield, at the **First Unitarian Church** on Hancock Street, in the nearby city of Quincy (*see p93*), are the crypts of two locally born US presidents – the second, John Adams, and the sixth, John Quincy Adams. And at **Holyhood Cemetery** on Heath Street, in Brookline, lie the parents of 35th president John F Kennedy: Joseph P and Rose Kennedy.

Ichabod Crane is not buried at **Sleepy Hollow Cemetery** in Concord (*see p233*); nor is his creator Washington Irving. But several major 19th-century writers and thinkers are. Laid to rest near their former homes are novelists Louisa May Alcott and Nathaniel Hawthorne, and essayist chums Ralph Waldo Emerson and Henry David Thoreau.

Meanwhile, more modern writers are well represented at the **Forest Hills Cemetery** in Jamaica Plain (*see p91*): you can seek out the tombs of confessional poet Anne Sexton, Nobel Prize-winning playwright Eugene O'Neill and poet ee cummings.

At the **Mount Auburn Cemetery** in Cambridge (*see p82*) is the grave of Henry Wadsworth Longfellow, who is linked to two others mentioned here – not only did he immortalize Paul Revere's ride in verse, he was also Nathaniel Hawthorne's college roommate. Here, too, lie a trio of highly influential women: philanthropist Dorothea Dix, who revolutionized the care and treatment of the mentally ill; Mary Baker Eddy, founder of Christian Science; and wealthy socialite and patron of the arts

Isabella Stewart Gardner, who founded a magnificent palazzo-style museum to house her collections (*see p64*).

In spooky Salem, the **Burying Point** on Charter Street is home to many of the victims of the 1692 Salem Witch Trials, including Giles Corey, the 83-year-old farmer who was crushed to death by heavy stones for refusing to stand trial. There are sinister tales down in southwestern Massachusetts city Fall River too. 'Lizzie Borden took an axe and gave her mother 40 whacks,' runs the old nursery rhyme. 'When she saw what she had done, she gave her father 41.' Lizzie was acquitted of the 1892 crime and, at **Oak Grove Cemetery** on Prospect Street, reposes with her mother and stepfather.

In **Edson Cemetery** on Gorham Street, in the mill town of Lowell, is the much-visited grave of Beat writer Jack Kerouac, who drank himself to death, at the age of 48, in 1969. Another victim of substance abuse, actor John Belushi, was a native Chicagoan, but the Massachusetts island Martha's Vineyard (*see p246*) was his favorite vacation spot, and it's here, in historic **Abel's Hill Cemetery** on South Road, in Chilmark, that his body lies.

SIGHTS

Get the local experience

Over 50 of the world's top destinations available.

FREE King's Chapel & Burying Ground

58 Tremont Street, at School Street (1-617 523 1749, www.kings-chapel.org). Gov't Center T. **Open** *Chapel* 10am-4pm Mon-Sat; 1.30-4pm Sun. *Burying Ground* 9am-4pm daily. **Admission** free. **Map** p272 K4.

Although the original King's Chapel – a small wooden structure – was built in the 1680s, the present one was designed by America's first architect, Peter Harrison, in 1754. The church was built on a plot of land excised from the cemetery next door after a decree from King James II (restive Bostonians were reluctant to comply with his order that land be sold at a fair price so a church could be founded to foist Anglicanism on the colonies, so the cemetery land was the only option). The burial ground is the city's oldest; eminent Bostonians who've found their final resting place here include Mary Chilton, the first woman to step off the *Mayflower*; John Winthrop, former governor of the Massachusetts Bay Colony; and Elizabeth Pain, said to be the model for the persecuted Hester Prynne in Nathaniel Hawthorne's *The Scarlet Letter*.

Old South Meeting House

310 Washington Street, at Milk Street (1-617 482 6439, www.oldsouthmeetinghouse.org). Downtown Crossing or State T. **Open** *Apr-Oct* 9.30am-5pm daily. *Nov-Mar* 10am-4pm daily. **Admission** $5; $1-$4 reductions. **Credit** AmEx, MC, V. **Map** p273 L4.

Second only to Faneuil Hall as a center of dissent during Boston's Revolutionary era, the Old South Meeting House (1729) combines the simple design of a Puritan meeting house with elements taken from Christopher Wren's then-fashionable Anglican church style, such as arched windows and a tall spire. Famously, it was the departure point of the Boston Tea Party: after a raucous debate on British taxation on 16 December 1773, the infuriated colonists, disguised as Mohawk Indians, marched to Boston Harbor under cover of darkness and hurled 342 crates of imported tea into the Atlantic.

FREE Park Street Church

1 Park Street, at Tremont Street (1-617 523 3383, www.parkstreet.org). Park St T. **Open** *Tours July-Aug* 9.30am-3.30pm Tue-Sat. *Services* 8.30am, 11am, 4pm, 6pm Sun. **Admission** free. **Credit** AmEx, MC, V. **Map** p272 K4.

Built in 1809, the Park Street Church was known as 'Brimstone Corner' during the war of 1812 – not for its fiery sermons about hellfire and damnation, but because gunpowder was stored in a basement crypt, emitting a constant (and sometimes overwhelming) smell of sulfur. It was here that William Lloyd Garrison gave his first anti-slavery oration and, in 1818, the nation's first Sunday School class took place. Sunday services are still held here.

A Public Garden **Swan Boat**. See p44.

FANEUIL HALL & AROUND

Gov't Center, Haymarket or State T.

Following either Washington Street or Tremont Street further north brings you to **Government Center**, which is dominated by **City Hall Plaza** (Congress Street, at Court Street). The result of 1960s urban 'renewal', City Hall Plaza was the site of Scollay Square, a boisterous, if somewhat seedy, riot of burlesque shows, jazz joints, penny arcades, movie houses, tattoo parlors and taverns. City planners leveled it and, in its place, built the hulking City Hall, stranded in a vast paved sea of brick that's used for public performances and festivals. Although City Hall was among America's most acclaimed works of architecture when it was completed in 1968, it has drawn vociferous local criticism for decades.

The main tourist attractions here are the colonial **Faneuil Hall** (pronounced *fan*-yell) and the adjacent 19th-century **Quincy Market**. The seat of the American Revolution, today Faneuil Hall is little more than part of a glorified mall. Locals refer to it and Quincy Market pretty much interchangeably, but the whole retail/restaurant conglomeration is called Faneuil Hall Marketplace. Although the gift shops, food stalls and chain stores have trivialized the importance of the historic building, it's worth bearing in mind that it was originally intended as a market and gathering place for the masses.

SIGHTS

In the earliest days of the American struggle for independence, the rebels frequently met here in tense, secret gatherings, under pain of execution for sedition, and fomented their plans for revolution. As the war began, Faneuil Hall was the heated centre of the struggle for the minds and hearts of the people of the colonies; later, it was here that George Washington toasted the giddy new nation on its first birthday. Through the years, the walls have heard the nation's most impassioned speakers, from the writer Oliver Wendell Holmes and early feminist Susan B Anthony, to Senator Ted Kennedy and President Bill Clinton.

Across the very busy Congress Street, at its intersection with State Street, is one of the most significant historical sites in the area: the spot where the **Boston Massacre** took place. It was under the balcony of the **Old State House** that British troops fired on protesting rebels, providing the spark needed to inflame the revolution. In typical Boston fashion, however, even this building is not sacrosanct. Almost unthinkably, its basement serves as an entrance to the T.

From Faneuil Hall, walk north to Blackstone Block (the block of streets off Blackstone Street, between Hanover and North Streets). Cozy, inviting pubs, along with one of the city's most famous restaurants, the **Union Oyster House** (see p116), line this cobblestoned area, making it an agreeable place to recover from a long afternoon's sightseeing with a pint of Harpoon IPA (a popular local brew) and a plate of gleamingly fresh raw shellfish.

Across the street in **Carmen Park** (at Congress and Union Streets) is the **New England Holocaust Memorial**. Six glass towers covered with six million etched numbers pay tribute to those who were killed. At night, steam rises from the transparent towers, and the dancing vapors make the monument particularly haunting.

FREE Faneuil Hall

15 State Street, at Congress Street (1-617 523 1300, www.faneuilhallmarketplace.com). Gov't Center, Haymarket or State Street T. **Open** 10am-9pm Mon-Sat; noon-6pm Sun. **Admission** free. **Map** p273 L4.

Built for the city by the wealthy merchant Peter Faneuil in 1742, the hall was later remodeled by ubiquitous Boston architect Charles Bulfinch. It had a dual function as a marketplace (on the ground floor) and a meeting hall (upstairs). During Revolutionary times it became known as the 'Cradle of Liberty', as colonial heroes such as Samuel Adams regularly roused the Boston populace against the British here – it still hosts the occasional political debate and symposium as a nod to its history. The building is part of Boston's

National Historic Park, and rangers provide brief historical talks in the Great Hall every half hour. *Photo p50.*

★ Old State House

206 Washington Street, at State Street (1-617 720 1713, www.bostonhistory.org). **Open** 9am-5pm daily. **Admission** $5; $1-$4 reductions. **Credit** AmEx, MC, V. **Map** p273 L4.

Incongruously but elegantly set in the midst of modern skyscrapers and congested traffic, this former legislative house is the oldest surviving public building in Boston. It was built in 1713 for the British governor (note the lion and unicorn still standing regally atop the building's façade) and the colonial legislature. Proclamations, including the 1776 Declaration of Independence, were read in this building, often from the balcony on the east side. The area below the balcony was the scene of the Boston Massacre in 1770 (commemorated by a ring of cobblestones), when British soldiers fired on an unruly crowd, killing five men.

Among them was Crispus Attucks, a black man recorded as the first casualty of the American Revolution. After Independence, the State House remained the seat of Massachusetts government until Bulfinch completed his imposing new legislative building on Beacon Hill (see p55). Today, it serves as the headquarters of the Bostonian Society, the historical society for the city, along with its library and museum. The collection covers the early colonial period to the present, including relics such as John Hancock's red velvet coat and embroidered waistcoat, tea from the famous Tea Party and an engraving of the Massacre by Paul Revere.

FREE Quincy Market

15 State Street, at Congress Street (1-617 523 1300, www.faneuilhallmarketplace.com). Gov't Center, Haymarket or State St T. **Open** 10am-10pm Mon-Sat; noon-6pm Sun. **Admission** free. **Credit** AmEx, MC, V. **Map** p273 L4.

Built in the mid 1820s, when Boston's population was rapidly outgrowing the smaller marketplace in Faneuil Hall, Quincy Market was originally right on the harbor (the shoreline has changed over time). Today, the neoclassical Colonnade building is lined with fast food stands. On either side of the central hall, rows of carts loaded with souvenirs and crafts lure tourists to part with still more dollars, as do the street performers who flock to the place. Flanking the Colonnade are the North and South Markets, which are likewise filled with shops. Old-time Boston restaurant Durgin Park (see p113) is touristy, but still retains an air of basic authenticity with dishes such as scrod and Indian pudding. The first stateside outpost of the London, UK noodle chain Wagamama has also arrived at the complex, drawing long lines.

▶ *One of the city's top comedy clubs, the Comedy Connection (see p229), is based here.*

Trail Blazers

Walk with purpose on one of these self-guided tours.

For the first-time visitor to Boston, the **Freedom Trail** (www.thefreedomtrail.org) provides a useful sightseeing starting point. The self-guided two-and-a-half-mile tour is clearly marked by a red line on the sidewalk, which has wended its way past 16 of the Hub's best-known historical sites since 1958. The Trail begins at the Visitor Information Center on Boston Common (147 Tremont Street, 1-617 426 3115), where you can pick up a map or hire an audio tour ($11), and ends at the Bunker Hill Monument (*see p74*).

More recently, historical organizations have jumped on the bandwagon with specialized rambles. The **Black Heritage Trail** traces the history of the African-American community in Boston from the late 18th and 19th centuries. Guided tours (1-617 725 0022) are offered daily from late May to early September, but a map (available at www.afroammuseum.org/trailmap.htm) lets you do it yourself. Starting at the Robert Gould Shaw and 54th Regiment Memorial (*pictured*), a relief sculpture on the Common in front of the State House that commemorates the valor of a young Boston Brahmin and the black regiment he commanded in the Civil War, the tour takes you past, among other sites, the Abiel Smith School (the country's first public school for African-American children)

and finishes at the African Meeting House (1806), the oldest black church in the US (both are part of the Museum of African American History; *see p55*).

The **Women's Heritage Trail** comprises ten separate, self-guided walking tours flung across Boston's neighborhoods (for maps and further details, visit www.bwht.org). In the North End, for example, you can stop by the birthplace of Rose Fitzgerald Kennedy, matriarch of the American political dynasty. Downtown, there's the statue of Mary Dyer, who was hanged on Boston Common in 1660 for her Quaker beliefs. On Beacon Hill are the homes of *Little Women* author, suffragette and abolitionist Louisa May Alcott, and Rebecca Lee Crumpler, who is generally considered to have been the first African-American woman doctor.

The **Irish Heritage Trail** is a self-guided tour (get a map at www.irishheritagetrail.com) that takes in museums, statues and memorials celebrating everyone from the city's first Irish-born mayor, Hugh O'Brien, to John Boyle O'Reilly, the 'poet, patriot, prisoner, sportsman and orator' who was one of the most influential Irish Americans of the 19th century. It winds up at the John F Kennedy Library & Museum (*see p89*) in Dorchester – a fitting conclusion for this tribute to 'the capital of Irish America'.

SIGHTS

SIGHTS

THE FINANCIAL DISTRICT

Downtown Crossing or State T.

Heading south from Faneuil Hall brings you to
the city's compact Financial District, roughly
bordered by Congress, Purchase and State
Streets. Amid the concrete labyrinth of one-way
streets and featureless skyscrapers are some
notable architectural curiosities. The **Custom
House** (3 McKinley Square, at Central Street,
1-617 310 6300), now a Marriott hotel, is an
extraordinary marriage of the original 1847
neoclassical structure and a tower stuck on
top in 1915 – which made it the city's tallest
building at the time. Around the corner, the
flamboyant 1892 Romanesque Revival **Flour
& Grain Exchange** building (177 Milk
Street, at India Street), formerly the meeting
hall for Boston's Chamber of Commerce,
echoes the work of prominent local architect
HH Richardson. Finally, **Post Office Square
Park** (between Pearl and Congress Streets)
provides a pleasant lunchtime oasis for office
workers, overlooked by such striking art deco
edifices as the John W McCormack **Post
Office and Federal Building** (31 Milk
Street, at Arch Street).

THE LADDER DISTRICT
& DOWNTOWN CROSSING

Downtown Crossing T.

West of the Financial District, where busy
main thoroughfare Washington Street meets
Winter Street, is the area known as **Downtown
Crossing**. It was once the home of Boston
department stores Jordan Marsh and Filene's,
but both are now defunct. The former is one
of Boston's most prominent casualties of the
economic recession: once scheduled to be a
looming tower of residential/retail/restaurant
development, the site is now nothing more than
a huge crater in the middle of the city. While
Mayor Thomas Menino has been vocal about
resuscitating development, plans are still
being vetted (*see p164* **The Basement Goes
Upmarket?**). Jordan Marsh, meanwhile, is now
a disappointing branch of **Macy's** (*see p157*).

The rest of Downtown Crossing is made up of
various discount and chain stores, cheap jewelers
and electrical goods emporia. The area has long
had a gritty, run-down feel to it – further south
on Washington Street is the last remnant of
the once-notorious red-light district the Combat
Zone, between Avery and Stuart Streets, which
now consists of a couple of strip clubs.

A few years ago, there was a flurry of
regeneration in the area, including the high-
profile hotel, the **Ritz-Carlton Boston**

Faneuil Hall (*see p47*)
& the **Custom House**.

Common (*see p97*), and the renovation of
the formerly dilapidated rococo **Opera House**
(*see p226*). Hip hangouts such as the retro
Silvertone Bar & Grill (*see p115*) and posh
pool bar **Felt** (*see p223*) started cropping up,
and the old appellation the 'Ladder District'
was resurrected to reinforce the impression of
an area on the up. The term, which had been in
wide use for almost a century, refers to the small
side streets running between main thoroughfares
Tremont and Washington Streets.

CHINATOWN &
THE THEATRE DISTRICT

Boylston, Chinatown or Tufts Medical Center T.

Towards the end of the 19th century, Chinese
immigrants began arriving in the city to work
on the railroads and provide cheap labor in
factories. By the early 20th century, there
were over 1,000 mostly Asian residents in the
area originally known as South Cove, and the
number expanded hugely after World War II.
Today, **Chinatown** is contained within a few
blocks around Kneeland, Essex, Beach and
Tyler Streets. It's still the best place in the city
to get a taste of authentic Asian cuisine (*see
p116*). Next to Chinatown, on Tremont Street,
is the compact **Theater District**. You can find
almost any sort of entertainment within about
a block, from cabaret to serious drama.

Beacon Hill
& the West End

It's where the other half lives – but that's only half the story.

From the FFBs (First Families of Boston) of old Brahmin money to the ghosts of torn-down tenements once housing the ethnic working class of Boston, the Beacon Hill and West End neighborhoods couldn't have more distinctively divergent roots.

Boston's most exclusive niche, **Beacon Hill** is synonymous with the city's original families. A short walk down any of its cobbled streets unveils centuries-old architectural treasures requiring a pirate's ransom to afford. You can, however, tour a couple of historic houses – and the sumptuous private library of the **Boston Athenæum** – to get a sense of how the other half lived during different epochs.

Charlestown Navy Yard
Cambridge
The North End & Charlestown
Old North Church
Beacon Hill & the West End
The Waterfront
State House
Faneuil Hall
Boston Common
Trinity Church
Downtown
ICA
Back Bay & the South End

Map p272　　**Restaurants**
Hotels p99　　**& cafés** p119
　　　　　　　　　Pubs & bars p144

The **West End**, once an urban renewal cautionary tale, is now home to some of Boston's best boutique hotels and the entertaining – and child-friendly – **Museum of Science & Charles Hayden Planetarium**.

BEACON HILL

Bowdoin, Charles/MGH or Park St T.

Boston's most lovingly preserved neighborhood, Beacon Hill is almost unfeasibly picturesque, with its red-brick row houses and mansions, gas lanterns and steep, narrow streets – some still cobbled. The quaint period charm is largely thanks to the establishment of the Beacon Hill Historic District in 1955, with its enforcement of strict architectural restraints.

The hill's name derives from the beacon lit when enemy ships were sighted out at sea by a lookout posted at the summit. This has been a lofty address – both literally and figuratively – since its development in the late 18th century. Originally there were three grassy hills (the other two were subsequently leveled), and the area was known as Tremontaine, giving nearby

Tremont Street its name. In Revolutionary times, it was little more than pasture land for cattle owned by politico John Hancock, who had his 'country estate' here, and the painter John Singleton Copley. But when construction began on Charles Bulfinch's new **Massachusetts State House** in 1795, well-to-do Bostonians with a nose for real estate began buying and building on the South Slope.

When the young, wealthy Charles Bulfinch left his family in Boston in 1786 for a European tour, he was expected to return home and begin life as a businessman. Bulfinch did come back, but, inspired by his travels, instead of starting in business, he thought he'd give his friends a few pointers on designing their homes first. The result of this 'help' changed the architectural landscape of Boston. And while Bulfinch's distinctive stamp can be seen throughout the city, it is most apparent in Beacon Hill, from

Walk Ups & Downs on the Hill

Experience the contrasting fortunes of Boston's historical communities.

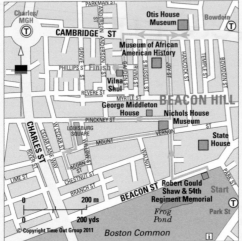

While Beacon Hill is known as Boston's Brahmin bastion, few are aware of the immigrants who left their mark – notably the free black community before the Civil War and late 19th century European Jews. This walk takes in the two sides of the hill.

Begin where they converge: the wealth and power of the **Massachusetts State House** (*see p55*) on Beacon Street, the work of Brahmin architect Charles Bulfinch; and, opposite, at the corner of Beacon and Park Streets, the **Robert Gould Shaw and 54th Regiment Memorial**. The bas-relief sculpture commemorates the first black regiment of the Union Army to fight in the Civil War (*see p24*). Colonel Shaw is depicted with drawn sword, leading his men to attack Fort Wagner; he and 62 of his soldiers would die in the battle.

Facing the State House, turn left along Beacon Street, then right on to Joy Street. Take the first left on to **Mount Vernon Street**, which Henry James hailed as the most respectable street in America. Perhaps that's because he once lived at no.131, alongside Julia Ward Howe, who wrote *Battle Hymn of the Republic* and invented Mother's Day (no.32), poet Robert Frost (no.88) and the orator Daniel Webster (no.57). On the right is the **Nichols House Museum** (*see p56*), home to suffragette,

and landscape gardener Rose Standish from 1885 to 1960.

Continue downhill along Mount Vernon Street until it opens into **Louisburg Square** – one of the city's wealthiest enclaves. Follow the gaze of the bust of Aristides (left) to Willow Street, then turn right into **Acorn Street**, a cobbled alley that lodged the Square's staff (and now itself a coveted address). Retrace your steps to Louisburg Square, and tarry for a moment at the doorstop of no.10, once home to Louisa May Alcott.

Walk north to Pinckney Street and turn right. It's less grand than Mount Vernon – in her earlier years, Alcott boarded at no.20. At no.15, Elizabeth Peabody founded one of the country's first kindergartens, while the **George Middleton House** (nos.5-7) is the oldest home on Beacon Hill built by African-Americans (1797), and the home of black liveryman and Revolutionary War veteran Middleton.

At the end of Pinckney Street, turn left into Joy Street and walk downhill. On your left, at no.46, is the **Abiel Smith School**, the country's first black public school and now part of the **Museum of African American History** (*see p55*). The **Black Heritage Trail** walking tour (*see p49* **Trail Blazers**) begins here. Behind the school, on Smith Court, is the **African Meeting House**, a gathering place for the community that was built by black artisans in 1806.

Further down Joy Street, at no.67, is the former home of Rebecca Lee Crumpler. The country's first black female doctor (1864). At the bottom of the hill, Joy Street dead-ends at Cambridge Street. Across the road, to the right, is the stately **Otis House Museum** (*see p56*), designed by Bulfinch in the 1790s for a prominent couple.

Walk west along Cambridge Street, turn left on to Garden Street, back up the hill, then right on to Phillips Street. The lovely **Vilna Shul** (no.18) is the only extant example of the 50 synagogues built by Boston's booming Jewish community in the early 20th century.

the State House, modeled after Somerset House in London, to the Federalist brick houses with classic Boston bow fronts (so called because they bulge in the middle).

Beacon Hill is closely associated with the 'First Families of Boston', or FFBs as they came to call themselves: the descendants of the original Puritan settlers who had become the American aristocracy. Ruthlessly exclusive, they were dubbed the 'Brahmin caste of New England' in 1861 by the writer Oliver Wendell Holmes; the sobriquet 'Boston Brahmin' stuck, and is still used today. Later, local wit JC Bossidy delivered a mocking toast at a Harvard dinner, which perfectly sums up their snobbish Yankee airs:

And this is good old Boston,
The home of the bean and the cod,
Where the Lowells talk only to Cabots,
And the Cabots talk only to God

Some of the grandest houses are on Chestnut and Mount Vernon Streets – on the latter, look out for the splendid, Bulfinch-designed residence of prominent Bostonian Harrison Gray at no.85. The poet Robert Frost lived at no.88, and Henry James's family had a house at no.131. Lodged between Mount Vernon and Pinckney is **Louisburg Square**. The city's only remaining private garden square, it is one of Beacon Hill's most coveted addresses. Louisa May Alcott moved to no.10 after the financial success of *Little Women*, while novelist and influential *Atlantic Monthly* editor William Dean Howells resided at nos.4 and 16 at different points. Senator John Kerry, defeated by Bush in the 2004 presidential race, lives in a former convent at no.19 with his wife, ketchup heiress Teresa Heinz. Between Mount Vernon and Chestnut Streets lies the tiny, cobbled **Acorn Street** – once occupied by servants of the square's inhabitants, and now reportedly the most photographed of the Hill's many picturesque byways.

In the 19th century, Boston's free black community was concentrated in what was then part of the West End, between Pinckney and Cambridge Streets, and on the North Slope of Beacon Hill, between Joy and Charles Streets. The **Black Heritage Trail** (*see p49* **Trail Blazers**) explores this community and the abolitionist movement through the area's historical sites, although as most of the buildings featured are private residences, visitors can only enter a couple of them. Together, the **African Meeting House** (8 Smith Court) and the adjacent **Abiel Smith School** (46 Joy Street), form the **Museum of African American History**.

Acorn Street.

Museum of African American History.

SIGHTS

Other points of interest on Beacon Hill include the **Otis House Museum**, which, along with the neighboring Federal-style **Old West Church** (1806), stands out on the traffic-choked thoroughfare of Cambridge Street, and the opulent **Nichols House Museum**. The **Boston Athenæum**, on Beacon Street, is a beautiful private library that contains some of George Washington's books. Tours take place twice a week, and there's an art gallery open to the public on the ground floor.

Charles Street, at the foot of the hill to the west, is lined with antiques shops, restaurants and, increasingly, chic boutiques such as **Holiday** and **Wish** (see p162). The handsome **Charles Street Meeting House**, built in 1807, now contains offices, cafés and shops.

Nearby on Beacon Street is one of the city's most popular tourist attractions, **Cheers** (see p144), located in the basement of former hotel Hampshire House. Once the Bull and Finch Pub, it is credited with inspiring the long-running TV sitcom. While the exterior is satisfyingly familiar – it featured in the opening shot for *Cheers* – the interior looks nothing like the show's set, and is best avoided by all but die-hard fans. A more authentic bet for sampling the Boston neighborhood bar experience is the unpretentious **Sevens Ale House** (see p145) on Charles Street. The area between Charles Street and the river is pleasant to stroll through and has a smattering of shops, including the delightful lingerie boutique **French Dressing** (see p167).

★ FREE **Boston Athenæum**

10½ Beacon Street, between Bowdoin & Somerset Streets (1-617 227 0270, www.bostonathenaeum. org). Park St T. **Open** *late May-early Sept* 9am-8pm Mon; 9am-5.30pm Tue-Thur. *Early Sept-late May* 9am-8pm Mon; 9am-5.30pm Tue-Thur; 9am-4pm Sat. *Tours* 3pm Tue, Thur. **Admission** free. **Map** p272 K4.

Founded in 1807 as a literary society, the Boston Athenæum published America's first literary magazine and acquired an extensive library of books and works of art. It moved to its current home, an imposing purpose-built structure, in 1847. The two upper floors, including the beautiful fifth floor reading room that featured in the Merchant Ivory film adaptation of Henry James's *The Bostonians*, were added in 1913-14, followed by further expansion and renovation at the turn of the century. Among its collections are books from George Washington's library and those given to the King's Chapel by William III in the 17th century.

The Athenæum helped to establish Boston's Museum of Fine Arts in the early 1870s in two of its four galleries, and much of its art collection moved with the museum. However, some notable works still remain on site, including busts of Washington, Franklin and Lafayette by Jean Antoine Houdon, and portraits by John Singer Sargent, Mather Brown and Thomas Sully. Although much of the library is accessible only to members or scholars, the ground floor gallery is open to the public, and free guided tours are conducted twice a week (you need to call in advance to reserve a place).

▶ For the Museum of Fine Arts, see p65.

SIGHTS

Boston Athenæum.

Massachusetts State House.

★ FREE Massachusetts State House
24 Beacon Street, at Park Street
(1-617 727 7030, www.sec.state.ma.us/trs).
Park St T. **Open** 9am-5pm Mon-Fri. *Tours*
10am-4pm Mon-Fri. **Admission** free.
Map p272 K4.
Designed by Bulfinch and completed in 1798, this magnificent structure replaced the old legislative building (*see p48*), which had been the headquarters of the British government. The dome, originally covered in copper by Paul Revere & Sons, was later sheathed in 23-carat gold. To this day, the shining bulb is one of Boston's best-known landmarks – although it was blacked out during World War II, due to the threat of air raids. The building is the seat of government for the state, and the stomping ground of the Senate and House of Representatives of the Massachusetts State Legislature. As it proved to be too small for the growing state, a somewhat incongruous yellow-brick extension was added in 1895, followed by two white marble wings in 1917.

Among the rooms covered by the guided tours (call ahead to reserve a place), are the Doric Hall, with its portraits and sculptures of historical politicos, and the House of Representatives and the Senate Chamber – in the public gallery of the House, look out for the Sacred Cod, an 18th-century carved wooden fish symbolizing the importance of the country's first industry (*see also above* **Inside Track**). Alternatively, visitors can also follow the tour unaccompanied, as well as sit in on meetings in the public galleries of the legislative chambers.

FREE Museum of African American History
46 Joy Street, at Smith Court (1-617 725 0022,
www.afroammuseum.org). Charles/MGH or Park
St T. **Open** *June-Aug* 10am-4pm Mon-Wed, Fri,
Sat; 10am-8pm Thur. *Sept-May* 10am-4pm Mon-
Sat. **Admission** free. **Map** p272 J3.
The museum's premises comprise the African Meeting House – the oldest black church in the country – and the Abiel Smith School, which was the nation's first public school for African-American children. The latter was named after a 19th-century white businessman who bequeathed $2,000 to the city for the education of black children. A few years after the school was built in 1834, controversy over segregated schooling began in earnest. In 1855, following much legal wrangling, a bill outlawing segregated schooling was finally passed. Children were allowed to attend the school closest to their homes, regardless of race, and the Abiel Smith School was closed. After extensive restoration works, it opened to the public in 2000, and now houses exhibitions.

Built by African-American artisans in 1806, the African Meeting House played an important role in the anti-slavery movement in the 19th century. Abolitionist William Lloyd Garrison founded the New England Anti-Slavery Society here in 1832 – earning it the moniker 'the black Faneuil Hall'. At the end of the century, when Boston's black population shifted further south, the building became a synagogue. Coinciding with the building's bicentenary, its management embarked on the final phase

SIGHTS

INSIDE TRACK
THE FIRST HOOKERS

Of the people represented by the statues that adorn the front of the **Massachusetts State House** (*see p55*), Major General 'Fighting Joe' Hooker surely has one of the most interesting backgrounds. A native of Hadley, Massachusetts, he not only distinguished himself as a Civil War general, but became notorious for his bodily appetites (ironically, the statue next to him is of the Quaker martyr Mary Dyer). An accomplished boozer, Major Hooker would allow loose women to prowl his troops' tents at night. These nocturnal guests became known as 'Hooker's Ladies' – and later, simply as 'hookers'.

of a 20-year restoration project in 2006, to return the interior to its mid 19th-century appearance.
▶ *Both buildings are stops on the Black Heritage Trail; see p49 Trail Blazers.*

Nichols House Museum

55 Mount Vernon Street, at Walnut Street (1-617 227 6993, www.nicholshousemuseum.org). Park St T. **Open** *Nov-Mar* noon-4pm Thur-Sat. *Apr-Oct* noon-4pm Tue-Sat. *Tours* every 30mins. **Admission** $7; free under-12s. **Credit** MC, V. **Map** p272 J4.

Nichols House, a Bulfinch design, was occupied from 1885 to 1960 by slightly wacky spinster, writer and landscape gardener Rose Standish Nichols – the last of her family to live there. In 1961, it became a museum. One of the few Beacon Hill homes open to the public, it's furnished with sumptuous oriental rugs, Flemish tapestries and American, European and Asian art. The tour offers a fascinating glimpse of how the other half lived in the late 19th century.

Otis House Museum

141 Cambridge Street, at Staniford Street (1-617 994 5920, www.historicnewengland.org). Bowdoin or Charles/MGH T. **Open** *Tours* (every 30mins) 11am-4.30pm Wed-Sun. **Admission** $8; $4-$7 reductions; free Boston residents. **Credit** AmEx, MC, V. **Map** p272 J3.

Built in 1796, this was the first of three residences designed by Bulfinch for his friend Harrison Gray Otis. A representative in the US Congress and, later, mayor of Boston, Otis lived here with his young wife for only four years (believe it or not, the impressive Federal-style mansion was considered merely a 'starter home' for the new couple). After Harry moved on, the house became a medical spa for ladies' complaints, with steam baths and massage, then a genteel boarding house. It has now

been painstakingly restored to its 18th-century appearance, and contains some of the original furniture. A 45-minute guided tour offers a vivid insight into the life of a Boston socialite. Even the fire bucket (all of the neighborhood residents were obliged to rush to the scene of a fire with a bucket in hand to create a water chain) is still in place, hanging behind the grand staircase.

THE WEST END

Bowdoin, Haymarket, North Station or Science Park T.

Unrecognizable as the vibrant neighborhood of 50 years ago, this area north of Cambridge Street now barely registers on many locals' radar, and it is hardly ever referred to by name. The West End was once a large residential area that formed a bridge between the North End and Beacon Hill. For many years an immigrant district, its winding streets and cramped tenements housed a sizeable low-income black, Jewish, Irish, Italian and Polish population.

Despite the problems such neighborhoods tend to endure – overcrowding and a run-down infrastructure being the most basic – the West End was a gritty but solid niche for many families, who dearly loved the area. Ironically, in a city that has had such difficulties with integration, it was one of Boston's true melting pots, with residents from a wide range of backgrounds living side by side. It was also known as a destination for visiting sailors, who patronized its shady bars and shadier brothels.

In the 1960s, under the flag of urban renewal, city planners leveled the neighborhood in favor of building luxury high-rises and expanding Massachusetts General Hospital. In the process, some 7,000 residents were displaced and the historic architecture was demolished. On a positive note, the destruction of the West End became a cardinal example of what not to do when seeking to improve a district, and other communities whose homes were up for 'urban renewal' banded together to stop the planners.

The character of the area is improving, however. The brooding stone Charles Street Jail, overlooking the river, has been turned into the dramatic boutique-style **Liberty Hotel** (*see p102* **Do Some time**). Meanwhile, the restored youth playing fields, **Teddy Ebersol's Red Sox Fields** (named in memory of a young baseball fan), have revitalized the stretch of Charlesbank called Lederman Park.

Between Longfellow and Harvard Bridges, the lovely, grassy **Charles River Esplanade** is crisscrossed by walking paths and anchored by the **Hatch Memorial Shell**, a pavilion best known for the annual Fourth of July concert (*see p181*) by the Boston Pops Orchestra. On summer weekends, the Esplanade becomes crowded with sun-worshippers, frisbee players, dog walkers, cyclists and skaters, and the river is dotted with sailboats.

To the north, the **Museum of Science** perches on the Charles River Dam between Boston and Cambridge. Featuring the Hayden Planetarium and a huge IMAX cinema, along with countless interactive exhibits, it's proved a hit with kids and parents.

As you head inland towards the North End, the dismantling of the ugly raised expressway that overshadowed the streets around North Station has made the area feel more open and less seedy. Now there is a new sense of space, and style-conscious businesses such as the **Onyx Hotel** (*see p101*) have joined the sports bars and fast-food joints clustered around the monolithic **TD Garden** (*see p217*). The stadium, renamed yet again after a merger absorbed its former sponsor, is on the site of the late, lamented Boston Garden. Though the old venue was mildewed, rickety and weathered, it was fondly regarded as the place where the Boston Celtics have won numerous NBA Championships in the 1980s, and where Boston Bruins legend Bobby Orr regularly sprayed ice with his skates. The Garden remains the only arena in town where both major sporting events and big rock concerts are staged, and also houses the **Sports Museum of New England**.

Museum of Science.

Museum of Science & Charles Hayden Planetarium

Science Park, between Storrow Drive & Edwin H Land Boulevard (1-617 723 2500, www.mos. org). Science Park T. **Open** 9am-5pm Mon-Thur, Sat, Sun; 9am-9pm Fri. **Admission** *Museum of Science* $17-$25; $14-$22 reductions. *Charles Hayden Planetarium & Mugar Omni Theater* $9; $7-$8 reductions. **Credit** AmEx, MC, V. **Map** p272 H2.

This extremely child-friendly museum is committed to providing an interactive and educational experience, making science accessible through a wealth of hands-on activities and engaging exhibits. Highlights here include the Thomson Theater of Electricity, which houses a giant Van de Graaf generator, providing a safe way to experience a dramatic lightning storm at close range; the domed Mugar Omni Theater for IMAX movies; and the new Butterfly Garden conservatory. At the multimedia Charles Hayden Planetarium, the Zeiss Star Projector reproduces a realistic night sky. There's an enormous gift shop, a decent café courtesy of celebrity chef Wolfgang Puck and a spectacular view of the river to admire from the vast windows at the back of the museum.

▶ *For a child-centric review of the museum's attractions, see p186.*

Sports Museum of New England

TD Garden, 1 Legends Way, at Causeway Street (1-617 624 1234, www.sportsmuseum. org). North Station T. **Open** 11am-5pm daily (subject to change). **Admission** $10; $5 reductions. **Credit** AmEx, DC, MC, V. **Map** p272 K2.

It's almost impossible to overstate the importance of professional sport in Boston. The exploits of the Red Sox, Patriots, Celtics and Bruins – never mind the New England Revolution, the Boston Marathon and beloved native sons such as Rocky Marciano – don't just represent entertainment. Sport is a deep-rooted passion in the region, a near religion that shapes the lives of fans across New England. The century-old traditions in this city of champions – in a state where basketball (and arguably baseball) was invented – receive the tribute they deserve here.

Located in the TD Garden, which is home to the Bruins and Celtics in the colder months, this museum offers a sweeping overview of the city's sporting history, via colorful displays of weathered artifacts, antique equipment and uniforms, faded front pages and game programs, and stunning photographs from across the decades. Whether you're interested in Bobby Orr and the Bruins, the Red Sox of Ted Williams or David Ortiz, or the century-spanning Harvard-Yale football rivalry, the SMNE's audio and video collections, interactive exhibits and knowledgeable staff will soon fill you in.

▶ *For more about Boston's 'big four' sports teams, see pp216-219.*

SIGHTS

Back Bay
& the South End

Offset consumer guilt with a culture glut.

Known predominately as the shopping hub of the Hub, **Back Bay** and the **South End** are also home to the most important architectural, artistic and sports-themed addresses in Boston.

These neighborhoods of brick and stone feel quaint but stylish, with hidden shady streets that give way to the cherished temple of sport, **Fenway Park**. Passers-by announce their status with over-sized shopping bags from haute couture **Newbury Street** establishments; warm light emanates from fashionable Victorian townhouses with cafés nestled below; the sound of a **Berklee School of Music** jazz band drifts out from a small underground bar.

The highbrow heart of the city, no visit to Boston is complete without dining in one of its restaurants after a browse through the superb duo of the **Museum of Fine Arts** and the **Isabella Stewart Gardner Museum**.

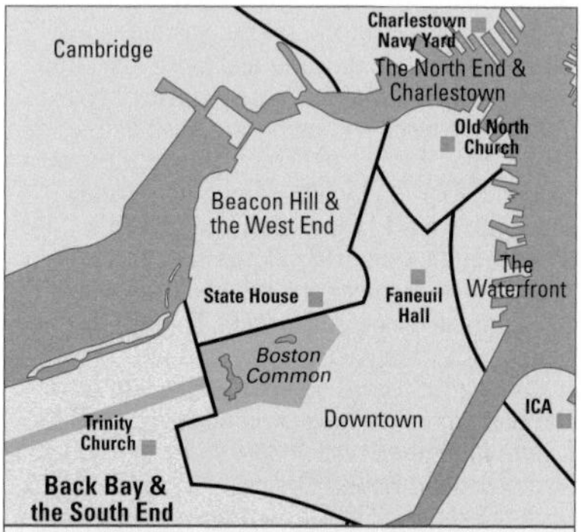

Map pp274-275 **Restaurants**
Hotels p103 **& cafés** p119
 Pubs & bars p145

Map pp274-275
Hotels p103
Restaurants
& cafés p119
Pubs & bars p145

BACK BAY

Arlington, Back Bay, Copley, Fenway, Hynes, Kenmore, Museum of Fine Arts, Prudential or Symphony T.

The expansive boulevards, ostentatious belle époque mansions and venerated cultural institutions give the impression of deep-rooted permanence, but in fact this district of the city is relatively new. Only 150 years ago, the entire area, from the Public Garden to the Fens, was submerged in swampland – it was, quite literally, Boston's back bay.

Largely due to immigration, the city's population soared from under 20,000 at the end of the 18th century to more than 300,000 in the mid to late 19th century. Boston was bursting at its seams. To expand the narrow neck of the peninsula along the Charles River,

the authorities set to work filling in mud flats along its south bank with gravel brought in by train from pits outside the city. Beginning in the 1850s, the massive landfill project, undertaken in stages, took 40 years. The reclaimed land was laid out in orderly grids, with broad avenues influenced by Haussmann's new boulevards in Paris. The finished product was an immediate hit with high society, who moved into the newly built mansions and row houses, and the area became the centre for the city's most important cultural institutions.

The heart of Back Bay is bracketed by the Public Garden to the east, Massachusetts Avenue to the west and Stuart Street and Huntington Avenue to the south. The area to the west known as the **Fenway**, home to two of the city's most important museums as well as the eponymous ballpark, is also covered in this chapter.

Today's Back Bay is a mix of affluent residential streets and commercial districts. Although it contains some of the city's most important architectural sights (for an overview, *see pp35-38*), this is the city's main shopping destination, where you'll find everything from global mega-chains to cutting-edge designer boutiques. Prime retail strip **Newbury Street** and elegant, residential **Commonwealth Avenue**, with its median swathe of parkland, are especially pleasant for strolling. Though the neighborhood has a conservative 'old Boston' reputation, there has been an influx of funkier businesses, not to mention the visible student presence from nearby Boston University, Berklee College of Music and Northeastern University.

Copley Square & Boylston Street

Despite the traffic rumbling through the intersection of Boylston and Dartmouth Streets, **Copley Square** is an expansive spot, anchored by two of the city's landmark structures: the recently restored neo-Romanesque **Trinity Church** and the imposing **Boston Public Library**. Looming behind the church, across St James Avenue, and providing a striking juxtaposition of period and style, is the 60-story glass sheath of the **John Hancock Tower**. The gleaming office block, designed by IM Pei, is the city's tallest building – although its observation deck closed after the 9/11 attacks. The building had a difficult beginning: during its construction in 1973, a flaw in the design caused dozens of the 500-pound windows to spontaneously pop out of their frames and

shatter on the sidewalk below. Miraculously, no one was hurt, but every single pane had to be replaced, and the frames that held them redesigned, at terrific expense. What's more, the weight of the tower damaged the foundations of Trinity Church; after a 12-year legal battle, the church received $11.6 million in compensation. Walk south along Dartmouth street for Boston's poshest mall, **Copley Place** (*see p158*).

While much of **Boylston Street** is a fairly characterless commercial thoroughfare, the stretch to the east of Copley Square has become more upmarket in recent years, with the arrival of retail development **Heritage on the Garden**, which houses such exclusive European labels as Hermès and Sonia Rykiel. America's oldest jeweler, **Shreve, Crump & Low** (*see p167*), established in 1796, has its headquarters on the corner of Berkeley Street, although the original premises were in the North End, across the street from patriot Paul Revere's workshop. Fans of ostentatious architecture should pause to gaze up at **The Berkeley** (420 Boylston Street, at Berkeley Street). Built in 1906, the office building looks like a giant wedding cake, with gleaming white spires and fussy adornments.

A block away is the considerably less embellished **Arlington Street Church** (351 Boylston Street, at Arlington Street, www.ascboston.org). It was built in the mid 19th century and boasts 16 Tiffany stained-glass windows, believed to be the largest collection in any church. The **Parish Café** (*see p121*) is a good place to refuel in the area.

In the other direction is the **Prudential Center**, with its 50th-floor observation deck

Copley Square.

SIGHTS

and shopping mall, which is connected to the swankier Copley Place by an enclosed, raised walkway. Adjacent is the Mandarin Oriental Hotel, which, along with new condos, seals the strip's transition from drab to deluxe. Nearby is the **Hynes Convention Center**, now eclipsed by the massive Boston Convention and Exhibition Center, which opened in the redeveloped waterfront area. Speaking of which, the **Boylston Fire Station** (941 Boylston Street), built in 1886 as the first combined fire and police station in the city, used to be the site of the Institute of Contemporary Art (*see p79*), now the waterfront's most celebrated occupant.

FREE Boston Public Library

700 Boylston Street, at Copley Square (1-617 536 5400, www.bpl.org). Copley T. **Open** 9am-9pm Mon-Thur; 9am-5pm Fri, Sat; 1-5pm Sun. Closed Sun June-Sept. **Admission** free. **Map** p275 G6.
The original structure, designed by Charles McKim and completed in 1895, is now the research library, while an extension opened in 1972 functions as a general library. The elegant granite exterior of the older building is generally classified as Italian Renaissance revival, although McKim cited various influences, including the Marshall Fields department store in Chicago. It's well worth visiting, and you can join an informal art and architecture tour, conducted by volunteers, most days (phone for times). At the center of the building is the cloistered courtyard, with its central fountain – a tranquil place to linger. Bates Hall (the expansive second-floor reading room named after an early benefactor) runs the entire length of the library, and features a majestic barrel-arched ceiling punctuated by half-domes at each end. Another highlight is John Singer Sargent's recently restored epic mural, the *Triumph of Religion*, which dominates the third floor gallery; there are also murals by 19th-century French painter Puvis de Chavannes, among others. The modern wing of the library – which echoes its parent's materials, lines and proportions in a modernist vocabulary – has had its critics but has aged well.
▶ *Downstairs, the library's restaurant, Novel, and the Map Room Café are worthy lunch spots.*

Prudential Center & Tower

800 Boylston Street, between Dalton & Exeter Streets (1-617 236 3100, www.prudentialcenter. com). Copley, Hynes or Prudential T. **Open** *Skywalk Observatory* Mar-Oct 10am-9.30pm daily. Nov-Feb 10am-8pm daily. *Shops* 10am-9pm Mon-Sat; 11am-6pm Sun. **Admission** *Skywalk Observatory* $11; $7.50-$9 reductions. **Credit** AmEx, MC, V. **Map** p275 G6.
A standard-issue shopping mall plus office complex hybrid, the Pru, as it's known commonly, is frequented by tourists as well as local workers. The mall (*see p158*) forms the base for the 52-story tower

Trinity Church.

above. Since the closure of the John Hancock observatory deck, the Skywalk Observatory on the 50th floor has been Boston's lone skyscraper viewing point. The glassed-in walkway offers a 360° perspective from a height of 750 feet; on a clear day, you can see as far as 80 miles in any direction, and two audio tours, picking out historical sites, are available.
▶ *The classic Top of the Hub Restaurant & Lounge, two floors up, is recommended more for the fabulous view than for the food.*

★ Trinity Church

206 Clarendon Street, at Copley Square (1-617 536 0944, www.trinitychurchboston.org). Copley or Back Bay T. **Open** 9am-6pm daily. **Admission** $5. **No credit cards**. **Map** p275 H6.
The unabashedly ornate Trinity Church is the visual centerpiece of Copley Square. And now that a $47 million restoration project is complete, its interior murals and stained-glass windows are equally impressive. The original church was on Summer Street, but was destroyed by fire in 1872. Commissioned to build a replacement, architect Henry Hobson Richardson rejected the Gothic Revival style prevalent at the time and instead took inspiration from the ancient churches of southern France.
It proved to be his masterpiece, so much so that the term 'Richardsonian Romanesque' entered the architectural jargon. The church is also known for its extensive murals – almost every inch of wall was handpainted by a team led by American artist John La Farge. The impressive stained-glass windows include four that were designed by the English Pre-Raphaelite painter Edward Burne-Jones and made by Arts and Crafts pioneer William Morris.

Newbury Street & around

Newbury Street has a reputation as the city's posh shopping street, and while this multi-purpose strip certainly has its share of luxe designer names (relatively recent arrivals include Marc Jacobs and Valentino), it also hosts everything from a hardware store to an outlet devoted to Boston bean memorabilia. The street's personality changes palpably from one end to the other. Generally speaking, the Arlington Street end, closer to the Public Garden, is more upmarket, with a mix of designer boutiques, antique stores and jewelers.

This is also a good place to head for a spot of pampering – there are more than 100 spas and salons on Newbury Street, as well as several cheap nail bars. A sceney vibe prevails on summer weekends, when locals promenade on the strip and linger at upmarket cafés such as the always busy **Stephanie's on Newbury** (no.190, between Dartmouth & Exeter Streets, 1-617 236 0990).

It's not all about conspicuous consumption: a high proportion of the city's galleries are clustered here (*see p195*), and you can spend an afternoon hopping from one to the next. The **Society of Arts & Crafts** (no.175, between Dartmouth & Exeter Streets, 1-617 266 1810, www.societyofcrafts.org), founded in 1897, has an upstairs gallery showcasing museum-quality thematic exhibitions, while the shop below, which represents more than 300 artists from across the country, sells more affordable items.

As you head toward Massachusetts Avenue, closer to Berklee College of Music and Boston University, the mood is more casual; high-priced cafés give way to younger fashion stores, pizza joints and ice-cream shops. Indie bookshop-cum-café **Trident Booksellers & Café** (*see p123*) is a well-loved hangout.

Running parallel to Newbury is the area's grandest residential street, **Commonwealth Avenue** (or Comm Ave, as it's universally known). Elegant mansions and townhouses line the thoroughfare, designed in 1865 to resemble a Parisian boulevard. The neo-Gothic **Burrage mansion** (no.314) is a particularly ostentatious example. The wide, tree-lined central promenade is a link in the Emerald Necklace series of parks designed by Frederick Law Olmsted (*see p64*). Dotted with statues, memorials and benches, it draws dog-walking locals and the homeless. On the corner of Clarendon Street is the **First Baptist Church**, Richardson's prelude to his ecclesiastical masterwork, Trinity Church, in Copley Square.

Crossing Newbury Street and Comm Ave are a series of streets that run in alphabetical order (from Arlington to Hereford). Cut down one of these, heading north towards the river, and

you'll come to Marlborough Street. Because of its rather odd configuration of one-way streets, Marlborough is the quietest and prettiest of Back Bay's streets. The French Academic-style residence at 273 Clarendon Street, between Marlborough and Beacon Streets, is the birthplace and former home of the Massachusetts Audubon Society, one of the country's first environmental organizations. Little more than a block south is the river, and the continuation of the **Esplanade** (*see p56*).

On Beacon Street, as you head toward Massachusetts Avenue, the stately environs are occasionally interrupted by fraternity houses – recognizable by the Greek letters hanging outside (and the riotous parties on weekends). More sedate is the **Gibson House** museum, which gives insight into the life of a well-to-do 19th-century family (and their staff) that lived in the neighborhood.

FREE First Baptist Church

110 Commonwealth Avenue, at Clarendon Street (1-617 267 3148, www.firstbaptistchurchofboston.org). Copley T. **Open** 11am-2pm Tue-Fri. **Admission** free. **Map** p275 H5.

Completed in 1871, a year before HH Richardson began work on Copley Square's Trinity Church, the First Baptist Church is a similar mix of stone and wood surfaces. Richardson commissioned the bas-relief encircling the top of the belltower from Frédéric Auguste Bartholdi, the sculptor of the Statue of Liberty.

Gibson House

137 Beacon Street, between Arlington & Berkeley Streets (1-617 267 6338, www.thegibsonhouse.org). Arlington T. **Tours** 1pm, 2pm, 3pm Wed-Sun. **Admission** $9; $3-$6 reductions. **No credit cards. Map** p275 H5.

INSIDE TRACK ODD SEAT OUT

Fenway Park (*see p64*), renowned as the oldest stadium in Major League Baseball, was first put to use in 1912. While fans perched in the cramped bleacher seats of the ballpark have been witness to a number of the sport's greatest moments, one seat stands out as having a history all its own. Of all the 30,000-plus places to sit in Fenway Park, only one is painted red, the rest a sea of green. It was to Section 42, Row 37, seat no.21 in the right-field bleachers that, on 9 June 1946, Ted Williams hit the longest home run ever recorded in the historic park: a 502-foot dinger that rung the bell of a fan when it struck the straw hat he was wearing.

SIGHTS

This Italian Renaissance-style townhouse, designed by local architect Edward Clarke Cabot and completed in 1860, was one of the first to be built in Back Bay. Although the brownstone and red-brick building isn't remarkable from the outside, the interior offers a rare glimpse into how wealthy Bostonians once lived. The house was impeccably and intentionally preserved by its last occupant, the idiosynchratic Charles Gibson Jr, and converted into a museum in 1957. Visitors on the hour-long tour can see four of the home's six floors, from the ground level where the servants labored, to the exquisite dining rooms, bedrooms and library above. Every room (except the servants' domain) is decorated with fine china, bronze sculptures and other accoutrements of 19th-century prosperity.

Massachusetts Avenue & around

The Back Bay stretch of this major thoroughfare, commonly referred to as Mass Ave, has a gritty, urban edge that feels a world away from smart Newbury Street. That said, deluxe streetwear emporium **Bodega** (whose hidden location behind a fake convenience store façade is no longer a hipsters' secret; *see p168*) sits on a side street amid the run-down fast-food joints and music stores. These establishments largely cater to the students at the **Berklee College of Music**, at the corner of Mass Ave and Boylston Street, one of the country's top music schools; its **Performance Center** (*see p207*) presents shows by both students and more established musicians.

The triangle formed by the intersection with Huntington Avenue is dominated by the imposing **Christian Science Plaza**, the world headquarters of the Church of Christ, Scientist, an organization established by Mary Baker Eddy, based on a system of spiritual, prayer-based healing. The plaza itself, with its dramatic 670-foot reflecting pool, was designed by IM Pei's firm in the 1960s, but the key buildings are much earlier. The 'Mother Church' is actually two churches: the more intimate Romanesque original, built in 1894, and the 1906 extension – a soaring, domed structure combining Byzantine and Renaissance elements, which can accommodate 3,000 worshippers. The adjacent 1930s neoclassical Mary Baker Eddy Library contains the **Mapparium**, one of the city's more unusual sights, along with interactive exhibitions about the faith and its founder. In 2006, the church announced plans to remodel the plaza for more public uses, including possible retail and residential space; in 2010, it unveiled further plans, which also include a potential bridge across the reflecting pool.

Almost directly across Mass Ave you'll find **Symphony Hall** (*see p206*), home of the Boston Symphony Orchestra. The attractive,

unfussy building, built in 1900, was partly inspired by the Leipzig Gewandhaus in Germany. The focus on the acoustics of the design was unprecedented; during the planning stages, the architects McKim, Mead and White consulted a Harvard physicist in order to achieve the best possible sound. Tours cover the groundbreaking acoustics in detail and provide some behind-the-scenes glimpses.

★ **Mapparium**
Mary Baker Eddy Library, 200 Massachusetts Avenue, at Clearway Street (1-888 222 3711, www.marybakereddylibrary.org). **Open** 10am-4pm Tue-Sun. **Admission** $6; $4 reductions; free under-6s. **Credit** AmEx, DC, MC, V. **Map** p274 F7. *See right* **Profile**.

Fenway & Kenmore Square

Huntington Avenue, home to Symphony Hall and the **Museum of Fine Arts** – Boston's smaller yet wide-ranging answer to New York's massive Met – was rather grandly rebranded the 'Avenue of the Arts' by Mayor Menino in 1998. While this seems somewhat hyperbolic, considering that only a handful of the city's cultural institutions reside in the vicinity (there's also the **Boston University Theatre** and the New England Conservatory, as well as the unmissable **Isabella Stewart Gardner Museum**, around the corner from the MFA), they are certainly among the most important.

North of Huntington Avenue are the Back Bay **Fens**, a lovely patch of parkland (and a legendary gay cruising spot), bordered by the Fenway and Park Drive. Once a foul-smelling swamp, the Fens is now an important link in the Emerald Necklace (*see p64* **Inside Track**).

With its freshwater creek and marshland, the Fens features both wild and landscaped spaces. The section behind the MFA contains the lovely **James P Kelleher Rose Garden**, established in 1930, with its rose-twined archways, formal flowerbeds and awning-shaded seats. Closer to Boylston Street, the northerly section is home to the **Fenway Victory Gardens** (www.fenway victorygardens.com). The seven-acre allotment site, planted during World War II, is open to the public – the main entrance is on the corner of Boylston Street and Park Drive. Further along the Riverway portion of the Emerald Necklace is **Olmsted Park**, which features a well-traveled path for cyclists and pedestrians, and straddles the Boston-Brookline border.

Near the Fens, **Kenmore Square** sits at the confluence of three major roadways: Commonwealth Avenue, Brookline Avenue and Beacon Street. The square can be easily identified by the giant, glowing Citgo sign on Beacon Street. Since its arrival in 1940, the sign

Profile The Mapparium

Journey to the center of the Earth.

Here's proof that Boston really is at the centre of the universe, or at least the world. The **Mapparium** (*see left*) – the world's largest walk-in globe – is among the city's quirkiest landmarks.

Located at the Mary Baker Eddy Library in the Christian Science Plaza, it is, essentially, a three-story model of the globe built to scale. The perfect sphere is 30 feet in diameter, traversed by way of the glass bridge. Bouncing off the globe room's non-porous glass walls, sound is amplified tenfold. The effect is pleasantly hallucinatory – whispers across the room register directly in your ear.

The 608 stained-glass panels that comprise the Mapparium recreate the planet as it was in the mid 1930s, when the project was completed. Most of the borders are outdated; several of the countries shown have long since been swallowed up by larger, hungrier, hardier entities.

Built in 1935 for the then-astronomical sum of $35,000, it was originally conceived as a symbol of the *Christian Science Monitor*'s global audience. Its creator, Boston-based architect Chester Lindsay Churchill,

designed the rest of the library as well. Ironically, it's the map's obsolescence that gives it a new and unexpected relevance today. Over the years, as its geography has grown ever increasingly antiquated, the giant map has become a gentle reminder that boundaries, and the powers that dictate them, are in a state of constant flux. There's a lesson here for every Ozymandias.

A number of technological improvements have given new life to the old globe. A proper lighting system, capable of generating 16 million color combinations, invigorates the map panels, and a multimedia presentation, 'A World of Ideas', has also been installed. You needn't be put off by its New Agey title – at seven minutes, the show is brief as well as totally doctrine-free.

The map itself, though, remains unchanged. Though it could easily have become just another kitsch relic, the enigmatic globe is still surprisingly dignified. As the Mapparium's admirers know, standing in the centre of world is an uplifting, if somewhat surreal, experience.

SIGHTS

OTHER WORLDLY
For the more conventional way of looking *from* the Earth, visit the **Charles Hayden Planetarium** (*see p57*).

INSIDE TRACK
THE EMERALD NECKLACE

Generally acknowledged as the father of landscape architecture, **Frederick Law Olmsted** (1822-1903) is perhaps best known as the designer (along with Calvert Vaux) of New York's Central Park. But his offices were based in the suburb of Brookline from 1883. And one of his greatest achievements was creating Boston's park system, a string of nine green spaces, collectively known as the **Emerald Necklace**, which cuts through some of the city's busiest districts. It's possible to walk the Necklace from end to end (it's about a seven-mile trek from Boston Common to Franklin Park), although sensible walking shoes are essential. You can download a map at www.emeraldnecklace.org.

has become a beloved point of reference for locals; attempts to remove it in the early '80s were met with such fierce resistance that they were ultimately dropped.

Over the years, Kenmore Square's function as a transportation corridor, combined with the seasonal nature of the visitors and inhabitants of its two main tenants, Boston University and Fenway Park, engendered the area with a sense of impermanence and confusion. The abundance of students created a natural market for cheap eateries and bars, all of which contributed to the square's slightly seedy air. But the past few years have seen a shift in character. Although it has yet to be transformed into quite the upmarket shopping and dining destination predicted by some of the local press, there are now some interesting shops, bars and restaurants clustered around the luxury **Hotel Commonwealth** (*see p105*), which opened in 2003, including repro Parisian brasserie **Eastern Standard** (*see p120*), jewelers **Persona** (*see p167*) and designer denim purveyor **Jean Therapy** (*see p163*).

Lurking behind Kenmore, **Lansdowne Street** has been the city's nightclub row for decades. The names have changed, but the clubs live on. In the early 20th century, retailer Eben Jordan (founder of now defunct local department store Jordan Marsh and the *Boston Globe*), built the structure at nos.13-15 as a stable for his horses and delivery trucks. In 1969, it became a psychedelic club called the Ark, before morphing into Boston Tea Party, a legendary rock haunt. In the 1970s, before moving to New York to open Studio 54, Steve Rubell took over and transformed the club into

a glittering disco. After a series of incarnations, the building became the site of Avalon and Axis in the 1990s and is now home to the Boston incarnation of the **House of Blues** (*see p207*).

Just steps from Lansdowne Street sits historic **Fenway Park** (*see p217*), home of the Boston Red Sox. The celebrated baseball stadium opened on 20 April 1912, just days after the *Titanic* sank. For decades, fans thought it must have been an omen, as the Sox didn't win a World Series for 86 years; this was also put down to the 'Curse of the Bambino', after owner Harry Frazee sold Babe Ruth to the New York Yankees in 1919. However, the spell was famously broken in 2004, an event depicted in the US film adaptation of Nick Hornby's novel *Fever Pitch*. The most famous part of the stadium is its 37-foot-high left-field wall, known affectionately as the Green Monster. The chances of getting your hands on a ticket are slim, due to the ballpark's small size and the large numbers of obsessive fans, but guided tours are available.

★ Isabella Stewart Gardner Museum

280 The Fenway, at Palace Road (1-617 566 1401, www.gardnermuseum.org). Museum of Fine Arts T. **Open** 11am-5pm Tue-Sun. **Admission** $12; $5-$10 reductions; free under-18s. **Credit** AmEx, MC, V. **Map** p274 D8.
As remarkable as its founder, the eccentric socialite and patron of the arts who was the inspiration for Isabel Archer in Henry James's *Portrait of a Lady*, the Gardner museum is a lavish reconstruction of a 15th-century Venetian palace, complete with a luxurious interior courtyard with a seasonally changing floral display. Initially conceived by Gardner and her husband Jack to house the growing collection of art and objects amassed during their extensive travels, the museum only came into being after Jack's death.

It opened in 1903, with the widowed Gardner residing on the fourth floor until she died in 1924. She wanted the arrangement of the architecture and artworks to engage the imagination, so every piece in the 2,500-piece collection, spanning European, Asian and Islamic art from classical times to the turn of the 20th century, is meticulously placed according to her personal instructions.

The result is an idiosyncratic mix of paintings, sculptures, tapestries, rare books and furniture. Among the many highlights are John Singer Sargent's *El Jaleo*, Titian's *Europa* and works by Botticelli, Rembrandt and Raphael. In 1990, 13 pieces, including Rembrandts, a Vermeer and Degas drawings, were stolen in America's largest art heist (*see p66* **Boston Illegal**), and the empty spaces – which can't be filled under the terms of Gardner's will – are a poignant sight. Many of the works aren't labeled, but you can buy or borrow a guide to the collections and the security staff are charming and helpful; there are also detailed floor plans on the

Museum of Fine Arts.

website. A modern building in the grounds by Italian architect Renzo Piano is under construction, and will accommodate exhibitions and events.
▶ *For more on the founder's eccentricities, see below, Inside Track.*

★ Museum of Fine Arts

465 Huntington Avenue, at Museum Road (1-617 267 9300, www.mfa.org). Museum of Fine Arts T. **Open** 10am-4.45pm Mon, Tue, Sat, Sun; 10am-9.45pm Wed-Fri. **Admission** $20; $7.50-$18 reductions; free under-6s; free under-17s weekdays after 3pm, weekends & school holidays. Free to all 4-9.45pm Wed. **Credit** AmEx, MC, V. **Map** p274 D8.
Founded in 1870, the MFA moved from Copley Square to its current home, a neoclassical granite building on Huntington Avenue – the so-called 'Avenue of the Arts' – in 1909. The globe-spanning collection encompasses 450,000 objects. Of particular note are the collection of American art, including Paul Revere's silver Liberty Bowl and paintings by John Singleton Copley; the Egyptian collection, much of which was acquired through excavations in conjunction with Harvard University in the first half of the 20th century; the Japanese collection (the first in America and one of the finest in the world); and the Impressionist and post-Impressionist paintings, including an impressive array by Monet – the second largest collection of his work in the US.

The Upper Rotunda in the center of the building is adorned by John Singer Sargent's spectacular murals, which pay tribute to the museum's role as guardian of the arts through references to Greek mythology. As well as the vast permanent collection, all of which is presented in an accessible way with a contemporary eye for design and placement, the MFA hosts major temporary exhibitions on such diverse themes as couture fashion and Spanish art during the reign of Philip III and retrospectives of greats such as Edward Hopper.

A new American wing (covering the art of North, Central and South America) and an enclosed courtyard, designed by the firm of British architect Norman Foster (*see p36* **A Fine Addition to the MFA**), famous for the contemporary revamp of the British Museum's Great Court, is set to add even more variety to the collection.

Refuelling options comprise two cafés and a more formal restaurant, Bravo. There's also a program of arthouse films and festivals and, increasingly, new and world music, in the Remis Auditorium and the Calderwood Courtyard.

INSIDE TRACK
AN ECCENTRIC HEIRESS

Boston is famous for its blue bloods, and there is probably none more extravagant and eccentric than **Isabella Stewart Gardner**, heir to her husband's shipping fortune and devoted patroness of the arts. 'Mrs Jack' was prone to much-discussed outbreaks of odd behavior: borrowing lion cubs from the zoo and walking them in the street; fraternizing with non-Brahmins; and wearing a Red Sox headband to Symphony Hall. She and her husband conceived a palazzo-style mansion to house their famous art collection, but he died before the plans were realized; the widowed Gardner left it to the public as a museum (*see left*), with the stipulation that it never be altered; in her honor, it offers free admission to all Isabellas.

THE SOUTH END

Back Bay, Mass Ave or Tufts Medical Center T, or Silver Line Washington St.

Between the commercial gloss of Back Bay and the working-class neighborhood of Roxbury, the South End was a shabby-chic 'gay ghetto' in the 1980s, where enterprising young urbanites found affordable period apartments in

SIGHTS

Boston Illegal The Gardner Heist

The great museum robbery.

In the wee hours of 18 March 1990, while most of Boston was celebrating St Patrick's Day, two men in Boston police uniforms came up to the side door of the **Isabella Stewart Gardner Museum** (*see p64*). There had been a disturbance on the grounds, they explained to the two guards on duty; could they come in to investigate?

Once inside, the 'officers' duct-taped the guards to poles in the basement, and set about stealing $300 million worth of art.

All told, the thieves got away with 11 paintings and drawings by Degas, Rembrandt, Vermeer, Manet and Govaert Flinck, as well as a Shang Dynasty Chinese bronze beaker and the finial of a Napoleonic banner. Included in the loot were some of the museum's most precious works. *The Storm on the Sea of Galilee* was Rembrandt's only known seascape, and *The Concert* by Vermeer was one of only a few dozen known paintings by the master; these two were worth about $50 million apiece.

To this day, the case is unsolved. Now that the statute of limitations on the robbery has expired, the US attorney in Boston has said he will not prosecute anyone connected with the crime. But the Gardner museum is still desperate to get the artwork back, and has offered a $5 million bounty for its return, no strings attached.

In 2005, on the 15th anniversary of the heist, the museum issued a renewed call for information. They also reached out publicly to an anonymous informer who, in 1994, had written a letter to the museum claiming to be able to facilitate the safe return of the stolen paintings, in exchange for $2.6 million and immunity from prosecution. If the museum was interested, the anonymous tipster wrote, they should arrange for the numeral '1' to be printed in the *Boston Globe*'s listing for the Italian lira in the US-foreign currency exchange on 24 May.

In exchange for a promise of an exclusive if the tip should lead to the artworks' recovery, the newspaper complied, and the anonymous informer responded. But a flurry of interest from law enforcement spooked the tipster, and he ceased corresponding with the museum. If the Gardner has heard from him since, they've kept quiet about it.

Rather than rearranging the collection after the robbery, the museum has left the spots where the pieces once hung blank, marked only by small cards with the names of the stolen paintings. There is supposedly a stipulation in Isabella Stewart Gardner's will stating that if any paintings do not hang in their original places, they must all be auctioned off and the proceeds sent to Harvard University. For the art-loving visitor, the stark spaces are a melancholy sight.

Speculation about who was behind the heist continues – fugitive mobster Whitey Bulger, famous art thief Myles Connor, disgruntled former museum director Rollin 'Bump' Hadley – but nothing's been proven. Many years after the robbery, in 2005, the *Globe* interviewed one of the security guards who had been on duty that night. At the time, he'd been a 23-year-old Berklee College of Music student who played in a rock band, sometimes smoked pot on the job and had given his notice to quit just days before the heist. The guard gave descriptions of the men after the robbery, but to no avail. 'One of them looked like Colonel Klink on *Hogan's Heroes*. That's all I can remember,' he said.

the heart of the city. Now as sought-after as its neighbor Back Bay, but a lot more trendy, it still has a large gay population. The area's high concentration of style-conscious residents explains the profusion of hip eateries and chic, independently owned homewares and gift shops in the area. Rainbow flags flying outside many businesses proclaim the area's gay pride and diversity.

A five-minute stroll south of Copley Square casts you into the **Landmark District**, near the junction of Clarendon and Tremont Streets. This is the core of the South End, and its name derives from its status as a protected neighborhood since 1983. It's an attractive, smartly arranged part of the city – the original street plan was laid out by celebrated Boston architect Charles Bulfinch, and the South End contains the largest collection of Victorian cast iron-girded rowhouse properties in the country.

While elaborately designed Back Bay was occupied by the upper crust, its near neighbor, with its neat, English-style squares, was built for the mercantile class. In the 20th century, however, the area fell into disrepair as economic depression struck. By the mid 1970s, many original buildings had been demolished; others fell victim to arson. But through the efforts of concerned citizens, who founded the South End Historical Society, the South End was restored and subsequently gained its protected status.

The South End's two parallel arteries, Tremont and Washington Streets, are at the centre of the area's thriving restaurant and bar scenes. It also has a rich cache of culture.

The sprawling **Boston Center for the Arts** occupies the block of Tremont Street between Berkeley and Clarendon Streets. An organ factory in the 19th century, the complex now contains four performance spaces and the large, light-filled **Mills Gallery** (*see p196*) as well as artists' studios. The headquarters of the Boston Ballet are also here. The building's centerpiece is the **Cyclorama**, a circular, domed structure built in 1884 to exhibit Paul Dominique Philippoteaux' massive painting of the Civil War battle of Gettysburg. The painting went on tour five years later, never to return – it's now on display in Gettysburg. The Cyclorama itself has served as a roller-skating arena, flower market and factory, and now hosts weddings, trade shows and the occasional performance. The most recent addition to the complex is the restaurant, bar and entertainment venue, the **Beehive** (*see p124*), which has been designed in collaboration with local artists; the funky decor includes bars made from reclaimed materials, and avant-garde loos.

The **Jorge Hernández Cultural Center** (85 West Newton Street, 1-617 927 0061, www.iba-etc.org), housed in a converted 19th-century church, is a dynamic neighborhood institution; the three-story **Villa Victoria Center for the Arts** (www.villavictoriaarts.org), sharing the same address, exhibits the artworks of contemporary Latino artists.

While there has been an artistic presence here since the 1960s, in recent years the area south of Washington Street, **SoWa**, has exploded with showrooms and studios. The converted warehouse at 450 Harrison Avenue houses more than 50 artists' studios and 15 exhibition spaces (www.sowaartistsguild.com; *see p195*). However, it seems only a matter of time before many artists get priced out of the 'hood, with upscale condos sprouting at a rapid rate.

Small shops, selling everything from kids' gear and pet accoutrements to fashion and chic home accessories, are dotted throughout the neighborhood. **Motley** (*see p173*) is a hip, cupboard-sized gift shop, and the delightfully camp **Aunt Sadie's General Store** (*see p172*) comes into its own at Christmas, when it's decked out in full yuletide regalia. **Turtle** (*see p162*) showcases local designers.

As you head southwest, towards Mass Ave and Roxbury beyond, the area has a rougher edge, but gentrification has spread here too; Ken Oringer's tapas bar **Toro** (*see p127*) has joined Joanne Chang's wonderful **Flour Bakery & Café** (*see p126*) on this stretch of Washington Street. But for an unmissable taste of pre-gentrified South End, sample the turkey hash at 1920s time-capsule lunchtime eaterie **Charlie's Sandwich Shoppe** (*see p124*) on Columbus Avenue. Not far away is self-styled 'lifestyle skate boutique' **Laced** (*see p168*).

Behind Columbus Avenue, the 4.7 mile **Southwest Corridor Park** cuts through the urban landscape, dotted with playgrounds and dog-exercising parks. Designed to be a 'new strand' of the Emerald Necklace (*see p64*), it starts at Back Bay T station and follows the Orange Line underneath it through the South End and Roxbury to Jamaica Plain.

Bay Village

Wedged between Back Bay, Downtown and the South End is the tiny residential neighborhood of Bay Village. Made up of just six square blocks, it was created on landfill in the 1820s, decades before the South End and Back Bay. It's worth a visit for its charming architecture – similar to that of Beacon Hill, though on a smaller scale, as it was colonized by the craftspeople who built the latter's townhouses. During Prohibition, a number of the city's speakeasies were secreted in this tucked-away enclave. Today, the underground element still lives on at Boston's best-known drag venue, **Jacque's Cabaret** (*see p200*).

SIGHTS

The North End & Charlestown

Revolutionary landmarks – and great gnocchi.

An ideal neighborhood for a stroll, the **North End** has a distinct character combining Italian heritage and a New England setting. The red brick buildings yield gastronomic treasures around every corner; small *salumerias*, bakeries and pastry shops are perfect for creating an impromptu picnic after a visit to the **Paul Revere House**.

Across the river is **Charlestown**, a working-class neighborhood given a facelift as young professionals move into the waterfront properties lining quaint alleyways and winding streets. Here you'll find colonial taverns and reminders of the Revolutionary War, such as the **Bunker Hill Monument** – climb to the top for a fantastic view of the city.

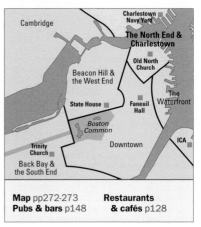

| **Map** pp272-273 | **Restaurants** |
| **Pubs & bars** p148 | **& cafés** p128 |

THE NORTH END

Haymarket or North Station T.

For decades quite literally cut off from the rest of the city, this historic area has been liberated by the Big Dig project. From the late 1950s until 2004, the massive iron girding holding up the elevated six-lane Central Artery created a 40-foot wall, separating it from the rest of downtown Boston – which may be one reason it has retained its distinctive identity. Now that the traffic that once congested the Central Artery has been re-routed underground to the southbound I-93 tunnel, and the unsightly and noisy hulk of steel dismantled, long-term residents marvel at the uninterrupted views of – and from – its streets. The resulting North End Park, part of the **Rose Kennedy Greenway** (*see p76*), is a beautiful place for a few minutes' rest in the heart of the city.

Settled in the early 1630s, the North End is one of Boston's oldest neighborhoods. For decades, it has been the city's Italian quarter,

and it's as famed for its restaurants as for being the starting point of silversmith Paul Revere's midnight ride to warn rebel troops in Lexington and Concord of the arrival of British Redcoats. (For more on Paul Revere, *see p20* **Artisans of the Revolution**.) As the childhood home of John F Kennedy's grandfather, John Fitzgerald, the North End also has links with that most famous of Boston political dynasties.

The early township at the tip of Shawmut Peninsula was a maze of two- and three-story clapboard houses known as saltboxes, but a number of fires – notably the devastating blaze of 1676 – ushered in the age of brick. The area's other memorable disaster was the great molasses flood (*see right* **Inside Track**).

Originally a blue-blood bastion, the neighborhood saw an influx of European immigrants in the mid to late 19th century. First came the Irish, then German, Russian and Polish Jews, followed by a smattering of Portuguese fishermen and, finally, the Italians. By 1920, some 90 per cent of the local population was from central and southern Italy.

Today, that figure has halved and a wave of high-income professionals has moved in to occupy a new crop of converted loft apartments. Nonetheless, the area retains its Italian flavor. With its tightly clustered red-brick row houses hung with wrought-iron fire escapes, traditional cafés and retro neon signs, all it needs is a Tony Bennett soundtrack to feel like a scene out of *GoodFellas*. Spurning the supermarket age, many locals still buy their provisions from *salumerias*, bakeries and greengrocers. Passers-by greet each other and chat in the streets, often in Italian. Elderly men cluster in modest social clubs or, when the weather is warm enough, drag their folding chairs on to the sidewalk to play backgammon and argue with gesticulating hands. In summer, thronging street festivals in honor of various saints take over the area nearly every weekend (*see p180* **Inside Track**).

However, since the dismantling of the Central Artery there are signs that 21st-century life is creeping in, with a sprinkling of stylish shops.

North Square

Three of the Freedom Trail's sites (*see p49* **Trail Blazers**) are in the North End. The best known is the house where Paul Revere once lived, at 19 North Square. Revere owned the house for 30 years and his silversmith's workshop was on nearby Clark's Wharf; some of his handiwork can be seen in the house today. While the **Paul Revere House** is a rare example of wooden 17th-century colonial architecture, it is Revere's own history that really makes it worth a visit.

On the other side of the courtyard stands the red-brick Georgian **Pierce/Hichborn House**. Revere's cousin and fellow Revolutionary Nathaniel Hichborn lived here from 1781 until his death in 1797. Separated by little more than 30 years, the architectural contrast between the two houses is fascinating – and while Revere's may appear the more primitive of the two, it was in fact a more impressive residence in its day.

Once Walt Whitman's place of worship, the 1833 **Sacred Heart Church** (no.12, 1-617 523 5638) is across picturesque, cobblestoned North Square. At no.2, a plaque marks the site of the Old North Meeting House, built in 1650, where Puritan preacher Increase Mather and his son Cotton used to preach.

While Revere's story is the area's main claim to fame, another American legend has its roots here. Congressman and former Boston mayor John 'Honey Fitz' Fitzgerald was born on Ferry Street and later lived at 4 Garden Court. There, he reared a daughter named Rose, who married a fellow named Kennedy. Her sons included President John F Kennedy, Attorney General Robert F Kennedy and Senator Ted Kennedy.

> ### INSIDE TRACK A STICKY END
>
> On 15 January 1919, a giant tank of molasses being stored on Commercial Street for rum-making exploded, sending 2.5 million gallons of the sticky liquid cascading through the streets. Rising to waves of up to 40 feet, the deluge crushed houses and vehicles and dragged 21 people (and 12 horses) to a sugary grave. Some claim that on a hot day you can still smell molasses on Commercial Street.

★ Paul Revere House & Pierce/Hichborn House

19 & 29 North Square, between Richmond & Prince Streets (1-617 523 2338, www.paulrevere house.org). Haymarket T. **Open** *mid Apr-Oct* 9.30am-5.15pm daily. *Nov-mid Apr* 9.30am-4.15pm daily. **Admission** $3.50; $3 reductions. **Credit** AmEx, MC, V. **Map** p273 L3.

Built in 1680 – making it the oldest surviving structure in downtown Boston – the Paul Revere House was constructed on the site of the parsonage that was home to Puritan preacher Increase Mather and his family (*see p71* **Inside Track**). The two-story, wooden post-and-beam structure may seem modest,

Paul Revere House.

SIGHTS

SIGHTS

Profile Old North Church

This Boston landmark is a witness to history.

Originally called Christ Church in Boston, **Old North Church** (*see p73*) – indeed, the city's oldest – was built in 1723, its design inspired by Sir Christopher Wren's London churches.

It played a critical role in the earliest days of the American Revolution: it was from Old North's steeple that lanterns were held aloft to warn the Minutemen of the movements of British forces. One lantern was to be displayed if the troops were seen moving by land, two if they were coming in by sea. They came by sea, and two it was, spurring Paul Revere to take his famous midnight ride – although Revere, a Puritan, never worshipped in this Anglican church.

The steeple itself wasn't part of the original church, but was added in 1740, with replacement steeples built in 1806 and 1954 after hurricanes tore the previous versions down. In the window where the two lanterns were hung sits a third lantern, lit by President Ford on 18 April 1975, symbolizing hope for the nation's next century of freedom.

The church's plain white interior also features its original chandeliers, lit for Christmas services, and wooden box pews.

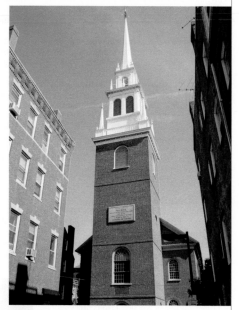

These were rented by local families, who were free to decorate them as they chose. The decor and positioning of each family's pew was a sign of their social status, with coveted centre pews attracting the highest rents. A bust of George Washington, housed within the church, is often considered to bear the best resemblance to the first president of the US.

Beneath the church rest the bodies of approximately 1,100 of the early colonists and British subjects in 37 tombs. The tombs have been sealed up since the early 20th century; however, archeologists are currently working with the church to learn more about the people buried there. Today, the church's rich history attracts a steady stream of visitors, and the converted chapel next door houses a tasteful gift shop.

TALKIN' 'BOUT A REVOLUTION For more on the US struggle for independence from Britain, *see pp17-22*.

but its high ceilings and large rooms (for the period) mark it out as a home for a family of means. Revere bought the house from its first owner, wealthy merchant Robert Howard, and lived here with his wife, children (he had 16 over 30 years, but only eight resided in the house at any one time) and mother from 1770 until 1800. The third story was removed in the 19th century, when the house fell into disrepair (at various times, it served as a flophouse, candy store, cigar factory and bank).

In 1902, it was nearly demolished, but the fortuitous intercession of Revere's great-grandson saved the place from the wrecking ball; six years later, the Paul Revere House opened to the public, one of the first 'house museums' in America. The ground floor is mainly furnished as it would have been when Howard occupied it, while upstairs is decorated in the style of Revere's time, with some original pieces of furniture that belonged to the family. There are also displays devoted to the silversmith's epic ride, along with examples of his work.

Across the courtyard – dominated by a 900lb iron bell cast by Paul Revere and Sons – is the Pierce/Hichborn House, one of the oldest brick buildings in Boston and a prime example of early Georgian architecture. It was built in 1711 for glazier Moses Pierce, and later purchased by Revere's cousin Nathaniel Hichborn, a shipbuilder. While the Paul Revere House is open to visitors, entry to the Pierce/Hichborn House is by guided tour only (usually twice daily; phone to check).

Hanover Street & around

With more than 100 restaurants packed into the small neighborhood, the North End has been a popular dining destination with Bostonians and tourists for decades. In the vicinity of the area's two main drags, Hanover Street and Salem Street, you can find everything from humble trattorias to chic *nuovo Italiano* eateries.

But it's not all about food. Among the Italian cafés and restaurants on Hanover Street is **St Stephen's Church** (24 Clark Street, 1-617 523 1230, 7.30am-5pm daily), the work of Boston-born architect Charles Bulfinch, and the only surviving example of his church designs in the city. Roughly bookended by St Stephen's and the **Old North Church** (*see left* **Profile**) is the brick-paved **Paul Revere Mall**, also known as the Prado. Its centerpiece is a statue of Revere, designed by Cyrus E Dallin in 1865 but only cast in 1940. As well as paying tribute to the North End's favorite son, the mall (between Hanover and Unity Streets) serves as a social hub in warm weather, where locals play cards, gossip and argue over sport scores. In the square, engraved tablets on the walls list the famous residents and places in the neighborhood. On Unity Street, to the left of the back gate of the Old North Church,

is the handsome Clough House. Built in 1712, it was once home to Ebenezer Clough, the master mason who helped build the church.

Now occupied by a clothing store, the former **Joseph A Langone Funeral Home** (383 Hanover Street) found notoriety as the site of the funeral for Nicola Sacco and Bartolomeo Vanzetti. The Italian anarchists were executed in 1927, following a controversial robbery and murder trial that preyed on the xenophobia of the era. Many believed the two were innocent; what is indisputable is that their case was railroaded through the courts to appease the angry, anti-immigrant zeitgeist, and the story of their fate remains a cause célèbre among anti-death-penalty groups worldwide.

Heading towards the waterfront, you'll pass a handful of trendy clothing stores, including **Injeanius** denim shop (no.441, 1-617 523 5326); around the corner at 12 Fleet Street is its dressier sibling, **Twilight** (1-617 523 8008).

At the opposite end of Hanover Street is the open-air produce, meat and fish market known as **Haymarket**, held on Blackstone Street between Hanover and North Streets. On Fridays and Saturdays it's a bustling, colorful scene, open from 5am 'until we sell out', according to one of the charismatic stallholders.

Salem Street & Copp's Hill

Unlike the Italians, other immigrants to the area didn't leave a lasting legacy. Salem Street is so named because it was once called Shalom Street – in the mid 19th century it was the primary home of the neighborhood's Jewish population. Today, none of the five synagogues that once stood in the North End remains, and virtually all traces of Jewish influence have vanished. Now the southern end of the street is dominated

---

INSIDE TRACK
NOBODY EXPECTS THE
SALEM INQUISITION

Perhaps the most famous Bostonians to be interred in **Copp's Hill Burying Ground** (*see p72*) are the Puritan preachers and arch-conservative theologians Cotton Mather and his father Increase. Famed for his literary prolificacy, Cotton is believed to have written more than 400 books and pamphlets. Father and son fell out of favour in subsequent years over their handling of the Salem Witch Trials. Both were influential enough to have halted the Salem inquisition, but neither condemned the mass hysteria that the trials unleashed until it was far too late.

SIGHTS

by old-fashioned food shops, including the 1930s **Polcari's Coffee** at no.105 (1-617 227 0786); foodies can sign up for one of resident expert Michele Topor's **Boston North End Market Tours** (1-617 523 6032, www.north endmarkettours.com), which take in the best. Gift shop **Shake the Tree** at no.67 (*see p173*) is a more recent arrival.

More importantly, Salem Street is the site of the **Old North Church**, the city's oldest place of worship and one of its most famous Revolutionary landmarks. After paying your respects, cross Salem Street and carry on up Hull Street to reach **Copp's Hill Burying Ground**, the highest point in the North End; below it on Commercial Street is Langone Park,

with its playing fields, children's playground and views of the Charlestown Navy Yard. Directly opposite the graveyard's entrance, **no.44 Hull Street** is Boston's narrowest house, measuring just ten feet wide. According to local lore, the sole purpose its original owners had in building it was to block their neighbors' view. Welcome to Boston, pal.

Nearby, 165 Prince Street, on the corner of Commercial Street, was the site of the 'Great Brink's Robbery' (*see below* **Boston Illegal**).

FREE Copp's Hill Burying Ground

Charter Street, at Snowhill Street (no phone). North Station T. **Open** 9am-5pm daily. **Admission** free. **Map** p273 L2.

Boston Illegal The Brink's Robbery

The original Brink's Job proves that crime doesn't pay.

On the evening of 17 January 1950, a group of armed gunmen in pea coats, chauffeur caps and rubber Halloween masks stormed the Brink's Building at 165 Prince Street in the North End. Within 20 minutes, they were gone – making off with an unheard-of $1.2 million in cash, and another $1.6 million in bonds and securities. A few months later, authorities found their getaway car – a brand-new green Ford truck, cut into pieces with an acetylene torch and wrapped in fiber bags – in a landfill in the suburban town of Stoughton.

The heist, unsolved for nearly six years, was considered 'the crime of the century', a daring and brilliant operation that was ultimately foiled not by a slip-up or canny police work, but by the robbers' own greed and bickering.

The gang – Tony Pino, Adolph 'Jazz' Maffie, James 'Specs' O'Keefe, Thomas 'Sandy' Richardson, Vincent Costa, James Faherty, Joe McGinnis, Mike Geagen, Henry Baker, Joseph Banfield and Stanley Gusciora – had meticulously cased the joint. Months before the heist, they stole the lock cylinders out of the doors one by one, had keys made by a local locksmith, and replaced them. They crept into the building dozens of times after hours to rehearse their plans. By the time the day of the job rolled around, they knew the Brink's building better than its own employees.

After making their getaway, the bandits divvied up some of the loot and made a pact not to touch it until six years had passed – the statute of limitations on

robbery in Massachusetts. But six months later, O'Keefe and Gusciora were arrested in Pennsylvania on an unrelated charge and sentenced to several years in prison. O'Keefe began putting pressure on his former associates to cough up money for his defense. Relations between the gang members soured, and when O'Keefe was released from prison, several attempts were made on his life.

Mere days before the statute of limitations on the Brink's job was due to expire, O'Keefe – in prison on yet another charge, and under extreme pressure from investigators – finally summoned an FBI agent. 'All right, what do you want to know?' he asked.

Today, the spot where the Brink's building once stood is a parking garage. In the 1970s, Dino De Laurentiis produced a film about the heist, *The Brink's Job*, much of it shot on location in Boston. Local lore has it that the film crew paid a North Ender $200 to take out an air conditioning unit for a shot, and the next morning, every window on the street had one.

After O'Keefe sang, the rest of the gang, most of whom were well known to police, were soon rounded up and convicted. Some died in prison, while others were paroled at ripe old ages. Richardson and Maffie marched in a Boston parade as guests of honor when *The Brink's Job* had its 1978 première.

As for the rat, O'Keefe? He never did time for the Brink's heist, eventually landed a job as Cary Grant's chauffeur, and died of a heart attack in 1976.

The final resting place for around 10,000 early Bostonians – including the Mathers (*see p71* **Inside Track**) – this cemetery was created on the northernmost hill of the Shawmut Peninsula in 1659. The British used the site's geographical advantage to launch cannon balls at the rebel army during the Battle of Bunker Hill; it is said that they warmed up by using some of the cemetery's gravestones for target practice. Also buried here is the slave and soldier Prince Hall, an early black leader in Boston. Hall lived in the free black community that originally settled the hill, and earned fame for his valour in the Battle of Bunker Hill.

FREE Old North Church

193 Salem Street, at Old Street (1-617 523 6676, www.oldnorth.com). Haymarket T. **Open** *Jan, Feb* 10am-4pm Mon-Fri; 9am-5pm Sat, Sun. *Mar-May, Nov, Dec* 9am-5pm daily. *June-Oct* 9am-6pm daily. **Admission** free. **Map** p273 L2. *See p70* **Profile**.

CHARLESTOWN

Community College T, or Haymarket T then bus 92 or 93, or North Station T then 10-15min walk.

A short walk across Charlestown Bridge from the North End, this neighborhood had for many years been known as the tough, working-class area on the edge of the Boston skyline – insular, with mob ties and a predominantly Irish-Catholic population. But its reputation, like that of many of the city's neighborhoods, is changing fast. Over the last two decades it has been infiltrated by young professionals, lured by its elegant waterfront properties and proximity to downtown Boston. Even so, the neighborhood maintains a small-town feel, with its tight, winding streets, clapboard 'triple-decker' three-family houses and corner pubs. Locals are still referred to as 'townies', a nickname that dates back to colonial times.

Charlestown may be on the edge of Boston proper, but it was once the centerpiece of the state. It was settled in 1628, two years before Boston (although once an independent town, it became part of its larger neighbor in the late 19th century). Its prosperity reflected the ebb and flow of business in the Navy Yard, founded in 1800 when the new republic, desperate to respond to attacks on merchant ships by Barbary pirates off the coast of North Africa, decided to beef up its navy. From that point on, it became one of the most critical and, during wartime, busiest shipbuilding and repair yards in the country – at the start of World War II, it employed 47,000 workers. Due to lack of demand, it closed in 1974, and some tough years

Bunker Hill Monument.

followed. Today, the **Charlestown Navy Yard** serves as a museum of American naval history. The most famous ship in the yard (if not in the country) is the USS *Constitution*, built in 1797. The adjacent **USS Constitution Museum** includes an interactive galley where visitors can load and fire a cannon or simulate steering a square-rigger at sea.

From the yard, you can see the obelisk of the **Bunker Hill Monument** shining in the near distance. Dominating picturesque Monument Square, it commemorates one of the most famous battles of the Revolutionary War, and its summit commands spectacular views. Just across the street, an airy museum recounts its bloody history. Not far from Bunker Hill, on Main Street and City Square respectively, and reflecting 1980s gentrification, are the first of celebrity chef Todd English's many restaurants, **Figs** (*see p130*) and **Olives**. Although the antique charm of the **Warren Tavern** (2 Pleasant Street, at Main Street, 1-617 241 8142) is somewhat marred by a blaring TV and modern bar fittings, it retains some of its period atmosphere. Named after Dr Joseph Warren, a popular revolutionary who died in the final clash in the Battle of Bunker Hill, the tavern was built just after most of Charlestown burned down in the

SIGHTS

late 18th century, making it one of the oldest structures in the area. Paul Revere presided over Masonic meetings as a grand master here, and George Washington visited as president. After closing in the 1960s, the tavern reopened in 1972, and has thrived ever since.

FREE Bunker Hill Monument
Monument Square, Breed's Hill (1-617 242 5641, www.nps.gov). Community College T. **Open** 9am-5pm daily. **Admission** free.
This 221ft granite obelisk, completed in 1842, commemorates the first major battle of the American Revolution. Technically speaking, it didn't go well for America: after a bloody conflict, the rebels had to retreat and the British declared victory. But England sustained severe casualties – almost half of its 2,200 troops were killed, compared to 440 American soldiers – and the fight emboldened the colonists. The legendary battle's name is actually a misnomer, as much of the fighting took place on Breed's Hill, the site of the monument – Bunker Hill is nearby, visible from the top of Breed's Hill. This isn't the first structure to commemorate the event; an 18ft wooden pillar with a gilt urn was erected in 1794.

Visitors can listen to free talks from park rangers, or climb the monument's 294 steps (a brisk ascent takes five minutes) for a breathtaking view of Boston. In front of the tower is a statue of Colonel William Prescott, an American officer whose instruction to troops in the Battle of Bunker Hill –

'Don't fire until you see the whites of their eyes!' – has become part of American military lore. Across the street, the Bunker Hill Museum, part of a $3.7 million restoration project, completed in 2007, features displays of weaponry, a 360° painting of the battle and an enormous diorama of fighting soldiers.

FREE Charlestown Navy Yard
Entrance at Gate 1, Constitution Road (1-617 242 5601, www.nps.gov). North Station T then 15min walk, or Haymarket T then bus 92, 93. **Open** *Visitor center* 9am-6pm daily. **Admission** free. **Map** p273 M1.
Established in 1800 at the point where the Mystic and Charles Rivers converge, this was once the country's premier naval dockyard. Its most famous occupant is the USS *Constitution*, which earned its nickname, 'Old Ironsides', during the War of 1812, when a sailor watched as shots fired by a British cannon bounced off its hull. The sailor is said to have shouted, 'Her sides are made of iron!' Although 'Ironsides' is actually made of oak, the nickname stuck. The *Constitution* is the oldest commissioned warship in the country – and although it has largely remained in dry dock since the late 19th century, in 1997 (its bicentennial year) it set sail for the first time in 116 years. The ship is also towed into Boston harbor and turned around once a year to ensure that the hull weathers evenly. Free tours are given daily. The *Constitution*'s neighbor is the restored naval destroyer USS *Cassin Young*, which during World War II served in the Pacific to provide early warning of air attacks to the rest of the fleet, and thereby suffered kamikaze suicide attacks by Japanese fighter pilots.

USS Constitution Museum
Building 22, Charlestown Navy Yard, off Constitution Road (1-617 242 5670, www.ussconstitutionmuseum.org). North Station T then 15min walk, or Haymarket T then bus 92, 93. **Open** *Museum* mid Apr-mid Oct 9am-6pm daily. Mid Oct-mid Apr 10am-5pm daily. *Ship* Apr-Sept 10am-6pm Tue-Sun. Oct-Mar 10am-3.50pm Thur-Sun. **Admission** free (donation suggested). **No credit cards**. **Map** p273 M1.
Built in 1797, this legendary old frigate became one of the most celebrated warships of its era, taking part in more than 30 battles and engagements. Ottoman polacres, French brigs and British privateers all felt the force of her guns. Today, 'Old Ironsides' is the oldest commissioned warship in America. Children can explore the inside of the ship, ask questions of guides decked out in period garb, then learn about the vessel's stormy history in the adjacent museum – where they can also try out sailors' hammocks for size. Located in a converted pumphouse in the Yard, the museum has exhibitions that relate both to the *Constitution* itself and to more general naval history. Interactive displays offer a simulated hands-on seafaring experience: the thrill of battle on deck and handling the ship's massive sails.

SIGHTS

USS Constitution.

The Waterfront

Coastal walks and contemporary art.

Although a section of the waterfront was developed decades ago, when the warehouses of **Commercial Wharf** and **Long Wharf** were converted into apartments, restaurants and other businesses, huge stretches of prime land remained untapped.

Following a $3.9 billion clean-up program launched in the 1980s after George Bush Sr called it 'the filthiest harbor in America', the city has been creating the 47-mile **HarborWalk**, an uninterrupted coastal path from East Boston to Dorchester. Much has already been completed; visit www.boston harborwalk.com for updates, as well as a map, points of interest and events.

Things appear to be picking up pace again, and the Waterfront now stands at the center of a flurry of development, both residential and commercial, that is changing the face of the area (*see p29*).

Charlestown
Navy Yard
The North End &
Charlestown
Cambridge
Old North
Church
Beacon Hill &
the West End
**The
Waterfront**
State House
Faneuil
Hall
*Boston
Common*
ICA
Trinity
Church
Downtown
Back Bay &
the South End

Map p273
Hotels p108

**Restaurants
& cafés** p130
Pubs & bars p149

LONG WHARF & CENTRAL WHARF

Aquarium T.

On the harborfront almost directly behind Faneuil Hall Marketplace lies **Long Wharf** (*photo p78*). Originally known as Boston Pier when it was constructed in the 17th century, it became the center of the city's shipping trade; the brick warehouses date from the 18th century. The shoreline has changed quite a bit since then: when the **Custom House** (*see p50*) was built in 1847, it stood at the edge of the water – today, the landmark building lies several blocks inland, across the **Rose Kennedy Greenway**.

The green space at the border of Long Wharf is **Christopher Columbus Park**. A huge wooden arbor, with vine-covered trellises and benches from which to admire the waterfront views, gives the spot a romantic air and there's a popular children's playground (*see p187*). Long Wharf is the departure point for whale-watching and sightseeing cruises or tours of the Boston Harbor Islands, while the hulking, concrete-and-glass **New England Aquarium** sits on neighboring Central Wharf.

New England Aquarium
1 Central Wharf, at Atlantic Avenue & Milk Street (1-617 973 5200, www.neaq.org).
Aquarium T. **Open** *July, Aug* 9am-6pm Mon-Thur; 9am-7pm Fri-Sun. *Sept-June* 9am-5pm Mon-Fri; 9am-6pm Sat, Sun. **Admission** $22; $14 reductions. **Credit** AmEx, MC, V.
Map p273 M4.
The breathtaking centerpiece of this excellent aquarium is the colossal 200,000-gallon salt-water replica of a Caribbean coral reef. The cylindrical tank, 40ft in diameter and three stories tall, is alive with moray eels, stingrays, gigantic sea turtles and menacing sharks. On a smaller scale, a touch tank exhibit lets children plunge their hands into the cold water of a tidal basin and get up close and personal with starfish, sea urchins and hermit crabs. The huge indoor penguin exhibit (constructed so almost all of the balconies overlook it) is a hoot. If the lines are too long, peek at the playful inhabitants of the outdoor seal enclosure instead. The IMAX theatre offers state-of-the-art 3D glasses to put viewers in the middle of the action. *Photo p76.*
▶ *From April to October, the Aquarium runs a naturalist-narrated whale watch boat trip, which visits one of the largest whale feeding grounds in the world; see www.neaq.org for details.*

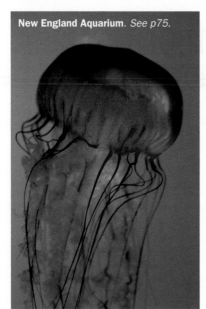

New England Aquarium. *See p75.*

FREE **Rose Kennedy Greenway**
*Along Atlantic Avenue (1-617 292 0020,
www.rosekennedygreenway.org). South Station,
Aquarium or Haymarket T.* **Open** 7am-11pm
daily. **Admission** free. **Map** p273 L3-L5.
The Greenway is one of the most celebrated results
of the now-infamous Big Dig (a kind of street-level
answer to New York's High Line). Formed when
I-93 was sunk underground, this verdant, mile-long
ribbon of grassy parks and outdoor resting places
invites the weary traveler (or office warrior) to stop
and take a moment to appreciate the city's fleeting
sunshine. There are also periodic festivals, events,
and parades located on or near the park.
▶ *For more about the Greenway and its genesis,
see p30 Going Green.*

BOSTON HARBOR ISLANDS

Some of the waterfront's least-exploited
assets are these 34 small islands, left by
a retreating glacier about 12,000 years ago.
In the 1990s, Congress designated them
national parkland, and they provide a thriving
wildlife habitat. Rare and endangered species
of birds such as plovers and ospreys have
been spotted here, and grey and harp seals
live in the harbor.

Although only six of the islands are
currently accessible by public ferry, special
arrangements can be made to visit most of the
others (1-617 223 8666, www.bostonislands.com).

In recent years, the islands' fate has become
a hot topic as waterfront renovation booms.
There had once been murmurs of developments
– B&Bs, amphitheaters, shops and even a water
slide – on the islands. Today, the city hosts
family events, yoga and vintage baseball
games in an attempt to bolster interest in these
forgotten resources. Largely unvisited, aside
from the fairly well-trafficked Fort Warren
on Georges Island, the islands make a pleasant
escape from the city on a warm afternoon.

Short of bringing your own boat, you can
catch a **Harbor Express** commuter boat
(1-617 222 6999, www.harborexpress.com)
from T Wharf (alongside Long Wharf Marriott).
The two most popular islands are Georges
Island and Spectacle Island. At 28 acres,
Georges Island is dominated by **Fort
Warren**, a massive structure used during the
Civil War as a Union training base and a prison
for captured Confederate soldiers (including,
most famously, the vice-president of the
Confederacy, Alexander Hamilton Stephens).
You can either take a guided tour or explore it
on your own. The 105-acre **Spectacle Island**
is the latest island to be opened up to the public.
A landfill for decades, it was capped off with
earth displaced by the Big Dig in 2005, and
now features a swimming beach, a large marina
and a visitors' center. The views of Boston from
atop its two hills are breathtaking.

Bumpkin Island, covering about 35 acres,
is tucked away in Hingham Bay and doesn't
see much traffic. From the early part of the
20th century to the 1940s it was used to
quarantine children with polio. Today it's one
of four islands, along with Peddocks, Grape
and Lovells, where camping is permitted.
In all cases, reservations must be made in
advance with park officials by calling the
number above. Also note that, inexplicably –
chalk it up to prim New England culture –
alcohol is not permitted on the islands.

Grape Island has never been developed;
the remains of a 19th-century farmhouse are
the only clue that the 50-acre island was once
inhabited. It has pristine shell and gravel
beaches, campsites and berries to pick.

Lovells Island covers 62 acres and
has a public swimming beach, hiking trails,
wooded hills and dunes. **Peddocks Island**,
at 188 acres, is the largest of the archipelago.
During the 1960s, a 4,100-year-old skeleton
was excavated on its shores. It's the only island
with residents all year round; when the Harbor
Islands were first turned into a state park,
the state granted the residents – most of them
fishermen – life-long leases; upon their death
the land reverts back to state ownership.
Peddocks, with its salt marshes and woods,
is great for picnicking, camping and hiking.

Faces & Places Jill Medvedow

Q&A with the ICA visionary.

As executive director of the Institute of Contemporary Art, and the driving force behind the construction of its impressive new waterfront building, Jill Medvedow has had a pronounced influence on the modern face of Boston. With its dramatic folding ribbon form and cantilever that extends to the harbor's edge, the new ICA (*see p79*) – the first art museum built in the city for nearly 100 years – makes a bold visual statement, signaling the transformation of a formerly barren district and putting Boston on the map as a destination for cutting-edge art.

TO: Why did you choose to live and work in Boston?
JM: It's a place that combines tremendous educational institutions with a fantastic location: it's very accessible to beautiful places in every direction, from the Boston Harbor Islands to Martha's Vineyard and Nantucket, Cape Ann, the Berkshires and Maine. And it's a fantastic place to raise a family, which is really important to me. Also, for a city, it's walkable.

TO: How has the city evolved?
JM: It's a much more lively, vibrant, financially healthy, diverse and active city than when I first moved here almost 20 years ago. There has been a big change in the South End in terms of galleries and restaurants, and the successful completion of the Big Dig.

TO: How has the new ICA galvanized the local arts community?
JM: It has brought tremendous national and international attention to Boston, as many people have called this the first 21st-century art museum to be built. It continues to play a critical role in making sure that the best art being made around the world is presented in Boston. Artists have an opportunity to experience that work, and our young people don't need to travel in order to participate.

TO: Was it difficult completing the project?
JM: Let's just say that for many years, this project had been characterized by a prevailing sense of skepticism; the widely held view was that it wasn't going

to happen. It was a difficult, thrilling, exhilarating and arduous process.

TO: What are your favorite places in the city?
JM: There are many great galleries. Barbara Krakow Gallery (*see p195*) and Samson Projects (*see p196*) are two places I visit frequently. First Fridays, the once-a-month South End open studios (*see p195*), is always exhilarating. The Harbor Islands (*see left*) are some of the best-kept secrets in Boston. For restaurants I like Barbara Lynch's Butcher Shop (*see p124*) and B&G Oysters (*see p124*), as well as Clio (*see p119*) and Toro (*see p127*). And in my own neighborhood of Brookline, I like La Morra (*see p138*).

TO: And your pet hates?
JM: Potholes, lack of signage, and litter.

SIGHTS

SIGHTS

FORT POINT CHANNEL

South Station T.

Fort Point, 16 December 1773: a group of 60 colonists disguised as Mohawk Indians dumps 342 chests of tea into Boston Harbor in protest at the tea tax imposed by King George III. The original ships involved are long gone (and the actual site was more towards the harbor, where the InterContinental hotel now stands), but re-enactments take place every year, complete with period costumes and a rambunctious crowd. Since the 1970s, the *Brig Beaver*, a replica of one of the Tea Party tea ships, was at the center of these celebrations; however, after a fire in 2002, it's been closed for repair and renovation. The new and improved **Boston Tea Party Ships & Museum**, at the Congress Street Bridge (1-617 269 7150, www.bostonteapartyship.com), is due to reopen in summer 2011, though that may be optimistic.

In the late 1970s, the warehouses of this former industrial area attracted artists, who defined the neighborhood. Although many have been forced out by developers over the last decade, several live/work buildings remain, including the looming structure at 300 Summer Street, which contains the **Fort Point Arts Community Gallery** (*see p197*). Check the FPAC's website (www.fortpointarts.org) for details of the annual open-studios weekend in the autumn, when more than 200 artists open their doors to the public (*see p183* **Inside Track**).

The run-down streets of derelict warehouses are gradually being smartened up and new businesses are moving in. Retro-style **Lucky's** on Congress Street (*see p149*) was one of the first bar/restaurants to arrive, serving classy cocktails and live music mostly in the Frank Sinatra vein. A slick, spacious branch of the **Flour Bakery & Café** (*see p126*) has established itself with the work crowd on Farnsworth Street, and celebrated chef Barbara Lynch has opened two restaurants, **Sportello** (*see p132*) and **Menton**, and a cocktail-lover's bar, **Drink** (*see p149*), on the lower floors of **FP3** (347-354 Congress Street), one of the city's hip condo projects.

Long Wharf. *See p75.*

Institute of Contemporary Art.

Longtime resident the **Children's Museum** (*see p188* **Profile**) underwent a 21st-century makeover, with a sleek glass extension and a new landscaped outdoor space and is one of the best places to bring kids in Boston. The oversized **Milk Bottle** (300 Congress Street) outside the museum is a Fort Point landmark that started life as a highway drive-in, and still serves ice-cream and snacks in summer.

SEAPORT DISTRICT

Silver Line Waterfront to World Trade Center.

Poised for major development, the area also known as the South Boston Waterfront is a hot topic around City Hall (*see p29*). The **Institute of Contemporary Art** currently stands in splendid isolation at the water's edge at Fan Pier, backed by a sea of parking lots that are gradually giving way to a tide of residential and retail construction. Further along Northern Avenue are the **Seaport Hotel** (*see p109*) and **World Trade Center** (*see p253*), while a few blocks inland is the impressive **Boston Convention & Exhibition Center** (*see p253*). But before the developers moved in, people came here for seafood. Although now eclipsed by more fashionable fish places, the classic restaurants are still lined up along the pier; the **No Name Restaurant** (15½ Fish Pier, at Northern Avenue, 1-617 338 7539) offers fried seafood galore, while **Anthony's Pier 4** (140 Northern Avenue, 1-617 482 6262, www.pier4.com) serves up baked cod and finnan haddie (smoked haddock) among

the driftwood and fishing nets. **Legal Sea Foods** has its headquarters here, and nearby is its **Legal Test Kitchen** (LTK; *see p130*), where you can get a preview of what the chain is cooking up. Beer-lovers can tour the **Harpoon Brewery** (306 Northern Avenue, 1-617 574 9551, www.harpoonbrewery.com) and taste the popular local brew.

Institute of Contemporary Art

100 Northern Avenue (1-617 478 3100, www.icaboston.org). Silver Line Waterfront to World Trade Center. **Open** 10am-5pm Tue, Wed, Sat, Sun; 10am-9pm Thur, Fri. **Admission** $15; $10 reductions; free under-17s. Free to all 5-9pm Thur. **Credit** AmEx, MC, V. **Map** p273 N5.

Once crammed into a tiny building in Back Bay, the ICA moved to its spacious new home in late 2006, and is now the cultural cornerstone of the waterfront. With its 65,000sq ft floor space, the dramatic, glass-walled building houses galleries, a theatre and a café.

The ICA prides itself on being a platform for challenging works – the permanent collection includes pieces by the likes of Julian Opie, Paul Chan and Mona Hatoum, while changing shows explore broader themes that unite different artists' work, or focus on individual luminaries (Louise Bourgeois, Philip-Lorca diCorcia and the like).

After you've contemplated the art, retreat to the deck outside, with its expansive vista over the harbor. The building has such unusual features as a downward-sloping Mediatheque that culminates in a front window framing a patch of water.
► *For an interview with the museum's director, see p77 Faces & Places.*

Cambridge

Explore the peaceful campuses and lively nightlife of student central.

The city just across the river from Boston is dominated by its two famous academic institutions: **Harvard University** and the **Massachusetts Institute of Technology (MIT)**. The high density of students and academics has created a liberal, bohemian vibe. Over the years, the traditionally affluent areas around Harvard Square have spread, pushing lower-income immigrant communities, intellectuals and artists to the outskirts.

While inflated property prices may make a mockery of its old moniker 'the People's Republic of Cambridge', it's still a free-thinking community – it hosted the country's first same-sex marriage in 2004. The residential areas are characterized by colorfully painted clapboard houses – from sprawling mansions to three-family triple-deckers in the once working-class neighborhoods.

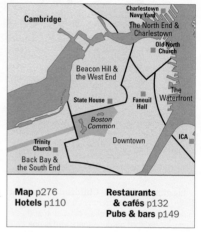

Map p276	Restaurants
Hotels p110	& cafés p132
	Pubs & bars p149

SIGHTS

HARVARD SQUARE

Harvard T.

It may be cool, but Cambridge is all about squares. The town is divided into small neighborhoods, which are themselves divided into a matrix of squares – although many of these are little more than glorified intersections, and almost none are square-shaped. The best known of these, and certainly one of the most popular, is **Harvard Square** (www.harvard square.com). It's a people-watcher's paradise, as the bustle of bookish Harvard students (a few actually wearing their sweaters tied over their shoulders), mohawked punks, camera-toting tourists, homeless panhandlers, buskers and harried businesspeople creates a diverse and colorful street scene.

Coming out of the Harvard Square T station, the biggest local landmark is right in front of you. **Out of Town News**, perched on an island at the confluence of Massachusetts Avenue, and Brattle and John F Kennedy Streets, stocks periodicals from all over the world, and is also the area's most popular

meeting place. Next to it is a pedestrianized space known as 'the Pit' – not much to look at when no one's around, but a hangout for kids since punk rock broke in the 1970s.

There are usually street performers on every corner of the square when the weather is fine, but a favorite spot is outside the local branch of bakery-café chain **Au Bon Pain** (1100 Massachusetts Avenue, 1-617 354 4144). The café itself is unremarkable, but it's a prime people-watching spot. Chess experts set up at the outdoor tables, and for a buck or two they'll let you challenge them; for a few more you can get a one-on-one lesson.

The streets of Harvard Square are lined with restaurants, cafés and shops. An influx of mega-chains, banks and high-end boutiques over the past couple of decades has pushed out characterful old establishments and undermined the neighborhood feel, yet there are some notable survivors including independent cinema the **Brattle Theatre** (*see p191*) and legendary folk venue **Club Passim** (*see p210*), which helped to launch the careers of Joan Baez and Suzanne Vega, among others. Retail stalwarts include **Cardullo's** (*see p171*),

80 Time Out Boston

a wonderfully eccentric gourmet food shop, and **Leavitt & Peirce** (1316 Massachusetts Avenue, 1-617 547 0576), an unchanging tobacconist established in 1883. Decorated with ancient Harvard crew oars and team photos, it has become a tourist attraction in its own right. You can still find a whiff of the old nonconformist spirit in time-honored hangouts **Café Algiers** (*see p132*) and **Mr Bartley's Burger Cottage** (*see p135*).

While it once laid claim to the most booksellers per square mile of any city in America, Cambridge is no longer the browsers' paradise it once was. Only a handful remain, protected by their passionate fan-base, including the **Grolier Poetry Book Shop** (*see p159*) and **Harvard Book Store** (*see p159*). You'll find graphic novels and regular visits by the people who create them at **Million Year Picnic** (99 Mount Auburn Street, 1-617 492 6763).

From Harvard Square it's a short stroll to the **Charles River**. Walk down John F Kennedy Street and you'll soon reach the embankment, along which there are walking paths in both directions. It's especially pleasant on summer Sundays, when Memorial Drive is closed to traffic, and runners, bladers and bikers take over the street. Head left for breathtaking views of Boston on the opposite bank.

In the opposite direction from Harvard Square, at Garden Street and Mass Ave, is the grassy **Cambridge Common**, where George Washington took control of the Continental Army in 1775 – a plaque marks the elm tree under which the troops were mustered. Nearby is the **Old Burying Ground**, dating from 1635, and **Christ Church** (Zero Garden Street, 1-617 876 0200, www.cccambridge.org), the site where

Harvard Square.

George and Martha once worshipped. Designed in 1761 by the country's first trained architect, Peter Harrison, Christ Church was a hotbed of rebel activity during the Revolutionary War: the walls are still peppered with bullet holes.

Nearby **Brattle Street** was once called Tory Row, and several of the mansions of its former wealthy merchant residents remain. The further you venture from Harvard Square on Brattle, the older and grander the houses become. Near the end is the HQ of the Cambridge Historical Society, which, appropriately, has set up shop in the oldest house in Cambridge, the 1688 **Hooper-Lee-Nichols House** (159 Brattle Street, 1-617 547 4252).

Further along Brattle or Mount Auburn Street is the vast **Mount Auburn Cemetery**, the country's first garden cemetery. It's a lovely and peaceful place, where many of the city's most famous residents are buried. To the north is **Fresh Pond** (take bus 72, 74 or 75 from Harvard Square), which was used in the 1800s as an ice source, and today is a peaceful reservoir with a two-mile perimeter and constantly changing scenery.

Carry on along Mass Ave from Cambridge Common and you will eventually reach Porter Square. While the square itself is unremarkable, the funky shops you'll find along the way are worth investigating – including the dazzling fair-trade and folk art emporium **Nomad** (no.1741, between Linnaean & Prentiss Streets, 1-617 497 6677, www.nomadcambridge.com) and the excellent children's bookshop **Barefoot Books** (no.1771, at Forest Street, 1-617 349 1610, www.barefootbooks.com).

Longfellow National Historic Site

105 Brattle Street, at Longfellow Park (1-617 876 4491, www.nps.gov/long). Harvard T. **Open** *Tours* June-Oct noon-4.30pm Wed-Sun. *Grounds* dawn to dusk year-round. **Admission** $3; free under-16s. **No credit cards. Map** p276 A2.

SIGHTS

Walk Harvard Architecture

Take a stroll through the hallowed grounds of academia.

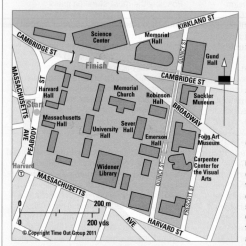

The most prominent entry to the yard is through **Johnston Gate** where, until the 1970s, the governor of Massachusetts arrived for students' graduation ceremonies in a carriage with scarlet-clad mounted lancers. Johnston Gate is flanked by **Massachusetts Hall** on the right and **Harvard Hall** on the left, two of the few remaining 18th-century Georgian buildings on the site.

Aligned with the gate is **University Hall**, a noble grey Chelmsford granite structure that has housed a series of administrative functions since 1813. Its architect, Charles Bulfinch, also designed the State House in Boston and is credited with proposing the system of interconnected yards that would guide Harvard's growth for the next century.

The challenging academics may take place inside Harvard's eclectic collection of buildings, but its outdoor spaces are the institution's heart and soul, offering a tree-lined vision of serenity amid the cut-throat Ivy League competition. Harvard Yard is the oldest; enclosed by buildings and a wrought iron fence, it feels a world away from its commercial counterpart, Harvard Square.

On the other side of University Hall is New Yard, dominated by **Widener Library** and **Memorial Church**, both built in the early 20th century. Between them stands one of Harvard's finest buildings, **Sever Hall**, designed by seminal American architect HH Richardson in 1878. Its monumental red-brick mass is penetrated

George Washington made this pretty, 28-room mansion his Continental Army headquarters from 1775 to 1776, before following the front line further south. In 1837 it became a boarding house, and a young Harvard professor, Henry Wadsworth Longfellow, moved in. When he married, his bride's father gave it to him as a wedding present, and he stayed until his death in 1882. In between entertaining such literary luminaries as Nathaniel Hawthorne, Ralph Waldo Emerson and Charles Dickens, Longfellow composed many of his best-known works here.

★ FREE Mount Auburn Cemetery

580 Mount Auburn Street, at Aberdeen Avenue (1-617 547 7105, www.mountauburn.org). Harvard T then bus 71, 73. **Open** *Cemetery* 8am-5pm daily. *Greenhouse* 8am-3.30pm Mon-Fri; 8-11.30am Sat. **Admission** free.
Mount Auburn Cemetery is the final resting place for Oliver Wendell Holmes, Henry Wadsworth Longfellow and Charles Bulfinch, along with some

86,000 others. In fact, the cemetery is now so full that locals who want to spend eternity here often settle for cremation. But there's plenty of life too. There are 4,000 types of tree and 130 species of shrub alone on its 175 acres, and excellent free guided tours to help you distinguish them.

FREE Old Burying Ground

Massachusetts Avenue, at Garden Street (no phone). Harvard T. **Open** dawn-dusk daily. **Admission** free. **Map** p276 A2.
One of the country's first cemeteries, the Old Burying Ground contains the remains of several early Puritan settlers as well as Revolutionary War veterans and victims.

Harvard University

Harvard has more than 400 buildings scattered around Cambridge and Boston, but for the campus you've seen in the movies, head to by a deep archway, and a fluid system of ornamentation gives an elemental strength to the building's many bays and towers.

A short walk through or around Sever leads to a court that opens on to Quincy Street. **Robinson Hall**, to the north, was designed by New York architects McKim, Mead and White and sits opposite the even grander **Emerson Hall**. Both halls are rendered in a refined classical style that speaks of early 20th-century America: wealthy, powerful, and increasingly led by the very people who wandered these walkways.

Across Quincy Street you'll see a remarkable series of buildings that challenge Harvard's stodginess (with various degrees of success). The most prominent is the **Carpenter Center for the Visual Arts** (*see p85*). A masterful sculptural composition of rectangular and curvilinear concrete forms built in 1960, it is the only building in America by Le Corbusier. The towering concrete columns and ramp allow views down into studios, reinterpreting the traditional tree-lined diagonal pathways of Harvard Yard for a community of artists and filmmakers.

Next door is the **Fogg Art Museum** (closed until 2013), which dates from 1925. It's a historicist hotchpotch: a Georgian Revival façade with a travertine replica of a 16th-century Italian courtyard, adjacent to gallery spaces in the 16th-century French and 17th-century English

styles. A minimalist 1990 addition by New York architects Gwathmey Siegal & Associates sits behind it.

Across the street is the **Arthur M Sackler Museum** (*see p84*), a 1981 effort from British architect James Stirling. Its pastiche of historical styles, more playful than the Fogg's, was considered inventive at the height of so-called 'post-modernism' but now looks cartoonish. Still, its vertiginous interior stairway and skylit galleries are worth exploring.

Anchoring the other side of Cambridge Street is John Andrew's **Gund Hall**, home to Harvard's Graduate School of Design since 1972. Four gargantuan concrete 'trays' holding open studios step upwards under a vast, sloping (and sometimes leaking) roof, giving dramatic expression to the work taking place inside.

Dominating the corner, and the skyline, is **Memorial Hall**. Although it looks like a cathedral, it actually houses the dining hall and Sanders Theatre (*see p206*). Its multicolored Victorian gothic masonry and steep slate roofs have gone in and out of fashion since 1878, when its doors opened to commemorate Harvard's contribution to the Civil War. Its neighbor is almost a century younger: the **Science Center** was the creation of Spanish architect and Design School dean Josep Lluís Sert in 1970. Its interior courtyards and walkways are a celebration of technology and community, from which future leaders will emerge.

SIGHTS

Harvard Yard (for tours, call 1-617 495 1573), a grassy, tree-lined quadrangle surrounded by red-brick buildings. First-year students still live in dormitories in the Yard, and you'll find them studying and reading (or flirting or sleeping) on the grassy sections of the quad.

As you enter the Yard from Mass Ave through Johnston Gate (a half-block walk from the Harvard T), look for **Massachusetts Hall** on the right. Built in 1720, the Hall sheltered the soldiers of the fledgling Continental Army during the Revolutionary War. Massachusetts Hall just edges out the **Wadsworth House** (built in 1726) as the oldest building in the Yard, though the latter's yellow clapboard structure is more picturesque. This building served as temporary headquarters for George Washington when he was leading the nation's army in 1775.

University Hall, designed by Charles Bulfinch in 1815, sits directly in front of the Yard's most popular sight: the **statue of**

John Harvard. Cast in 1884 by Daniel Chester French (who also sculpted the Lincoln Memorial in Washington, DC), it's known as the 'statue of three lies'. Its inscription reads 'John Harvard, Founder, 1638', which is three times untrue since John Harvard was a donor, not a founder; the college was set up in 1636; and nobody knows what he really looked like – French used a Harvard student as a model. Touching John Harvard's shoe is rumored to bring good luck, so tourists line up accordingly, but students know better: peeing on the foot is an undergraduate rite of passage.

So are liaisons among the stacks of **Widener Library**, which sits on the quiet square directly behind University Hall. The imposing, classically styled building houses the headquarters of the oldest university library in the country and the largest academic library system in the world; it holds 3.2 million volumes.

Though most visitors don't venture beyond the main quad, it's worth exploring further in order to see the neo-Gothic **Memorial Hall** (45 Quincy Street), which houses the Sanders Theatre (*see p206*), and the **Carpenter Center for the Visual Arts** (24 Quincy Street), designed in 1963 by the French modernist architect Le Corbusier – his only North American building. Other notable buildings on campus include the **Science Center**, just north of the central quad – which is said to look like a Polaroid camera, and is one of several buildings at Harvard designed by Josep Lluís Sert. (For an architectural tour of the campus, *see p82* **Walk**.)

Outside Harvard Yard

The 12 houses that serve as Harvard's undergraduate dorms are clustered near Harvard Square: walk down Plympton Street, past the gold cupola of **Adams House**, and turn right on to Mount Auburn Street and past the enormous blue bell tower of **Lowell House**. Lying between Harvard Yard and Memorial Drive is the **Harvard Lampoon Castle** (44 Bow Street), offices of the satirical publication the *Harvard Lampoon*, which has spawned countless writers and comedians, including John Updike and Conan O'Brien. You can't go inside, but it's still worth seeing the exterior. It's wedged on to a tiny sliver of land between Mount Auburn and Bow Streets, but architects Wheelwright & Haven made the most of the site in 1909, creating a cartoonish, miniature castle that reflects its mischievous inhabitants.

Harvard has an impressive array of museums that range from the authoritative to the bizarre. Casualties of the 'shoot it and stuff it' school of science fill several halls in the **Museum of Natural History** (26 Oxford Street, 1-617

495 3045, www.hmnh.harvard.edu), which also houses a collection of intricate, minutely detailed flowers modeled out of glass and Vladimir Nabokov's meticulous catalogue of butterfly genitalia. The spoils of 100 years of excavations in the Near East are free for anyone to view at the **Semitic Museum** (6 Divinity Avenue, 1-617 495 4631). Thanks to the lofty aspirations and generous donations of generations of Harvard alumni, the collections on display in the Harvard art museums – the **Arthur M Sackler Museum**, and currently closed Fogg Art and Busch-Reisinger museums – are impressive.

Arthur M Sackler Museum

485 Broadway, at Quincy Street (1-617 495 9400, www.artmuseums.harvard.edu). Harvard T. **Open** 10am-5pm Mon-Sat; 1-5pm Sun. **Admission** (with Fogg Art & Busch-Reisinger Museums) $9; $6-$7 reductions; free under-18s. Free to all 4.30-5pm daily, 10am-noon Sat. **Credit** AmEx, MC, V. **Map** p276 B2.

The Sackler is the place to peruse ancient objects, from Romanic gambling artifacts to ancient coins. With two floors of display cases and one floor for special exhibitions, the museum is dedicated to Asian, Islamic and later Indian art. It houses the widest collection of Chinese jades outside China, an unrivalled showcase of Korean ceramics, and an outstanding collection of Thai illuminated manuscripts. With the Fogg and Busch-Reisinger Museums across the street closed for renovations, the Sackler currently plays host to the best of all three institutions. The large permanent collections are displayed on a rotating basis; its sister museums should reopen (freshened by star architect Renzo Piano) in 2013.

INSIDE TRACK **INVENTED HERE**

Whether it's due to an overabundance of education or just something in the water, Yankee ingenuity is a strong tradition here. There's no shortage of gadgets and gizmos with a local pedigree, from the disposable razor (invented by King Camp Gillette) to the differential analyzer – a forerunner of today's computers (invented by Vannevar Bush). The iconic Thomas Edison got his start as a young inventor in Boston; his first patented invention, an electric vote counter, was created here. Over a century later, MIT students are now working on ways to transmit electricity through space without using wires.

FREE Carpenter Center for the Visual Arts/Sert Gallery

24 Quincy Street, at Harvard Yard (1-617 495 3251, www.ves.fas.harvard.edu). Harvard T.
Open 10am-11pm Mon-Sat; 1-11pm Sun.
Admission free. **Credit** AmEx, MC, V.
Map p276 B2.

In the Le Corbusier-designed Carpenter Center for the Visual Arts, the ground-floor main gallery and the Sert Gallery on the third floor host regular exhibitions by prominent artists. The focus is on contemporary work, with a particular emphasis on photography.

Peabody Museum of Archaeology & Ethnology/Museum of Natural History

11 Divinity Avenue, at Kirkland Street (1-617 496 1027, www.peabody.harvard.edu). Harvard T.
Open 9am-5pm daily. **Admission** $9; $6-$7 reductions. **Credit** AmEx, MC, V. **Map** p276 B2.

The Peabody features fossils and anthropological artifacts from as far back as the Palaeolithic period, with exhibitions on North American Indians and Central America. Connected to the Peabody is Harvard's Museum of Natural History (*see p186*), which exhibits dinosaur fossils, mineral and rock collections and a menagerie of stuffed animals that includes pheasants once owned by George Washington. A highlight of the museum is the world's only mounted kronosaurus, a 42ft-long prehistoric marine reptile.
▶ *For other highlights, see p81 Inside Track.*

CENTRAL SQUARE

Central T.

Although undoubtedly gentrified, Central Square has kept its distinct, rather gritty, identity. There is still a black and immigrant presence in what was predominantly a working-

INSIDE TRACK WEIRD SCIENCE

If there's a mad-scientist capital of the world, it's surely **MIT** (*see p86*). The MIT Media Lab, in particular, is an incubator of bizarrely wonderful ideas – like Eigenradio, a project to create 'statistically optimal' music by analyzing pop radio. (There's not much practical use for it, but their 2004 album, *A Singular Christmas*, was an internet hit.) MIT's Artificial Intelligence Lab, where researchers are developing 'sociable' robots, is another think tank whose resident geniuses are stretching the limits of what technology can do.

class neighborhood. Over the past decade or so, it's become a desirable location for young professionals – high-priced condos and the ubiquitous chains have followed. On the plus side, so have some great restaurants, such as **Rendezvous** (*see p135*), and stylish bars including the **Enormous Room** (*see p149*).

With a high concentration of eating and drinking options, Central Square is a popular spot for going out. Fabled rock clubs the **Middle East** (*see p209*) and **TT the Bear's Place** (*see p210*) share the same block. Other hangouts include Irish pub the **Field** (*see p149*) and ultra-chilled lounge bar **ZuZu** (*see p152*).

During the day, the square's sprinkling of unusual shops, such as venerable vintage emporium **Great Eastern Trading Co** (*see p165*), second-hand vinyl fixture **Cheapo Records** (*see p176*) and kitsch general store/gift shop **Buckaroo's Mercantile** (*see p172*), makes for an interesting browse.

SIGHTS

Harvard Yard. *See p83.*

About a 15-minute walk up Prospect Street from Central, at the intersection of Hampshire and Cambridge Streets, is **Inman Square**, an up-and-coming hipster zone graced with a high concentration of reasonably priced restaurants, including Brazilian eateries run by the local immigrant community, quirky shops and wonderful ice-cream at **Christina's** (*see p133*).

KENDALL SQUARE

Kendall/MIT T.

Harvard notwithstanding, some incredibly bright folks attend that other top Cambridge college, the **Massachusetts Institute of Technology** in Kendall Square, a short walk from Central Square along Mass Ave. MIT was founded in 1861 and rose to prominence during World War II, when radar was invented in its labs. The architecture of its various buildings is wildly diverse, ranging from the neoclassical walls of Building Ten to some striking modern structures by Eero Saarinen, Alvar Aalto, IM Pei and, latterly, the Frank Gehry-designed **Ray & Maria Stata Center**. (For more on MIT's architecture, *see p40*.)

At the heart of it all, cutting through the centre of campus and radiating out from under the university's imposing dome, is the so-called 'Infinite Corridor', a long passage – punctuated by unexpected art installations – that connects many of the institute's departments.

MIT has its share of impressive museums, from the cutting-edge **List Visual Arts Center** to the multimedia **MIT Museum**. Sculptures by the likes of Alexander Calder and Henry Moore also dot the grounds. Below MIT's famous dome, in Building 10, the **Compton Gallery** (1-617 253 4444) features alternating shows that draw on the institute's historical collections of art and scientific objects. Hidden away in the back of the fourth floor of Building Four is the Edgerton Center's **Strobe Alley**. The narrow passage displays the work of Harold ('Doc') Edgerton, the pioneer of high-speed photography, who shot the famous images of a bullet explosively tunneling through an apple and a crown-shaped splat of milk. The center carries on his research in high-speed and scientific imaging.

MIT doesn't have the same connection with Kendall Square that Harvard has with its eponymous square, so the area lacks a striking identity. But you'll find some good bars and restaurants and a popular arthouse cinema, the **Kendall Square Cinema** (*see p193*).

List Visual Arts Center

20 Ames Street, at Main Street (1-617 253 4680, http://web.mit.edu/lvac). Kendall/MIT T. **Open** *Oct-June* noon-6pm Tue-Thur, Sat, Sun; noon-8pm Fri. **Admission** free ($5 suggested donation). **No credit cards. Map** p276 C4. Located on the Wiesner Building's first floor, the List Visual Arts Center holds between five and eight shows a year, featuring American and international artists, working in wide variety of media. From conceptual installations to digital displays and video projects, the exhibitions typically push the boundaries of contemporary art.

★ MIT Museum

265 Massachusetts Avenue, at Front Street (1-617 253 4444, http://web.mit.edu/museum). Central or Kendall/MIT T. **Open** 10am-5pm

Charles River. See p81.

daily. **Admission** $7.50. Free to all 3rd Sun of each mth. **No credit cards**. Map p276 C4. Five blocks from MIT's campus, this fascinating museum serves as a historical record of the institute and a showcase for its amazing inventions and related art. In its four on-site collections – general MIT history (including the famous pranks), science and technology, architecture and design, and holography – plus marine engineering at the Hart Nautical Gallery on main campus, you can see everything from exploding chairs and robotic hands to historic lasers developed for NASA.

Alexander Graham Bell carried out research on the MIT campus, so there's a retrospective of early telephonic devices too. Also on display are the kinetic sculptures of Arthur Ganson – ingenious, often hilarious machines that seem to have minds of their own – and the world's largest collection of holographic art, featuring a morphing image of the busts of various scientific geniuses and a woman transmogrifying into a tiger.
▶ *When you've finished being amazed, swing over to nearby Toscanini's (see p136) to refresh yourself with delicious ice-cream or tea.*

Boston Illegal MIT Takes Las Vegas

A calculated risk pays off for student gamblers.

It was pretty heady stuff, for a bunch of fresh-faced math geeks from MIT: checking into Vegas hotels disguised as Russian arms traders, dating strippers and major-league cheerleaders, stashing wads of $100 bills under the laundry in their dorm rooms and walking through airport security with hundreds of thousands of dollars strapped to their bodies under their clothes.

Never mind that what they were doing was technically legal. The MIT Blackjack Club was toying with the most powerful players in Vegas, and Vegas has its own rules. Students were beaten up, threatened at gunpoint and – even worse – audited by the IRS.

Any serious gamblers will be well aware that blackjack players can minimize the house edge to almost nothing just by using correct tactics. As the dealer plays out the deck, the odds shift subtly, and a player who knows how to watch the deck can win big. A deck with a lot of high cards tilts the odds in the players' favor. By counting cards, keeping track of which cards have already been played and bidding high when the deck is 'hot', a player can gain a tiny advantage that will eventually yield big wins – if no mistakes are made.

But most card counters are easy to spot, and casinos have an arsenal of measures against them, from high-tech surveillance to simply harassing players who win more often than they ought to. If you bid high when the deck gets hot, and lower your bids when

there are fewer high cards left in play, you are bound to attract unwelcome attention from casino security before you can make off with much of the house's money.

The MIT team fooled the pit bosses by playing in teams, and by using casinos' profiling techniques against them – disguising a geeky Asian kid as the son of a rich foreign executive, or a red-headed, miniskirted business student as a wide-eyed novice. With tight discipline and immaculate play, they made millions, raking in up to $400,000 on a good weekend.

But, like all good things, it came to an end. Under tremendous pressure, the team split into factions. One group was busted by security fraternizing with each other outside the casino, and their cover was blown. In the end, they became so notorious that it was impossible for them to play anywhere without attracting attention.

Local author Ben Mezrich told the incredible story in two bestselling books, *Bringing Down the House* and *Busting Vegas*. Researching the books, Mezrich tagged along with players, playing blackjack on their massive bankrolls and smuggling cash through airport security.

Mezrich used pseudonyms and composite characters to conceal his subjects' identity. A few have since come forward – most prominently Semyon Dukach, who still lives in Brookline and teaches blackjack seminars. And fictional versions appear in the stylized film *21* (2008), based on Mezrich's first book and starring Kevin Spacey.

SIGHTS

Other Neighborhoods

Discover Kennedy's legacy, lush greenery and a vibrant boho buzz.

Boston's layout is a patchwork of distinct districts, connected by nebulous roads that confuse even life-long residents: just ask for directions from Somerville to Jamaica Plain. While many of these areas are simply neighborhoods others are separately administered cities, such as Cambridge (*see p80*) and Brookline, which feel like parts of Boston.

Ironically, given the city's reputation for liberalism and its association with the 19th-century Abolitionist movement, Boston's working-class neighborhoods were largely segregated by race in the 20th century, although widespread immigration and gentrification have latterly created a more diverse ethnic mix in all quarters of the city.

Map pp270-271	**Restaurants**
Pubs & bars p152	**& cafés** p136

ROXBURY & DORCHESTER

Roxbury: Jackson Sq, Mass Ave, Roxbury Crossing or Ruggles T, or Silver Line Washington St. Dorchester: Ashmont, Fields Corner, JFK/UMass, Savin Hill or Shawmut T.

Roxbury is considered the heart of Boston's African-American community, although it hasn't always been a likely tourist stop. The inner-city neighborhood is emerging from hard times: in the 1980s and early '90s it was known for its high crime rate and low employment, with the warehouses and factories that once generated a booming manufacturing trade long abandoned. In recent years, however, the area has been receiving more constructive attention. Community events, grassroots activism and a boost in state funding have helped revitalize the neighborhood.

Attracted by the low rents, artists have set up studios and experimental galleries such as **HallSpace** (950 Dorchester Avenue, www.hallspace.org); and cultural venues such

as the **Roxbury Center for Arts** have been established (182-186 Dudley Street, 1-617 849 6324). While the neighborhood can still feel quite threatening to visitors, **Discover Roxbury** (183 Roxbury Street, 1-617 427 1006, www.discoverroxbury.org) is gaining recognition for its historical and cultural tours.

Founded in 1630 by British colonists, Roxbury flourished first as a farming community, and later as a bustling industrial centre. During the 1950s, it became famous for its swinging jazz scene. It was during this period that Roxbury's most illustrious resident moved to town. For several years, Malcolm Little, aka Malcolm X, lived here with his half-sister Ella.

One sight worth visiting is the beautiful **First Church of Roxbury** (10 Putnam Street, at Dudley Street, 1-617 445 8393), near John Eliot Square. Built in 1803, this is the oldest wooden church in Boston, with a bell that was cast by patriot and silversmith Paul Revere. Also in the area lies the **Shirley-Eustis House** – one of the few remaining examples of pre-Revolutionary architecture. The **Eliot Burying Ground**

(Eustis Street, at Washington Street), which was established in 1630, is another surviving site. Several colonial governors, as well as Reverend John Eliot (who was known as the 'Apostle to the Indians', for translating the Bible into their native Algonquin), are buried here. Although Roxbury is home to many immigrant groups, its recent history as a predominately black neighbourhood is reflected in the **Museum of the National Center of Afro-American Artists**, on Walnut Avenue.

Nearby Dorchester, known locally as Dot, is, geographically, Boston's largest neighborhood. It has also seen its fair share of crime and poverty, but began to be gentrified in the 1980s. The restored mansions in the affluent Ashmont Hill area, lining Ocean Street and Welles Avenue, for example, are as impressive as any you'd find in Cambridge, and expensive condos are replacing old triple-decker apartment buildings. The area's prime draw for visitors is the **John F Kennedy Presidential Library & Museum**, which shares Columbia Point with the University of Massachusetts (UMass) Boston campus.

★ John F Kennedy Presidential Library & Museum

Columbia Point, off Morrissey Boulevard, Dorchester (1-617 514 1600, www.jfklibrary.org). JFK/UMass T then free shuttle bus. **Open** 9am-5pm daily. **Admission** $10; $7-$8 reductions; free under-12s. **Credit** AmEx, MC, V.

A looming concrete-and-glass monolith designed by IM Pei (completed in 1979), this shrine to the life and

work of the 35th US president overlooks the outer harbor from the top of the Columbia Point peninsula.

On the ground floor, the stunning 115ft-tall atrium commands panoramic views of the sea and the city. Downstairs, the museum contains an extensive display of memorabilia, as well as temporary shows. Presented as a series of multimedia retro room sets and visitor-friendly displays, the permanent exhibition comprises a timeline of Kennedy's rise to power (including excerpts from his famous televised debate

SIGHTS

John F Kennedy Presidential Library & Museum.

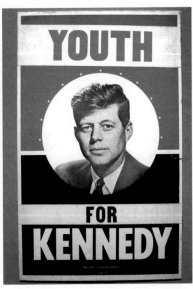

with Nixon, and documentary footage on the Cuban Missile Crisis), achievements (promoting the space race), his family life and reproductions of the Oval Office and the office of JFK's brother, Attorney General Robert F Kennedy.

The historical archives, which can only be viewed by appointment, include an extensive collection of Ernest Hemingway's letters and papers, donated by his wife Mary – Kennedy allowed her to re-enter Fidel Castro's Cuba in order to remove the writer's effects from their abandoned home in Havana.

▶ For JFK's birthplace, see right.

Museum of the National Center of Afro-American Artists

300 Walnut Avenue, at Dennison Street, Roxbury (1-617 442 8614, www.ncaaa.org). Ruggles T then bus 22. **Open** *1-5pm Tue-Sun.* **Admission** *$4; $3 reductions.* **No credit cards.**
The NCAAA's museum, affiliated with the Museum of Fine Arts (*see p65*) in Back Bay, is the only place in New England committed exclusively to African, Caribbean and Afro-American visual arts. Its Victorian mansion in Roxbury houses diverse exhibitions, including a permanent display recreating a Nubian king's burial chamber.

Shirley-Eustis House

33 Shirley Street, between Dudley & George Streets, Roxbury (1-617 442 2275, www.shirley eustishouse.org). Ruggles T then bus 15. **Open** *June-Sept noon-4pm Thur, Fri, 2nd wknd of each mth. Oct-May by appt.* **Admission** *$5; $3 reductions.* **No credit cards.**
This Georgian mansion, the only remaining house in America that was built by a royal colonial governor, is a National Historic Landmark. It went up between 1747 and 1751, and was built by William Shirley, who was appointed to his post by King George II. After that, the building played host to a who's who of historical figures: used as barracks for Revolutionary forces during the war, and later home to federal governor William Eustis, its illustrious visitors have included George Washington and Benjamin Franklin. Today, guided tours show off the restored marble floors and lovely period furniture of this perfectly preserved slice of pre-Revolutionary Roxbury.

JAMAICA PLAIN

Forest Hills, Green St or Stony Brook T.

Jamaica Plain – or JP, as it's called – has been slowly evolving for decades. As well as being one of Boston's densest Latino neighborhoods, its impressive Victorian properties coupled with low rents have been attracting young, arty types for years, creating a bohemian buzz. Trendy restaurants and bars such as the **Centre Street Café** (*see p137*) and **Ten Tables** (*see p137*) sit alongside Latino bakeries and barber shops.

Once a quirky bowling alley cum club cum restaurant, the **Bella Luna Restaurant & Milky Way Lounge** (*see p152*) has since reopened – without the bowling alley – in a new, higher-rent location in the Brewery Complex. Art studios abound – once a year, many are opened to the public for the Jamaica Plain Open Studios weekend (www.jpopenstudios.com). the main drag, Centre Street, is especially vibrant, with murals decorating the sides of buildings.

Landmark Irish pub **Doyle's** (*see p152*), sporting atmospheric murals of colonial times, has been drawing politicos for decades – Mayor Thomas Menino is a regular and even has a room decorated in his honor, although staff says he modestly prefers to sit elsewhere.

Blessed with acres of parkland, JP is easily one of the most verdant parts of the city. In the spring, the **Arnold Arboretum**, a sprawling botanical park, explodes with colorful blossoms, attracting eager walkers, joggers and cyclists. **Franklin Park**, a somewhat careworn 527-acre spread, features a woodland reserve, golf course and zoo (*see p185*). Landscape architect Frederick Law Olmsted, who designed the park as part of Boston's Emerald Necklace (*see p64* **Inside Track**), considered it to be his masterwork – which makes its current dilapidation, despite efforts of local activists, all the more unfortunate. Across the way, **Forest Hills Cemetery** contains the graves of several literary notables and colonial heroes.

★ FREE Arnold Arboretum

125 Arborway, at Centre Street (1-617 524 1718, www.arboretum.harvard.edu). Forest Hills T. **Open** *Grounds dawn-dusk daily. Visitors' center 9am-4pm Mon-Fri; 10am-4pm Sat; noon-4pm Sun.* **Admission** free.
The arboretum, one of the world's leading centers for plant study, was established in 1872. In a beautiful,

INSIDE TRACK TOP DOGS

Yes, **Castle Island Park** (*see p92*) is home to Fort Independence, where Edgar Allan Poe served for five months – allegedly inspiring 'The Cask of Amontillado'. And, yes, it also offers a great view of Boston Harbor and is perfect for an early morning walk. But the main reason to come to the park is for the hot dogs at **Sullivan's** (www.sullivanscastleisland.com). First opened in 1951, it has locals lining up out of the door from February to November for its $1.60 dogs or $1.80 hamburgers. They then head back to their cars for a front row seat as the planes take off from and land at Logan Airport.

265-acre park setting, this living museum is administered by Harvard University. Open to the public, it provides the opportunity to see more than 7,000 specimens of trees and plants from around the world. Free guided tours are available on designated days throughout the year – phone for details.

▶ *In May, Lilac Sunday is a day-long celebration of the fragrant, flowering shrub; see p180.*

FREE Forest Hills Cemetery
95 Forest Hills Avenue, at Route 203 (1-617 524 0128, www.foresthillstrust.org). Forest Hills T. **Open** 8.30am-dusk daily. **Admission** free.

Literary giants ee cummings, Eugene O'Neill and Anne Sexton are all buried here, as is the prominent abolitionist William Lloyd Garrison. The mile-long Contemporary Sculpture Path, established in 2001, gives the cemetery the feel of an open-air museum.

Loring-Greenough House
12 South Street, at Centre Street (1-617 524 3158, www.lghouse.org). Green St T then 15min walk, or Forest Hills T then bus 39. **Open** 10am-noon Sat; noon-2pm Sun; or by appt. **Admission** $5. **No credit cards.**

Built in 1760 for a wealthy British naval officer, this house was used as a hospital during the Revolutionary War, then housed five generations of another prosperous family before becoming a museum in 1924. Its decor spans a variety of periods, and includes collections of Victorian card cases and late 19th-century clothing. Visitors can freely roam its two acres of landscaped lawns and gardens, but may only enter the house with a guided tour.

Samuel Adams Brewery
30 Germania Street, at Brookside Avenue (1-617 368 5080, www.samueladams.com). Stony Brook T. **Tours** noon-3pm Tue-Thur; noon-5.30pm Fri; 11am-3pm Sat. **Admission** $2. **No credit cards.**

This local lager, named after the brewer turned Revolutionary leader, is on tap around the city and beyond. Brewery tours allow you to follow the beer-making process, from the selection of ingredients to the finished product – which you get to sample.

▶ *For more on Samuel Adams, see p18 Profile.*

BROOKLINE

Brookline Village, Cleveland Circle, Coolidge Corner or Longwood T.

Located four miles west of downtown Boston, Brookline is one of its prettiest and most affluent suburban communities. Cinephiles should check out the restored art deco **Coolidge Corner Theatre** (*see p193*), Greater Boston's only not-for-profit cinema; across the street, **Brookline Booksmith** (*see p159*) is a treasure trove of new and used titles.

Arnold Arboretum.

The birthplace and boyhood home of the town's most famous son, **John F Kennedy**, is a short walk away. The small house was carefully restored after the assassinated president's death under the supervision of his mother, Rose.

If cars are your thing, check out America's oldest collection of automobiles, at the **Larz Anderson Auto Museum**, in the vast, verdant Larz Anderson Park. The **Frederick Law Olmsted National Historic Site** (99 Warren Street, at Dudley Street, 1-617 566 1689) is a draw for garden-lovers, but has been closed for renovations for a few years and may not reopen until 2011.

John F Kennedy Birthplace
83 Beals Street, at Harvard Avenue (1-617 566 7937, www.nps.gov/jofi). Coolidge Corner T. **Open** *May-Sept* 10am-4.30pm Wed-Sun. **Admission** $3; free under-17s. **No credit cards.**

The modest former home of the country's 35th president has been restored to its appearance at the time of his birth in 1917. It includes the earliest of presidential artifacts: the bed in which JFK was born, and the piano he learned to play on. Tours are available of the house and surrounding neighborhood.

Larz Anderson Auto Museum
Larz Anderson Park, 15 Newton Street (1-617 522 6547, www.larzanderson.org). Cleveland Circle or Reservoir T then bus 51. **Open** 10am-4pm Tue-Sun. **Admission** $10; $5 reductions; free under-5s. **Credit** MC, V.

SIGHTS

Larz Anderson Auto Museum.
See p91.

In the early 20th century, the 64-acre Larz Anderson Park was the private estate of distinguished couple Larz and Isabel Anderson; it was bequeathed to the town of Brookline after the widow's death in 1948. The motorcar-mad couple's collection of vintage vehicles is contained in their former carriage house. The non-profit museum also displays rotating automotive exhibitions, and hosts weekend car shows in the summer, when models are displayed on the lawn.

SOUTH BOSTON

Broadway or Andrew T.

Known as Southie, this area feels quite cut off from central Boston. That's partly due to the wasteland of disused piers and warehouses that lies between them, but as the development of this stretch of waterfront gathers pace, it's starting to become more integrated. Perhaps because of its physical isolation, the blue collar, Irish-Catholic community remained virtually unchanged for almost a century. Dominated by organized crime in the 20th century, it gained a reputation as one of Boston's toughest areas. But like nearly every corner of the city, it's now been colonized by young graduates looking for affordable rents. The mood on Southie's two main thoroughfares is changing accordingly.

Smart new eateries and shops have been popping up on East and West Broadway, most notably designer boutique **Habit** (703 E Broadway, 1-617 269 1998, www.habitshop.com). **Woody's L Street Tavern** (658A East 8th

Street, at L Street, 1-617 268 4335), has been given a facelift, but is still recognizable as the dive where Matt Damon and Ben Affleck hung out in *Good Will Hunting*. Be warned, it's a long walk (or a ride on the no.9 bus) from the T.

The area's signature 'triple-decker' homes reflect its past as a purpose-built immigrant district, dating from the early 19th century, but there's not much in the way of tourist sights, apart from the **Dorchester Heights Monument** (Thomas Park, south of Broadway and G Street). Built in 1898, it marks the site of a former military encampment used by the troops of General George Washington when he was pushing the British out of Boston. It's said that when Washington brought his forces up to Dorchester Heights on 17 March 1776, he ordered his troops to use the password 'Saint Patrick', which explains why St Patrick's Day (a huge celebration) is also called Evacuation Day here.

On the coast, **Castle Island** used to live up to its name, but was connected to the mainland in the 1930s when streetcars served the beach at Pleasure Bay. On the peninsula sits the National Historic Landmark, **Fort Independence**.

FREE Castle Island Park & Fort Independence
East end of William J Day Boulevard, at Shore Road (1-617 727 5290). Broadway T then bus 9, 11. **Open** *Park* 24hrs daily. *Fort* 7pm-midnight Thur; noon-3.30pm Sat, Sun. **Admission** free.
South Boston lays claim to one of the city's most appealing shoreline parks: 22-acre Castle Island. It's also among the oldest fortified military sites in North America, centered on Fort Independence, a pentagonal granite structure that was finished in the 1850s. Prior to its construction, seven other forts had been built and destroyed in the area, occupied by American and British troops in turn. Today, the island's wide-open green spaces make for a pleasant outing.
▶ *For a snack here, see p90 Inside Track.*

INSIDE TRACK
PRESIDENTIAL PARKING TICKETS

Long before he was the so-called leader of the free world, President Barack Obama lived in Somerville while studying law at Harvard University – and did he ever rack up some parking tickets. While living at 365 Broadway, Obama was cited for 17 violations – seven in one eight-day stretch – including parking at bus stops and in 'resident only' areas, and failing to pay meters. The chief of state dodged the law for 17 years before paying off the $400 in fines in 2007.

SIGHTS

QUINCY

Quincy Center T.

Although most of this neighboring city – about seven miles south-east down the coast from downtown Boston – looks like an average suburb, with strip malls and pizza parlors, it's earned the right to declare itself 'the Birthplace of the American Dream'. Founding Fathers (and cousins) John and Samuel Adams (*see p18* **Profile**) and John Hancock were born here, and another of its native sons, John Quincy Adams, was the country's sixth president (1825-29). The Romanesque **Thomas Crane Public Library** in the town centre (40 Washington Street, 1-617 376 1301, www.thomascrane library.org), built in 1881 by Trinity Church architect HH Richardson, is also worth a look. Quincy (locals pronounce it 'Quinzy') was also an important center for shipbuilding, which reached its peak during World War II.

Adams National Historical Park

1250 Hancock Street, at Saville Avenue (1-617 770 1175, www.nps.gov/adam). Quincy Center T. **Open** *Visitor center* 19 Apr-10 Nov 9am-5pm daily. 11 Nov-18 Apr 10am-4pm Tue-Fri. *Tours* (19 Apr-10 Nov) 9am-3pm. **Admission** $5; free under-16s. **Credit** AmEx, MC, V.
Trolleys depart from the visitor center (which contains a medley of historical displays) to take you to the park for a guided tour with a ranger (around two hours in total). The park contains three important houses: the saltbox-style home where John Adams, the second American president, was born; the larger colonial home where his son (and America's sixth president) John Quincy Adams was born; and the Old House, a mansion built in 1731 that both used during their presidencies as the summer White House. Nearby is the Stone Library, built in 1873, which contains more than 14,000 books owned by the family. The grounds include an 18th-century-style formal garden and a lovely orchard.

SOMERVILLE

Davis T.

There isn't much in the way of sightseeing in this city just to the north of Cambridge, but interesting shops, bars and restaurants – mainly concentrated around buzzing **Davis Square** – have sprung up to cater to the young creatives who live here. It's not just for locals, though; Bostonians and Cantabridgians think nothing of making the short T or car journey to Davis. In the space of a few blocks, you'll find the live music venues **Johnny D's Uptown Restaurant & Music Club** (*see p212*) and the **Somerville Theatre** (*see p208*). On weekend evenings, the vintage boxcar **Rosebud Diner** (381 Summer Street, 1-617 666 6015, www.rosebuddiner.com) hosts local musicians. In addition to the diner, eating options include **Redbones** (*see p138*) for barbecue and beer, and the slightly more upscale **Gargoyles on the Square** (*see p138*). For a sweet snack, head for the charming **Petsi Pies** (*see p138*). There's also an intriguing collection of shops, including **Magpie** (*see p172*) for offbeat gifts.

SIGHTS

Adams National Historical Park.

Consume

Neptune Oyster. *See p128.*

Hotels

Forget the Midnight Ride – get a comfortable sleep instead.

Occupying a city seeped in US history, Boston hoteliers have found fertile ground for the chic and boutique, adding dimension to the old-school opulence and business-class options that have long been considered standard fare.

Smaller, smart hotels thrive in Back Bay, where shopping and culinary options within walking distance add to a savvy Boston experience, while the much-publicized opening of the **W Hotel** in the Theater District compliments a performance at the newly refurbished Paramount. And as the hotels around the South Boston Seaport shift their focus from business travelers looking for a harbor view, a new clientele is discovering Fort Point's vibrant galleries, restaurants and bars.

But while choices are expanding and the number of available rooms is growing, remember to book in advance, especially during college graduation season.

STAYING IN BOSTON

Before the arrival of the first bona fide boutique hotel, **XV Beacon** (*see p99*), in 1999, the choices for visitors were limited to old-school luxury establishments, homey guesthouses or bland corporate chains. That's all changing. After 80 years, the much-loved Back Bay landmark Ritz-Carlton was taken over by Indian luxury group **Taj** (*see p103*) in 2007, making its modern property across the Common the flagship. Meanwhile, the grande dame **Fairmont Copley Plaza** (*see p104*), which once housed the city's Museum of Fine Arts, recently received a $34 million facelift. Many new luxury and moderately priced properties have recently sprouted up around Boston, with ten opening in the last four years, including the **Hotel Veritas** (*see p110*) in Cambridge, a $10 million designer affair situated across from the Zero Arrow Theatre on Massachusetts Avenue.

CHOOSE YOUR PATCH

At the heart of the action, Back Bay – with its lively dining, shopping and arts scene – is the most popular area for visitors, and has a good choice of high-end and more moderately priced hotels. There's a modest sprinkling of small-scale accommodation in the hip South End, a prime spot for dining, drinking and taking in some culture, and Beacon Hill, which offers a glimpse of historic Boston. Luxury names are lining up on the waterfront to take advantage of the harbor views and space freed up after the Big Dig, which also provided the welcome green space of the Rose Kennedy Greenway (*see p76*).

Reflecting the needs of its most frequent visitors – academics and parents of students – Cambridge accommodation tends to be of the guesthouse or chain variety, with some notable exceptions.

INFORMATION AND PRICES

Boston can be a pricey place to lay your head: the projected average rate for hotel rooms in 2011 is $202.50. However, finding a good deal on lodging is relatively easy given the many travel discount websites. It's wise to book ahead, particularly in the traditionally busy autumn season, and during May and June, when over 60 college graduation ceremonies take place in the Boston area. Prices may change according to season and do not include the 12.45 per cent sales tax.

Note that unless otherwise stated, breakfast is not included in the room rates.

> ❶ Red numbers given in this chapter correspond to the location of each hotel on the street maps. *See pp272-276.*

CONSUME

DOWNTOWN
Deluxe

Ritz-Carlton Boston Common
*10 Avery Street, at Washington Street, Boston,
MA 02111 (1-617 574 7100, www.ritzcarlton.
com). Boylston T.* **Rates** $355-$495 double.
Credit AmEx, DC, MC, V. **Map** p272 K5 ❶
Though efforts have been made to smarten up this
part of Downtown, overlooking the Common near
the Theater District, it's still a work in progress. The
hotel, however, offers all the luxury associated with
the Ritz-Carlton name – although it eschews old-
fashioned opulence in favor of contemporary styling.
A creamy, neutral palette creates a warm, relaxing
atmosphere and the suites are fabulous, with sweeping floor-to-ceiling windows and imposing fireplaces.
There's a slick (and expensive) in-house restaurant
and bar, Jer-Ne, along with a chic bar/restaurant, Blu,
and the vaguely health-oriented Blu Café. The vast
Sports Club/LA is next door (guests pay a $15 fee per
room, per day), along with the Splash Spa.
*Bars/cafés (2). Business center. Concierge.
Disabled-adapted rooms. Gym. Internet
(wireless & high-speed, $6/3hrs). Parking ($39).
Restaurants (2). Room service. TV: pay movies.*

Expensive

Hilton Boston Financial District
*89 Broad Street, at Franklin Street, Boston,
MA 02110 (1-800 445 8667, www.hilton.com).
State T.* **Rates** $240-$400 double. **Credit** AmEx,
DC, MC, V. **Map** p273 L4 ❷
Built in 1928, this Downtown art deco landmark,
known as the Batterymarch building, was the city's
first skyscraper. It once housed the Department of
Transportation – hence the painting in the domed
entrance depicting various modes of travel. The lobby
itself oozes elegance, with its dark wood paneling and
1920s fixtures and fittings. Guest rooms, some of
which overlook the waterfront, are generously proportioned and were recently renovated in a sleeker,
more modern style. The airy restaurant, Caliterra,
serves a fusion of West Coast and Tuscan cuisine.
*Bar/café. Business center. Concierge. Disabled-
adapted rooms. Gym. Internet (wireless, free).
Parking (paid). Restaurant. Room service.
TV: pay movies.*

Langham Hotel Boston
*250 Franklin Street, at Post Office Square,
Boston, MA 02110 (1-617 451 1900, www.
boston.langhamhotels.com). State T.* **Rates**
$240-$450 double. **Credit** AmEx, DC, MC, V.
Map p273 L4 ❸
The Boston outpost of this small, international
luxury chain is housed in the 1920s former Federal
Reserve Bank on pretty Post Office Square. To
locals, however, it is best known for its Saturday

Ritz-Carlton Boston Common.

The Chain Gang
Stay with someone you know.

In addition to the hotels listed in
this chapter, many moderately priced
chains have outposts in Boston and
Cambridge. **Marriott** (1-888 236 2427,
www.marriott.com) has several branches
downtown and beyond, including the
remarkable Custom House in the
landmark tower (*see p50*) and the
Courtyard Boston Tremont, housed
in a splendid 1920s building.
  Westin and **Sheraton** (1-888
625 5144, www.starwood.com) offer
comfortable options in convenient
locations downtown, and the **Hyatt**
chain (1-888 591 1234, www.hyatt.com)
has a downtown address as well as its
unusual pyramid-style property overlooking
the Charles River in Cambridge. More
budget-conscious options include **Best
Western** (1-800 780 7234, www.best
western.com), and the veteran franchise
Howard Johnson, which originated in
nearby Quincy, and has an outpost on
Boylston Street in the Fenway (1-800
446 4656, www.hojo.com).

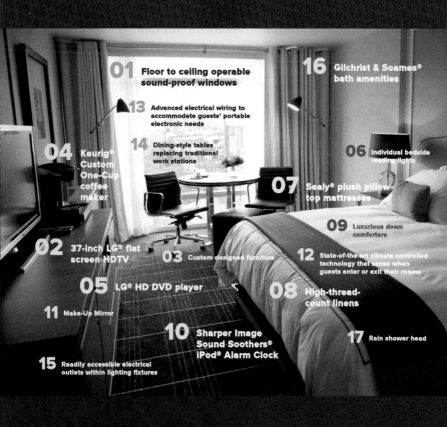

Chocolate Bar. Served in the Café Fleuri restaurant, it's a gloriously rich, indulgent buffet of all things chocolatey, from tortes to truffles and fondue. Those whose taste in interiors is unfussy and minimalist are advised to steer well clear of the Langham: polished bronze and ornate woodwork abound, and the Renaissance Revival-style public rooms are supremely opulent. The gilded Julien Bar and Lounge, with its carved doorways, magnificent chandeliers and gold paneled ceiling, is a masterpiece of overstatement. The health club has a gym, saunas and a 40ft pool.
Bar/café. Business center. Concierge. Disabled-adapted rooms. Gym. Internet (high-speed, free). Parking (paid). Pool (indoor). Restaurants (2). Room service. Smoking rooms. Spa facilities. TV: pay movies.

Millennium Bostonian

26 North Street, at Faneuil Hall Marketplace, Boston, MA 02109 (1-617 523 3600, www. millenniumhotels.com). Gov't Center or Haymarket T. **Rates** $159-$359 double. **Credit** AmEx, DC, MC, V. **Map** p273 L3 ❹
Part of the British hotel chain, the Millennium underwent extensive renovations in 2007. The hotel was thoroughly revamped, exchanging its English country inn demeanor for a more modern design. Housed within two adjoining converted warehouses and arranged around a central brick courtyard, the hotel boasts an excellent location next to Faneuil Hall Marketplace, with the harbor, Financial District and North End within easy walking distance. The ground floor Atrium Lounge is a nice retreat from Faneuil Hall's summer tourist bustle, with 180-degree floor-to-ceiling windows that provide superb people-watching opportunities.
Bar/café. Business center. Concierge. Disabled-adapted rooms. Gym. Internet (high-speed, free). Parking (paid). Restaurant. Room service. Smoking rooms. Spa facilities. TV: pay movies.

★ Nine Zero

90 Tremont Street, at Bosworth Street, Boston, MA 02108 (1-617 772 5800, www.ninezero.com). Park St T. **Rates** $270-$550 double. **Credit** AmEx, DC, MC, V. **Map** p272 K4 ❺
When it opened in 2002, Nine Zero was one of a select sprinkling of boutique-style hotels in Boston. Now part of the Kimpton group, it retains its aura of chilled-out chic – 'relax' is etched in brass lettering on the sidewalk outside the entrance as a welcome mantra – and exclusivity. The white-painted rooms are sleekly modern, with plush bed linens and oversized black vinyl headboards (with slight dominatrix overtones). Extras here include Kimpton's signature leopard-print robes, free Wi-Fi and a complimentary 'wine hour' in the evening. Celebrated local chef and restaurateur Ken Oringer opened a deluxe steak house, KO Prime, in 2007, which operates as the hotel's in-house kitchen for room service too.

Bar/café. Business center. Concierge. Disabled-adapted rooms. Gym. Internet (wireless, free). Parking (paid). Restaurant. Room service. Smoking rooms. TV: pay movies.

Omni Parker House

60 School Street, at Tremont Street, Boston, MA 02108 (1-617 227 8600, www.omnihotels.com). Park St T. **Rates** $170-$459 double. **Credit** AmEx, DC, MC, V. **Map** p272 K4 ❻
Established in 1855 as the Parker House, this is the oldest continuously operating hotel in the country. No opportunity is missed to remind guests that Charles Dickens once stayed here, holding court in the Last Hurrah bar – which became a famous literary hangout for the likes of Longfellow, Hawthorne and Emerson. And that's not all: Ho Chi Minh and Malcolm X were both among the staff, and romantics can dine at the very corner table where JFK proposed to Jackie (it's best to book it in advance).
Bars/cafés (2). Concierge. Disabled-adapted rooms. Gym. Internet (high-speed, $10). Parking (paid). Restaurant. Room service. Smoking rooms. TV: pay movies.

W Hotel

100 Stuart Street, at Tremont Street, Boston, MA 02116 (1-617 261 8700, www.whotels.com/ boston). Boylston T. **Rates** $259-$529 double. **Credit** AmEx, MC, V. **Map** p275 J6 ❼
This trailblazing, chic and ever-so-slightly snooty urban hotel chain continues to expand around the country, but it hasn't yet reached the point at which hip and fashionable turns to yesterday's thing. For that, full credit goes to the design, which eschews grand flourishes in favor of a simple and unobtrusive stylishness in both the rooms and the public spaces. Immediately on entering the hotel, you'll find yourself in a buzzing lobby bar, crowded with visitors and after-work locals making the scene.
Bar/café. Business center. Concierge. Conference facilities. Gym. Internet (high-speed, $15). Restaurant. Spa facilities. TV: DVD & pay movies.

BEACON HILL

Deluxe

XV Beacon

15 Beacon Street, at Park Street, Boston, MA 02108 (1-617 670 1500, www.xvbeacon.com). Park St T. **Rates** $350-$500 double. **Credit** AmEx, DC, MC, V. **Map** p272 K4 ❽
In a former office building not far from the State House, XV Beacon opened in 1999, introducing contemporary boutique chic to Boston. Although there's more competition now, XV's air of discretion and exclusivity still carries considerable cachet. The sleek, spacious guest rooms are decorated in a lively mix of stripes and patterns, browns and beiges, and feature

marble bathrooms and a lounge area with a grand gas fireplace (which, inexplicably, seems to emit heat whether you want it or not, battling with the air conditioning). The modern four-poster beds are a bit twee, although recent updates have introduced flatscreen TVs. Swanky restaurant Mooo offers steakhouse dining with a tongue-in-cheek twist. The hotel's free chauffeured car service is a boon, especially in winter, although its prime Beacon Hill location is just steps away from the Financial District and Back Bay.
Bar/café. Concierge. Disabled-adapted rooms. Gym. Internet (wireless, free). Parking (paid). Restaurant. Room service. Smoking rooms. TV: pay movies.

Expensive

★ Beacon Hill Hotel & Bistro
25 Charles Street, at Branch Street, Boston, MA 02114 (1-888 959 2442, www.beaconhill hotel.com). Arlington or Charles/MGH T. **Rates** (incl breakfast) $285-$305 double. **Credit** AmEx, DC, MC, V. **Map** p272 J4 ❾
The location for this charming hotel couldn't be lovelier: on Beacon Hill's pretty main drag, steps away from the Common and Public Garden, and a short stroll to Back Bay. Rooms are airy, decorated in an unfussy, updated New England style to maximize space, and equipped with flatscreen TVs and free Wi-Fi. The busy ground floor French bistro and tiny, popular corner bar are open to the general public, but only guests can relax in the simple but comfy second-floor lounge or out on the private roof deck.
Bar/café. Disabled-adapted rooms. Internet (wireless, free; shared terminal, free). Restaurant. Room service. TV: pay movies.

★ Liberty Hotel
215 Charles Street, at Cambridge Street, Boston, MA 02114 (1-617 224 4000, www.libertyhotel. com). Charles/MGH T. **Rates** $285-$685 double. **Credit** AmEx, DC, MC, V. **Map** p272 H3 ❿
See p102 **Do Some Time**.
Bar/café. Business center. Concierge. Disabled-adapted rooms. Gym. Internet (wireless & high-speed, free). Parking ($39). Restaurants (2). Room service. TV.

Moderate

John Jeffries House
14 David G Mugar Way, at Charles Street, Boston, MA 02114 (1-617 367 1866, www. johnjeffrieshouse.com). Charles/MGH T. **Rates** (incl breakfast) $139-$155 double. **Credit** AmEx, DC, MC, V. **Map** p272 H3 ⓫
Named after the co-founder of a free eye clinic for Boston's poor (now the renowned Massachusetts Eye and Ear Infirmary), this building was originally a nurses' residence. These days it's a comfortable guesthouse, modestly done up with reproduction Victorian

decor, but kept quite simple. Rooms range from small studios to full suites; most include a kitchenette, complete with refrigerator, stove and microwave. Continental breakfast is served each morning in the common room on the ground floor, and there's free wireless internet access. The shops and restaurants of Beacon Hill's Charles Street are on your doorstep, and Back Bay is within strolling distance.
Disabled-adapted rooms. Internet (wireless, free). Parking (paid). TV.

WEST END
Moderate

Onyx Hotel
155 Portland Street, at Causeway Street, Boston, MA 02114 (1-866 660 6699, www.onyxhotel. com). Haymarket or North Station T. **Rates** $159-$480 double. **Credit** AmEx, DC, MC, V. **Map** p272 K3 ⓬
A tasteful bolthole in what was a style wasteland by major sports/performance venue TD Garden. The small rooms are decorated with clean, elegant lines and a bold red, black and taupe color scheme. It may be short on space, but the Onyx doesn't skimp on style or service. Top-of-the-line amenities are in abundant supply, from feather-down pillows to wireless internet access and video games. In-room spa services are available at an extra charge, and there's a complimentary early evening wine hour in

Beacon Hill Hotel & Bistro.

CONSUME

Do Some Time

Spend the night in prison – in style.

Fancy spending the night in a cell? It's a lot more appealing than it sounds at the luxurious **Liberty Hotel** (*see p101*), set inside the former Charles Street Jail, which has housed a number of famous – and infamous – inmates: Malcolm X; Sacco and Venzetti, whose controversial trial and subsequent execution are often employed as evidence against the death penalty; and Bay State politician James Michael Curley.

The 220 cells in the former penitentiary by the Charles River near Beacon Hill were 8 feet by 10 feet; drunks and assorted villains were once locked up in the tiny cubicles in what is now the bar. Built in 1851, the Charles Street Jail was a model prison for the times – but by the 1970s, the facility was outmoded and in disrepair, known for its dire conditions. A district court ruled that the jail violated prisoners' constitutional rights, and it finally closed in 1990.

Needless to say, there's no trace of its former squalor. For its conversion into a luxury hotel, some $120 million was pumped into renovations and the construction of an adjacent 16-story wing,

which contains most of the 300 guest rooms. As the jail is a National Historic Landmark, the refurbishment has preserved the cruciform-shaped building's original features. The airy 90-foot central rotunda, which houses the main lobby, is topped by a cupola that was formerly covered over, and magnificent, original floor-to-ceiling windows overlook the landscaped patio. The catwalks that link the jail's public spaces were also kept, along with the cells in the cocktail lounge, Alibi.

Inside the restored landmark are two restaurants, Clink and Scampo, which also milk the vestiges of prison architecture for all they're worth. The food at Clink, the fine-dining option, treats local ingredients with modern American flair, but has received mixed reviews. Scampo is a more casual affair, with brick-oven pizzas and other dishes couched in Italian cuisine.

Rooms are more comfortable than cutting edge, with pale, neutral decor, mahogany furniture and handmade patchwork throws. Luxuries abound, from plush bed linen and Molton Brown toiletries to flatscreen HD-LCD TVs, wireless internet and VoIP telephones.

the lobby. The daringly designed – more bright red in the curving banquette – Ruby Room café and bar is a cozy hangout if you're too lazy to venture out to the plethora of pubs and bars around the lively North Station area. *Photo p104.*

Bar/café. Business center. Concierge. Disabled-adapted rooms. Gym. Internet (wireless & high-speed, free). Parking ($38). Restaurant. Room service. TV: pay movies.

BACK BAY

Deluxe

Four Seasons

200 Boylston Street, at the Public Garden, Boston, MA 02116 (1-800 338 4400, www.fourseasons.com/boston). Arlington T. **Rates** $425-$695 double. **Credit** AmEx, DC, MC, V. **Map** p272 J5 ⑬

The five-star Four Seasons is known for its famous guests. When the Stones roll into town, this is where they set up camp. Problem: there's only one Presidential Suite, an apartment complete with baby grand piano and dedicated maid or butler service. So who gets it, Mick or Keith? Or do they bunk up together? Apparently, Keith defers to his Glimmer Twin and takes the less lavish – but still deluxe – Ambassador Suite. Built on the site of a former Playboy Club, the hotel boasts an ideal location in the Back Bay, with swooning views of the Public Garden and impeccable amenities (such as a 44ft swimming pool, fitness center and spa – none of which is open to the public) and service. Traveling with Pongo? Pampered pooches can chow down from a dedicated pet room service menu, while their owners bask in the Brahmin splendor of the Bristol Lounge and haute dining room, Aujourd'hui.

Bars/cafés (2). Concierge. Disabled-adapted rooms. Gym. Internet (wireless & high-speed, free). Parking (paid). Pool (indoor). Restaurants (2). Room service. Smoking rooms. TV: pay movies.

★ Taj Boston

15 Arlington Street, at Newbury Street, Boston, MA 02116 (1-877 482 5267, www.tajhotels. com). Arlington T. **Credit** AmEx, DC, MC, V. **Map** p275 H5 ⑭

Few saw it coming, but in early 2007 the venerable Ritz-Carlton on Arlington Street was taken over by the Indian hotel group Taj. While tea at the Taj may not have quite the same ring to it as tea at the Ritz, very little has changed about the old girl really. As the Ritz, it had already undergone refurbishment that kept to its old-world European style. Decor is unremarkable but pleasantly pastel, with plenty of ruffled window adornments and dark woods, creating a classic, elegant feel. Rooms vary from standard deluxe and garden view (the only difference being they overlook the Public Garden) to the 1,540sq ft

THE BEST FOR A SPLURGE

Charles Hotel
Everything under one roof: renowned restaurants, a cool bar and live jazz.
See p110.

Fairmont Copley Plaza
The grande dame of the Back Bay.
See p104.

Taj Boston
The former Ritz keeps the luxury alive.
See below.

Presidential Suite, with its own jacuzzi, parlor, kitchen and a dining area to seat six. Taj Boston Club guests have members-only services and privileges and a dedicated, catered lounge. As the Ritz, the place had a mystique engendered by decades of famous guests, from Frank Sinatra to Winston Churchill. It may look basically the same, but there's no doubt that an era ended when the new nameplate went up. *Photo p105.*

Bar/café. Business center. Concierge. Disabled-adapted rooms. Gym. Internet (high-speed, $10). Parking (paid). Restaurants (2). Room service. Smoking rooms. TV: pay movies.

Expensive

Back Bay Hotel

350 Stuart Street, at Berkeley Street, Boston, MA 02116 (1-617 266 7200, www.doylecollection. com). Back Bay T. **Rates** $215-$535 double. **Credit** AmEx, DC, MC, V. **Map** p275 H6 ⑮

Housed in the former headquarters of the Boston Police Department, the Back Bay is a modern, pleasingly eccentric luxury hotel. The classic 1920s exterior is in sharp contrast to the contemporary, playful interior design, which features a fantastic glass staircase, a waterfall, a two-story fireplace and disco-psychedelic elevators. Guest rooms are superb and spacious, eschewing minibars in favor of fridges that guests can fill with their own goodies. There's a trio of eating and drinking options on site: Cuffs bar (popular with locals); the Stanhope Grille; and an airy café and lounge on the second floor. But with this location, the city's dining scene is on your doorstep.

Bar/café. Business center. Disabled-adapted rooms. Gym. Internet (wireless & high-speed, free). Parking (paid). Restaurant. Room service. Smoking rooms. TV: DVD.

Boston Park Plaza

50 Park Plaza, at Arlington Street, Boston, MA 02116 (1-888 625 5144, www.bostonparkplaza. com). Arlington T. **Rates** $170-$435 double. **Credit** AmEx, DC, MC, V. **Map** p275 J6 ⑯

Onyx Hotel. *See p101.*

When the Park Plaza, which celebrated its 80th anniversary in 2007, was first built it doubtlessly looked out over the lovely Public Gardens, but development put it in the shadows. A recent cosmetic overhaul has brought it somewhat up-to-date, upgrading the rooms with flatscreen TVs and high-thread-count bed linen. But the Park Plaza was built in gentler times and its cramped standard rooms, which are average at best, have no sound insulation; you can hear every clatter from your neighbors. The opulently decorated, chandeliered lobby houses the main restaurant, Swan's Café. Apart from Todd English's Bonfire Steakhouse (owned by the hotel, not local superstar chef English), the street-level restaurants and bars are independently operated.
Bars/cafés (2). Business center. Concierge. Disabled-adapted rooms. Gym. Internet (high-speed, $11). Parking (paid). Restaurants (5). Room service. Smoking rooms. TV: pay movies.

Colonnade

120 Huntington Avenue, at West Newton Street, Boston, MA 02116 (1-800 962 3030, www.colonnadehotel.com). Prudential T. **Rates** $199-$599 double. **Credit** AmEx, DC, MC, V. **Map** p275 G7 ⑰
Out went fuddy-duddy floral decor and in came sleek, modern elegance: the genteel Colonnade Hotel's renovations are boutique hip, but with a smart, individual edge to the design. Rooms are a blend of geometric patterns, blond woods, chrome and soothing chocolate browns with purple accents. A shimmering rooftop pool, 11 stories above the city streets, is another enticement to check in. The art deco-inspired bar offers great cocktails and happy hour deals, and the excellent ground floor restaurant, Brasserie Jo (*see p119*), was well ahead of Boston's current taste for authentic French brasseries. If its coq au vin and steak frites don't appeal, the South End's myriad eateries and bars are close at hand.
Bar/café. Business center. Concierge. Disabled-adapted rooms. Gym. Internet (wireless & high-speed, $14). Parking ($36). Pool (outdoor). Restaurant. Room service. Smoking rooms. TV: pay movies.

Fairmont Copley Plaza

138 St James Avenue, at Copley Square, Boston, MA 02116 (1-866 540 4417, www.fairmont.com/copleyplaza). Copley T. **Rates** $209-$469 double. **Credit** AmEx, DC, MC, V. **Map** p275 H6 ⑬
This little sister to New York's Plaza Hotel occupies a prime spot overlooking Copley Square, in the heart of Back Bay. Built in 1912, its mirrored and gilded lobby and function rooms are quite spectacular, with beautiful murals and ornate ceilings. But this place also has the air of an old family business, with black labrador Catie holding court in the lobby. A major renovation has introduced modern comforts while preserving the old-fashioned charm; rooms have high-speed internet access as well as stately club chairs and marble bathrooms. On the fourth floor, the discreet Fairmont Gold hotel-within-a-hotel has its own dedicated check-in and concierge, business center and lounge. The Fairmont's mahogany-paneled bar and restaurant, the Oak Room, is a Boston institution.
Bar/café. Business center. Concierge. Disabled-adapted rooms. Gym. Internet (high-speed, $14). Parking (paid). Restaurant. Room service. TV: pay movies.

Hotel Commonwealth

*500 Commonwealth Avenue, at Kenmore Square,
Boston, MA 02215 (1-866 784 4000, www.hotel
commonwealth.com). Kenmore T.* **Rates** (incl
breakfast) $199-$485 double. **Credit** AmEx, DC,
MC, V. **Map** p274 D6 ⑲

Rumors of Kenmore Square's rise are as greatly
exaggerated as those of Hotel Commonwealth's fall.
While Kenmore, a stone's throw from Fenway Park,
is taking its time in 'coming up', the Commonwealth
lost none in recovering from its early hiccups. Yes,
Bostonians hated its fiberglass, faux 19th-century
façade so much it was redone at huge expense, only
to be met with more pained sighs of disapproval. But
inside, the spacious suites and rooms have a rustic,
boutique elegance, along with superior technological
conveniences. The lauded Radius Group runs the
adjoining seafood restaurant and bar, Great Bay,
while room service comes courtesy of Eastern
Standard (*see p120*), a hip adjacent brasserie that's
made waves on the city's dining scene. Good sound-
proofing and superbly comfortable, Italian linen-clad
beds are further plus points.

*Bar/café. Concierge. Disabled-adapted rooms.
Gym. Internet (wireless & high-speed, free).
Parking (paid). Restaurant. Room service.
Smoking rooms. TV: DVD.*

Lenox

*61 Exeter Street, at Boylston Street, Boston, MA
02116 (1-800 225 7676, www.lenoxhotel.com).
Copley T.* **Rates** $235-$485 double. **Credit**
AmEx, DC, MC, V. **Map** p275 G6 ⑳

The privately owned Lenox, which first opened in
1900, boasts a prime location next to the Boston
Public Library (*see p60*). The hotel's old-style gold
and blue decor oozes quiet elegance, while its rooms
feature brass chandeliers, dark wood furniture and
marble bathrooms; several also boast working fireplaces, as does the charmingly restored lobby. The
Lenox also houses the independently owned restaurant Azure – superb New England cuisine with a
twist, courtesy of young, vivacious chef Andy
Fathman – and the chic City Bar and City Table.

*Bars/cafés (2). Business center. Concierge.
Disabled-adapted rooms. Gym. Internet (wireless,
free). Parking (paid). Restaurant. Room service.
Smoking rooms. TV: pay movies.*

Moderate

★ Charlesmark Hotel

*655 Boylston Street, at Copley Square,
Boston, MA 02116 (1-617 247 1212,
www.thecharlesmark.com). Copley T.* **Rates**
(incl breakfast) $119-$279 double. **Credit**
AmEx, DC, MC, V. **Map** p275 G6 ㉑

Converted from a private residence, the slender
Charlesmark is a beacon of minimalist boutique elegance on busy Boylston Street. The chic lounge and
patio, opened in 2005, draws a local crowd. There's

no restaurant, but Back Bay's culinary wealth more
than compensates. The hotel is the work of local
architect Dennis Duffy – a man responsible for
some of the hippest restaurant, commercial and private revamps in town – whose clean, simple aesthetic
is perfect for maximizing space in the modestly
proportioned rooms. *Photo p106.*

*Bar/café. Business center. Disabled-adapted
rooms. Internet (wireless, free). Parking ($20).
Smoking rooms. TV: pay movies.*

Copley Square Hotel

*47 Huntington Avenue, at Exeter Street, Boston,
MA 02116 (1-866 891 2174, www.copleysquare
hotel.com). Back Bay or Copley T.* **Rates** $179-
$399 double. **Credit** AmEx, DC, MC, V.
Map p275 G6 ㉒

Back Bay's first hotel, Copley Square opened for
business in 1891; decades later, Ella Fitzgerald,
Billie Holiday and Duke Ellington lit up its now
defunct jazz bar, Storyville. These days, the hotel's
somewhat of an oddity. The general style is old-
fashioned, with rooms decorated in somewhat
dowdy, countrified ginghams and florals. Yet it's
also home to super-slick, self-styled 'nitery' Saint
(*see p215*) and a sleekly modern Italian trattoria,
Domani. Still, the hotel's reputation is solid and the
staff friendly and efficient.

*Bars/cafés (2). Business center. Concierge.
Disabled-adapted rooms. Internet (wireless, free).
Parking ($36). Restaurants (3). Room service.
Smoking rooms. TV: pay movies.*

CONSUME

Taj Boston. *See p103.*

Charlesmark Hotel. *See p105.*

Gryphon House

9 Bay State Road, at Beacon Street, Boston,
MA 02215 (1-617 375 9003, www.inboston.com).
Kenmore T. **Rates** (incl breakfast) $189-$265
double. **Credit** AmEx, MC, V. **Map** p274 E6
Housed in an old townhouse, tucked between Back
Bay and Kenmore Square, this comfy, upscale bed
and breakfast couldn't be accused of minimalism. If
you're not averse to a bit of Victorian-style clutter, it's
a charming, warm retreat, pleasantly situated off the
main drag. Each of the eight suites is individually decorated; some have gas fireplaces and all are equipped
with refrigerators and your own cocktail or 'wet' bar.
Internet (wireless & high-speed, free; shared
terminal, free). Parking ($15). TV: DVD.

★ Hotel 140

140 Clarendon Street, at Stuart Street, Boston,
MA 02116 (1-800 714 0140, www.hotel140.com).
Copley T. **Rates** (incl breakfast) $129-$199
double. **Credit** AmEx, MC, V. **Map** p275 H6 ㉔
Sharing a landmark 1920s building with original
tenant the YWCA, private apartments and the Lyric
Stage Company, Hotel 140 is great value. While it
may not be the pinnacle of luxury – the modern
decor is plain but unassuming, with blond woods
and neutral colors – the rooms come with all modern conveniences (including high-speed internet and
nice bathroom products), the staff are very friendly
and the Back Bay location is hard to beat.
Business center. Disabled-adapted rooms.
Gym. Internet (high-speed, free). Parking ($20).
Restaurant. Room service. Smoking rooms. TV.

Hotel Buckminster

645 Beacon Street, at Kenmore Square,
Boston, MA 02215 (1-800 727 2825, www.
bostonhotelbuckminster.com). Kenmore T.
Rates $100-$180 double. **Credit** AmEx, DC,
MC, V. **Map** p274 D6 ㉕
Built in 1897 by architect Stanford White, whose
firm McKim, Mead and White designed several
prominent buildings in the city, the Buckminster is
one of the oldest hotels in Boston. (The first network
radio broadcast took place here in 1929, when
WNAC radio moved into a studio on the premises.)
Its reputation and decor are a little faded these days,
but this friendly, comfortable, centrally located hotel
offers one of the best deals in town. Rooms are
equipped with microwaves and refrigerators, and
there are coin-op laundry facilities too – making it a
good option for budget and long-stay visitors.
Disabled-adapted rooms. Internet (high-speed,
free). Parking ($18). TV.

Newbury Guest House

261 Newbury Street, between Gloucester
& Fairfield Streets, Boston, MA 02116
(1-800 437 7668, www.newburyguesthouse.com).
Hynes T. **Rates** (incl breakfast) $139-$200 double.
Credit AmEx, DC, MC, V. **Map** p274 F6 ㉖
Perfect for shopaholics or anyone who wants to stay
on Boston's chic-est strip, this pleasant townhouse
B&B is set amid retail heaven. Rooms are fitted out
with reproduction Victorian furnishings, in keeping
with the building's hardwood floors and high ceilings. There's a homey atmosphere, though the bustle from the street does filter in. A breakfast buffet
is served in a bright parlor that opens on to a small
terrace. It's good value for the location – and what
you save on hotel rates you can spend in the shops.
Concierge. Disabled-adapted rooms.
Internet (wireless, free). Parking ($15).
Smoking rooms. TV.

Oasis Guest House

22 Edgerly Road, at Stoneholm Street, Boston,
MA 02115 (1-617 267 2262, www.oasisgh.com).

THE BEST
FOR A UNIQUE EXPERIENCE

Beacon Hill Hotel & Bistro
Local color. *See p101.*

Clarendon Square Inn
A South End gem. *See p108.*

XV Beacon
Eclectic elegance. *See p99.*

W Hotel
Design meets decadence. *See p99.*

Hynes or Symphony T. **Rates** (incl breakfast) $99-$159 double. **Credit** AmEx, MC, V.
Map p274 F7 ➋

With its peaceful yet central location and reasonable prices, the Oasis is a welcome find. Its clean, comfortable rooms boast up-to-date amenities, including Wi-Fi, attracting non-expense-account business travelers as well as tourists. Continental breakfast is served in the cozy lounge – which, like the outdoor deck areas, is a pleasant place to relax. There's also a kitchen for guests.
Disabled-adapted rooms. Internet (wireless, free). Parking ($15). Smoking rooms. TV: pay movies.

Budget

Florence Frances Guest House

458 Park Drive, at Beacon Street, Boston, MA 02215 (1-617 267 2458). Fenway or St Mary's Street T. **Rates** $97 double. **No credit cards.**
Former actress Florence Frances offers three guest rooms in her 19th-century townhouse. Each is lovingly decorated around a theme – take the flamenco-fabulous 'Spanish' room, which features a bold red and black color scheme and decorative fans. Depending on your taste, you'll either find it delightfully kitsch or bordering on tacky – the communal bathroom (there are no private ensuites) features a toilet seat inlaid with half-dollar coins. There's also a comfortable lounge, a roof terrace, laundry facilities and free parking at the back.
Parking (free).

Hosteling International Boston

12 Hemenway Street, at Boylston Street, Boston, MA 02115 (1-617 536 9455, www.bostonhostel. org). Hynes T. **Rates** (incl breakfast) $30-$48 dorm; $80-$130 private single/double. **Credit** AmEx, MC, V. **Map** p274 E7 ➋
If you're in Boston on a modest budget, hoping to hang out and hook up with fellow travelers, this outpost of the backpackers' standby is for you. Most rooms are dormitory style, sleeping up to six people; some are mixed sex. The Back Bay location is great, and private rooms are available – but if you're spending $100 on a double, you might as well upgrade to a hotel.
Disabled-adapted rooms. Internet (wireless, free; shared terminal, $2). TV.

YMCA

316 Huntington Avenue, at Northeastern University, Boston, MA 02115 (1-617 536 7800, www.ymcaboston.org). Northeastern T. **Rates** $35 single; $66 double. **Credit** AmEx, MC, V. **Map** p274 F8 ➋
The YMCA only takes male guests for most of the year, but allows women from May to August. It offers reasonable, if basic, budget accommodation in private rooms with shared bathrooms (private facilities are available for an extra charge). The

Hotel 140.

CONSUME

rooms are austere but clean and comfortable, and fresh linen is offered daily – although guests staying for more than one night can opt to be environmentally friendly and reuse.

Disabled-adapted rooms. Gym. Internet. Pool (indoor). Restaurant. Smoking rooms. TV.

SOUTH END
Moderate

Chandler Inn
26 Chandler Street, at Berkeley Street, Boston, MA 02116 (1-800 842 3450, www.chandlerinn. com). Back Bay T. **Rates** $115-$260 double. **Credit** AmEx, DC, MC, V. **Map** p275 H7 ③⓪
If you fancy staying in Boston's hippest residential neighbourhood, book a room at this gay-friendly South End guesthouse. Guest rooms have ensuite bathrooms and are equipped with all mod cons: satellite TV, voicemail and complimentary wireless internet access. Several have been revamped as 'deluxe' rooms with boutique-style design and amenities, including plasma TVs, iPod docks and marble bathrooms with walk-in showers. Complimentary coffee and tea are offered throughout the day in the lobby. The Fritz Lounge sports bar, located on the ground floor, can be noisy at weekends; non-party people are advised to request a room on the upper floors. *Bar/café. Concierge. Internet (wireless, free). TV.*

INSIDE TRACK
HAUNTED HOTELS

If your idea of sightseeing involves ghost sightings, who you gonna call? These three hotels that go bump in the night are good places to start. The **Omni Parker House** (*see p99*) has a long history of spooks and is said to be haunted by the hotel's founder, Harvey Parker. Be sure to get a room on the 10th floor, the focal point of paranormal activity. The TV show *Ghost Hunters* had reason to believe the **Hawthorne Hotel** (*see p239*) in Salem – Massachusetts' epicenter of witches and weirdness – was under a spell. Ask for suite 612 or room 325 for some added excitement, free of charge. Lastly, the infamous **Lizzie Borden Bed & Breakfast** in Fall River (92 Second Street, 1-508 675 7333, www.lizzie-borden.com, $150-$250 double) is where the 33-year-old woman allegedly hacked her father and stepmother to pieces with an axe over a century ago. The hotel has been restored to look just as it did in 1892 and is stocked with all types of Borden curios, to ensure pleasant dreams during your stay.

★ Clarendon Square Inn
198 West Brookline Street, between Tremont Street & Warren Avenue, Boston, MA 02118 (1-617 536 2229, www.clarendonsquare.com). Back Bay or Prudential T. **Rates** $115-$375 double. **Credit** AmEx, MC, V. **Map** p275 H8 ③①
Housed in a beautifully renovated 1860s merchant's townhouse, this luxury bed and breakfast is a far cry from Boston's staid image – take the rooftop hot tub, for instance, with its views over Back Bay. Guest rooms are individually designed and furnished with impeccable attention to detail, mixing carefully chosen antiques with sleek contemporary pieces. Some rooms have original fireplaces, but they're now only for decoration. Marble and limestone bathrooms and high-thread-count linens add to the appeal, although there are no king-sized beds, only queens. The Clarendon suite, with its splendid freestanding Victorian bath, is popular with romantics. Wireless internet access is complimentary, and limited guest parking (reserved in advance) is a boon in the area. *Internet (wireless, free). Parking ($20). TV: DVD.*

Budget

YWCA/Berkeley Residence
40 Berkeley Street, between Gray & Appleton Streets, Boston, MA 02116 (1-617 375 2524, www.ywcaboston.org). Arlington or Back Bay T. **Rates** (incl breakfast) $70 single; $99 double; $120 triple. **Credit** MC, V. **Map** p275 H7 ③②
Although the name hasn't changed, this centrally located YWCA is now unisex year round. Men have a designated floor, and the communal bathrooms are segregated by sex too. Though comfortably furnished, it's a no-frills operation. The rooms have no telephones or TV – there is a 24-hour television room – but free Wi-Fi is gradually being introduced throughout the building.
Internet (wireless, free; shared terminal, $2/20mins). Restaurant. TV room.

WATERFRONT
Deluxe

Boston Harbor Hotel
70 Rowes Wharf, Boston, MA 02110 (1-617 439 7000, www.bhh.com). Aquarium T. **Rates** $380-$900 double. **Credit** AmEx, DC, MC, V. **Map** p273 M4 ③③
The Big Dig blighted the Harbor Hotel's west side for years, but now – overlooking the Rose Kennedy Greenway (*see p76*), as well as the harbor – the hotel is having the last laugh. It's in a superbly central location, close to the North End's Italian restaurants, Faneuil Hall (*see p47*) and the Financial District. Rooms and suites are appointed with every little luxury, from plush bathrobes and slippers to an umbrella – a thoughtful touch, considering Boston's famously changeable weather. Although the decor

InterContinental Boston.

up with international travelers' off-kilter body clocks. The inviting rooms are chic and contemporary, but warm woods and rich accent colors save them from clinical minimalism. Some have splendid canopied four-poster beds, others stunning harbor views; all are kitted out with the latest high-tech gear, including widescreen HD TVs. Club InterContinental offers high flyers a dedicated floor of extra pampering and exclusive business services. *Bar/café. Business center. Concierge. Disabled-adapted rooms. Gym. Internet (high-speed, $7/hr or $14/day). Parking ($39). Pool (indoor). Restaurants (3). Room service. Spa facilities. TV: pay movies.*

Seaport Hotel
1 Seaport Lane, at Northern Avenue, Boston, MA 02210 (1-617 385 4000, www.seaport boston.com). Silver Line Waterfront to World Trade Center. **Rates** $189-$449 double. **Credit** AmEx, DC, MC, V. **Map** off p273 N5 ㉟
Before the harbor area development, the Seaport was a lone beacon, accommodating business types attending the adjacent Seaport World Trade Center. Now that the nearby Institute of Contemporary Art (*see p79*) has broadened its attractions and Fort Point is blossoming, putting up here offers a different perspective on the city. Facilities are faultless: the spa is highly recommended, while the third-floor fitness center has a wonderful 50ft pool with sky views and underwater music. There's also plentiful parking in the adjacent garage, and a good in-house restaurant, Aura. Innovations include the touchscreen in-room 'Seaportal' service, which provides guests with VoIP telephone calls, information on local dining spots, cultural attractions and events, and the latest flight information from Logan International's website – all at the tap of the monitor screen. *Photo p110.*
Bar/café. Business center. Concierge. Disabled-adapted rooms. Gym. Internet (wireless & high-speed, free). Parking ($29; valet $37). Pool (indoor). Restaurants (2). Room service. Spa facilities. TV: pay movies.

Moderate

Harborside Inn
185 State Street, at Commercial Street, Boston, MA 02109 (1-888 723 7565, www.harborsideinn boston.com). Aquarium T. **Rates** $140-$270 double. **Credit** AmEx, DC, MC, V. **Map** p273 L4 ㊱
Occupying a converted warehouse at a prime downtown address, the sister hotel to the Charlesmark (*see p105*) in Back Bay is one of the city's best bargains. Guest rooms feature atmospheric exposed brick walls and simple, classic furnishings, such as mahogany sleigh beds and hand-woven Middle Eastern rugs, plus the usual modern amenities. The lobby – a bright, eight-story atrium – is gorgeous. Although the building once bordered the harbor, due to the changing coastline there are no water views:

is old-fashioned by most hotel standards – New England country-house-style florals and heavy woods – it's understated, not fussy, and the lobby's high ceilings and cool marble add an air of classic elegance. Rowes Wharf Bar has the atmosphere of a gentlemen's club, while the stunning restaurant Meritage (*see p113*) offers first-class dining; the Intrigue Café is less formal. The hotel's spa and fitness rooms are among the best in the city, with a welcomingly warm 60ft pool as the centerpiece. *Bar/café. Business center. Concierge. Disabled-adapted rooms. Internet (wireless, free). Parking ($22-$32). Pool (indoor). Restaurants (2). TV: pay movies.*

Expensive

InterContinental Boston
510 Atlantic Avenue, at Pearl Street, Boston, MA 02210 (1-617 747 1000, www.intercontinental boston.com). South Station T. **Rates** $375-$450 double. **Credit** AmEx, DC, MC, V. **Map** p273 L5 ㉞
What the InterContinental lacks in front entrance grandeur – an understatement, given the hazardous forecourt right on the busy street – it makes up for with a snazzy, Vegas-style glamour. One thing's for sure: when it opened in 2007, the hotel was a smash hit with Bostonians, who immediately designated the circular bar RumBa a place to party. Another attraction is Sushi-Teq, an unusual hybrid of a sushi bar that also specializes in premium aged tequilas. The sunny restaurant Miel (*see p115*), meanwhile, serves excellent Provence-inspired food 24/7, to keep

Seaport Hotel. *See p109.*

just the bustle of business-oriented State Street and the lively bar scene around Faneuil Hall.
Concierge. Disabled-adapted rooms. Internet (wireless, free). Parking ($26.50). TV.

CAMBRIDGE

Deluxe

Hotel Veritas
1 Remington Street, at Massachusetts Avenue, Harvard Square, Cambridge, MA 02128 (1-617 520 5000, www.thehotelveritas.com). Harvard T. **Rates** $379-$489 double. **Credit** AmEx, MC, V. **Map** p276 B3 ➌➐
Smack in the middle of staid Harvard Square, this delightfully lush boutique hotel is turning heads. The 31-room property is old Cambridge meets Italian minimalism – hints of which can be found everywhere from the crown molding in every room to the luxurious Anichini bed linens. Raised on the site of a former apartment complex and auto-body shop, the sweeping floor to ceiling windows wrapping around its lower level are a nod to its automotive past. Although it fits well into its environment, they've banished any hint of roughness from the space.
Bar/café. Concierge. Internet (wireless, free).

Expensive

★ Charles Hotel
1 Bennett Street, at Harvard Square, Cambridge, MA 02138 (1-800 882 1818, www.charleshotel. com). Harvard T. **Rates** $260-$400 double. **Credit** AmEx, DC, MC, V. **Map** p276 A2 ➌➑
Utterly modern, the purpose-built Charles Hotel has an air of relaxed refinement that befits its smart Harvard Square location. Rooms are kept simple, with a New England aesthetic that includes Shaker furniture and handmade quilted comforters on the beds. DVD players, flatscreen TVs and sleek Seura 'in mirror' bathroom televisions add to the air of unobtrusive luxury. The Charles is home to an impressive line-up of bars and restaurants: the renowned Rialto (*see p136*); Henrietta's Table, whose menu highlights organic and local produce; the seductive bar Noir (*see p151*); and the Regattabar (*see p212*), a nationally recognized jazz hotspot. In winter, a skating 'pond' is set up in the hotel's courtyard, while during the summer months the famed Legal Seafoods hosts a popular raw bar here. All in all, a unique place to stay. *Bars/cafés (3). Business center. Concierge. Disabled-adapted rooms. Gym. Internet (high-speed, free; shared terminal, free). Parking ($34). Pool (indoor). Restaurants (2). Room service. TV: DVD & pay movies.*

Hotel Marlowe
25 Edwin H Land Boulevard, at Charles Street, Cambridge, MA 02142 (1-800 825 7140, www. hotelmarlowe.com). Lechmere T then 10min walk.
Rates $200-$450 double. **Credit** AmEx, DC, MC, V. **Map** p272 H2 ➌➒
The nondescript exterior of this modern block near the Cambridgeside Galleria mall doesn't prepare you for the flamboyant melange of fake animal prints and rich colors within. The decor may be loud, but the atmosphere is laid-back, unpretentious and fun. The early evening complimentary wine hour – an institution of the California-based Kimpton chain – offers the opportunity to unwind and meet other guests in the lobby lounge, with its huge fireplace. Although the hotel feels removed from the main cultural and commercial areas of the city (the mall notwithstanding), it's only a short walk and a subway stop to the excellent restaurants and funky nightlife of Central Square. If you don't feel like commuting, Bambara restaurant is a decent dining option also frequented by non-residents. Some of the rooms offer wonderful views over the river. *Bar/café. Business center. Concierge. Disabled-adapted rooms. Gym. Internet (high-speed, free). Parking ($20). Restaurant. Room service. Spa facilities. TV: pay movies.*

Inn at Harvard
1201 Massachusetts Avenue, at Bow Street, Harvard Square, Cambridge, MA 02138 (1-800 458 5886, www.theinnatharvard.com). Harvard T. **Rates** $240-$500 double. **Credit** AmEx, DC, MC, V. **Map** p276 B2 ➍➊
This little gem of a place is just a stone's throw from Harvard Yard. Designed by Harvard alumnus Graham Gund in 1992, the red-brick structure is intended to mimic the architectural style prevalent

at America's most prestigious university. The hotel's 111 rooms are arranged over four floors around a glassed-in courtyard, designed to recall an Italian villa, and the atrium is a pleasant place for morning coffee, afternoon tea or a quiet dinner. The rooms themselves are somewhat predictable in their florals and frills, but comfortable enough, with all the usual amenities. The shortest of strolls takes you to the campus, the T station and a bevy of pubs and cafés. *Business center. Disabled-adapted rooms. Gym. Internet (wireless, free). Parking ($40). Restaurant. Room service. TV: pay movies.*

Moderate

A Bed & Breakfast in Cambridge

1657 Cambridge Street, at Trowbridge Street, Harvard Square, Cambridge, MA 02138 (1-617 868 7082, www.cambridgebnb.com). Harvard T. **Rates** (incl breakfast) $95-$200 double. **Credit** AmEx, MC, V. **Map** p276 B2 ④①

Minutes away from Harvard University, this family-run B&B offers three rooms (with shared bathroom), each furnished in keeping with the Colonial Revival-era house, built in 1897. Breakfast features home-baked pastries, waffles and jams, and, deliciously quaintly, guests are offered complimentary afternoon tea or a glass of sherry. But old customs meet New Age here – the proprietor is also an Alexander Technique teacher, handy should you wish to book a session or two during your stay. *Concierge. Internet (wireless, free). TV.*

A Cambridge House Bed & Breakfast Hotel Inn

2218 Massachusetts Avenue, at Rindge Avenue, Davis Square, Cambridge, MA 02140 (1-617 491 6300, www.acambridgehouse.com). Davis or Porter T. **Rates** (incl breakfast) $129-$249 double. **Credit** AmEx, MC, V.

On busy Mass Ave, a few miles north of Harvard Square, this lovely Greek Revival house was constructed in 1882. It offers 16 rooms, furnished in a somewhat fussy – but lovely for its type – Victorian style. The hotel may be off the beaten track, but free parking is available. If you plan to explore further than Cambridge and Boston, it offers easy access to all points west and north. *Disabled-adapted rooms. Internet (wireless, free). Parking (free). TV.*

Budget

Monastery of the Society of Saint John the Evangelist

980 Memorial Drive, at John F Kennedy Park, Harvard Square, Cambridge, MA 02138 (1-617 876 3037, www.ssje.org). Harvard T. Self-directed retreat $75/person; $40 reductions. *Self-directed retreat* $100/person; $50 reductions. **Credit** MC, V. **Map** p276 A3 ④②

Run by an order of monks affiliated with both the Anglican and American Episcopal churches, the Italianate monastery is a short walk from Harvard Square. This is a place for peaceful reflection and spiritual renewal: many guests are on directed religious retreats, and silence is a strict rule. That applies even in the tiny guest rooms, which served as monk's cells for eight years before the main monastery and its beautiful church were built in 1936. Guests are welcome to breakfast with the monks in the refectory, but there's no chit-chat over coffee. The white-painted rooms are small and sparsely furnished, and although there is one double room, the order of silence means most couples find it easier to lodge in separate cells. There are no TVs or phones, and mobile phone usage is kept to a minimum, permitted only in the common room or out in the garden.

BED & BREAKFAST AGENCIES

Whether you're after a more 'authentic' taste of local life or all the comforts of home in your own apartment, B&B agencies can hook you up with accommodation in Boston and beyond. Rates start from as little as $70 per night off-season for a single room with a shared bath.

Bed & Breakfast Agency of Boston

47 Commercial Wharf No.3, Boston, MA 02110 (1-800 248 9262, www.boston-bnbagency.com). Aquarium T. **Credit** AmEx, MC, V.

This agency offers high-quality, child-friendly accommodation in central Boston, ranging from waterfront lofts to rooms in historic Victorian Back Bay homes. It's especially good at finding short-term studios and apartments.

Bed & Breakfast Associates Bay Colony

PO Box 57166, Babson Park Branch, Boston, MA 02457 (1-800 347 5088, www.bnbboston.com). **Open** *Office* 8.30am-7pm Mon-Fri; 9am-5pm Sat; 11.30am-4pm Sun. **Credit** MC, V.

With a far-reaching list of accommodation in B&Bs, inns, suites and furnished apartments throughout the city and surrounding suburbs, this agency also covers the coast, Nantucket and Martha's Vineyard.

THE BEST GOOD-VALUE STAYS

Charlesmark Hotel
Boutique on Boylston – on a budget.
See p105.

Hotel Buckminster
Front row to Fenway. See p106.

Hotel 140
A landmark, low-frills lodging. See p106.

CONSUME

Restaurants & Cafés

Adventurous, global, retro – Boston's cuisine goes far beyond the bean.

Perhaps it's the ubiquity of farmers markets in the summer, the Earth-conscious liberal sentiment prevalent among its residents, or simply a reflection of universal foodie trends, but Boston embraces a 'buy local' philosophy when it comes to food. Sure, seafood has always been a staple of the New England diet, from the cod fish reeled in off the Atlantic coast to the quahog clam particularly abundant off the Cape Cod shore.

However, a small-farm push from Vermont to Connecticut has restaurants embracing locally grown vegetables and grass-fed proteins as well, which make for spectacular seasonal menus in a wide variety of cuisines from Vietnamese to Cape Verdean. The panorama of choices also includes a number of fine, smaller restaurants with less overhead, ensuring Bostonians can not only eat well, but affordably.

THE DINING SCENE

Like Cajun, Southwestern and soul food before it, New England cooking is finally getting its due in the rest of the country, with raw bars dispensing shucked-to-order shellfish popping up on the plains and clam shacks coming to roost in the Rockies. And why not, considering its cornucopia of sparkling seafood and such patriotically tinged produce as pumpkins, cranberries and corn? But while foodies from elsewhere rally round New England's traditional cuisine, its main city's dining scene continues to expand and diversify.

Bostonians are, as a rule, proud sponsors of little guys and underdogs (as evidenced by their Revolutionary history and unwavering devotion to the Red Sox). Add to that the city's long-term absorption of ever-changing waves of immigrants and starving students, and you can rest assured that Beantown is a haven for eats of the cheap, ethnic and/or mom-and-pop variety as well as the pricier creations by the Boston area's celebrity chefs (*see p115* **Inside Track**).

> ❶ Blue numbers given here correspond to the location of each restaurant or café on the street maps. *See pp272-276.*

Downtown and the Back Bay may be hotspots of conspicuous consumption, but chowhounds need venture only slightly further afield to strike gold among East Boston's taquerias, Dorchester's roti huts or the Portuguese hideaways of East Cambridge and Somerville. Chinatown has more worthwhile holes-in-the-wall per square inch than you can believe without seeing. And then, of course, there's the North End: the city's celebrated Little Italy may be gentrifying, but it still shelters a few red-checked pasta-and-pizza parlors, serving up hearty, unpretentious fare.

Bear in mind that the price range given for main courses in the listings is approximate.

DOWNTOWN

Avila

1 Charles Street South, at Stuart Street (1-617 267 4810, www.avilarestaurant.com). Arlington or Boylston T. **Open** 11.30am-3pm, 5-10pm Mon, Tue, Sun; 11.30am-3pm, 5-11pm Wed-Sat. **Main courses** $18-$42. **Credit** AmEx, MC, V. **Map** p275 K5 ❶ Mediterranean

For all the architectural drama befitting its Theater District location (soaring ceilings, sweeping lines, sun-baked hues), Avila is a surprisingly comfortable and laid-back place to dine, especially if you sit at the elliptical bar, where you can mix and match plates from both the snack and full menus. The bolder the Mediterranean flavors, the bigger the payoff – so here's your chance to test your threshold for salty fish and strong cheese. Halloumi, pan-fried in ouzo with dates and cashews, packs quite a punch.

Durgin Park

340 Faneuil Hall Marketplace, Commercial Street (1-617 227 2038, www.durgin-park.com). Aquarium, Gov't Center, Haymarket or State T. **Open** 11.30am-10pm Mon-Sat; 11.30am-9pm Sun. **Main courses** $11-$40. **Credit** AmEx, DC, MC, V. **Map** p273 L3 ❷ **American**

As Faneuil Hall tourist traps go, this cheerfully creaky joint maintains surprising integrity. Plain old-fashioned Yankee cooking carries the day – as it has done every day for going on 200 years. Highlights include whole heaps o' steamers, prime rib you can practically eat with a spoon and the quintessential Indian pudding.

▶ *For more about Indian pudding and other local specialties, see p117 Classic Tastes.*

★ Locke-Ober

3 Winter Place, off Winter Street (1-617 542 1340, www.lockeober.com). Downtown Crossing or Park Street T. **Open** 5-10pm Mon-Fri; 5-11pm Sat. **Main courses** $39-$62. **Credit** AmEx, MC, V. **Map** p272 K5 ❸ **American**

Some things never change. All carved mahogany and polished silver, stained glass and tinkling crystal, the dining room at Locke-Ober looks much as it did when it opened 130-plus years ago (a day you'd be forgiven for imagining some of the starched, bow tie-clad waiters must recall first-hand).

Other things change for the better. Under co-owner Lydia Shire's watchful eye, the kitchen has ushered the menu into the 21st century: curry, wasabi, *guanciale* and ancho chilies find their place among the escargots, filet mignon, calf's liver and dover sole (although a few classics, including JFK's lobster stew, brook no alteration).

Meritage

Boston Harbor Hotel, 70 Rowes Wharf, at Atlantic Avenue (1-617 439 3995, www.meritage therestaurant.com). Aquarium or South Station T. **Open** 5.30-10.30pm Tue-Sat; 10.30am-2pm Sun. **Main courses** $32. **Credit** AmEx, DC, MC, V. **Map** p273 M4 ❹ **Creative contemporary**

CONSUME

Union Oyster House. *See p116.*

Hard Rock CAFE

SEE THE SHOW BOSTON

22-24 CLINTON ST.
+1-617-424-7625 • HARDROCK.COM

Ensconced on the second floor of a waterfront hotel in a space so minimalist it seems half-furnished, Meritage can produce an odd sense of dislocation, both from downtown Boston and in general. So much the better for losing yourself in the experience Daniel Bruce's artful, enocentric menu affords, we say. Listing its dishes according to the type of wine they're designed to complement, it's foolproof yet flexible, and educational rather than dogmatic. (Granted, its portion-to-price ratio may end up teaching spendthrifts a less pleasant lesson.)

★ Miel

InterContinental Boston, 510 Atlantic Avenue, at Pearl Street (1-617 217 5151, www.inter continentalboston.com). South Station T. **Open** 24hrs daily. **Main courses** $14-$28. **Credit** AmEx, DC, MC, V. **Map** p273 L5 ❺ French
See p139 **Paris, Massachusetts**.

★ O Ya

9 East Street, between Atlantic Avenue & South Street (1-617 654 9900, www.oyarestaurant boston.com). South Station T. **Open** 5-10pm Tue-Thur; 5-11pm Fri, Sat. **Small plates** $8-$20. **Credit** AmEx, MC, V. **Map** off p273 L5 ❻ Japanese
Bite for bite, this self-styled Japanese tavern is arguably serving the most expensive food in the city of Boston. It's also, less arguably, some of the most thrilling cuisine – daring yet meticulous, and delicate but rarely precious. Sushi isn't the half of it: chef Tim Cushman transforms the humblest fare, from miso soup to *tonkatsu*, into luxuries, which sommelier Nancy Cushman pairs with sakés from her select list.

Pigalle

75 Charles Street South, at Stuart Street (1-617 423 4944, www.pigalleboston.com). Arlington, Boylston or Tufts Medical Center T. **Open** 5-10pm Tue-Fri; 5.30-10.30pm Sat; 5-9.30pm Sun. **Main courses** $24-$40. **Credit** AmEx, DC, MC, V. **Map** p275 J6 ❼ French
A husband and wife team runs this Theater District fixture – which may account for the intimate glow emanating from its petite bar and plush, brown-toned dining room. But it's their individual contributions that really make the Pigalle shine. Chef Marc Orfaly is a whizz at massaging bistro classics into modern, Asian- and Italian-accented shapes, while gracious general manager Kerri Foley is charm itself.

Radius

8 High Street, at Summer Street (1-617 426 1234, www.radiusrestaurant.com). South Station T. **Open** 11.30am-2.30pm, 5.30-10pm Mon-Thur; 11.30am-2.30pm, 5.30-11pm Fri, Sat. **Main courses** $35-$45. **Credit** AmEx, DC, MC, V. **Map** p273 L5 ❽ Creative contemporary

From the semicircular dining room, aglow with silver and scarlet, to the piped-in trance soundtrack, Michael Schlow' subtly hedonistic flagship would make a great backdrop for some latter-day Fellini – who would undoubtedly cast his leads straight from the jet- and trend-setting clientele who descend here. Of course, it's the glamorous New French cuisine that would steal the scene. If dinner is too pricey for your budget, cut to the bar for top-notch cocktails and finger food.

$ Silvertone Bar & Grill

69 Bromfield Street, at Tremont Street (1-617 338 7887, www.silvertonedowntown.com). Downtown Crossing or Park Street T. **Open Kitchen** 11.30am-11pm Mon-Fri; 6pm-11pm Sat. **Bar** 11.30am-2am Mon-Fri; 6pm-2am Sat. **Main courses** $7-$14. **Credit** AmEx, DC, MC, V. **Map** p272 K4 ❾ American/bar
Forward-thinking in its backward-looking ways, the subterranean Silvertone Bar & Grill was a local pioneer of the trend for classic cocktails and American comfort food – and the long wagon train of regulars it immediately formed remains firmly hitched. The owners' good-natured commitment to a bygone era manifests itself in everything from the old prom pictures and liquor ads that line the walls to the confoundingly low prices charged for smart wines by the glass, served alongside such much-loved staples as macaroni and cheese, quesadillas and meatloaf.

INSIDE TRACK
CELEBRITY CHEFS

Where the legacy of adopted Cantabrigian Julia Child lingers, the cult of the chef thrives – and those at its center play their part with dynamism, from winners of prestigious awards to reality show competitors. **Clio** (*see p119*) mastermind Ken Oringer has kept himself on his toes by dabbling in tapas (**Toro**; *see p127*), tacos (**La Verdad**; *see p123*) and T-bones (at his steakhouse, **KO Prime**, in boutique hotel Nine Zero; *see p99*). Todd English runs a score of restaurants in Greater Boston, from seafood to steakhouse; he opened his flagship venture, **Olives**, in Charlestown in 1989. Meanwhile, the mighty powerhouse behind **No.9 Park** (*see p119*), Barbara Lynch (*see p121* **Faces & Places**), continues to put her distinctive stamp on street corners from the glam South End to the up-and-coming Seaport District, where her empire also now includes **Drink** (*see p149*), a posh bar that creates cocktails with techniques somewhere between art and science.

CONSUME

CONSUME

$ Sultan's Kitchen

116 State Street, at Broad Street (1-617 570 9009, www.sultans-kitchen.com). Aquarium or State T. **Open** 11am-8.30pm Mon-Fri; 11am-4.30pm Sat. **Main courses** $5-$11. **Credit** AmEx, MC, V. **Map** p273 L4 ❿ **Turkish**

In an area swarming with chowder-chugging tourists and chop-chomping financiers, this Turkish eaterie is an unlikely sensation – and has been for the past quarter-century. The space (for lack of a better term) is cramped, and the counter service brusque; the eats, however, are anything but utilitarian. Split the huge, garlicky, pita-wrapped doner kebab so you can sample at least one of the aromatic veggie dishes too.

★ Union Oyster House

41 Union Street, at Marshall Street (1-617 227 2750, www.unionoysterhouse.com). Gov't Center or Haymarket T. **Open** *Kitchen* 11am-9.30pm Mon-Thur, Sun; 11am-10pm Fri, Sat. *Bar* 11am-midnight Mon-Sat; noon-midnight Sun. **Main courses** $18-$30. **Credit** AmEx, DC, MC, V. **Map** p273 L3 ⓫ **Fish & seafood**

America's oldest restaurant, established in 1826, may be targeted at tourists – as is every establishment within a block of Faneuil Hall – but as long as you turn a blind eye to the gift shop, the wooden booths and whitewashed walls beyond manage to project some sense of authenticity. The Yankee cooking, not so much. Stick with the historic wooden raw bar, where affable shuckers will ply you with Blue Points and cherrystones – best paired, of course, with a pint or two. *Photo p113.*

Les Zygomates

129 South Street, at Kneeland Street, Waterfront (1-617 542 5108, www.winebar.com). South Station T. **Open** 11.30am-2pm, 6-10.30pm Mon-Fri; 6-11.30pm Sat. **Set meal** $32. **Credit** AmEx, DC, MC, V. **Map** off p273 L5 ⓬ **French**

Vintage posters and red banquettes, a zinc bar and a live jazz line-up – Ian Just's *vrai, vrai français* bistro has long been one of the lone bright spots in the nightly deserted Leather District. And all that glitters is not vibe. A fiercely eclectic and fairly priced wine list accompanies Les Zygomates' carte of slightly tweaked standards: wonderful wilted salads, earthy vegetarian crêpes and precision-cooked steak frites.

CHINATOWN

Kaze

1 Harrison Avenue, at Essex Street (1-617 338 8283, www.kazeshabushabu.com). Chinatown T. **Open** 11.30am-1am Mon-Thur; 11.30am-3am Fri, Sat; noon-1am Sun. **Main courses** $11-$22. **Credit** AmEx, MC, V. **Map** off p272 K5 ⓭ **Japanese**

If the Japanese phenomenon known as *shabu-shabu* has yet to make a splash in Boston, it's no fault of this hot-pot spot, which is rather stylish by Chinatown standards. Both the range and quality of the ingredients at your disposal are impressive, and the effort made by Kaze's friendly staff to explain the cooking process is commendable. The ritual of dipping, say, ribbons of rib-eye with discs of lotus root into tea-like Chinese herbal broth can be so mesmerizing that the meal it leads to just seems like a bonus.

New Shanghai

21 Hudson Street, at Kneeland Street (1-617 338 6688, www.newshanghaiboston. com). Chinatown T. **Open** 11.30am-10pm Mon-Thur; 11am-11pm Fri; 11am-11pm Sat; 11am-10pm Sun. **Main courses** $10-$38. **Credit** AmEx, MC, V. **Map** off p272 K5 ⓮ **Chinese**

Even during its regular dinner service, the New Shanghai makes dim sum-style dining an option – and a delight. Its panoply of steamed or fried pies and buns, filled with chives, soupy ground pork, bean paste and the like, counts among the area's best, while an array of cold appetizers – pickled, salted and smoked – beckons the bold of palate. Other intriguing options include giant-sized lion's head meatballs (juicy pork goodness in a fine gravy) and sweet-and-spicy garlic pork, served in spongy rice-flour 'pockets'.

Peach Farm

4 Tyler Street, at Beach Street (1-617 482 1116). Chinatown T. **Open** 11am-3am daily. **Main courses** $10-$30. **Credit** AmEx, DC, MC, V. **Map** off p272 K5 ⓯ **Chinese**

If the name conjures up bucolic landscapes, Peach Farm's dowdy basement digs promptly erase them. Happily, the Hong Kong-style seafood soon makes amends. Spiced dry-fried eel, enormous steamed oysters in black bean sauce, and lobster stir-fried with ginger and scallions are all superlative.

Penang

685 Washington Street, at Kneeland Street (1-617 451 6373, www.penangusa.com). Chinatown T. **Open** 11.30am-11.30pm Mon-Thur, Sun; 11.30am-midnight Fri, Sat. **Main courses** $10-$23. **Credit** MC, V. **Map** off p272 K5 ⓰ **Malaysian**

The menu of this funky, bamboo-and-brick-lined Malaysian joint is riddled with mysterious warnings ('Please ask server for advice before you order!!!'), which will whet the appetite of the challenge-starved – as well it should, when applied to pungent staples such as the tamarind- and chili-drenched anchovies known as *assam ikan bilis*. Tentative newbies may prefer to start with *roti canai* – a savory pancake, enriched by curried chicken dip – or the surprisingly light oyster omelette.

Classic Tastes

Dip into the dishes of Beantown.

A little starvation finally taught Bostonians' kidney-and-crumpet-craving colonial forebears to acquire a taste for their new home's native crops and produce – the building blocks of a regional cuisine founded on simple (sea-) creature comforts. Humble cod begat proud scrod – young small fry typically broiled with herbed breadcrumbs. Soft-shell clams proved just the stuff for steamers, served – as at the Waterfront's **Barking Crab** (*see p130*) – in heaps with drawn butter and lemon, as well as their own sweet broth. And beans baked in molasses – a byproduct of the city's once-thriving rum industry – became the fodder for its nickname, Beantown. To sample prime examples of such local specialties, here's where to head.

CLAM CHOWDER

A really good chowder – originally and most simply defined as a seafood stew – is a triumph of moderation. Its milk or cream base isn't broth-thin, but neither is it paste-thick; and though it stars the oh-so-handsome clam (in the best-known instance), it's hardly a one-mollusk show – pork, potato, onion and perhaps a pinch of herbs (parsley or dill), used judiciously, make an ideal supporting cast. Relying on its parent chain Legal Sea Foods' definitive recipe, **LTK** (*see p130*) ladles up a fine cup.

LOBSTER ROLL

Cold with mayo or hot with butter? For lobster-roll diehards from Maine or Connecticut (respectively), the question rivals 'to be or not to be?' But being in the geographical middle, Massachusettsans can go either way. Since there are worse undertakings than trying both and deciding for yourself, we suggest hitting **Neptune Oyster** (*see p128*) for the buttery variety and **B&G Oysters** (*see p124*) for the mayo-daubed sort. If money is an object, you can get the taste without the trimmings at **Charlie's Kitchen** (*see p133*), where you can sample two rolls for less than many a burger goes for these days.

BOSTON CREAM PIE

First popularized by the Parker House hotel (now the **Omni Parker House**; *see p99*) some 150 years ago, this dessert doesn't

actually qualify for pie status except in its midsection, where it's layered with vanilla pastry cream; the sponge base and topmost layer of chocolate icing make it a cake. And for its beauty of a rendition, **Flour Bakery & Café** (*see p126*) takes the cake.

INDIAN PUDDING

While the hasty pudding of the motherland contained wheat, oats, barley or rye, the Stateside variant evolved to incorporate local (hence 'Indian') corn in the form of meal, which was mixed with milk and molasses and ultimately baked as well as boiled. It's mainly just for tourists these days, but you can spoon up an uncompromisingly lowbrow bowlful at the likewise delightfully downmarket **Durgin Park** (*see p113*), or at the stately last Brahmin bastion that is **Locke-Ober** (*see p113*).

CONSUME

Discover the city from your back pocket

Essential for your weekend break, over 30 top cities available.

POCKET SIZED
from £6.99/ $11.95

Taiwan Café
34 Oxford Street, at Beach Street (1-617 426 8181). Chinatown T. **Open** 11am-1am Mon-Sat; 11am-midnight Sun. **Main courses** $9-$14. **No credit cards. Map** off p272 K5 ⑰
Taiwanese

Down a side street and up a flight of stairs, Taiwan Café is hard to find – but once you have, you'll soon be back. Though seafood figures prominently – and wonderfully, as with salt-and-pepper-fried squid – the kitchen has range: choice examples include unctuous julienned beef, sautéed with longhorn peppers and tangy, sweet braised aubergine with basil.

BEACON HILL

Bin 26 Enoteca
26 Charles Street, between Beacon & Chestnut Streets (1-617 723 5939, www.bin26.com). Charles/MGH or Arlington T. **Open** noon-10pm Mon-Thur; noon-11pm Fri; 10am-11pm Sat; 10am-10pm Sun. **Main courses** $13-$35. **Credit** AmEx, DC, MC, V. **Map** p272 J4 ⑱
Italian

When wine bottles serve as lamp bases and wine labels as wallpaper, you know you're in for a good glass of grape juice. The 25-page list at this stylish rendezvous is ever-evolving, and refreshingly full of enological wit and wisdom. Savor several sample pours or linger over a carafe paired with exquisitely simple Italian plates, including apt assortments of cheese and charcuterie.

Grotto
37 Bowdoin Street, between Beacon & Cambridge Streets (1-617 227 3434, www.grottorestaurant. com). Bowdoin or Park St T. **Open** 11.30am-3pm, 5-10pm Mon-Fri; 5-10pm Sat, Sun. **Main courses** $31-$50. **Credit** AmEx, DC, MC, V. **Map** p272 K3 ⑲ Italian

Set below street level on the back slope of Beacon Hill, this Italian restaurant is as quirky as its angle. Red paint, lace curtains and close-set tables define its design, and couples of all ages its customer base. The sheer vigor of the fare is born of chef-owner Scott Herritt's muscular cooking style. Both the garlic soup with parmesan and truffles and the gnocchi with short ribs and gorgonzola are eye-rollingly memorably rich. *Photo p120.*

Lala Rokh
97 Mount Vernon Street, at West Cedar Street (1-617 720 5511, www.lalarokh.com). Charles/MGH or Park St T. **Open** noon-3pm, 5.30-10pm Mon-Fri; 5.30-10pm Sat, Sun. **Main courses** $14-$19. **Credit** AmEx, MC, V. **Map** p272 J4 ⑳ Persian

Armed with the recipes their mother brought with her when she emigrated from Azerbaijan, the brother and sister team Azita and Babak Bina have been acting as culinary cupids for well over a decade, causing Bostonians to fall in love with intricately perfumed Persian cuisine – and each other – while on dates at this tastefully romantic Beacon Hill hideaway.

No.9 Park
9 Park Street, at Beacon Street (1-617 742 9991, www.no9park.com). Park St T. **Open** 11.30am-2.30pm, 5.30-10pm Mon-Fri; 5.30-10pm Sat. **Main courses** $32-$45. **Credit** AmEx, DC, MC, V. **Map** p272 K4 ㉑ Italian/French

Although the word 'timeless' is much bandied about by No.9's admirers, Barbara Lynch's flagship can also (despite its head-on view of Boston Common) seem oddly placeless, thanks to its sleekly cosmopolitan air. The former mansion's good looks demonstrate how 'smooth' and 'sharp' can be synonyms; the service – from the remarkable bartenders to the splendid sommelier, Cat Silirie – hits the heights of professionalism. And the French/Italian-based cuisine? Rarely less than luscious, for all its elegance – especially the finely wrought pastas.
▶ *For an interview with Barbara Lynch, see p121.*

Paramount
44 Charles Street, between Mount Vernon & Chestnut Streets (1-617 720 1152, www. paramountboston.com). Charles/MGH or Park Street T. **Open** 7am-4.30pm, 5-10pm Mon-Thur; 7am-4.30pm, 5-11pm Fri; 8am-4.30pm, 5-11pm Sat; 8am-4.30pm, 5-10pm Sun. **Main courses** $13-$20. **Credit** AmEx, DC, MC, V. **Map** p272 J4 ㉒ American

Admittedly greater than the sum of its parts, this once-classic greasy spoon (established in 1937) is now a knowingly jazzy version of its original self. Though the old stainless steel grill, Formica tabletops and cafeteria-style service at breakfast and lunch proudly advertize its blue-collar roots, blue cheese and spinach omelettes, turkey burgers and sweet potato fries hint at a yuppie bent. Either way, people-watching during Sunday brunch is the biggest treat of all.

BACK BAY

Brasserie Jo
Colonnade Hotel, 120 Huntington Avenue, at West Newton Street (1-617 425 3240, www. brasseriejoboston.com). Prudential T. **Open** 11am-1am Mon-Thur; 11am-1.30am Fri, Sat. **Main courses** $18-$25. **Credit** AmEx, DC, MC, V. **Map** p275 G7 ㉓ Brasserie
See p139 **Paris, Massachusetts.**

★ Clio
Eliot Hotel, 370 Commonwealth Avenue, at Massachusetts Avenue (1-617 536 7200, www.cliorestaurant.com). Hynes T. **Open** 5.30-10pm Mon-Thur; 5.30-10.30pm Fri-Sun. **Main courses** $32-$40. **Credit** AmEx, DC, MC, V. **Map** p274 E6 ㉔ French

CONSUME

Grotto. *See p119.*

The taupe and cream color scheme says 'refinement'; the leopard-print rug says 'excitement'. The menu says both at once – and the cooking that first earned Ken Oringer his celebrity status bears out that promise. In the tiny kitchen of the Eliot Hotel's ever-buzzing special-occasion destination, Oringer sculpts miniature New French masterpieces from foie gras, lobster, game and exquisite produce you've never heard of – while the deft chefs behind the counter at Uni, Clio's cozy adjoining sashimi bar, do likewise with seafood flown in weekly from Tokyo's Tsukiji market (threadfish bream, anyone?).

Douzo

131 Dartmouth Street, between Stuart Street & Columbus Avenue (1-617 859 8886, www. douzosushi.com). Back Bay or Copley T. **Open** 11.30am-3pm, 4.30pm-midnight daily. **Main courses** $20-$30. **Credit** AmEx, DC, MC, V. **Map** p275 H7 ㉕ **Japanese**

Scallop-kiwi maki, sea urchin tempura, shining baubles of monkfish pâté – Back Bay was more than ready for such heady fare, as Douzo has proven since day one. A date favorite for its multi-level nooks and mood lighting, it's no less welcoming to loners who score seats at the sushi bar, getting the inside scoop on daily specials direct from the chefs.

★ Eastern Standard

Hotel Commonwealth, 528 Commonwealth Avenue, at Beacon Street (1-617 532 9100, www.easternstandardboston.com). Kenmore T. **Open** 7am-midnight daily. **Main courses** $18-$28. **Credit** AmEx, MC, V. **Map** p274 D6 ㉖ **Brasserie**

For some it evokes the Gare du Nord, for others New York's Balthazar – but among them all, this big, bustling American brasserie is a smash hit, accessible in every sense of the word. It's open early and closes late, is staffed by energetic sorts (including expert mixologists) and frequented by equally lively folks: the huge bar and heated patio are rocking. The menu is deceptively simple but appealing, sneaking in oodles of offal between the chilled shellfish and such comfort classics as steak frites and schnitzel.
▶ *For French brasseries in Boston, see p139 Paris, Massachusetts.*

L'Espalier

Mandarin Oriental, 30 Gloucester Street, at Newbury Street (1-617 262 3023, www.lespalier. com). Hynes T. **Open** 11.30am-2.30pm, 5.30-10.30pm Mon-Fri; noon-1.45pm, 5.30-10.30pm Sat, Sun. **Set meal** $75 (3 courses); $94 (7 courses). **Credit** AmEx, MC, V. **Map** p274 F6 ㉗ **French**

Marriage proposals and six-figure deals are par for the course at chef-owner Frank McClelland's New French New England legend. Make that par for seven courses, rather: the main menu is a prix-fixe degustation, breathtaking in its creativity, scope, execution and, of course, price. Served in a posh, intimate brownstone by hyper-attentive waiters, it has no local equal – and the cellar wine director Erik Johnson has built is tremendous too. L'Espalier makes its home in the posh Mandarin Oriental hotel.

Grill 23 & Bar

161 Berkeley Street, between Stuart Street & Columbus Avenue (1-617 542 2255, www. grill23.com). Arlington T. **Open** 5.30-10.30pm

Mon-Thur; 5.30-11pm Fri; 5-11pm Sat; 5.30-10pm Sun. **Main courses** $30-$40. **Credit** AmEx, DC, MC, V. **Map** p275 H6 ❷ **American**
It looks like all the other beef barns in town: high ceilings, marble columns, white tablecloths and white-jacketed waiters; lawyers and brokers whooping it up with trophy wives over trophy wines; and chops that very nearly cost their weight in gold. But Jay Murray is a real chef, whose seasonal menu transcends steakhouse clichés, while Alex DeWinter is a gracious sommelier, whose thoughtful recommendations reveal not a whit of mere showiness or salesmanship.

Parish Café
361 Boylston Street, at Arlington Street (1-617 247 4777, www.parishcafe.com). Arlington T. **Open** 11.30am-2am Mon-Sat; noon-2am Sun. **Main courses** $9-$14. **Credit** AmEx, DC, MC, V. **Map** p275 H5 ❷ **American /bar**
What's better than cramming the city's most celebrated chefs into a single kitchen? Giving them room to think, so they can contribute from afar to a single menu comprising the city's most celebrated sandwiches instead. Besides signature faves from East Coast Grill's Chris Schlesinger, Blue Ginger's Ming Tsai, Radius's Michael Schlow and others, there's

Faces & Places Barbara Lynch

A top restaurateur gives the dish on Boston.

Following no less auspicious a debut than the nationally acclaimed **No.9 Park** (*see p119*), chef-restaurateur Barbara Lynch – born and bred in South Boston – earned the clout to tackle just about any project she chose – and so she has, from a raw bar (**B&G Oysters**; *see p124*) and a charcuterie (the **Butcher Shop**; *see p124*) to a designer market (**Plum Produce**) and a rare cookbook library and demonstration kitchen, **Stir**. And that's not all. The newest additions to Lynch's empire include a trio of properties in the Waterfront area: upscale French dining with a hint of Italian influence at **Menton**; Italian luncheonette **Sportello** (*see p132*); and cocktail paradise, **Drink** (*see p149*).

TO: So what's kept you in Boston?
BL: [Before No.9 Park opened in 1998] the city felt like an empty palette that you could fill in however you wanted. The chefs were fabulous, but the restaurants were all being built the same, by the same designers, and they all gave you the same feeling, like 'You're lucky to get a table, you're lucky to eat here.' I felt we needed an upgrade in management; we needed to bring back maître d's and the whole dining experience.

TO: How does the city inspire you?
BL: Actually, it's the underground of really talented artists: architects, cabinetmakers, craftspeople, bookbinders, authors… There's just a bunch of creative people in this city, more than are ever perceived.

TO: But you can see their work in your restaurants, where decor closely reflects concept.
BL: Yes, a lot of francophiles come to the Butcher Shop who actually get that,

who have a special place in their hearts for the design.

TO: What would you tell visitors not to miss?
BL: Well, it's not in Boston, but the DeCordova Museum [in Lincoln; *see p235*]. It's so cool. There's a big garden where you can picnic, surrounded by New England sculpture. I also think the city's really lucky to have Louis Boston (*see p156*). Not only does it have the clothes, but it has a marketplace where you can get cookbooks and cutlery and linens.

TO: What would you tell visitors to avoid?
BL: The highway.

Bags packed, milk cancelled, house raised on stilts.

You've packed the suntan lotion, the snorkel set, the stay-pressed shirts. Just one more thing left to do – your bit for climate change. In some of the world's poorest countries, changing weather patterns are destroying lives.

You can help people to deal with the extreme effects of climate change. Raising houses in flood-prone regions is just one life-saving solution.

Climate change costs lives.
Give £5 and let's sort it _Here & Now_

www.oxfam.org.uk/climate-change

Oxfam is a registered charity in England and Wales (No.202918) and Scotland (SCO039042). Oxfam GB is a member of Oxfam International.

Be Humankind ⚘ **Oxfam**

always something new to sample; local bartenders get equally creative on the cocktail list. What never changes is the kinetic energy both inside the snug, multicolored café and out on the mega-popular patio.

▶ *For our review of East Coast Grill, see p134. For Radius, see p115.*

Petit Robert Bistro

468 Commonwealth Avenue, near Charlesgate West, Kenmore (1-617 375 0699, www.petit robertbistro.com). Kenmore T. **Open** 11am-11pm daily. **Main courses** $12-$20. **Credit** AmEx, MC, V. **Map** p274 E6 ③⓿ **French**

Simplicity isn't simple: Boston's dearth of authentic French bistros is proof enough of that. Or was, until Maître Cuisiner de France Jacky Robert came along and made it all look supremely easy. Comfortable, unfussy and affordable, his townhouse kitchen is reacquainting diners with the hearty joys of proper *quenelles*, no-nonsense *soupe à l'oignon gratinée* and *boeuf bourguignon* – topped off with a terrific, rustic tarte tatin.

Other locations 480 Columbus Avenue, at Rutland Square, Back Bay (1-617 867 0600).

$ Snappy Sushi

144 Newbury Street, at Dartmouth Street (1-617 262 4530, www.snappysushi.com). Copley T. **Open** noon-9pm Mon-Wed, Sun; noon-9.45pm Thur-Sat. **Set meal** $6-$12. **Credit** AmEx, MC, V. **Map** p275 G6 ③❶ **Japanese**

Along the stairs leading down from Newbury Street into this literal bargain basement of a sushi bar, it's often standing room only – but the few tables in the tiny dining room turn over quickly, a good sign for freshness freaks and speedniks alike.

Sonsie

327 Newbury Street, between Hereford Street & Massachusetts Avenue (1-617 351 2500, www.sonsieboston.com). Hynes T. **Open** 11.30am-2.30pm, 6-11pm Mon, Tue; 11.30am-2.30pm, 6pm-midnight Wed-Fri; 11.30am-3pm, 6pm-midnight Sat; 11.30am-3pm, 6-11pm Sun. **Main courses** $17-$35. **Credit** AmEx, MC, V. **Map** p274 F6 ③❷ **Creative contemporary**

With French doors opening out on to ever-chic Newbury Street and waiting staff as attractive as the scenery, Sonsie should by rights be a tourist trap. The fact that its eclectic, oft-changing menu is actually engaging – think wasabi-baked oysters with asparagus tempura or grilled trout with crayfish waffles – is a testament to the skills of long-term chef Bill Poirier. Still, people-watching from the café tables over cappuccinos or cocktails takes priority for the chic Back Bay denizens who frequent it.

★ Sorellina

1 Huntington Avenue, at Dartmouth Street (1-617 412 4600, www.sorellinaboston.com). Back Bay or Copley T. **Open** 5-11pm Mon-Thur, Sun;

5pm-midnight Fri, Sat. **Main courses** $15-$60. **Credit** AmEx, MC, V. **Map** p275 G6 ③❸ **Italian**

Even more striking in its black and white stripes than older sibling Mistral, Sorellina looks as much like a modern design showroom as an Italian restaurant. The menu is equally glamorous. The ingredients are posh, sauces sparing; even the signature spaghetti and meatballs (make that *maccheroncelli*) contains Kobe beef and a splash of Barolo. Of course, you'll find plenty of the latter on the largely high-end Cal-Ital wine list as well. *Photo p125.*

▶ *For our review of Mistral, see p127.*

Trattoria Toscana

130 Jersey Street, at Queensberry Street, Fenway (1-617 247 9508). Fenway or MFA T. **Open** 5-10pm Mon-Sat. **Main courses** $13-$20. **Credit** MC, V. **Map** p274 D8 ③❹ **Italian**

There isn't a street corner in Italy without at least one simple, family-run trattoria, a place where hospitality goes hand in hand with homemade pasta. The fact that Trattoria Toscana would blend in so easily there is precisely what makes it stand out here, among Boston's many corny macaroni joints. Dotted with ceramics and landscapes of *la campagna*, it's as tastefully unpretentious as the food it serves: try robust bread-based soups such as *pappa al pomodoro* or *ribollita*, followed by pretty much anything made with liver or own-made sausage – then sit back and relax with a textbook cappuccino.

Trident Booksellers & Café

338 Newbury Street, at Hereford Street (1-617 267 8688, www.tridentbookscafe.com). Hynes T. **Open** 9am-midnight daily. **Main courses** $10. **Credit** AmEx, DC, MC, V. **Map** p274 F6 ③❺ **Café**

A bohemian ambience permeates this bright, airy in-store café. It hops all day with Berklee students and writerly types, poring over glossies from an edgy, globe-spanning magazine rack while polishing off breakfast burritos, tuna and swiss cheese melts, yam fries and smoothies.

$ La Verdad

1 Lansdowne Street, at Ipswich Street (1-617 351 2580, www.laverdadtaqueria.com). Kenmore T. **Open** 11am-1am Tue-Thur; 11am-2am Fri, Sat. **Main courses** $3-$18. **Credit** AmEx, MC, V. **Map** p274 E7 ③❻ **Mexican**

Wonderfully shadowy, looking as if it might belong on the corner of some dusty Mexican plaza, Ken Oringer's *taqueria* nonetheless caters largely to *Yanquis* (though not, mind you, to Yankees – Fenway Park isn't even half a block away). But, like its siblings Uni and Toro (*see p127*), it's authentic unto itself. Lovingly crafted little tacos are the menu's mainstay, accompanied by all manner of salsas. Hot, fresh cotija cheese-sprinkled tortilla chips with guacamole and elaborate *tortas* are memorable too – provided you manage to keep your tequila consumption in check, that is.

CONSUME

CONSUME

THE BEST LOCAL FLAVORS

Durgin Park
Home of the baked bean. *See p113.*

Locke-Ober
Brahmin-era dining room. *See p113.*

Lower Depths
$1 Fenway franks. *See p146.*

Via Matta

79 Park Plaza, at Arlington Street (1-617 422 0008, www.viamattarestaurant.com). Arlington T. **Open** 11.30am-2.30pm, 5.30-10pm Mon-Thur; 11.30am-2.30pm, 5.30-11pm Fri; 5-11pm Sat. **Main courses** $10-$20. **Credit** AmEx, DC, MC, V. **Map** p275 J6 **⑤** **Italian**
The Crazy Way, as the name translates, takes an admirably streamlined approach to contemporary Italian cuisine. The strikingly bare setting reflects this ethos, from the dining room – as stark white and echoey as an art gallery – to the dark, generally quiet wine bar. Meanwhile, stripped-down, spot-on specialties such as crunchy eggplant and *spaghetti aglio e olio con pomodoro* convey an easy breeziness, borne by waiters whose smoothness and efficiency is a hallmark of every Michael Schlow venture.

THE SOUTH END

Addis Red Sea

544 Tremont Street, at Clarendon Street (1-617 426 8727, www.addisredsea.com). Back Bay or Tufts Medical Center T. **Open** 5-11pm Mon-Fri; noon-11pm Sat, Sun. **Main courses** $8-$15. **Credit** AmEx, MC, V. **Map** p275 H7 **⑧** **Ethiopian**
If you've never scooped up a dollop of *kitfo* with a hunk of soft, spongy *injera* while seated around a multicolored *mesob*, or if you don't even know what all that means, then this much-loved Ethiopian charmer will come as an eye-opening treat. Brightly hued woven baskets act as tables, flatbread replaces flatware and a typical meal centers on spicy, stew-like mélanges, with the soothing counterbalance of honey wine. There are plenty of options for vegetarians too.

★ B&G Oysters

550 Tremont Street, at Waltham Street (1-617 423 0550, www.bandgoysters.com). Back Bay or Tufts Medical Center T. **Open** 11.30am-10pm Mon; 11.30am-11pm Tue-Fri; noon-11pm Sat; noon-10pm Sun. **Main courses** $16-$24. **Credit** AmEx, MC, V. **Map** p275 H7 **⑨** **Fish & seafood**
'Bivalves', reads a hand-shaped sign on the gate, pointing you towards Barbara Lynch's diminutive, understated oyster bar. Decor so coolly clean that

it's practically scrubbed sets the tone for an ever-changing array of oysters from both coasts, complemented by dozens of mostly white wines offered by the glass. The menu is supplemented by a small but sparkling (if rather costly) selection of seafood-centric appetizers and mains.
▶ *The Butcher Shop (see below), also owned by Barbara Lynch, is just across the road.*

Beehive

Boston Center for the Arts, 541 Tremont Street, between Berkeley & Clarendon Streets (1-617 423 0069, www.beehiveboston.com). Back Bay or Tufts Medical Center T. **Open** 5.30pm-2am Mon-Fri; 11.30am-4pm, 5.30pm-2am Sat, Sun. **Main courses** $14-$27. **Credit** AmEx, MC, V. **Map** p275 H7 **⑩** **Creative contemporary**
An annex of the Boston Center for the Arts, Beehive is a madly buzzing bohemia. Whimsical textiles, wild paintings and other odd objets offset the loft-like restaurant, bar and entertainment venue's exposed-brick grittiness, while some of the city's best-known bartenders mix the drinks. In short, Beehive is a capital-S Scene. The kitchen whips up fun, Mediterranean-tinged nibbles, salads and communal platters to fuel the revelry, plus a few main courses for square-meal sticklers.
▶ *For information about the Boston Center for the Arts, see p226.*

★ Butcher Shop

552 Tremont Street, at Waltham Street (1-617 423 4800, www.thebutchershopboston.com). Back Bay or Tufts Medical Center T. **Open** 11.30am-3.30pm, 4.30-10pm Mon, Sun; 11.30am-3pm, 4.30-11pm Tue-Sat. **Main courses** $18-$24. **Credit** AmEx, MC, V. **Map** p275 H7 **⑪** **French/bar**
It's polished, it's chic, it's packed with designer-clad South Enders swirling wine goblets and nibbling on pâté, it's... a butcher's shop? Yes, indeed – as well as a cozy soapstone-and-slate wine bar. Owner Barbara Lynch stocks the display cases with every delicacy, from pigs' heads and whole hams to quails' eggs and truffle butter, and fills the short menu with equally delicious, simple fare. Own-made charcuterie and antipasti can be washed down with a selection of mostly European boutique reds.
▶ *After a bite or two, regulars often cross the street to B&G Oysters, also owned by Barbara Lynch, to complete their surf-and-turf crawl.*

★ $ Charlie's Sandwich Shoppe

429 Columbus Avenue, between Braddock Park & Holyoke Street (1-617 536 7669). Back Bay or Mass Ave T. **Open** 6am-2.30pm Mon-Fri; 7.30am-1pm Sat. **Main courses** $4-$8.
No credit cards. **Map** p275 G7 **⑫** **American**
Perched on a windy stretch of Columbus Avenue, this greasy spoon (established in 1927) is pure bygone Americana. Chrome stools literally on their last legs line the counter, oilcloth covers the tables

Sorellina. *See p123*.

and yellowed photos of famous customers plaster the walls – while the impassive hash-slingers and crammed-in regulars radiate local color. Speaking of hash, Charlie's turkey-based version is a staple, though the fluffy omelettes and even fluffier pancakes are as trusty as the turkey clubs, tuna melts and chili dogs.

Don Ricardo's

57 West Dedham Street, at Ivanhoe Street (1-617 247 9249, www.donricardoboston.com). Back Bay T. **Open** 11.30am-10pm Mon-Thur; 11.30am-11pm Fri, Sat; 3-10pm Sun. **Main courses** $10-$14. **Credit** MC, V. **Map** p275 H8 ⑬ **Brazilian/Peruvian**
A true gentleman and his smiling wife run this sweetly modest Peruvian-Brazilian side-street find. Still a favorite with neighborhood couples after more than two decades, it offers credible ceviche and incredible *albondigas rellenas* (meatballs stuffed with chopped olives, eggs and peppers). Robust beer-braised lamb tastes even better with a side of *tostones*, while the wine list is very reasonably priced.

★ $ Flour Bakery & Café

1595 Washington Street, at Rutland Street (1-617 267 4300, www.flourbakery.com). Mass Ave T, or Silver Line Washington St to Newton St. **Open** 7am-9pm Mon-Fri; 8am-6pm Sat; 9am-3pm Sun. **Main courses** $8-$15. **Credit** AmEx, MC, V. **Map** p275 H9 ⑭ **Bakery-café**
Some years back, Flour put this then-desolate stretch of Washington Street on the culinary map – and X still marks Joanne Chang's sweet spot for baked-treasure hunters. Pastel hues and a chalkboard menu make this place as cute as a cupcake –

or any of the other goodies gracing the counter, for that matter, from sticky buns to fat chocolate-chip macaroons that could convert even sworn coconut-loathers. The sandwiches are no mere afterthought – curried tuna salad and BLTs are the hot sellers. **Other locations** 12 Farnsworth Street, Fort Point Channel, Waterfront (1-617 338 4333); 190 Massachusetts Avenue, Central Square, Cambridge (1-617 225 2525).

Franklin Café

278 Shawmut Avenue, at Hanson Street (1-617 350 0010, www.franklincafe.com). Back Bay or Tufts Medical Center T. **Open** 5pm-2am daily. **Main courses** $9-$19. **Credit** AmEx, DC, MC, V. **Map** p275 J7 ⑮ **Creative contemporary**
The small but perfectly formed Franklin is a neighborhood hangout for the whole city. What's it got that your average corner joint hasn't? The culinary talents – and the constant commitment to honing them – that you'd expect from dining destinations charging twice the price. Tiny, dark and pretty much packed from happy hour onwards, it requires patience from its patrons but eventually rewards them with quality cocktails and foodie delights such as soy-marinated chicken livers or scallop and artichoke casserole.

★ Gaslight, Brasserie du Coin

560 Harrison Avenue, at Waltham Street (1-617 422 0224, www.gaslight560.com). Tufts Medical Center T. **Open** 11.30am-1.30am Mon-Fri; 10.30am-1.30am Sat, Sun. **Main courses** $17-$24. **Credit** AmEx, DC, MC, V. **Map** p275 J8 ⑯ **Brasserie**
See p139 **Paris, Massachusetts**.

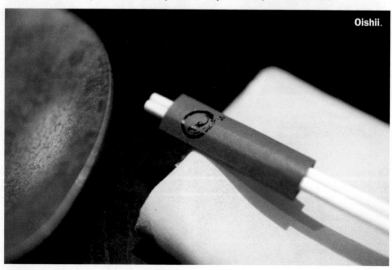

Oishii.

Hamersley's Bistro

*553 Tremont Street, at Clarendon Street
(1-617 423 2700, www.hamersleysbistro.com).
Back Bay or Tufts Medical Center T.* **Open** 5.30-
9.30pm Mon-Fri; 5.30-10pm Sat; 11am-2pm, 5.30-
9.30pm Sun. **Main courses** $24-$39. **Credit**
AmEx, DC, MC, V. **Map** p275 H7 ⓐ **French**
With its sleek black light fixtures, white tablecloths,
ceiling beams and creamy yellow walls, Gordon
Hamersley's South End institution seems half French
country cottage, half metropolitan boîte. The twain
do indeed meet in the kitchen, where pickled fiddle-
head ferns (a New England specialty in spring) might
jazz up duck rillettes, and garlic soup comes spiked
with curry and mint. The wine list generally plays it
safe, but amid one too many cabs and chards there
are some curios to be uncorked.

Mistral

*223 Columbus Avenue, at Cahner's Place (1-617
867 9300, www.mistralbistro.com). Back Bay T.*
Open 5.30-11pm Mon-Sat; 5.30-10pm Sun. **Main
courses** $18-$44. **Credit** AmEx, DC, MC, V.
Map p275 H6 ⓐ **French/Mediterranean**
With its stone floors and potted cypresses, sunnily
sophisticated Mistral brings a touch of swish Saint
Tropez to the edge of the Mass Pike. This place has
been on the A-listers' shortlist since it opened. For
our part, we wish chef-owner Jamie Mammano
would tinker a tad more often with the items on his
rarely changing French-Mediterranean menu –
exquisite though they may be – and with their ever-
rising prices a little less. But the tête-à-têtes among
the beauties and powermongers lining the bar are
meaty enough to make eavesdropping over cocktails
synonymous with feasting.

Oishii

*1166 Washington Street, at Perry Street (1-617
482 8868, www.oishiiboston.com). Tufts Medical
Center T.* **Open** 5pm-midnight Tue-Sat; 5-10pm
Sun. **Main courses** $40-$60. **Credit** AmEx,
MC, V. **Map** p275 J7 ⓐ **Japanese**
Cross a Zen meditation garden with a slick postmodern lounge, and what do you get? Something
like the urban outpost of Oishii – which is to say
nothing like the modest 15-seat original in suburban Chestnut Hill. And that's just fine: if anyone's
earned the right to a little flashy immodesty, it's the
folks who brought Bostonians their first taste of
Tokyo-grade sushi. Hype, you scoff? Go for the
omakase (house special) before you answer that
question. The spectacularly colorful combinations
look as sensational as they taste.
Other locations 612 Hammond Street, Chestnut
Hill (1-617 277 7888).

Orinoco: A Latin Kitchen

*477 Shawmut Avenue, at Concord Street
(1-617 369 7075, www.orinocokitchen.com).
Mass Ave T.* **Open** noon-2.30pm, 6-10pm Tue-Sat;

11am-3pm Sun. **Main courses** $10-$14.
Credit MC, V. **Map** p275 H8 ⓐ **Venezuelan**
Amid the twee boutiques and dog bakeries of the
hyper-gentrified South End, this twinkling little tribute to the Venezuelan roadside restaurant known as
a *taguarita* comes as a total surprise. So does the
bold yet delicately nuanced food, served in a mask-
and basket-lined dining room. The smaller plates in
particular burst with flavors and textures: after a
round of *antojitos* such as cheese-filled, deep-fried
plantain chunks and rich, gooey bacon-wrapped
dates, share a couple of the stuffed corn pockets
called *arepas* – the shredded beef and mojo-laced
roast pork really stand out.

★ Pops

*560 Tremont Street, near Clarendon Street
(1-617 695 1250, www.popsrestaurant.net). Back
Bay or Tufts Medical Center T.* **Open** 5-10pm Mon-
Wed; 5pm-midnight Thur, Fri; 10.30am-2.30pm,
5pm-midnight Sat; 10.30am-2.30pm, 5-10pm Sun.
Main courses $16-$20. **Credit** AmEx, MC, V.
Map p275 H7 ⓐ **Creative contemporary**
The just-right place at the just-right time, Pops is
helping to fill the Goldilocksian gap in the Boston
dining scene where all the mid-range eateries should
be. Patterned wallpaper, etched-glass dividers and
mini-chandeliers strike an unusual truce between
quaintness and contemporary cool, while chef-owner
Felino Samson gives the cliché that is 'creative comfort food' a fresh meaning, turning out salads chock-
full of unexpected goodies (fried oysters, poached
eggs, cantaloupe, chickpeas), creamy pastas and
delicious bread pudding.

Toro

*1704 Washington Street, between West
Springfield & Worcester Streets (1-617 536
4300, www.toro-restaurant.com). Mass Ave T.*
Open 5.30pm-midnight Mon-Wed, Sun; 5.30pm-
1am Thur-Sat. **Main courses** $20-$35. **Credit**
AmEx, DC, MC, V. **Map** p275 H9 ⓐ **Spanish**
Ken Oringer's smash take on a *taperia* is an atmospheric spot. With its exposed brick and wooden
beams, central communal table and blackboard

CONSUME

chalked with drink specials, it effortlessly captures the rustic spirit of Spain – which its customers invariably catch in turn, swigging wine from juice glasses or cava from *porrónes*. The food is superb. Buttery, cider-simmered foie gras sausage, immaculate salt cod croquettes and seasonal treats showcasing glass eels or green chickpeas prove the much-touted grilled corn with alioli and crumbled cotija (pungent aged cheese) is no fluke.

THE NORTH END

Antico Forno
93 Salem Street, at Wiget Street (1-617 723 6733, www.anticofornoboston.com). Haymarket T. **Open** 11.30am-10pm Mon-Thur, Sun; 11.30am-10.30pm Fri, Sat. **Main courses** $14.50-$22. **Credit** AmEx, MC, V. **Map** p273 L3 ⑤ Italian
The North End is notoriously ridden with sloppy, corner-cutting imitations of authentic trattorias. But Antico Forno is the genuine article, quietly eschewing red-checked clichés as it upholds Italian-American traditions. From aubergine rolls to rigatoni with sausage or thin-crust pizza, pretty much anything that emerges from the brick oven, oozing ricotta and proper tomato sauce, is a winner. The pasta plates also please, especially the cloud-soft gnocchi. The kitchen is open all day for impatient appetites.

Bricco
241 Hanover Street, between Cross & Parmenter Streets (1-617 248 6800, www.bricco.com). Haymarket T. **Open** 5-11pm Mon, Sun; 5pm-2am Tue-Sat. **Main courses** $21-$46. **Credit** AmEx, MC, V. **Map** p273 L3 ⑥ Italian
With name chefs blowing in and out of its kitchen, this dark, suave neighborhood pioneer of *alta cucina* has hit its share of rough patches over the years. But its capacity for comebacks is astounding. Give it a go when you're feeling flush – chances are you'll score some marvelously silky pasta (the meatball-studded *timpano* is a wonder), rounded out by intriguing seasonal *contorni*-like foie gras-laced butternut squash or potatoes mashed with pink grapefruit. Meanwhile, the allure of the obscure tints the all-Italian wine list.

THE BEST SEAFOOD

LTK
Chowder fit for a king, and at least a few presidents. *See p130.*

Neptune Oyster
God of the sea(food). *See right.*

Union Oyster House
The country's oldest restaurant. *See p116.*

$ Caffe Vittoria
290-296 Hanover Street, between Prince & Parmenter Streets (1-617 227 7606, www.vittoriacaffe.com). Haymarket T. **Open** 8am-midnight Mon-Thur, Sun; 8am-12.30am Fri, Sat. **No credit cards. Map** p273 L2 ⑤ Café
Fusing the freshly scrubbed look of a small-town soda fountain with the vintage spirit of *un bar italiano*, this is one of the North End's quintessential coffeehouses. A scattered array of antique espresso urns and French presses attests to this – and the rich, foamy cappuccino sprinkled with cocoa confirms it. The imported sodas and a smattering of grappas make their case too.
▶ *After hours, head downstairs to cigar bar Stanza dei Sigari, a Prohibition-era speakeasy that still looks the part.*

Daily Catch
323 Hanover Street, between Richmond & Prince Streets (1-617 523 8567, www.daily catch.com). Haymarket T. **Open** 11am-10pm Mon-Thur, Sun; 11am-11pm Fri, Sat. **Main courses** $20-$59. **No credit cards. Map** p273 L3 ⑥ Fish & seafood
When people talk about the true character of the 'old' North End, chances are they're envisioning the Daily Catch. It's essentially a kitchen nook with a blackboard menu, juice glasses in lieu of stemware and skillets that double as plates. It doesn't take credit cards, or even have a bathroom. But boy, has it got calamari – fried, stuffed, marinated and chilled, chopped and pressed into delicious meatballs. Squid ink, meanwhile, gives the linguine a kick – as does garlic galore.

Maurizio's
364 Hanover Street, at Clark Street (1-617 367 1123, www.mauriziosboston.com). Haymarket T. **Open** 5-10pm Mon-Fri; noon-10.30pm Sat; 11am-10pm Sun. **Main courses** $17-$28. **Credit** AmEx, MC, V. **Map** p273 L2 ⑤ Italian
Little Maurizio's keeps a lower profile but higher standards than the majority of Hanover Street's eateries. Delivered by generally earnest waiters, along with the occasional complimentary glass of bubbly, Sardinian curiosities such as gnocchi-like *malloreddus* and hearty *mazzamurru* (a thick bread-and-tomato stew topped with egg and cheese) are as stout as their names.

Neptune Oyster
63 Salem Street, at Morton Street (1-617 742 3474, www.neptuneoyster.com). Haymarket T. **Open** 11.30am-11pm Mon-Wed, Sun; 11.30am-midnight Thur-Sat. **Main courses** $15-$34. **Credit** AmEx, MC, V. **Map** p273 L3 ⑤ Fish & seafood
Established in 2004, Neptune Oyster is a delightful paradox – at once exemplary and exceptional. This place looks and feels exactly as an East Coast raw

Neptune Oyster.

bar should: tiny, lined with pressed tin, subway tiles and etched glass, it possesses retro gleam and unmistakable charm. If the daily oyster roster is definitive, the rest of the menu is startlingly original. The fearless eatery will try just about anything – pairing fried oysters with pickled beef tongue, say – and so will the adventurers he's made of his fiercely loyal regulars (of whom there are many – expect long waits at peak hours). Grab a marble topped table or a seat at the bar, and you're in for a treat.

★ Pizzeria Regina
11½ Thacher Street, at North Margin Street (1-617 227 0765, www.pizzeriaregina.com). Haymarket T. **Open** 11am-11.30pm Mon-Thur; 11am-midnight Fri, Sat; noon-11pm Sun. **Main courses** $10-$18. **No credit cards.** **Map** p273 L2  **Pizza**
With a magic oven that yields a beautifully bubbly crust on every pizza and a stalwart crew of Boston-bred tray-slingers, Pizzeria Regina's reputation precedes it. So, often, does the line to get in. Though it has spawned numerous mall outlets, none can compare to the original, which opened in 1926 and has barely changed since. Park yourself in a wooden booth, call for a pitcher of beer and a pizza napoletana or the whopping three-pound, multi-topping giambotta, and get set to *mangia* like you've never *mangia'd* before.

Prezza
24 Fleet Street, between Moon & Garden Court Streets (1-617 227 1577, www.prezza.com). Haymarket T. **Open** 5.30-10pm Mon-Thur, Sun; 5-10.30pm Fri, Sat. **Main courses** $22-$40. **Credit** AmEx, MC, V. **Map** p273 L2 **Italian**

The achievement of local boy-done-good Anthony Caturano, Prezza combines the urbane musculature of a downtown steakhouse with the intimacy of the North End trattorias that surround it – which is why you'll glimpse as many back-slapping businessmen at the bar as you will canoodling couples in the booths. Caturano's cooking boasts similar breadth: follow an order of *arancini* – a Sicilian street snack, here transformed with luxe fillings such as lobster and mascarpone – with a hefty, expertly wood-grilled chop, and you'll discover as much for yourself.

Taranta
210 Hanover Street, at Cross Street (1-617 720 0052, www.tarantarist.com). Haymarket T. **Open** 5.30-10pm daily. **Main courses** $19-$30. **Credit** AmEx, MC, V. **Map** p273 L3 **Italian/Peruvian**
In the hands of a lesser chef-owner, Taranta might have been a mere novelty. Under José Duarte – a visionary in the kitchen and a charmer in the dining room – this southern Italian-Peruvian joint is one of the most consistently exciting (yet warm and relaxing) eateries around. The cross-cultural fusion not only yields the piquant likes of yuca gnocchi with lamb ragù, and pork chops with sugar cane and *rocoto* pepper glaze, but also determines the scope of the wine list, extending from Sicily, Campania and Apulia to Argentina and Chile.

★ $ Volle Nolle
351 Hanover Street, between Prince & Fleet Streets (1-617 523 0003). Haymarket T. **Open** 11am-4pm daily. **Sandwiches** $7-$9. **No credit cards.** **Map** p273 L2 **Café/Italian**

A sandwich constructed with care from fine ingredients ought to be the rule, not the exception, to the glut of stale, mass-produced products. This quirky little shop sets things to rights, handling classics such as *cubanos* and *muffulettas* correctly while bearing a few standards of its own – take, for instance, the gratifyingly messy chicken with prosciutto, fresh mozzarella, romaine and walnut pesto, served on griddled french bread.

CHARLESTOWN

Figs

67 Main Street, at Monument Avenue (1-617 242 2229, www.toddenglish.com). Community College T. **Open** 5.30-10.30pm Mon-Sat; 5-9.30pm Sun. **Main courses** $11-$19. **Credit** AmEx, MC, V. **Map** p272 K1 ⓺ Pizza

While Todd English has gone on to become a fully fledged celebrity chef, his tiny pizzeria remains a sentimental favorite. These days it's a tad the worse for wear (chipped paint, torn cushions and all), but its exposed brickwork and copper trim still exude a cozy charm. The pizzas are as distinctive as ever – oblong and free-form, with crusts whose edges snap like crackers and toppings that run the gamut from mushroom purée to mustard aïoli – not to mention that famed, heady fig and balsamic vinegar jam. **Other locations** 42 Charles Street, Beacon Hill (1-617 742 3447).

$ Sorelle

100 City Square, at Route 99 (1-617 242 5980, www.sorellecafe.com). Haymarket T then 10min walk. **Open** 7am-7pm Mon-Fri; 8am-7pm Sat; 8am-5pm Sun. **Sandwiches** $6-$8. **Credit** AmEx, DC, MC, V. **Map** p272 K1 ⓸ Bakery-café

It's as sleek – indeed quasi-industrial – as bakery-cafés come: think exposed pipes, stone floors, pastel plastic chairs and black banquettes (not to mention a two-seat wine bar). It's also as conveniently situated as can be: right on the Freedom Trail, minutes from Old Ironsides. In short, Sorelle's a nifty pit stop for fresh pastries, gourmet sandwiches and super-charged coffee concoctions to fuel any sightseeing jaunt. **Other locations** 1 Monument Avenue, Charlestown (1-617 242 2125).

▶ *For visits to the USS Constitution, see p74.*

THE WATERFRONT

Barking Crab

88 Sleeper Street, at Northern Avenue (1-617 426 2722, www.barkingcrab.com). Silver Line Waterfront to Courthouse. **Open** 11.30am-12.30am daily. **Main courses** $10-$26. **Credit** AmEx, MC, V. **Map** p273 M5 ⓺ Fish & seafood

Set right on Boston Harbor, this red-shingled seafood shack and open-air tent is party central all summer long for local desk jockeys as well as for the tourists who crowd the picnic tables beneath lamps made of Christmas light-strung lobster traps. Plastic buckets of indifferently fried clams or peel-and-eat shrimps come second to the beer-fueled festivities.

★ Channel Café

300 Summer Street, at A Street, Fort Point (1-617 426 0695, www.channel-cafe.com). South Station T. **Open** 8am-3pm Mon-Wed; 8am-10pm Thur, Fri. **Main courses** $15-$19. **Credit** AmEx, MC, V. **Map** off p273 M5 ⓺
Café/creative contemporary

This underground café caters to Fort Point's population of creatives who inhabit the up-and-coming neighborhood's loft spaces, as well as Financial District office drones willing to make the trek across the bridge. In addition to a vibrant menu full of locally sourced favorites and a rotating list of specials, the artsy eaterie (the space doubles as a gallery) offers tasty espresso coffees and an array of baked goods.

LTK

225 Northern Avenue, at D Street (1-617 330 7430, www.ltkbarandkitchen.com). Silver Line Waterfront to World Trade Center. **Open** *Kitchen* 11am-10pm Mon-Wed, Sun; 11am-11pm Thur-Sat. *Bar* 11am-1am Mon-Wed, Sun; 11am-2am Thur-Sat. **Main courses** $10-$26. **Credit** AmEx, MC, V. **Map** off p273 N5 ⓺
Creative contemporary

The monogram stands for Legal Test Kitchen; the look is as casually edgy as the name. But while the high-tech gimmickry defining this offshoot of Boston-born restaurant chain Legal Sea Foods is a hoot (PDAs and touch screens, iPod docks and credit card portals are all part of the dining experience), the eclectic eats and cocktails are, at their best, equally enthusiastic. Skip the ethnic imitations (bland pho, fish tacos) in favor of such fusion-inspired, flavor-filled nibbles as fried stuffed mussels and skillet-roasted fresh cheese with chickpeas.

Sel de la Terre

255 State Street, at Long Wharf (1-617 720 1300, www.seldelaterre.com). Aquarium T. **Open** 11.30am-2.30pm, 5-10pm Mon, Tue, Sun; 11.30am-2.30pm, 5pm-12.30am Wed-Fri; 11am-2.30am, 5pm-12.30am Sat. **Main courses** $26. **Credit** AmEx, MC, V. **Map** p273 M4 ⓺
Mediterranean

The glimpse of Long Wharf you'll catch before entering L'Espalier's half-sibling will soon fade as the Mediterranean comes into focus – a dining room mural depicting a village on the Riviera, which in turn betokens Geoff Gardner's sunny provençal-inspired cuisine. Gardner polishes his rustic repertoire, from savory tarts to satisfyingly chunky pâtés, until it shines – as you'll discover once you finally tear yourself away from the splendid home-baked breads.

▶ *For information about sightseeing on and around Long Wharf, see p75.*

Sportello. *See p132.*

CONSUME

★ Sportello
*348 Congress Street, at A Street, Fort Point
(1-617 737 1234, www.sportelloboston.com).
South Station T.* **Open** 11.30am-10pm Mon-Thur;
11.30am-11pm Fri; 10.30am-11pm Sat; 10.30am-
10pm Sun. *Bakery* 7am-7pm Mon-Fri; 10.30am-
7pm Sat, Sun. **Main courses** $13-$18. **Credit**
AmEx, MC, V. **Map** off p273 M5 **69** **Italian**
Tucked away in Fort Point, chef Barbara Lynch's
sleek iteration of the classic diner offers supremely
tasty trattoria-inspired Italian cuisine. Sit at the
large communal counter that showcases the action
in the kitchen, or grab a bite to go from the bakery
counter's rotating selection of pastries, soups and
sandwiches and find a bench along the channel for
a waterside picnic. *Photo p131.*
▶ *Have a post-prandial drink at Drink; see p149.*

CAMBRIDGE

Baraka Café
*80½ Pearl Street, at Auburn Street, Central
Square (1-617 868 3951, www.barakacafe.com).
Central T.* **Open** 11.30am-3pm, 5.30-10pm Tue-
Sat; 5.30-10pm Sun. **Main courses** $9-$17. **No
credit cards**. **Map** p276 C4 **70** **North African**
Small wonder this vivid, richly colorful North African
café remains unknown even to many Central Square
locals – with only 25 seats, this is one little secret that
devotees tend to keep to themselves. And once you've
tasted the complex yet zesty spicing of meze such as
merguez (lamb and beef sausage) and *karentika*
(harissa-laced chickpea custard), washed down with
stellar *cherbat* (lemonade infused with rose petals),
you'll be hard put to blame them. Well-organized
types can call three days before their visit to order the
remarkable *bastilla*, a fragrant squab pie.

Blue Room
*1 Kendall Square, between Cardinal
Madeiros Avenue & Hampshire Street
(1-617 494 9034, www.theblueroom.net).
Kendall/MIT T.* **Open** 5.30-10pm Mon-Thur;
5.30-10.30pm Fri, Sat; 11am-2.30pm, 5.30-10pm
Sun. **Main courses** $19-$26. **Credit** AmEx,
DC, MC, V. **Creative contemporary**
Following an indie flick at arthouse Kendall Square
Cinema (*see p193*), Cambridge's culture vultures convene to refuel at this eclectic, welcoming hideaway.
Best known for its frisky, fairly priced wine list and
funky Sunday brunch buffet, it cultivates the spirit
of adventure at dinner time too, incorporating far-
flung influences and interesting ingredients such as
game and offal into its regularly changing repertoire.

Café Algiers
*40 Brattle Street, at Church Street, Harvard
Square (1-617 492 1557). Harvard T.* **Open**
8am-11pm daily. **Main courses** $10-$20.
Credit AmEx, MC, V. **Map** p276 A2 **71**
Café/Middle Eastern

Intricate lanterns, copper urns, swatches of Arabic
calligraphy… if it weren't for the sweatshirted students monopolizing the octagonal wooden tables,
nose-deep in textbooks, you could easily forget you
were in Harvard Square. The menu's Middle
Eastern basics, supplemented by omelettes and
sandwiches, are fine for study breaks, but it's the
beverages that really suit the setting, particularly
the house mint tea and coffee.

$ Café Pamplona
*12 Bow Street, at Arrow Street, Harvard Square
(1-617 492 0352). Harvard T.* **Open** 11am-
midnight daily. **Main courses** $4-$7. **Credit**
AmEx, MC, V. **Map** p276 B3 **72** **Café**
With a colorful history as a Harvard Square fixture
run by a Spanish expat, this wee coffeehouse is where
Cantabrigians go to get closer to Europe. Outdoor
seating and decades of mythology ensure that
Pamplona looms large in the minds of those looking
for the authentic Harvard Square experience.

Cambridge, 1
*27 Church Street, at Palmer Street, Harvard
Square (1-617 576 1111). Harvard T.* **Open**
11.30am-midnight daily. **Main courses** $13-$25.
Credit AmEx, MC, V. **Map** p276 B2 **73** **Pizza**
There's nothing remotely parlor-like about this
Harvard Square pizza parlor, as austere as you
might expect a former fire station overlooking a
graveyard to be. But there's plenty to like about its
no-nonsense attitude, reflected in a streamlined
menu of elegantly simple salads and thin-crust pizzas. The latter are charcoal-grilled and topped with
the likes of lobster or chicken sausage, with flavor-
some fresh herbs and infused oils.

INSIDE TRACK
CAMBRIDGE'S DEEP SOUTH

Three Cambridge restaurants have taken
Southern food to the next level in three
very distinct ways. **East Coast Grill** (*see
p134*), known for its Hell Night hot chilli
parties, has been serving a delicious
combination of seafood and barbecue
for 25 years. Not far away is **Tupelo**
(1193 Cambridge Street, at Tremont
Street, 1-617 868 0004, www.tupelo
02139.com), which focuses on comfort
food with affordable prices and a Southern
flair – try the gumbo or come for brunch.
Lastly, **Hungry Mother** (*see p135*) is
the high-end version of the genre, serving
fantastic cocktails against a backdrop
of mouth-watering sweet and salty
combinations. Who knew crossing the
Mason-Dixon Line in Boston could be
as easy as crossing into Cambridge?

Clover Food Lab MIT.

$ Charlie's Kitchen

10 Eliot Street, at Winthrop Street (1-617 492 9646). Harvard T. **Open** 10.30am-1am Mon-Wed; 10.30am-2am Thur, Fri; 11am-2am Sat; 11am-1am Sun. **Main courses** $4-$10. **Credit** MC, V. **Map** p276 A2 ⑳ **American**

Despite the rampant fancifying of everything within a five-mile radius of Harvard, the stalwart Charlie's Kitchen has hardly changed a bit. This place may be known as the double cheeseburger king, but the loud, ready-to-drink crowd of punks, students, professors and local rock luminaries pile into the upstairs bar for the massive glasses of Hoegaarden, cheap eats, snippy waitresses and the best damn jukebox in Cambridge.

Chez Henri

1 Shepard Street, at Massachusetts Avenue, Porter Square (1-617 354 8980, www.chezhenri. com). Harvard or Porter T. **Open** 6-10pm Mon-Thur; 5.30-10pm Fri, Sat; 5.30-9pm Sun. **Main courses** $24-$39. **Credit** AmEx, DC, MC, V. **Map** p276 A1 ⑳ **French/Cuban**

If ever there were a place to do as the locals do (besides Rome, of course), this French-Latin haunt is it. And what is it they do? They pass up on the sometimes hit-and-miss quasi-fusion dishes the dining room offers in favor of the tasty Cuban fare (think grilled chorizo, chicken empanadas, slow-roasted pork sandwiches…) and cocktails served at the moody bar.

$ Christina's Homemade Ice Cream

1255 Cambridge Street, at Prospect Street (1-617 492 7021, www.christinasicecream.com). Central T then 15min walk or bus 83, 91.

Open 11.30am-11pm Mon-Thur, Sun; 5.30-11pm Fri, Sat. **Ice-cream** $3-$5. **No credit cards**. **Map** p276 C2 ⑯ **Ice-cream**

Whether or not they advertise the fact, many local restaurants scream for ice-cream from this Inman Square shop to supplement their dessert menus. Among the painstakingly crafted, beautifully realized seasonal flavors, keep your eyes peeled – and your mouth primed – for fresh rose, burnt sugar and ginger molasses.

★ $ Clover Food Lab MIT

20 Carleton Street, at Amherst Street, Kendall Square (no phone, www.cloverfoodlab.com). Kendall/MIT T. **Open** 8am-7pm Mon-Fri. **Sandwiches** $5. **Credit** AmEx, MC, V. **Creative contemporary/vegetarian**

Clover Food Lab is actually a food *truck*, a concept fairly new to Bostonians. You'll find the MIT outpost nestled between a few other frontrunners in the mobile food phenomenon just outside the MIT Medical Building, bringing inventive and nutritious locally sourced breakfasts, lunches, dinners and snacks to the Kendall Square area. The rosemary fries are always a crowd-pleaser, as is the ever-changing beverage menu, where you'll find creative concoctions such as blueberry *agua fresca* and basil lemonade.

★ Craigie on Main

853 Main Street, at Massachusetts Avenue, Central Square (1-617 497 5511, www.craigie onmain.com). Central T. **Open** 5.30pm-1am Mon-Sat; 11am-2pm, 5.30pm-1am Sun. **Main courses** $21-$36. **Credit** AmEx, MC, V. **Map** p276 C3 ⑰ **Creative contemporary**

The buzz surrounding this culinary hotspot has been palpable since renowned chef Tony Maws moved his tiny bistro into a new, larger space. It's retained the quirkiness of the previous location, while expanding its capacity to better accommodate the growing number of devotees who pack the house most nights for Maws' latest Franco-American creations – each born of his intense dedication to using the best local, organic ingredients. Craigie on Main's knowledgeable and friendly staff (including a handful of smiling cocktail mavens) will guide you through the seasonal menus. The ten-course tasting menu is a favorite, and might include crispy-fried Florida frog's legs, hirmasa sashimi salad or rhubarb-hibiscus mousse.

Cuchi Cuchi

795 Main Street, off Massachusetts Avenue, Central Square (1-617 864 2929). Central or Kendall/MIT T. **Open** 5.30pm-12.30am Mon-Sat. **Small plates** $7-$23. **Credit** AmEx, DC, MC, V. **Map** p276 C3 ⑦ **Global**

It's hard to think that a Charo-inspired space could be anything but tacky, but here it is. The decor was inspired by the intensity of the Latina siren's performance on *The Ed Sullivan Show* in the '70s, combined with belle époque beauty and early Hollywood glamour. The result is surprisingly intimate and romantic, the perfect place to share a cocktail and a few small plates with a date. Just don't call it a tapas place; the owners will be quick to correct you – tapas are from Spain exclusively, while Cuchi Cuchi traffics in globe-trotting international fare.

Dante

Royal Sonesta Hotel Boston, 40 Edwin H Land Boulevard, at Cambridgeside Place, Lechmere (1-617 497 4200, www.restaurantdante.com). Lechmere or Science Park T. **Open** 6.30am-2.30pm, 5.30-10pm Mon-Thur; 6.30am-2.30pm, 5.30-11pm Fri; 7am-2.30pm, 5.30-11pm Sat; 7am-2pm, 5-9pm Sun. **Main courses** $22-$36. **Credit** AmEx, MC, V. **Map** p272 H2 ⑦ **Mediterranean**

Named after its young gun of a chef-owner, this cool Med eatery has got the goods to generate a major happy-hour buzz: a spacious lounge, a seasonal patio, a front-row view of the Charles River – and, of course, sharp cocktails and fancy snacks. But it usually delivers at mealtimes too, via dishes whose twists and turns can come as unexpectedly as those in the roads along the cliffs of the Riviera.

$ Darwin's Ltd

148 Mount Auburn Street, at Brewer Street, Harvard Square (1-617 354 5233, www.darwins ltd.com). Harvard T. **Open** 6.30am-9pm Mon-Sat; 7am-9pm Sun. **Sandwiches** $6-$8. **Credit** MC, V. **Map** p276 A2 ⑧ **Café**

Tucked away from the preppy hubbub of Harvard Square proper, this quirky sandwich shop caters to

Cuchi Cuchi.

locals looking for quality sandwiches (all named after surrounding neighborhood streets, therefore differing from the menu at its Cambridge Street counterpart) and a place to hang with free Wi-Fi. The shabby-chic deli also offers beer and wine, local bakery breads, take-out dinners, loose tea and plenty of homemade goodies.

Other locations 1629 Cambridge Street, between Roberts Road & Trowbridge Street, Harvard Square (1-617 491 2999).

East by Northeast

1128 Cambridge Street, at Elm Street, Inman Square (1-617 876 0286, www.exnecambridge. com). Central Square or Lechmere T. **Open** 5-10pm Tue-Sun. **Small plates** $4-$10. **No credit cards.** **Chinese**

This small Chinese bistro is located slightly outside Inman Square, but it's worth the extra few minutes of travel time to sample chef Phillip Tang's nuanced take on his family's oldest recipes. Small plates of noodles, dumplings and pickled vegetables make up the bulk of the menu, with daily specials ensuring that there is always something new to try. Bring a few adventurous friends who like to share, and don't forget to check out the cocktail list – it's as inventive as the cuisine.

East Coast Grill

1271 Cambridge Street, at Prospect Street, Inman Square (1-617 491 6568, www.east coastgrill.net). Central T, then 15min walk

or bus 83, 91. **Open** 5.30-10pm Mon-Thur;
5.30-10.30pm Fri, Sat; 11am-2.30pm, 5.30-10pm
Sun. **Main courses** $15-$26. **Credit** AmEx,
MC, V. **Map** p276 C2 ⑪ **Fish & seafood**
On paper, the concept must have looked pretty
fuzzy: how could the then-unknown Chris
Schlesinger possibly pull off a tropically tinged
seafood shack/barbecue pit complete with raw bar
and tiki lounge? But the disparate elements proved
wildly harmonic; a quarter of a century on, the
chow's still as spicy as the attitude, and the crowd's
full of jumping beans.

$ Friendly Toast
*Building 300, 1 Kendall Square (1-617 621 1200,
www.thefriendlytoast.net). Kendall/MIT T.* **Open**
8am-10pm Mon; 8am-midnight Tue-Thur; 8am-
1am Fri, Sat; 8am-9pm Sun. **Main courses**
$8-$12. **Credit** AmEx, MC, V. **Café**
The Kendall Square representative of this quirky
Portsmouth, New Hampshire-based diner is quickly
becoming a local favorite. Breakfast is served all
day, and their appetizing combinations and overflowing portions make it a great place to linger over
brunch – though you can also grab lunch on the go.
Sit at the bar for a better view of the deliciously
bizarre (and somewhat macabre) decor.

Hungry Mother
*233 Cardinal Medeiros Avenue, between Bristol
& Hampshire Streets, Kendall Square (1-617
499 0090, www.hungrymothercambridge.com).
Kendall/MIT T.* **Open** 5pm-12.30am Tue-Sun.
Main courses $18-$24. **Credit** AmEx, MC, V.
American
This adorable spot manages to combine a commitment to sourcing ingredients locally with inspiration from far away – specifically from the base of
the Mississippi River Delta. The concise menu
bursts with Southern tastes and flavors, from
shrimp *escabeche* to cornmeal catfish with dirty rice.
Conveniently located across from the Kendall
Square Cinema, dinner here before 6pm will result
in discounted movie tickets – Hungry Mother will
even pick them up for you.
▶ *For information about the Kendall Square
Cinema, see p193.*

★ $ Mr Bartley's Burger Cottage
*1246 Massachusetts Avenue, at Plympton
Street, Harvard Square (1-617 354 6559,
www.mrbartley.com). Harvard T.* **Open**
11am-9pm Mon-Sat. **Main courses** $6-$13.
No credit cards. Map p276 B2 ⑫
American
There's barely room to move amid the memorabilia
that clutters this Harvard Square institution, never
mind the crush of diners scoffing thick, juicy burgers and even thicker frappes (New England-speak
for milkshakes). But don't let that stop you; the tight
squeeze is all part of the fun.

★ Oleana
*134 Hampshire Street, at Elm Street,
Inman Square (1-617 661 0505, www.oleana
restaurant.com). Central T, then 15min walk
or bus 83, 91.* **Open** 5.30-10pm Mon-Thur,
Sun; 5.30-11pm Fri, Sat. **Main courses** $23-$28.
Credit AmEx, MC, V. **Map** p276 C3 ⑬
Mediterranean
Two tiny, coolly pretty dining rooms and an enormously popular garden patio provide a showcase
for chef-owner Ana Sortun's passion for and mas-
tery of the hauntingly aromatic cuisines of Turkey,
Greece, Armenia, Morocco, Egypt and Sicily. Most of
the small plates are memorable, while many of the
desserts are downright extraordinary. *Photo p136.*

Rendezvous
*502 Massachusetts Avenue, at Brookline
Street, Central Square (1-617 576 1900,
www.rendezvouscentralsquare.com). Central T.*
Open 5-10pm Mon-Thur, Sun; 5-11pm Fri, Sat.
Main courses $18-$26. **Credit** AmEx, MC, V.
Map p276 C3 ⑭ **Mediterranean**
Local loyalty to Rendezvous' Steve Johnson runs jus-
tifiably deep. As a host, he's discreetly perceptive; as
a chef, he's equally judicious, arranging exuberant
Mediterranean ingredients within a delicate frame-
work (which a simply decorated dining room showcases in turn). Lemon buttermilk pudding with a
seasonally changing berry sauce is a lovely example.

Friendly Toast.

CONSUME

★ Rialto

Charles Hotel, 1 Bennett Street, at Eliot Street, Harvard Square (1-617 661 5050, www.rialto-restaurant.com). Harvard T. **Open** 5-11.30pm Mon-Sat; 5-10.30pm Sun. **Main courses** $30-$43. **Credit** AmEx, MC, V. **Map** p276 A2 🆖 **Italian**

For its tenth birthday a few years ago, Jody Adams gave Harvard Square's premier celebration destination a head-to-toe makeover. The now breezy, spruce interior mirrors a menu stripped of its former pan-Mediterranean flourishes to reveal a regional Italian core. Which isn't to imply that the new order is minimalist – Adams' cooking remains as luscious as ever, staying true to its rustic roots while branching out in deluxe directions.

$ S&S Restaurant

1334 Cambridge Street, at Oak Street, Inman Square (1-617 354 0777, www.sands restaurant.com). Central T then 15min walk or bus 83, 91. **Open** 7am-10pm Mon-Wed; 7am-11pm Thur, Fri; 8am-11pm Sat; 8am-10pm Sun. **Main courses** $8-$15. **Credit** AmEx, MC, V. **Map** p276 C2 🆖 **Jewish/American**

After 90-plus years in the business, this sprawling deli is an Inman Square institution; frumpy decor and strictly utilitarian service are all part of the package. The fare can be pretty ordinary, be it the all-day breakfast, Jewish-style classics such as pastrami on rye, or timeless comfort food such as roast chicken. But sometimes, the schlock of the old trumps the shock of the new.

Tealuxe

Zero Brattle Street, at John F Kennedy Street, Harvard Square (1-617 441 0077, www.tealuxe.com). Harvard T. **Open** 8am-10pm Mon-Thur; 8am-10.30pm Fri; 8.30am-10.30pm Sat; 8.30am-10pm Sun. **Credit** AmEx, DC, MC, V. **Map** p276 B2 🆖 **Tearoom**

This cozy tea sanctuary appeals to everyone from little old ladies to trucker-capped hipsters who linger over muffins, scones and freshly brewed pots of loose-leafed goodness. There are dozens and dozens of varieties of teas to choose from, including such rarities as second-flush darjeeling. The infused hot chocolate and rotating flavors of bubble tea ensure they have something to entice in all seasons.

$ Toscanini's

899 Main Street, at Massachusetts Avenue, Central Square (1-617 491 5877, www.tosci.com). Central T. **Open** 8am-11pm daily. **Ice-cream** $3-$6. **Credit** AmEx, MC, V. **Map** p276 C3 🆖 **Ice-cream**

The *New York Times* called it the best ice-cream in the world. *People* magazine said they've got the best vanilla ice-cream in the United States. Not bad, but the folks at Toscanini's aren't ones to rest on their laurels – and that's what makes them one of our

favorites. They are constantly coming up with such new and intriguing flavors as the amazing burnt caramel – which was actually created by accident.

UpStairs on the Square

91 Winthrop Street, at John F Kennedy Street, Harvard Square (1-617 864 1933, www.upstairs onthesquare.com). Harvard T. **Open** 11am-3pm, 5-10pm Mon-Thur; 11am-3pm, 5-11pm Fri, Sat; 10am-3pm, 5-10pm Sun. **Main courses** $16-$40. **Credit** AmEx, DC, MC, V. **Map** p276 A2 🆖 **Creative contemporary**

Straight from the design team of Barbie and Matisse – or so it would seem from the pink and gold decor of the Soirée Room and the Fauvist palette of the Monday Club Bar – this eye-popping double-decker in Harvard Square is apt to scandalize your pearl-choked Aunt Muckety-Muck. So don't take her. Instead, bring a date you can get to know over artful cocktails and contemporary cuisine that's usually as tasty as it is playfully intriguing.

DORCHESTER

Ashmont Grill

555 Talbot Avenue, at Dorchester Avenue (1-617 825 4300). Ashmont T. **Open** 5-10pm Mon-Thur; 5-11pm Fri; 10am-3pm, 5-11pm Sat;

Oleana. See p135.

10am-3pm, 4-10pm Sun. **Main courses** $12-$26. **Credit** AmEx, MC, V. **American/bar**
First on the scene of the up-and-coming Ashmont Hill section of Dorchester, this bar and grill brought a bit of class to the neighborhood. The sleek decor, addictive appetizers and tasty main courses keep the locals coming back again and again, but it's the patio space out back that makes the Ashmont Grill worth the trek out to the end of the Red Line. The high, vine-coated fence blocks out the sounds and sights of the bustling neighborhood beyond, creating a cozy, twinkling nook for cocktails and conversation.
▶ *For more about sightseeing in the Dorchester neighborhood, see p89.*

Tavolo Ristorante
1918 Dorchester Avenue, between Ashmont & Bailey Streets (1-617 822 1918, www.tavolo ristorante.com). Ashmont T. **Open** 5pm-1am daily. **Main courses** $9-$19. **Credit** AmEx, MC, V. **Italian**
This new Italian spot is helmed by a pair of chefs who live by the motto 'Good food is everything' – but we're calling their bluff. It's not just the perfectly turned out pizza and pasta dishes that could be classified as 'good', but also the sleek decor, friendly staff and strong cocktails.

JAMAICA PLAIN

Centre Street Café
669A Centre Street, at Seaverns Avenue (1-617 524 9217). Green Street T then 10min walk. **Open** 11.30am-3pm, 5-10pm Mon-Fri; 9am-3pm, 5-10pm Sat; 9am-3pm Sun. **Main courses** $8-$16. **Credit** MC, V. **Global**
Just as miscellany marks the menu, diversity defines the diners who throng at this wood-paneled, homey café. Among the legion of cuisines that the kitchen borrows from (Asian, Mediterranean, Middle Eastern), Tex-Mex and vegetarian are the most prevalent and successful; hence the wild popularity of the weekend brunch, which emphasizes both.

$ JP Licks
659 Centre Street, at Starr Lane (1-617 524 6740, www.jplicks.com). Green Street T or bus 39. **Open** 6am-midnight daily. **Ice-cream** $3-$6. **Credit** AmEx, MC, V. **Ice-cream**
As one might gather from the name, the Jamaica Plain shop is the flagship location of what has become a Boston institution (other shops have popped up on Newbury Street, Coolidge Corner, Davis Square, and Harvard Square, among other areas). The local chain is known for its funky atmosphere, hip scoopers and flavors so good they'll bring you to your knees, so expect to wait in line on hot days. But don't worry, it just gives you more time to decide between the wild Maine blueberry or the brownie batter.
Other locations throughout the city.

THE BEST
SMALL PLATES

Butcher Shop
Meaty bites from Barbara Lynch.
See p124.

Dalí
Tapas at their most *auténtico*.
See p138.

East by Northeast
Modern Chinese made to share.
See p134.

Ten Tables
597 Centre Street, between Pond Street & Parley Avenue (1-617 524 8810, www.tentables.net). Green Street T then 10min walk. **Open** 5.30-10pm Mon-Thur; 5.30-11.30pm Fri, Sat; 3-10pm Sun. **Main courses** $16-$21. **Credit** MC, V. **Creative contemporary**
On any given night, the lucky few who manage to get reservations at this diminutive bistro have front-row seats for the show put on by the crew in the open kitchen. Then they get to enjoy the results, distinguished by owner Krista Kranyak's commitment to locally grown organic produce and own-made fare, from charcuterie and pastas to ice-cream. The superb fish stews warrant special mention.

★ $ Ula Café
284 Armory Street, at the Brewery Complex (1-617 524 7890, www.ulacafe.com). Stony Brook T. **Open** 7am-7pm Mon-Fri; 8am-7pm Sat, Sun. **Main courses** $5-$8. **Credit** MC, V. **Café/vegetarian**
Truly a JP gem, Ula was founded with the intention of creating a friendly neighborhood space for locals and visitors to interact – and dine on some amazing and healthy food. An impressive range of baked goods round out the solid menu of creative sandwich and salad options, attracting a diverse crowd to the patio.

BROOKLINE

Dok Bua
411 Harvard Street, at Fuller Street (1-617 232 2955, www.dokbua-thai.com). Coolidge Corner T, then 10min walk or bus 66. **Open** 11am-11pm daily. **Main courses** $8-$16. **Credit** AmEx, DC, MC, V. **Thai**
The kitsch will tickle you; the kitchen will floor you. This gaudy former grocery serves up some of Boston's freshest, most fiery Thai fare. The sprawling menu grants diners numerous opportunities to nosh on something new, be it ground pork mixed with steamed egg, sour curry with root vegetables

or black sesame dumplings. The familiar favorites are all there too, from tom yum soup to red curry.

La Morra

48 Boylston Street, near Washington Street (1-617 739 0007, www.lamorra.com). Brookline Village T. **Open** 5.30-10pm Mon-Thur; 5.30-10.30pm Fri, Sat; 11am-2.30pm, 5.30-9pm Sun. **Main courses** $19-$24. **Credit** AmEx, MC, V. Italian

From the outside, it's a nondescript building on a major thoroughfare. Inside, Josh and Jennifer Ziskin's two-story eaterie evokes a cozy Tuscan farmhouse, serving cuisine to match. Ziskin relishes blurring the lines between humble and elegant, hearty and delicate, be it chicken livers glazed with *vin santo*, marrow risotto or wood-grilled chops with herbed polenta. Looking for something slightly lighter? Settle in at the ground-floor bar for a sampling of what Venetians call *cicchetti* – an anchovy between fried sage leaves here, a *crostino* slathered with salt cod there.

Taberna de Haro

999 Beacon Street, at St Mary's Street (1-617 277 8272). St Mary's T. **Open** 5.30-10pm Mon-Thur; 5.30-11pm Fri, Sat. **Tapas** $8-$25. **Credit** MC, V. **Map** p276 C5 Spanish

Eschewing the hoopla that surrounds greater Boston's better-known tapas bars, low-key Taberna de Haro – whose owners used to run an eaterie in Madrid – enjoys something of a cult following. Simply but cheerfully decorated and always filled to capacity, the little dining room is dominated by an open kitchen, whence emerge all manner of rustic, ultra-appealing *pinchos* and *raciones* (as well as the occasional crowd-thrilling jet of flame). Own-made *butifarra* (veal sausage) with lemony aïoli, garlicky frogs' legs, exemplary *papas arrugadas*, blue cheese whipped with brandy – the cooks keep it coming, while the de Haros' catalogue of little-known regional wines and sherries goes down a treat.

Zaftigs

335 Harvard Street, at Babcock Street (1-617 975 0075, www.zaftigs.com). Coolidge Corner T. **Open** 8am-10pm daily. **Main courses** $10-$13. **Credit** AmEx, MC, V. Jewish/American

At this ridiculously popular Jewish deli (emphasis on the -ish), Brookline's preppy pram-pushers and hungover co-eds wait in line to get their weekend brunchtime fix of gefilte fish or pastrami on rye – not to mention smoked salmon quesadillas or ham and cheddar omelettes. Kosher the enormous menu ain't.

SOMERVILLE

Dalí

415 Washington Street, at Beacon Street (1-617 661 3254, www.dalirestaurant.com). Harvard or Sullivan Square T, then bus 86.

Open *Kitchen* 5.30-11pm Mon-Sat; noon-11pm Sun; *Bar* 5.30pm-12.30am daily. **Main courses** $19-$25. **Tapas** $4-$9. **Credit** AmEx, DC, MC, V. **Map** p276 C2 ❾⓿ Spanish

It glitters and glows, shimmers and shines – one look at Somerville's extravagantly decorated Spanish stronghold and you'll know why the surrealist icon is its patron saint. Luckily, the menu forgoes ant swarms and melting clocks in favor of mostly traditional tapas. Solid if not swoon-generating, they're backed up by an exceptional list of wines and sherries, and great sangría.

Gargoyles on the Square

219 Elm Street, at Summer Street, Davis Square (1-617 776 5300, www.gargoyles onthesquare.com). Davis T. **Open** *Kitchen* 5.30-10pm Mon-Thur, Sun; 5.30pm-10.30pm Fri, Sat. *Bar* 5pm-1am daily. **Main courses** $18-$27. **Credit** AmEx, MC, V. Creative contemporary

Since it opened in the mid-1990s, Gargoyles has gone from Davis Square secret to suave foodie fave. In a dining room as dim, hushed and plush as the bar is airy and gregarious, guests are constantly surprised by the menu's daring. Smoked blueberries? Mimolette dust? Sweet potato ice-cream? Even more surprising is that the kitchen crew has the talent to carry off the majority of its experiments.

Petsi Pies

285 Beacon Street, at Sacramento Street, Porter Square (1-617 661 7437, www. petsipies.com). Porter T then 10min walk or bus 83. **Open** 7am-7pm Mon-Fri; 8am-4pm Sat; 8am-2pm Sun. **Credit** MC, V. **Map** p276 B1 ❾❶ Bakery-café

Cartoonishly pretty fruit pies line the window of this otherwise plain little bakery and coffee shop. Savory tarts, cookies and more beckon from the display cases inside, all bearing testament to owner Renee McLeod's wonderful way with pastry and dough of all descriptions. Resistance is not merely futile but simply foolish; the scones at Petsi Pies, in particular, are sublime.

Other locations 31 Putnam Avenue, at Green Street, Cambridge (1-617 499 0801).

★ Redbones

55 Chester Street, at Elm Street, Davis Square (1-617 628 2200, www.redbones.com). Davis T. **Open** 11.30am-12.30am Mon-Sat; noon-12.30am Sun. **Main courses** $8-$19. **Credit** AmEx, MC, V. Barbecue

Expect sensory overload at this popular barbecue joint. The walls are covered in fluorescent colors, the ribs slathered in sauce – and the crammed-in patrons are pleasantly steeped in beer. Actually, the global selection of brews are superior to the 'cue, though the fried catfish and corn fritters are mouth-watering. But the party atmosphere's the point.

ALLSTON

Soul Fire BBQ

182 Harvard Avenue, between Glenville & Commonwealth & Avenues (1-617 787 3003, www.soulfirebbq.com). Harvard Ave T. **Open** 11.30am-10pm Mon-Thur; 11.30am-11pm Fri, Sat; noon-10pm Sun. **Main courses** $10-$25. **Credit** AmEx, MC, V. **Map** p276 A5 ⑫ **Barbecue**

The folks at Soul Fire BBQ are mighty serious about their barbecue. They respect the process as both a science and an art – and their dedication shows in the results. Quality meats are slathered in an assortment of dry rubs and different sauces to suit every taste, and regulars love paying just $2.50 for the draft beer to wash them down with. Sure, they have great, meatless sides such as mac and cheese, and baked beans, but this is not a venue for sensitive vegetarians.

Paris, Massachusetts

From brasseries to provençal cuisine – who need to fly to France?

Raw bars? Check. Spaghetti houses? Double check. Irish pubs? A check on every corner. But French brasseries, here, in hard-nosed Beantown? *Mais oui.* Granted, 'brass' rather than 'French' may be the operative word, as the enormous success of **Eastern Standard** (*pictured; see p120*) – a sprawling, sexy, but staunchly Stateside spin on the genre – suggests. Still, with restaurateurs jumping on the bandwagon left and right, it's never been easier to get a taste of homegrown Gallicism.

For years the city's only source of genuine French cuisine, **Brasserie Jo** (*see p119*) may still be its most authentic. If it's *les plats classiques* you crave – piquant yet succulent steak tartare; bubbly, beefy onion soup; profiteroles awash in chocolate sauce – then this big, bright Back Bay workhorse is still one of your best bets. And the bar – whose design suggests, just obviously enough, post-war Paris – is a genuinely cozy affair on a wintry late afternoon.

Gaslight, Brasserie du Coin (*see p126*) is the latest contender to the brasserie title. Rustic yet urbane, retro yet of-the-moment, evoking the Left Bank yet firmly entrenched in the South End, its intent to flash both sides of the gastro-cultural coin has already been established. Belly up to the bar or an oh-so-Euro communal table to pair a local microbrew with a *pissaladière*, or a half carafe of gewürztraminer with a hearty burger.

Provence, not Paris, is the inspiration for **Miel**'s 24/7 hotel kitchen (*see p115*), which mostly does justice to a menu designed by Michelin-starred French chef Jacques Chibois: mussels in any guise are a must, as is the cold berry soup with candied olives. The regional theme may or may not explain (or excuse) the atypically frou-frou, countrified decor – but a stunning view over Boston Harbor, from inside or out on the patio, more than makes amends.

CONSUME

Pubs & Bars

Beautiful old Irish boozers, sleek lounges and authentic dives.

Boston's bar scene has changed dramatically in the past few years. What was once a city dotted with old haunts is now brimming with drinkeries of every size and description. Small spaces and tame closing times (2am at the latest) have contributed to shaping local nightlife into the bustling, clustered, crawl-prone network of hot spots that it is.

Luckily for visitors, you can head to virtually any neighborhood in the city and find a handful of worthwhile places to settle in for a few drinks, or to mingle and dance. Our advice? Find a place to drink close to your hotel: the subway service stops at 12.30am and you don't want any part of the cab-hunting madness that commences come last call.

DOWNTOWN

Also worth a try are the delightfully retro-style **Silvertone Bar & Grill** (*see p115*) and chic wine bar **Les Zygomates** (*see p116*).

Bell in Hand Tavern

45-55 Union Street, at Marshall Street (1-617 227 2098, www.bellinhand.com). Gov't Center or Haymarket T. **Open** 11.30am-2am Mon-Sat; noon-1am Sun. **Credit** AmEx, DC, MC, V. **Map** p273 L3 ❶

Though it claims to be the oldest tavern in town (1795), you'd hardly know it from the Bell in Hand's interior decoration (think exposed brick walls and neon). The clientele is largely young regulars, and you'll find them nose to elbow Tuesday to Saturday, when the bar has live music.

Black Rose

160 State Street, at India Street (1-617 742 2286, www.irishconnection.com). Aquarium or State T. **Open** 11.30am-2am Mon-Sat; 10.30am-1am Sun. **Credit** AmEx, MC, V. **Map** p273 L4 ❷

One of the older Irish pubs in the city, the Black Rose plays its part well: photos of martyred patriots adorn the walls, and flags from every county hang from the ceiling. But its true selling point is the nightly

> ❶ Green numbers given in this chapter correspond to the location of each pub or bar on the street maps. *See pp272-276*.

program of live Irish music (there's sometimes a cover of up to $5). If you're up for a rowdy, Guinness-fuelled sing-along with friendly locals and fellow tourists, this is the place to go.

★ District

180 Lincoln Street, at Beach Street (1-617 426 0180, www.districtboston.com). South Station or Chinatown T. **Open** 11.30am-2.30pm Mon; 11.30am-2.30pm, 5-10pm Tue; 11.30am-2.30pm, 5pm-1am Wed-Fri; 6pm-1am Sat. **Credit** AmEx, MC, V. **Map** off p273 L5 ❸

While District sits apart from most of the Leather District's foot traffic, after work and on weekends the place really picks up – and it's no mystery why. In a town not taken with high design, it makes its mark with Lucite furnishings, walls of birch and ornate black and white florals working (along with a deft team of DJs) to give this bar a notably cosmopolitan vibe. Careful when ordering the Kiss Goodnight cocktail – it ain't kidding.

Good Life

28 Kingston Street, at Summer Street (1-617 451 2622, www.goodlifebar.com). Downtown Crossing T. **Open** 11.30am-2am Mon-Fri; 6pm-2am Sat. **Credit** AmEx, MC, V. **Map** p272 K5 ❹

One of several upmarket spots that have helped to drag downtown Boston out of late-night wasteland, this is one of the most popular – and for good reason. With its orange vinyl walls, wood panelling, Rat Pack soundtrack and *GoodFellas* ambience, the Good Life is a smirky tribute to lounge bars of the 1950s.

Green Dragon

*11 Marshall Street, at Union Street (1-617 367
0055, www.celticweb.com/greendragon). Gov't
Center T.* **Open** 11am-2am daily. **Credit** AmEx,
DC, MC, V. **Map** p273 L3 ⑤

A stone's throw from the Bell in Hand Tavern (*see
left*), this bar dates back (though not in its present
form) to 1773. The spot on which it stands is 'the
birthplace of American freedom', where the sons of
liberty gathered over a few pints to plot the down-
fall of the British. A glass case on the wall contains
some of the implements – muskets and so forth –
used to achieve that end. Still, this is a congenial
place with live music, attentive staff, carpeted
nooks and faded wallpaper.

▶ *For more on this turbulent period of Boston's
history, see pp17-22.*

Hennessy's

*25 Union Street, at Salt Lane (1-617 742
2121). Gov't Center or Haymarket T.* **Open**
11am-2am daily. **Credit** AmEx, MC, V.
Map p273 L3 ⑥

A warm, brightly lit place, with peat fires and *seisiún*
music, this is a welcoming refuge from the bustle of
nearby Faneuil Hall Marketplace. If you're aching
to hear voices that ring with the musical cadences
of Ireland, you can pop in here to have a nice drop
of Guinness. And, like many of its more rural
cousins back in the old country, Hennessy's comes
equipped with a mini grocery store, selling tea, oatmeal and various other staples. *Photo p143.*

Hub Pub

*18 Province Street, between School & Bosworth
Streets (1-617 227 8952). Park Street T.* **Open**
11am-2am daily. **Credit** AmEx, MC, V.
Map p272 K4 ⑦

About as unpretentious as they come, the Hub is a
throwback to a time before bars had to be trendy.
What you see is what you get: a Golden Tee Golf
machine, a projection TV to watch the Sox and a

INSIDE TRACK
WHERE THE BARTENDERS GO

Looking to get a late night bite for a
bargain? Want to sample from an eclectic
cocktail and beer menu? For all that, and
to rub shoulders with those really in the
know – the best bartenders, chefs and
servers in town – Downtown's **Silvertone
Bar & Grill** (*see p115*) is the place to go.
Long before it was de rigueur to carry more
than two kinds of bourbon or use fresh
fruit instead of sour mix, this retro-themed
institution was doing it for service-industry
workers who initially came because the
kitchen was open late and they had a solid
2am last call. (If you're too shy to chat
up a bartender for advice on where to go,
check out Lauren Clark's excellent website
www.drinkboston.com instead.)

---

laminated bar adorned with mementos from Boston's
past. Bar staff are friendly, the beer's cold and the
cheese fries are top-notch. What more do you need?

Intermission Tavern

*228 Tremont Street, at Stuart Street (1-617 451
5997, www.intermissiontavern.com). Boylston or
Chinatown T.* **Open** 10.30am-2am daily. **Credit**
AmEx, DC, MC, V. **Map** p275 J6 ⑧

The Theater District wasn't always an entirely
savory place to hang out. After the curtain calls, the-
atergoers have long been known to scuttle off
toward posh spots by the park, or to the clubs off
Boylston Street across the Common. The
Intermission, though, holds court in the 'hood as one
of the only down-to-earth joints where you can grab
some quality pub grub and a pre-show beer – or a
post-show cocktail, if it's not too crowded.

▶ *For details of Boston's theater scene, see p225.*

CONSUME

District.

Whatever your carbon footprint, we can reduce it

For over a decade we've been leading the way in carbon offsetting and carbon management.

In that time we've purchased carbon credits from over 200 projects spread across 6 continents. We work with over 300 major commercial clients and thousands of small and medium sized businesses, which rely upon our market-leading quality assurance programme, our experience and absolute commitment to deliver the right solution for each client.

Why not give us a call?

T: London (020) 7833 6000

www.CarbonNeutral.com

★ Jacob Wirth
*31-37 Stuart Street, at Washington Street,
Chinatown (1-617 338 8586, www.jacobwirth.
com). Chinatown or Boylston T.* **Open** 11.30am-
8pm Mon; 11.30am-10pm Tue-Thur; 11.30am-
midnight Fri; 11.30am-11pm Sat. **Credit** AmEx,
MC, V. **Map** p 275 J5
Walking into Jacob Wirth (established 1868) feels
like stepping back in time. The ceilings are high, the
bar is ornate and the staff are decked out in black
and white finery. But this is an informal place. Slosh
your mug of fine import lager and tuck into a heaped
plate of schnitzel or bratwurst and red cabbage.

JJ Foley's
*21 Kingston Street, at Summer Street (1-617 695
2529). Downtown Crossing T.* **Open** 10am-2am
daily. **Credit** AmEx, MC, V. **Map** p272 K5
This low-key, low-lit bar is an institution in Boston
– a hangout for bike messengers, tattooed masses,
business suits and borderline bums. Anyone who
has lived in Boston for long has met someone at
Foley's, or broken up with someone at Foley's, or
met and broken up with them there on the same
evening – or knows someone who has.
Other locations 117 East Berkeley Street,
at Cortes Street, South End (1-617 728 0315).

Kinsale
*2 Center Plaza, at Government Center (1-617
742 5577, www.classicirish.com). Gov't Center T.*
Open 11am-2am daily. **Credit** AmEx, MC, V.
Map p272 K3
Built in Ireland and shipped to the Hub piece by
piece, the Kinsale is Irish pub as theme park. And
for all that effort, it looks about as inauthentic as an
Irish pub can look. That said, the Irish staff are

pleasant and pull a fine pint of Guinness. The central location (right across the street from brutalist
Boston City Hall) means it can get crowded fast, but
great pub grub and occasional live music make up
for any stepped-on toes or spilled suds. The food
menu abandons the Emerald Isle in favor of global
eclecticism – quesadilla, grilled shrimp and mango
salad, and clam chowder are among the offerings.

Kitty O'Shea's
*131 State Street, at India Street, Financial District
(1-617 725 0100, www.kittyosheasboston.com).
Aquarium or State T.* **Open** 11am-2am daily.
Credit AmEx, MC, V. **Map** p273 L4
Despite the fact that it's part of an international
chain, Kitty O'Shea's is one of the city's nicer Irish
pubs. With its cosy rooms, stained-glass windows,
dark mahogany bar and ornate plaster ceilings, it's
not a far cry from some of the old pubs you'd find in
Dublin. The Irish bartenders reinforce the authenticity, and the Guinness is some of the best around.

Mr Dooley's
*77 Broad Street, at Milk Street (1-617 338
5656). Aquarium or State T.* **Open** 11.30am-2am
Mon-Fri; 11am-2am Sat; 9am-2am Sun. **Credit**
AmEx, DC, MC, V. **Map** p273 L4
Named after the fictional, opinion-rich barkeep of
writer FP Dunne's syndicated newspaper columns,
this Financial District mainstay has a loyal clientele
of journalists and politicians, and lives up to its own
billing as 'a great place for a pint and a chat'.

Remington's
*124 Boylston Street, between Charles
& Tremont Streets (1-617 574 9676,
www.remingtonsofboston.com). Boylston T.*

CONSUME

Hennessy's. *See p141.*

Open 11.30am-2am Mon-Sat; 11am-2am Sun.
Credit AmEx, MC, V. **Map** p272 J5 ⓮
An unpretentious Theater District hangout, Remington's is the sort of place that seems ever rarer: a pub where quiet conversation with the bartender or the guy on the stool next to you is its main selling point. Don't expect it to be hopping, even when there's stand-up comedy downstairs – but that's how the regulars like it at this mellow pub.

Rock Bottom
115 Stuart Street, at Tremont Street (1-617 742 2739). Boylston T. **Open** 11.30am-midnight Mon-Thur, Sun; 11.30am-1am Fri, Sat; 11am-1am Sun.
Credit AmEx, MC, V. **Map** p275 J6 ⓯
It may be part of a national chain (which specializes in the beer styles of the West Coast), but Rock Bottom is a fine establishment for beer-lovers. In the heart of Boston's rejuvenated Theater District, it holds up well against stiff local competition. Brewmaster Gerry O'Connell hails from Tralee, in County Kerry, and his beers (especially when he selects the big, chocolatey Oatmeal Stout as his rotating dark beer selection) can sometimes show the influence of his homeland.
▶ *For more locally produced pints, see p147 Brewed in Boston.*

Tam
222 Tremont Street, between Lagrange & Stuart Streets (1-617 482-9182). Boylston T. **Open** 8.30am-1am Mon-Fri, Sun; noon-2am Sat.
No credit cards. Map p275 J6 ⓰
A dive bar for dive bar connoisseurs, the Tam is a Boston legend – and rightly so. Everything here is just as it should be: the beer is cheap, the whisky is plentiful, the neon is garish, the music is loud, and the toilets… er, have running water. An eccentric, eclectic crowd gathers to sample its delights.

BEACON HILL & THE WEST END

21st Amendment
150 Bowdoin Street, at Mount Vernon Street (1-617 227 7100, www.21stboston.com). Park St T. **Open** 11.30am-2am daily.
Credit AmEx, MC, V. **Map** p272 K4 ⓱
On the surface, there's nothing particularly striking about this small, low-ceilinged bar. Just across the way, however, is the State House, which leads to the happy spectacle of power brokers, legislators, journalists, tourists and local ne'er-do-wells sharing a drink together. The 21st is the ultimate off-hour politico bar; you may well spot some in there on 'business lunches'.
▶ *To see the politicians at their official duties, visit the Massachusetts State House; see p55.*

6B
6 Beacon Street, at Somerset Street (1-617 742 0306, www.6blounge.com). Gov't Center
or *Park St T.* **Open** 11am-2am Mon-Fri, 6pm-2am Sat, Sun. **Credit** AmEx, MC, V.
Map p272 K4 ⓲
Like most places within spitting distance of the State House, the folks who stuff themselves into 6B towards the end of the working day are a mishmash of Financial District go-getters and the legislative fat cats they go get it for. Surprisingly, everyone seems to get along – we think it has something to do with the crazy bright blue martinis the girls all seem to be drinking.

Beacon Hill Pub
149 Charles Street, at Cambridge Street (1-617 625 7100). Charles/MGH T. **Open** 11am-2am Mon-Sat; noon-2am Sun. **No credit cards.**
Map p272 H3 ⓳
The debate rages over whether the understated Beacon Hill Pub, perched at the end of posh Charles Street, is really a legitimate dive bar (sort of an inverted diamond in the rough) or a reservoir for high-earning post-grads who haven't managed to let go of their devotion to cheap Buds and Brubakers. Who cares? With not a frill to be found, but plenty of seats and inexpensive drinks, it's the perfect spot for much more interesting arguments.

Cheers
84 Beacon Street, at Brimmer Street (1-617 227 9605, www.cheersboston.com). Arlington T. **Open** 11am-2am daily. **Credit** AmEx, DC, MC, V.
Map p272 H4 ⓴

Cheers.

THE BEST COCKTAIL SHAKERS

Cuchi Cuchi
Vintage cocktails for the more
adventurous. *See p134.*

Drink
The name says it all. *See p149.*

Eastern Standard
Pure class. *See p120.*

You'll recognise the façade of Cheers from the once-popular sitcom of the same name. Snap a picture and move on, Norm, because that's where the similarities end. Nobody here knows your name, and unless there's a wait for a table, no one wants to know it. The burgers are legendary – for their high prices. The replica Cheers in Faneuil Hall Marketplace (*see p47*) feels even less authentic. Don't be fooled by either; you don't really need another T-shirt, anyhow.

Grand Canal

57 Canal Street, between Causeway & New Chardon Streets (1-617 523 1112, www.grand canalboston.com). Haymarket or North Station T. **Open** 11am-2am daily. **Credit** AmEx, MC, V. **Map** p272 K2 ㉑
The Grand Canal boasts one of the finest façades in the city of Boston. While billed as an Irish pub, there's something very English about the place – although the no-frills menu is decidedly American. Live music on Friday and Saturday nights and a cheery atmosphere have made it enormously popular with a young crowd.
▶ *For more live music venues, see pp208-212.*

★ Sevens Ale House

77 Charles Street, between Mount Vernon & Pinckney Streets (1-617 523 9074). Charles/MGH T. **Open** 11.30am-12.45am daily.
No credit cards. Map p272 J4 ㉒
Though often prohibitively crowded, this unpretentious little Beacon Hill pub is a good spot to seek respite from a hard day of sightseeing and antiques-hunting. The Sevens provides some welcome knuckle and grit to the relative daintiness of the area. Find a booth in the corner, settle down with a Guinness or a Bass, and you might find the Freedom Trail ends right here.

BACK BAY

29 Newbury

29 Newbury Street, at Arlington Street (1-617 536 0290, www.29newbury.com). Arlington T. **Open** 11.30am-11pm Mon-Thur, Sun; 11.30am-1am Fri, Sat. **Credit** AmEx, DC, MC, V. **Map** p275 H5 ㉓

Though primarily a restaurant (and a pretty good one), 29 has a thriving little bar where Boston's PR and media power players convene to slam martinis ('doing lunch'), order second bottles of Burgundy ('catching up') and pop Cristal ('keeping it simple'). A sure thing in the spring and summer, the petite patio is about as glam as it gets.

An Tua Nua

835 Beacon Street, at Munson Street, Fenway (1-617 262 2121, www.antuanuabar.com). Fenway or Kenmore T. **Open** 11am-1am Mon-Wed; 11am-2am Thur-Sun. **Credit** AmEx, MC, V.
An Tua Nua (Gaelic for 'the new beginning') is an odd duck: a hybrid Irish pub and dance club, as popular with its friendly daytime regulars as with the nightly hordes from BU up the way. A fine place to stop in for a quiet afternoon pint or shoehorn yourself into seething masses of sweaty co-eds grinding to surprisingly solid selections of underground dance. The weekly goth night Ceremony (www.ceremonyboston.com) has been going for more than a decade. There's a $5 cover charge for club nights.

Back Bay Social Club

867 Boylston Street, at Gloucester Street (1-617 247 3200, www.backbaysocialclub.com). Hynes T. **Open** 8am-2am daily. **Credit** AmEx, MC, V. **Map** p274 F6 ㉔
Casual charm and a mean classic cocktail have returned to the Back Bay. With a large dining room, extensive patio seating and a sprawling speakeasy-style lounge, you have your pick of destinations within this single establishment. While the decor is excellent, it's gratifying to see that the focus here is on the food and drink. The curving crimson booths are lovely, but you'll want to be right at the bar where the action is, chatting with their knowledgeable and adventurous bartenders. Try the white russian – their smooth and creamy version contains a house-made coffee liquer that is aged for over a month.

Bar Lola

160 Commonwealth Avenue, at Dartmouth Street (1-617 266 1122, www.barlola.com). Copley T. **Open** 4pm-2am daily. **Credit** AmEx, MC, V. **Map** p275 G6 ㉕
What with the tucked-away tranquility of the Commonwealth Mall, Bostonians are continually stymied in their quest for a spot to relax and rehydrate along its green grandeur. Bar Lola answers this call with subterranean chic and Mediterranean treats. Its cool, cavey, dimly lit interior is a romantic option, but hit the patio for a livelier scene. The Lolita martini sports an edible orchid, and the house sangria recipe has to be be sampled to be believed – try the jacked-up 'Matador' version if you're feeling feisty.

Baseball Tavern

1270 Boylston Street, at Yawkey Way (1-617 867 6526, www.thebaseballtavern.com). Fenway or

CONSUME

Kenmore T. **Open** 11am-2am Mon-Sat; noon-2am Sun. **Credit** AmEx, MC, V. **Map** p274 D7 ㉖
One could refer to the rooftop deck of the Baseball Tavern as the 'cheap seats' – you can kinda sorta see Fenway's Jumbotron – but to do so would be to downplay the three spacious plasma-studded floors of sports fan utopia. If you aren't in the market for fly balls on the roof, you can always catch a good local band in the basement club.
▶ *For more about the Red Sox, see p216.*

Boston Beer Works
61 Brookline Avenue, at Lansdowne Street, Fenway (1-617 536 2337, www.beerworks.net). Fenway or Kenmore T. **Open** 11.30am-12.45am daily. **Credit** AmEx, MC, V. **Map** p274 D7 ㉗
With its perfectly positioned location across the street from Fenway Park, Boston Beer Works can be overrun with baseball fans between April and September. But it's worth popping in here at any time of year, if only for the beer, made on the premises, such as the crisp Fenway Pale Ale and the hearty Boston Red. There's also a menu of above-par burgers and other munchables.
Other locations 110 Canal Street, West End (1-617 896 2337).

★ Bukowski Tavern
50 Dalton Street, at Scotia Street (1-617 437 9999). Hynes T. **Open** 11.30am-2.30am daily. **No credit cards**. **Map** p274 F7 ㉘
If you don't mind a backdrop of loud rock, the beer selection (more than 100 choices) in this tiny bar is fit for any beer geek. If your taste runs to spirits, go elsewhere. As one employee aptly put it, 'it's all about the beer' – but for hopheads, this perch above the Massachusetts Turnpike is heaven in a shoebox.
Other locations 1281 Cambridge Street, at Prospect Street, Inman Square, Cambridge (1-617 497 7077).

Flash's Cocktails
312 Stuart Street, at Columbus Avenue (1-617 574 8888, www.flashscocktails.com). Arlington T. **Open** 11.30am-midnight Mon-Thur; 11.30am-1am Fri, Sat; 5pm-1am Sun. **Credit** AmEx, MC, V. **Map** p275 J6 ㉙
Wedged between the edge of Back Bay and the South End, a cute space that once housed a busy cafeteria is now Boston's hippest little cocktail spot, renowned citywide for its penchant for turning classics upside down (which then turn the patrons upside down). As convenient to several choice neighborhoods as it is to a spread of high-end hotels, it draws a mix of people that's almost as complex as the drinks.

★ Foundation Lounge
500 Commonwealth Avenue, at Kenmore Square (1-617 859 9900, www.thefoundationlounge.com). Kenmore T. **Open** 5pm-2am Tue-Sun. **No credit cards**. **Map** p274 D6 ㉚

Kenmore Square's days as the epicenter of Boston's punk underbelly may be long gone, but none of the foxed-up fashionistas who hang in the ultra-modern Foundation Lounge seem to notice – nor do the tourists from the Hotel Commonwealth upstairs, for that matter. They're too busy downing rule-flaunting martinis and munching their way through delicious Japanese *zensai* snacks. Oh, and making sure their fancy handbags can be seen.
▶ *For a bed within stumbling distance, book into the Hotel Commonwealth; see p105.*

Lower Depths
476 Commonwealth Avenue, between Charlesgate West & Kenmore Street (1-617 266 6662). Kenmore T. **Open** 11.30am-1am Mon-Sat; noon-1am Sun. **No credit cards**. **Map** p274 E6 ㉛
We'll cut to the chase – the Lower Depths' claim to fame is their $1 Fenway Franks. Located just steps away from 'The Park' itself, this subterranean hangout is packed on game nights with rowdy fans taking advantage of the above-average beer selection and casual but stylish atmosphere. Sure beats paying $7.50 for a watery brew that you're just going to spill on your way back to the nosebleed section.

★ Otherside Café
407 Newbury Street, at Massachusetts Avenue (1-617 536 8437, www.theothersidecafe.com). Hynes T. **Open** 11am-1am Mon-Thur; 11am-2am Fri; 10am-2am Sat; 10am-midnight Sun. **Credit** MC, V. **Map** p274 E6 ㉜
At the tail end of Newbury Street, across Mass Ave from the more fashionable parts of Back Bay, the aptly named Otherside attracts a different kettle of clientele. Scruffy and bohemian (that is to say, chock full of hipsters), this crowd is equally at home sipping carrot-based concoctions or quaffing a few beers.
▶ *This is also probably one of the most casually vegetarian-friendly establishments in all Boston.*

Pour House
907 Boylston Street, at Gloucester Street (1-617 236 1767, www.pourhouseboston.com). Copley or Hynes T. **Open** 8am-2am daily. **Credit** DC, MC, V. **Map** p274 F6 ㉝
The bloody marys are immense, the burgers are dirt cheap and darn tasty, and the booths are a little tight. In short, a drink and a snack at the Pour House will seldom let you down and never break the bank – hence the pun. Be warned: the later it gets, the more mobbed it grows. The enormous frosted drafts and frozen mudslides flow, and instances of 'Mojito Madness' (and the like) can break out at any time.

Sonsie
327 Newbury Street, between Hereford Street & Massachusetts Avenue (1-617 351 2500, www.sonsieboston.com). Hynes T. **Open** 11.30am-2.30pm, 6-11pm Mon, Tue; 11.30am-2.30pm, 6pm-midnight Wed-Fri; 11.30am-3pm,

Brewed in Boston

Get a taste of local flavor.

Boston's love affair with fermented beverages is a long one. On 9 November, 1620, as the *Mayflower* bobbed off the Cape Cod coast, it was decided to come ashore early in Plymouth. The pilgrims were tired and hungry. And thirsty. 'We could not now take much time for further search or consideration,' wrote soon-to-be Plymouth Colony governor William Bradford, 'our victuals being much spent, especially our beere.'

The American Revolution was famously plotted in ale houses and taverns, and founding father Samuel Adams (*see p18* **Profile**) was also a brew master. And throughout the 19th century, Boston had more breweries per capita than anywhere in the United States, the massive factories built by German and Irish immigrants – AJ Houghton, Eblana, H&J Pfaff – churning, clanging and issuing great billows of hoppy steam as they turned out barrel after barrel of pilsners, ales and stouts.

Alas, the adoption of the 18th Amendment back in 1920 ensured that most of those breweries' recipes have been lost to the ages. And by the early '60s – three decades after Prohibition's repeal in 1933 – there were barely more than three dozen breweries in the entire country, most of them producing thin, flavorless lagers. But happily, the last couple of decades have seen a renaissance in craft brewing in the United States, with New England (and Greater Boston in particular) one of its epicenters.

Much of this has to do with Jamaica Plain's own **Samuel Adams Brewery** (*see p91*), founded by Jim Koch in 1985. When he began brewing his great-great-grandfather's recipe, rich and flavorful beers were all but forgotten in the US. He was able to get his Boston Lager sold at local bars only after carrying chilled bottles in his briefcase for impromptu taste tests with skeptical publicans. Nowadays, the brewery offers guided tours of its scaled-down operation – followed, of course, by generous samples.

Elsewhere in Boston and its environs, beer fans can choose among several exemplary brewpubs with vast selections of fine ales and lagers. With locations across from both Fenway Park and the TD Garden, **Boston Beer Works** (*see left*)

Boston Beer Works.

CONSUME

is one of the more centrally located brewpubs, and one of the best. They're always pouring 15 or so fine ales, ranging from staid classics such as the nutty Boston Common Ale and the hoppy Back Bay IPA to more adventurous offerings, such as the Bunker Hill Blueberry, which features real berries bouncing up and down in ever-so-slightly fruity beer.

Just across the river, near MIT, is the **Cambridge Brewing Company**. Founded in 1989, it's one of the oldest brewpubs in the east. Its staples — the German-style Regatta Golden or the sweetish Cambridge Amber — are excellent. But it's when head brewer Will Meyers struts his stuff, with a nuanced Belgian ale, or a warming barley wine, that the CBC really shines.

Up the road from MIT is Harvard and, not to be outdone, America's oldest university has a brewpub of its own. The interior of **John Harvard's Brew House** (*see p150*) is dark and cavernous, much like an English pub. And the beers therein, such as the copper-colored John Harvard's Pale Ale or the potent Mid-Winter's Strong Beer, wouldn't be out of place in one. Nor would the delectable fish and chips.

6pm-midnight Sat; 11.30am-3pm, 6-11pm Sun.
Credit DC, MC, V. **Map** p274 F6 ③④
Known mainly as a restaurant, with talented Bill
Poirier in the kitchen, the tasteful (if slightly
touristy) Sonsie is a premier hangout for the Back
Bay elite and those who want to meet them. A goat's
cheese and roasted sweet pepper-topped gourmet
pizza, a couple of glasses of wine and a little marble
table that faces the Newb (that's Newbury Street,
darling) all add up to an utterly Bostonian gazing
and grazing opportunity.

TC's Lounge
*1 Haviland Street, at Massachusetts Avenue
(1-617 247 8109). Hynes T.* **Open** 11am-2am
daily. **No credit cards**. **Map** p274 F7 ③⑤
This is the quintessential dive bar, featuring cheap
beer, a rocking jukebox, 50-year-old furniture, a
vending machine with snacks and an electric log
fireplace. What more could you ask for in a bar? The
clientele is a mix of students from nearby Berklee
College of Music, punk rockers and old-time regulars. Beware the hefty shots – and your propensity
to overlook their heftiness.

THE SOUTH END

Chef Barbara Lynch's hugely popular wine
bar/charcuterie the **Butcher Shop** (*see p124*)
has a great selection of wines by the glass;
although most spaces are reserved for diners,
you can sidle up to the soapstone bar if you
order one of the exquisite small plates.

Lively restaurant/nightspot the **Beehive**
(*see p124*) boasts some of the best bartenders
in town and live entertainment. **Wally's** (*see
p212*) is a wonderfully divey hole-in-the-wall
jazz haunt. Eateries the **Franklin Café**
(*see p126*) and **Toro** (*see p127*) both have
excellent bars that are worth nipping into.

Anchovies
*433 Columbus Avenue, at Braddock Park
(1-617 266 5088). Back Bay or Prudential T.*
Open 4pm-2am daily. **Credit** AmEx, MC, V.
Map p275 G7 ③⑥
If you're all bistro'd out (always a risk in the South
End), Anchovies is the perfect antidote. A cosy little hole in the wall with simple, tasty Italian vittles,
a solid beer selection and a bar packed with the
friendliest regulars you're likely to find in town –
which means get there earlyish.
▶ *For more South End restaurants, see p124.*

Clery's
*113 Dartmouth Street, at Columbus Avenue
(1-617 262 9874). Back Bay or Copley T.* **Open**
11am-midnight Mon, Tue; 11am-2am Wed-Sun.
Credit AmEx, MC, V. **Map** p275 H7 ③⑦
Clery's is one of the few remaining joints in the South
End where you can still order a Bud without feeling

like a pariah. The clientele is a mix of sporty youngsters and a slightly unbuttoned after-work crowd,
with a few locals thrown in for good measure. Clery's
serves solid but unspectacular American food, but the
broad windows make for great people-watching.

★ Delux Café
*100 Chandler Street, at Clarendon Street (1-617
338 5258). Back Bay T.* **Open** 5pm-1am Mon-
Sat. **No credit cards**. **Map** p275 H7 ③⑧
A wall of record sleeves, graffiti-covered restrooms
and a low-budget, laid-back feel make this place a
favorite with locals, passing bike messengers and
people from all over town who appreciate a cheap
drink or two. Friendly bartenders and the Cartoon
Network on the TV add to the kind of jolly atmosphere that can only be found at a place that keeps a
fake Christmas tree on the bar all year long. The
Delux, in all its kitsch glory, is a hidden treasure.

Red Fez
*1222 Washington Street, at Perry Street
(1-617 338 6060, www.theredfez.org). Silver
Line Washington St to East Berkeley St.* **Open**
11am-2am daily. **Credit** AmEx, DC, MC, V.
Map p275 J8 ③⑨
The Red Fez serves Middle Eastern cuisine that's a
little uneven, but the bar is often crowded, and for
good reason. While the drinks list – good wines,
great cocktails – is impressive enough, it's worth
checking this place out just for the colorful, quasi-
Middle Eastern decor and sunny side patio.

THE NORTH END

Goody Glover's
*50 Salem Street, at Cross Street (1-617 367
6444, www.goodyglovers.com). Haymarket T.*
Open 11am-1am daily. **Credit** AmEx, MC, V.
Map p273 L3 ④⓪
The Italian North End is one of the areas in Boston
you'd least expect to find an Irish pub, but Goody
Glover's – named for a local Irish-Catholic woman
who was hanged as a witch in 1688 – occupies
pride of place at the corner of Salem Street. The
Guinness is delicious, of course, but so is the
unusual menu, offering fried reubens and grilled
potato and cheese sandwiches.

THE BEST FOR THE BEER

Deep Ellum
A hidden microbrew haven. *See p155.*

Delux Café
No-frills boozing. *See above.*

Independent
The best Guinness in town. *See p154.*

THE WATERFRONT

★ Drink
*348 Congress Street, at A Street, Fort Point
(1-617 695 1806, www.drinkfortpoint.com).
South Station T.* **Open** 4pm-1am daily.
Credit AmEx, MC, V. **Map** off p273 M5 ㊶
This underground bar been firmly planted at the top
of local and national cocktail-enthusiasts' must-see
lists for its personal approach to mixology. Master
bartenders present you not with a menu but with an
ear to listen to your preferences, crafting artisinal tip-
ples from their stock of premium spirits and mixers.
▶ *Drink is part of Barbara Lynch's mini empire,
as is Sportello around the corner; see p132.*

★ Lucky's
*355 Congress Street, at A Street (1-617
357 5825, www.luckyslounge.com). South
Station T.* **Open** 11am-2am Mon-Fri; 5pm-2am
Sat; 10am-2am Sun. **Credit** AmEx, MC, V.
Map off p273 N5 ㊷
Hidden away in a beautiful old warehouse near Fort
Point Channel, Lucky's is easily missed. In true
speakeasy style, there's no sign – look out for the
orange glow radiating from the basement windows
– which fits with the louche, retro vibe inside. The
big night at Lucky's is Sinatra Sunday; far from
drawing nostalgic pensioners, young hipsters flock
to hear the Al Vega Trio pay tribute to Ol' Blue Eyes.
Lucky's also features live funk, soul and R&B from
Wednesday to Saturday, beginning around 9.30pm.

CAMBRIDGE

Low-key hangouts the **Lizard Lounge**
(*see p208*) and the **Toad** (*see p209*) are best
known for their live music. **Central Bottle
Wine & Provisions** (*see p170*) runs
Thursday Wine Bar evenings.

Cambridge Brewing Company
*Building 100, 1 Kendall Square, at Hampshire
Street (1-617 494 1994). Kendall T.* **Open**
11.30am-11pm Mon; 11.30am-midnight Tue-
Thur; 11.30am-12.45am Fri; noon-12.45am Sat;
noon-11pm Sun. **Credit** AmEx, MC, V.
Boston is a serious beer town – and Cambridge has
never been one to be outdone. Thus, the Cambridge
Brewing Company approaches the challenge with
panache, brewing classic styles such as the Regatta
Golden, as well as bolder cask-conditioned brews and
seasonals such as the Arquebus Barleywine. Grab a
seat on the nifty patio and enjoy a sampling session.

Charlie's Kitchen
*10 Eliot Street, at Winthrop Street (1-617 492
9646). Harvard T.* **Open** 10.30am-1am Mon-
Wed; 10.30am-2am Thur, Fri; 11am-2am Sat;
11am-1am Sun. **Credit** AmEx, MC, V.
Map p276 A2 ㊸

Despite the rampant fancifying of everything
within a five-mile radius of Harvard, the stalwart
Charlie's Kitchen has hardly changed a bit. This
place may be known as the double cheeseburger
king, but the loud, ready-to-drink crowd of punks,
students, professors and local rock luminaries pile
into the upstairs bar for the massive glasses of
Hoegaarden, cheap eats, snippy waitresses and the
best jukebox in Cambridge.

Daedalus Restaurant & Bar
*45½ Mount Auburn Street, at Bow Street,
Harvard Square (1-617 349 0071, www.daedalus
harvardsquare.com). Harvard T.* **Open** 11am-
1am Mon-Wed; 11am-2am Thurs-Sat; 10am-1am
Sun. **Credit** AmEx, MC, V. **Map** p276 B3 ㊹
While the bar and lounge areas are standard, locals
flock to Daedalus in good weather to snag a seat
on the roof deck. Sure, patio-appropriate weather
can be hard to come by in the Hub, but so are last
calls as late as 2am – another one of this Harvard-
area hangout's major draws.

★ Enormous Room
*567 Massachusetts Avenue, at Pearl Street
(1-617 491 5550, www.enormous.tv). Central T.*
Open 5.30pm-1am Mon-Wed, Sun; 5.30pm-2am
Thur-Sat. **Credit** AmEx, MC, V. **Map** p276 C3 ㊺
Easily one of the most popular places in Central
Square, the Enormous Room is not exactly enormous, but cordon yourself some space on the long,
oriental carpet-clad platforms, or sink into a cushy
leather sofa, and your personal space issues will be
well and truly sorted. There are DJs every night,
usually spinning classy house, raw soul or deep
dance cuts. Kick off your shoes, try some infused
bourbon and order a generous platter of Moroccan
goodies to share – just take care no one steps in your
falafel and aubergine dip.

Field
*20 Prospect Street, at Massachusetts Avenue,
Central Square (1-617 354 7345, www.thefield
pub.com). Central T.* **Open** noon-1am Mon-Wed,
Sun; noon-2am Thur-Sat. **No credit cards.**
Map p276 C3 ㊻
You really don't want to get into the discussion of
what qualifies as a real Irish pub in this town.
Suffice it to say, the Field does – perhaps because
it doesn't try too hard. Staff pour a good Guinness,
and do so with a smile. As a result, its two rooms
fill up each night with a mix of Irish imports and
Cambridge townies. Darts, anyone?

Grafton Street
*1230 Massachusetts Avenue, at Plympton Street,
Harvard Square (1-617 497 0400, www.grafton
streetcambridge.com). Harvard T.* **Open** 5pm-
midnight Mon-Wed; 5pm-2am Thur, Fri; 10.30am-
2am Sat; 10am-1am Sun. **Credit** AmEx, MC, V.
Map p276 B3 ㊼

A welcoming spot on the edge of Harvard Square, Grafton Street overflows in summer, when its big french windows allow interaction with the square's fascinating parade. Expect no leprechaun logos or fiddledy-dee music at this new-school Irish pub – Grafton Street favors upscale modernism over stereotypical kitsch. Be sure to sample the haute pub grub and excellent cocktails.

Grendel's Den
89 Winthrop Street, at John F Kennedy Street, Harvard Square (1-617 491 1050, www.grendels den.com). Harvard T. **Open** 11.30am-1am daily. **Credit** AmEx, MC, V. **Map** p276 A2 ㊽
This unpretentious little basement bar continues to attract throngs of thirsty Harvard students. From 5pm until 7.30pm (plus 9pm until 11.30pm Sunday to Thursday), everything on the menu is half price after you've bought a $3 drink. You'd be surprised how much tomorrow's leaders could use a bargain now and again.

Hong Kong
1238 Massachusetts Avenue, at Plympton Street, Harvard Square (1-617 864 5311, www.hong kongharvard.com). Harvard T. **Open** 11.30am-2am Mon-Wed, Sun; 11.30am-2.30am Thur; 11.30am-3am Fri, Sat. **Credit** AmEx, MC, V. **Map** p276 B2 ㊾
Despite the gaudy 1950s-style sign out front, this Chinese restaurant-cum-bar – a Harvard institution in an area of vanishing institutions – is slightly lacking in the decor department. But atmosphere? Oh, there's plenty of that. Witness ten medical students crowded around a scorpion bowl, or a gaggle of comedians retelling the jokes they told in the comedy club upstairs, and you'll see that it's the people that make this place such a kick.
▶ *For more about the Comedy Studio, see p229.*

★ John Harvard's Brew House
33 Dunster Street, at Mount Auburn Street, Harvard Square (1-617 868 3585, www.john harvards.com). Harvard T. **Open** 11.30am-12.30am Mon-Thur; 11.30am-1am Fri, Sat; 11.30am-midnight Sun. **Credit** AmEx, MC, V. **Map** p276 B2 ㊿
A longtime favorite with local students, this large basement brewpub in Harvard Square offers basic but solid American cooking and a selection of own-brewed beers – try the delicious Old Willy IPA.

★ Lord Hobo
92 Hampshire Street, at Windsor Street, Kendall Square (1-617 354 0766, www.lordhobo.com). Central T then 15min walk or bus 83, 91. **Open** 5pm-1am Mon-Wed; 5pm-2am Thur, Fri; 10am-2am Sat; 10am-1am Sun. **Credit** MC, V.
Leaving behind the diner/bar legacy of its predecessor, Lord Hobo has embraced the booze-snob trend, bringing Cambridge locals quality after-work

cocktails and late night micro-brewed pints – at a cost. Still, the clientele that crowds the dim space is an intriguing mix of young professionals, Inman Square-based indie kids and MIT students.

★ Middlesex
315 Massachusetts Avenue, between State & Village Streets (1-617 868 6739, www.middlesex lounge.com). Central T. **Open** 11.30am-2pm, 5pm-1am Mon-Wed, Sun; 11.30am-2pm, 5pm-2am Thur-Sat. **Credit** AmEx, MC, V. **Map** p276 C4 ㊱
Though the DJs spin the best vintage hip-hop, classic electro and underground dance, and while the clientele has been known to kick off their shoes and fill the floor, Middlesex is still more of a lounge than a full-blown nightclub. The room is filled with little metal benches on wheels that can be artfully arranged to accommodate even the most disorganised of parties – just one of many functionally futuristic design flairs that keep the queues outside stretching into the night.

Miracle of Science Bar & Grill
321 Massachusetts Avenue, between State & Village Streets, Central Square (1-617 868 2866, www.miracleofscience.us). Central T. **Open** 7am-1am daily. **Credit** AmEx, MC, V. **Map** p276 C4 ㊲
The Miracle of Science combines ultra-modern design, a well-selected variety of beers and a comfortable, sun-bathed interior, thanks to its huge windows looking out over Mass Ave. In honor of the many MIT students who frequent the place, the menu is laid out like the periodic table.

River Gods.

CONSUME

INSIDE TRACK
HOTEL GIN JOINTS

If your accommodation is less than four-star, get a taste of the deluxe life at one of the top hotel watering holes: the **Bar at the Taj** (formerly the Ritz; *see p103*) has retained its old-school elegance; the **Bristol Lounge** in the Four Seasons (*see p103*) exudes understated class; and the high-ceilinged, wood-paneled **Oak Bar** at the Fairmont Copley Plaza (*see p104*) is an institution.

Noir

Charles Hotel, 1 Bennett Street, at Eliot Street, Harvard Square (1-617 661 8010, www.noir-bar.com). Harvard T. **Open** 4.30pm-2am daily. **Credit** AmEx, MC, V. **Map** p276 A2 ⑬

This lovely little lounge in the Charles Hotel stays true to its name, with its decor (deep blacks, flashes of red, thick drapes of metal beads) re-imagining the film noir era. The candlelit atmosphere makes this the perfect place for a romantic drink. Things are also kept era-appropriate with happening events, such as weekly *Mad Men* viewing parties during the show's season. The stylish interior and thoughtful concoctions keep the locals showing up, and the feisty late-night hotel guests make for an interesting mix. Try the American Beauty – a velvety tango of Courvoisier and port.

▶ *Sleep it off at the Charles Hotel; see p110.*

Om Restaurant & Lounge

92 Winthrop Street, at John F Kennedy Street, Harvard Square (1-617 576 2800, www.om restaurant.com). Harvard T. **Open** 3pm-1am Mon, Tue; 3pm-2am Wed-Fri; 11.30am-2am Sat; 11.30am-1am Sun. **Credit** AmEx, DC, MC, V. **Map** p276 A3 ⑭

If inner peace ever struck you as a bit dull, you'll love the Om, where a selection of 'aromatherapy martinis' (no wait, come back!) find even the most cynical Harvard brat sinking into a leather sofa and nursing a concoction of violet, vodka, saké and jasmine (that'd be the Violent Femmes). Funky lighting, video art, hot people… You might as well stop by for a look.

People's Republik

878 Massachusetts Avenue, at Lee Street, Central Square (1-617 491 6969, www.noir-bar.com). Central or Harvard T. **Open** noon-1am Mon-Wed, Sun; noon-2am Thur-Sat. **No credit cards.** **Map** p276 C3 ⑮

In the spot that used to house the divey little bar Drumlin's, the People's Republik has jazzed things up considerably. In the daytime, you'll find postal workers from down the street cozying up to the bar. At night, though, it becomes a seething cauldron of

youth. With old communist propaganda pasted all over the walls and a giant mock bomb hovering above the window, the Republik plays around with a revolutionary theme, which has led local wags to rename it Kremlin's. Be warned: it's easy to pass hours here without realizing it.

Phoenix Landing

512 Massachusetts Avenue, at Brookline Street (1-617 576 6260, www.noir-bar.com). Central T. **Open** 11am-1am Mon-Thur; 11am-2am Fri; 9am-2am Sat; 9am-1am Sun. **Credit** AmEx, MC, V. **Map** p276 C3 ⑯

Invariably packed and loud, and often somewhat steamy, this was one of the first Irish bars in the area to realize the potential of combining a dance club with a pub. At night, the Landing is the center of the local electronic scene, showcasing up-and-coming DJs and producers, as well as some international floor-filling talent – and its intimate digs make dancing a blast. Besides pulling a very decent pint of Guinness, the bar shows English football at weekends, coupled with delicious, artery-clogging full-Irish breakfasts.

★ Plough & Stars

912 Massachusetts Avenue, at Hancock Street, Central Square (1-617 576 0032, www.plough andstars.com). Central T. **Open** 11.30am-1am Mon, Tue, Sun; 11am-2am Wed-Sat. **Credit** AmEx, MC, V. **Map** p276 B3 ⑰

The spiritual forefather of Greater Boston's thriving Irish pub business, the Plough has been going for some 30 years. In the daytime, it offers the best pub grub in town. At night, the tiny bar is transformed into a hotbed of clashing elbows and live music. Your chances of meeting a novelist just went up by 90%.

Redline

59 John F Kennedy Street, at Eliot Street (1-617 491 9851). Harvard T. **Open** 4pm-1am Mon-Wed, Sun; 4pm-2am Thur-Sat. **Credit** AmEx, DC, MC, V. **Map** p276 A3 ⑱

Occupying the site of the fabled Crimson Sports Bar & Grille (a place where the Bud flowed freely and the sports coverage never stopped), Redline has tried to up the ante a little, with its granite bar top and cosy booths, not to mention a full lunch and dinner menu. After 10pm, the DJ shows up and the place transforms into a miniature disco. But there are still a couple of large-screen TVs, so the Harvard students who continue to flock here can catch a game from time to time.

★ River Gods

125 River Street, at Kinnaird Street, Central Square (1-617 576 1881, www.rivergodsonline. com). Central T then 10min walk. **Open** 3pm-midnight Mon; 3pm-1am Tue-Sat; 3-11pm Sun. **Credit** MC, V. **Map** p276 B3 ⑲

The Irish owners serve a great pint of Guinness, but you won't find any shamrocks hanging on the walls here. River Gods is contemporary yet cosy, carved

CONSUME

into a cute residential neighborhood just outside Central Square. The tiny space fills up quickly around 9pm as the DJs, who rotate nightly, do their (incredibly varied) thing – get here early to score a table. The beer selection is good, cocktails are reasonably priced and tasty food is served every night until 10pm. All in all, this is easily one of the most original hangouts in town (exemplified by the gigantic mermaid hanging over a throne in the back of the room).

Shay's Lounge
58 John F Kennedy Street, at South Street, Harvard Square (1-617 864 9161). Harvard T. **Open** 11am-1am Mon-Sat; noon-1am Sun. **Credit** AmEx, MC, V. **Map** p276 A3 ⑥⓪
Owned and operated by English expats, Shay's is one of the nicer bars in the area. Sunk a few feet below the sidewalk and sporting a handy outdoor patio, the bar itself is rather poky. It attracts a lively mix of academics, artists and die-hard regulars. Though many patrons quaff from the bar's extensive beer menu, this is primarily a wine bar – and there are no spirits.

Simple Truth Lounge
Hotel Veritas, 1 Remington Street, at Massachusetts Avenue, Harvard Square (1-617 520 5000, www.thehotelveritas.com). Harvard T. **Open** noon-11pm daily. **Credit** AmEx, MC, V. **Map** p276 B3 ⑥①
The sitting area of the Hotel Veritas deserves special mention. With a carefully edited array of local cheese and charcuterie, smart cocktails, and a short but power-packed beer and wine list – not to mention beautifully understated furnishings, an outdoor patio, and some of the best background music in Cambridge – this is a gem that locals in the know are beginning to discover. The lounge is small but luxurious, perfect for a lingering date; an intimate spot for two next to the fireplace may even turn things up a few degrees.

Temple Bar
1688 Massachusetts Avenue, at Sacramento Street, Porter Square (1-617 547 5055, www.templebarcambridge.com). Harvard or Porter T. **Open** 5pm-1am Mon-Fri; 11am-1am Sat, Sun. **Credit** AmEx, DC, MC, V. **Map** p276 B1 ⑥②
Despite its name, an Irish pub this ain't. Emblematic of the current vogue for neo-lounge bars, it attracts the nouveau-riche, mobile-phone-wielding, martini-clinking crowd, as well as grown-up rockers and junior foodies. The atmosphere is serene, and the food a little classier (lobster bisque, artichoke pizza) than your usual pub grub.

Tory Row
3 Brattle Street, at JFK Street, Harvard Square (1-617 876 8769, www.toryrow.us). Harvard T. **Open** 7am-1am Mon-Fri; 9am-1am Sat, Sun. **Credit** AmEx, MC, V. **Map** p276 B2 ⑥③

Patrons on stylish metal stools appear ready to topple out into the street on warm, busy nights. Is it the consistently packed house or the prime location that gives Tory Row it's air of self importance? No matter – the people watching is superb, the nibbles fairly and resonably priced, and the beer and wine selection features a smattering of locally produced favorites.

ZuZu
474 Massachusetts Avenue, at Brookline Street, Central Square (1-617 864 3278, www.zuzubar.com). Central T. **Open** 5.30pm-1am Mon-Wed, Sun; 5.30pm-2am Thur-Sat. **Credit** AmEx, MC, V. **Map** p276 C3 ⑥④
Sandwiched between the two rooms of its parent – famed music venue the Middle East – ZuZu is one of Central Square's gems. With its muted red and orange tones and walls busy with local art, this is a place to have a drink, nibble on Latin-Lebanese mezze and browse one seriously schooled jukebox. ZuZu is a haven for local musicians, and when they're not sipping the bar's creative cocktails, they're playing. Every night starting at 10.30pm, it features oddball DJs and eclectic live music, from Latin to rock 'n' roll.
▶ *For our review of Middle East, see p209.*

JAMAICA PLAIN

★ Bella Luna Restaurant & the Milky Way Lounge
284 Armory Street, at the Brewery Complex (1-617 524 6060, www.milkywayjp.com). Stony Brook T or bus 39. **Open** 5-11.30pm Mon, Tue, Sun; 5pm-midnight Wed; 5pm-1am Thur, Fri; 11am-1am Sat. **Credit** AmEx, MC, V.
What used to be JP's beloved bowling alley, dance club and restaurant combo has relocated to the Brewery Complex. Conspicuously absent are the lanes, but the new space features the same familiarly kooky decor, a pool table and a rad patio on which you can enjoy craft beers and slices of gourmet pizza.

Brendan Behan Pub
378 Centre Street, at Sherridan Street (1-617 522 5386). Jackson Square T. **Open** 1pm-1am daily. **No credit cards.**
This is one of the jewels of Boston's popular Irish pub scene. Named after the Irish playwright, it once hosted standing-room-only *seisiúns*, attended by the likes of Patrick McCabe and JP Donleavy. Behan's is not a fancy place – it's small and dimly lit, with no food on offer – but that's part of its charm. Locals love it because they are encouraged to bring their own food – usually from the various take-out joints that dot Centre Street – to nibble on between pints from the incredible beer selection.

★ Doyle's
3484 Washington Street, at Williams Street (1-617 524 2345). Green Street T. **Open** 9am-midnight daily. **Credit** AmEx, MC, V.

Bella Luna Restaurant &
the Milky Way Lounge.

In business for more than a century, this old Irish charmer has long been popular with politicos. Times have changed, however; the room once named after JFK's grandfather, 'Honey Fitz', is now named after Mayor Menino – of Italian descent. The ceilings are lofty, the rooms capacious, and the murals high on the walls (scenes of colonial Massachusetts) are gorgeous. The generous portions of comfort food and wide selection of ales and scotches are its other strengths.

▶ *If you're lucky, you may get to taste a brand new brew from the Samuel Adams Brewery (see p91), which makes beer just down the road and sometimes tests out recipes at Doyle's.*

Haven
2 Perkins Street, at Centre Street, Jamaica Plain (1-617 524 2836, www.thehavenjp.com). Jackson Square T. **Open** 5pm-1am Mon-Fri; 10am-1am Sat, Sun. **Credit** AmEx, MC, V.
Greater Boston's most authentic Scottish pub is actually located in Jamaica Plain. Sure, the great beer selection, Scottish party music and nifty antler chandelier are all well and good, but you've really come out this way for the haggis and neeps (those patrons less enthused by dining on sheep organs will appreciate the tomato bridie or barley risotto, made from locally foraged mushrooms). For dessert, make sure to order something with the Drambuie whipped cream.

BROOKLINE

Matt Murphy's
14 Harvard Street, at Webster Place (1-617 232 0188, www.mattmurphyspub.com). Brookline Village T. **Open** 11am-2am daily.
No credit cards.

One of the better Irish pubs in a city that has no shortage of them, Matt Murphy's is well worth a journey into the Brookline outlands. The Guinness poured here is sublime, but what makes the pub such a hit among locals is its grub. The fish and chips (served wrapped in newspaper, naturally) is deservedly famous and the shepherd's pie superb. The kitchen even makes its own ketchup. If it's not as youth-oriented as some of the city's Irish bars, Murphy's still gets its customers moving once the music starts – if they're capable of moving after dinner, that is.

★ Publick House
1648 Beacon Street, at Winthrop Road (1-617 277 2880, www.eatgoodfooddrink betterbeer.com). Washington Square T. **Open** 5pm-2am Mon-Fri; 4pm-2am Sat, Sun. **Credit** AmEx, MC, V.
Beer is the thing here, and ale aficionados flock from miles around for its voluminous list of lambics, witbiers and dubbels from the world over. Even better is the menu, which suggests which beers should be ordered with which meal (try the sausage sandwich with the rare Belgian mustard beer). If you come alone, you can always gaze at the large collection of European brewery memorabilia adorning the walls.

SOMERVILLE

Barbecue joint **Redbones** (*see p138*) is a beer connoisseur's favourite for its 25 rotating taps, flowing with craftbrews from New England and the Northwest, plus potent Belgian ales.

Burren
247 Elm Street, at Chester Street, Davis Square (1-617 776 6896, www.burren.com). Davis T. **Open** 11am-1am daily. **Credit** AmEx, MC, V.

CONSUME

CONSUME

A Davis Square mainstay, the Burren is one of the most popular (and largest) Irish pubs on the north side of the river. During the afternoon, the front room – with its wooden floors and a gentle light pouring through the windows – is full of folks tucking into bowls of beef stew, sipping pints of Guinness (or any number of local brews) and listening to informal Irish *seisiúns*. At night, the Burren is packed, largely with students from nearby Tufts University, who crowd the large back room to hear live (and loud) roots rock.

Independent

75 Union Square, at Stone Avenue (1-617 440 6022, www.theindo.com). Harvard T then bus 86. **Open** *4.30pm-1am Mon-Thur; 4pm-2am Fri, Sat; noon-1am Sun.* **Credit** *AmEx, MC, V.*
Marked by the comfort of a neighborhood haunt and a low-key sort of elegance, 'the Indo' is a Somerville favourite. The kitchen produces delicious, adventurous dishes – raclettes, trout fritters, fried almonds – until 1am. And the adjoining bar is Irish without being too much so, with a fine wine list and one of the better pints of Guinness in town. Every other Friday night, it plays host to 'Mash Ave', a DJ night featuring the latest and greatest mash-ups and bootlegs.

▶ *For more about the neighborhood, see p93.*

Orleans

65 Holland Street, at Wallace Street, Davis Square (1-617 591 2100, www.orleans restaurant.com). Davis T. **Open** *11am-1am daily.* **Credit** *AmEx, MC, V.*
Half restaurant and half lounge, with both sections sharing the same large, airy expanse, Orleans is of two minds. At night, it can get crowded as the drinks flow and the DJ pumps louder and louder music over the crowd. The next morning, however, it's a fine and mellow place to indulge in some eggs Benedict and a bloody mary, as the large windows are thrown open to let in the sun and offer views of the passers-by outside.

PJ Ryan's

239 Holland Street, at Broadway, Davis Square (1-617 625 8200, www.pjryans.com). Davis T. **Open** *3pm-1am Mon-Wed; noon-1am Thur, Sun; noon-2am Fri, Sat.* **Credit** *AmEx, MC, V.*
PJs does the Irish pub thing with tasteful restraint. A couple of Jack Yeats paintings, a perfectly pulled pint and live music at the weekend create the right vibe. With its intimate size, dark-wood paneling and homey feel, it's the perfect place to grab a beer and watch the world go by through its expansive front windows. Take note: on Tuesdays PJs has a popular trivia night that can make getting through the door a challenge. On big days for rugby or soccer, this is the place to be, with the shades drawn and the game on satellite.

Precinct

70 Union Square, at Washington Street (1-617 623 9211, www.precinct.com). Davis T then bus 87. **Open** *9pm-2am daily.* **Credit** *AmEx, DC, MC, V.*
Precinct is upscale without being too pretentious, and big enough (with several different rooms) to offer variety while retaining an intimate feel. Irish music evenings from Sunday to Wednesday are free, while themed nights held during the rest of the week require a small cover charge.

Sligo Pub

237A Elm Street, at Davis Square (1-617 623 9561). Davis T. **Open** *11am-1am daily.* **No credit cards.**
The Sligo – small, dimly lit, still serving Pabst Blue Ribbon for two bucks a pint, with oldies on the jukebox – is one of the last bastions of Davis Square's blue-collar traditions. Although it's now been infiltrated by Tufts University students, it still serves generous shots of the hard stuff to guys who look like they've been regulars for decades.

Thirsty Scholar Pub

70 Beacon Street, between Smith Avenue & Cooney Street, Inman Square (1-617 497 2294, www.thirstyscholarpub.com). Harvard T then 15min walk. **Open** *11am-1am daily.* **Credit** *AmEx, MC, V.*
Map 276 C2 ⑥⑤
With its charming exposed brick walls and an Irish pub-style interior, the Thirsty Scholar is an ideal place to hole yourself away with a special someone for a quiet drink. But it's also a large room, with big TVs to watch the game, and filled to the rafters with a lively crowd of regulars (especially on weekends). So if you'd rather come out and be sociable, well, that's OK too.

★ Trina's Starlite Lounge

3 Beacon Street, at Cambridge Street, Inman Square (1-617 576-0006, www.trinasstarlite lounge.com). Central T then bus 83. **Open** noon-4pm, 5pm-1am Mon; 5pm-1am Tue-Sun. **Credit** AmEx, MC, V. **Map** p276 C2 ⑥⑧

Rising from the ashes of the classic-but-grimy Abbey Lounge, the Inman Square space has remained a meeting spot for savvy locals. Trina's low lighting and dark wood paneling are brightened up by retro images just about everywhere you look (the bathrooms are wallpapered in mid-century magazine pages), but it's the menu full of diner-style comfort food that really keeps the clientele smiling into their expertly executed cocktails. Head here for brunch on Mondays to recover from the weekend's excesses.

ALLSTON

Deep Ellum

477 Cambridge Street, between Beacon Street & Brighton Avenue (1-617-787-2337). Harvard Ave T or bus 57, 66. **Open** 11.30am-1am Mon-Fri; 11am-1am Sat, Sun. **Credit** AmEx, MC, V. The decor is plainspoken, but the beer list is superb. And so are the cocktails, with bartenders willing and able to mix up any old-fashioned or off-the-wall concoction you can think of. The eclectic menu runs from chilli dogs to veggie lentil stew. Taking its name from the jazz-rich area of Dallas, this relative newcomer is generating a buzz among booze connoisseurs.

Model Café

7 North Beacon Street, at Cambridge Street (1-617 254 9365). Harvard Ave T or bus 57, 66. **Open** 6pm-2am Mon-Fri, Sun; 5pm-2am Sat. **No credit cards.**

The Model started off as an unpretentious little neighborhood dive and then one day, through no fault of its own, suddenly became enormously pretentious, playing host to the cream of the countercultural community (who inexplicably started calling it the 'Mow-dell'). Nowadays, the trendy crowd and the divey neighborhood crowd share the place. The jukebox is among the best around.

Sunset Grill

130 Brighton Avenue, at Harvard Avenue (1-617 254 1331, www.allstonsfinest.com). Harvard Ave T or bus 57, 66. **Open** 11.30am-1am daily. **Credit** AmEx, DC, MC, V. **Map** p276 A5 ⑥⑦

The Sunset Grill serves beer. Great beer, beer of all types, from all over the world, in every color and flavor and consistency. And it serves a lot of it. The list of ales and lagers is vast: 380 bottles, with 112 on tap. The decor is nothing spectacular, and unless you have a thing about college students, the clientele won't knock your socks off.

Wonder Bar

186 Harvard Avenue, at Commonwealth Avenue (1-617 351 2665, www.wonderbarboston.com). Harvard Ave T or bus 57, 66. **Open** 5pm-2am daily. **Credit** AmEx, MC, V. **Map** p276 A5 ⑥⑧

Wonder Bar makes no bones about wanting to move in higher circles, what with its votive candles and lazily spinning ceiling fans. All the same, it's located smack in the middle of Boston's student epicenter (it's near BU and BC, among others). So even as it hosts classy jazz performances to go along with its modest dinner menu every Friday and Saturday night, it's a different place after 10pm – the DJ sets up shop, the college kids arrive and the beer starts flowing.

CONSUME

Trina's Starlite Lounge.

Shops & Services

Get the plastic out: compact hunting grounds encourage spending sprees.

In the shadow of New York's overflowing retail cornucopia, Boston isn't known as a major shopping destination, but that sort of setback has always brought out the local competitive spirit. Coveted designer names such as Marc Jacobs and Jimmy Choo have set up shop in Back Bay. Barneys has opened a slick, two-floor space in the Copley Place mall, to the delight of designer-label lovers.

More interestingly, there has been an explosion of independent shops around the city, in the South End, the North End and corners of Cambridge and Somerville, as well as consumer center Back Bay. For more on shopping areas, *see p157* **Where to Shop**. Another good reason to shop in Boston: there's no sales tax on clothing purchases totaling less than $175.

General

DEPARTMENT STORES

Barneys New York
Copley Place, 100 Huntington Avenue, at Exeter Street, Back Bay (1-617 385 3300, www.barneys. com). Back Bay, Copley or Prudential T. **Open** 10am-8pm Mon-Sat; 11am-6pm Sun. **Credit** AmEx, MC, V. **Map** p275 G7.
This two-level branch of the super-chic New York department store within the city's premier mall has been criticised by some for bringing a less interesting selection of labels to Boston than those found in its parent store – but, given the compact size, it seems inevitable that the number of lines would be more limited. There's no doubt it's a welcome addition for style-conscious shoppers looking for contemporary designer fashion (Dior Homme by Hedi Slimane, Martin Margiela and Doo.Ri, for example), shoes and accessories hitherto hard to find in the city, as well as less ubiquitous cosmetics. *Photo p158.*
▶ *There's a second, much smaller, outpost in the Mall at Chestnut Hill; see p158.*

Lord & Taylor
760 Boylston Street, at Fairfield Street, Back Bay (1-617 262 6000, www.lordandtaylor.com). Copley or Prudential T. **Open** 10am-9.30pm Mon-Fri; 10am-9pm Sat; 11am-7pm Sun. **Credit** AmEx, MC, V. **Map** p275 G6.
A small, classic department store with a conservative air, selling designer and brand-name men's, women's and children's clothing, sportswear and shoes, as well as cosmetics, jewelry and accessories.

★ Louis
60 Northern Avenue, at Courthouse Way, Waterfront (1-617 262 6100, www.louisboston. com). Courthouse T. **Open** 11am-6pm Mon-Wed; 11am-7pm Thur-Sat; 11am-5pm Sun. **Credit** AmEx, MC, V. **Map** p275 H5.
Before a branch of Barneys opened in Copley Place, this was Boston's answer to the hip New York designer temple. Having just completed a grand move to the waterfront, Louis sells carefully selected fashion, beauty products and homewares

CONSUME

in an exquisite setting. A variety of gifts, attractively packaged foodstuffs, fashion and home accessories are artfully displayed – you might find jeweled espresso cups and vintage handbags in the mix. A central CD station is manned by a DJ, and satellite rooms are devoted to bed, bath and cult beauty products. Also included are men's and women's collections from the likes of Marni, Dries Van Noten and Jane Mayle. *Photo p159.*

Macy's

450 Washington Street, at Summer Street, Downtown (1-617 357 3000, www.macys.com). Downtown Crossing or Park St T. **Open** 10am-9pm Mon-Sat; 11am-8pm Sun. **Credit** AmEx, MC, V. **Map** p272 K5.

Macy's replaced Boston institution Jordan Marsh in 1996 (there's even a plaque outside commemorating the dearly departed store), but in fact it was more of a conversion than a hostile takeover, since Federated Department Stores, Macy's umbrella company, already owned Jordan's. Macy's sells brand-name clothing, cosmetics, homewares, furniture and lingerie, but those expecting the scale or choice of the famous New York store will likely be disappointed by this more modest Boston outpost.

Neiman Marcus

5 Copley Place, at Dartmouth Street, Back Bay (1-617 536 3660, www.neimanmarcus.com). Back Bay or Copley T. **Open** 10am-8pm Mon-Sat; noon-6pm Sun. **Credit** AmEx. **Map** p275 G6.

Situated in the posh Copley Place mall, Neiman Marcus is the place to come for big-name international designer fashion and accessories. Customer service is excellent, and the cosmetics department has a good selection of cult brands such as Darphin and Laura Mercier.

Saks Fifth Avenue

Prudential Center, 800 Boylston Street, at Gloucester Street, Back Bay (1-617 262 8500, www.saks.com). Copley or Prudential T. **Open** 10am-9pm Mon-Sat; noon-6pm Sun. **Credit** AmEx, MC, V. **Map** p274 G6.

Entered from the Pru mall or Ring Road, the formerly staid (and much smaller) branch of the famous New York store got a slick revamp a few years ago. The

---

Where to Shop

A neighborhood by neighborhood guide.

DOWNTOWN
Once the city's main shopping area, crowded Downtown Crossing has been in decline since it lost one of its landmark department stores. It's now primarily the domain of discount chains, mobile-phone outlets and electrical stores. There are more global chains (and tourist gift shops) at Faneuil Hall Marketplace.

BEACON HILL
Antiques shops dominate the main street, but a handful of stylish boutiques has moved in; cut down River Street for a hidden cache.

BACK BAY
This area has the highest concentration of clothing stores, from international chains to exclusive designer salons, several department stores and a couple of malls, plus a good sprinkling of intriguing independent boutiques. Newbury Street is the retail backbone, but shops are spreading out to Boylston Street, which has a string of ultra-exclusive names in the Heritage on the Garden complex at the corner of Arlington Street. Newbury Street gets funkier as it progresses west from the Public Garden.

SOUTH END
Although this hip district is choked with restaurants and bars, its shops are spaced further apart (though the gaps are rapidly being filled in). Thanks to the stylish gay population, the area has become a hub for chic home and gift shops, but there are also scattered fashion boutiques, cool children's shops and pet-accessory emporia.

NORTH END
Boston's Italian quarter is known for its old-fashioned specialist food shops, but a smattering of fashion boutiques adds to its retail attractions.

CAMBRIDGE
Across the Charles River, student-dominated Harvard Square has a few survivors of what was once a thriving bookstore enclave. While some offbeat independent shops remain, the area has become increasingly bland. For more unusual shopping ops, either head north up Massachusetts Avenue towards Porter Square, or south to Central Square, which counts a legendary second-hand record shop among its handful of idiosyncratic gems.

CONSUME

Barneys New York. *See p156.*

ground-floor designer accessories department is arranged in mini 'boutiques', while cosmetics is similarly divided up into individually labeled stands. It's a good place to snap up popular young sportswear labels such as Vince, but service can be patchy.

MALLS

CambridgeSide Galleria
100 CambridgeSide Place, off Edwin H Land Boulevard, Cambridge (1-617 621 8666, www. cambridgesidegalleria.com). Kendall/MIT T then free shuttle bus, or Lechmere T. **Open** *10am-9.30pm Mon-Sat; 11am-7pm Sun.* **Map** *p272 H2.*
The only major retail oasis within striking distance of curiously shop-free Kendall Square, the Galleria is good for stocking up on inexpensive basics from the likes of J Crew, Old Navy and Abercrombie & Fitch. It also has one of the Boston area's Apple Stores (*see p161*) – a bonus for students from nearby MIT.
▶ *There's a free shuttle bus service to and from the Kendall/MIT T station every 20 minutes.*

Copley Place
100 Huntington Avenue, at Ring Road, Back Bay (1-617 369 5000, www.simon.com). Back Bay or Copley T. **Open** *10am-9pm Mon-Sat; 11am-6pm Sun.* **Map** *p275 G6.*
This upmarket mall gets better and better: cool designer department store Barneys New York recently moved in, with the socialites' favorite footwear brand, Jimmy Choo, hot on its heels. Copley Place has an 11-screen cinema, two hotels and 100 stores, including Gucci, Louis Vuitton, Tiffany, Neiman Marcus and less rarefied names such as Banana Republic, J Crew and Victoria's Secret, plus gems such as a branch of New York

cult apothecary CO Bigelow. A glass-enclosed bridge connects it to its more pedestrian counterpart at the Prudential Center.

Mall at Chestnut Hill
199 Boylston Street, off Route 9, Chestnut Hill (1-617 965 3037, www.mallatchestnuthill.com). Chestnut Hill T then 15min walk, or Kenmore T then bus 60. **Open** *10am-9.30pm Mon-Fri; 10am-8pm Sat; noon-6pm Sun.*
This mall is geared towards a customer base of affluent suburbanites. It houses New England's only two Bloomingdale's stores – one for women's clothing and accessories, and one at the other end of the mall for men's clothing and homewares – and a mix of mid-range and designer fashion brands, including Brooks Brothers, Coach, local chain Jasmine Sola, a small outpost of Barneys New York, beauty emporium Sephora, local traditional jewellers Shreve, Crump & Low and an Apple Store.
▶ *While you're in the area check out the nearby Atrium Mall (www.atrium-mall.com), which has MAC cosmetics, Anthropologie and Williams-Sonoma homewares, among other stores.*

Shops at Prudential Center
800 Boylston Street, between Fairfield & Gloucester Streets, Back Bay (1-800 746 7778, www.prudentialcenter.com). Copley, Hynes or Prudential T. **Open** *10am-9pm Mon-Sat; 11am-6pm Sun.* **Map** *p274 F6.*
Packed with workers from the landmark 52-floor office tower, this shopping center gets a bit manic at lunchtime. The majority of stores are mid-range chains (Club Monaco, Ann Taylor, Sunglass Hut) and useful retailers, such as the Travel 2000 luggage store, Olympia Sports, Barnes & Noble Booksellers and cosmetics emporium Sephora. The complex also encompasses department stores Saks and Lord & Taylor. Vending carts selling tourist merchandise clutter the corridors, but there are some convenient facilities, such as cash machines, a post office and a tourist information desk. There are also plenty of places to eat, from pizza stands to sushi restaurants.

MARKETS

For farmers' markets, *see p171.*

SoWa Open Market
540 Harrison Avenue, at Union Park Street, South End (www.southendopenmarket.com). Silver Line Washington St to Union Park St. **Open** *May-Oct 10am-4pm Sun.* **No credit cards.** **Map** *p275 J8.*
As part of SoWa's transformation into a hip art destination, artists and vendors set up stalls in a parking lot every Sunday during the warmer months to sell their work. Antiques, art, handmade jewelry and other accessories are among the mix, along with a few bakers and other food sellers.

Specialist

BOOKS & MAGAZINES

General

Borders Books & Music has a large outpost downtown (10-24 School Street, at Washington Street, 1-617 557 7188, www.bordersstores.com). In Cambridge, student standby the **Harvard Coop** (1400 Massachusetts Avenue, at John F Kennedy Street, 1-617 499 2000, www.the coop.com) has a large selection across all categories and, often, discount tables. For **Trident Booksellers & Café**, *see p123*.

Brookline Booksmith
279 Harvard Street, at Beacon Street, Brookline (1-617 566 6660, www.brookline booksmith.com). Coolidge Corner T. **Open** 8.30am-11pm Mon-Fri; 9am-11pm Sat; 10am-8pm Sun. **Credit** AmEx, MC, V.
It's easy to find what you're looking for at this cheery Coolidge Corner bookstore, with its friendly staff and fine selection of new books. There's a charming children's reading area in the back, near a gift section stocked with greeting cards, toys and novelties. In the used-book cellar, shelves are pushed aside for readings with local and emerging writers.

Louis. *See p156.*

Harvard Book Store
1256 Massachusetts Avenue, at Plympton Street, Harvard Square, Cambridge (1-617 661 1515, www.harvard.com). Harvard T. **Open** 9am-11pm Mon-Sat; 10am-10pm Sun. **Credit** AmEx, MC, V. **Map** p276 B2.
This independent bookseller in Harvard Square works hard to rival the larger chain stores with its varied selection of general-interest books and helpful staff, always ready to recommend a title or two. Students crowd the substantial philosophy and cultural theory sections. Meanwhile, local bibliophiles make a beeline for the basement, where the used and remainder book shelves are packed with everything from dog-eared cookbooks to gorgeous art books, all at a hefty discount.

Specialist

Curious George Goes to WordsWorth
1 John F Kennedy Street, at Brattle Street, Harvard Square, Cambridge (1-617 498 0062, www.curiousg.com). Harvard T. **Open** 10am-7pm daily. **Credit** AmEx, MC, V. **Map** p276 B2.
Its parent shop, WordsWorth, has closed, but the children's branch (named after the fictional monkey whose creator, Margret Rey, used to frequent the old bookstore) lives on. The jungle-themed upstairs room offers parenting and baby books, board books, picture books, early readers and non-fiction tomes; older readers will find chapter books, Tintin, Asterix and anime works downstairs. But beware: your kids may not even notice the books among the profusion of toys, games and art supplies.

★ Grolier Poetry Book Shop
6 Plympton Street, at Massachusetts Avenue, Harvard Square, Cambridge (1-617 547 4648, www.grolierpoetrybookshop.com). Harvard T. **Open** 11am-7pm Tue, Wed; 11am-6pm Thur-Sat. **Credit** MC, V. **Map** p276 B2.
Down a side street from the Harvard Book Store, the tiny Grolier has been catering to the voracious appetites of Cambridge poetry lovers for more than 80 years. Every available surface is piled with new books of verse, ranging from anthologies for casual readers to collections by obscure poets in translation. The Grolier further encourages the appreciation of poetry through its annual prizes and well-attended readings. *Photo p160.*

Used & antiquarian

Ars Libri
500 Harrison Avenue, at Randolph Street, South End (1-617 357 5212, www.arslibri.com). Back Bay T, or Silver Line Washington St to E Berkeley St. **Open** 9am-6pm Mon-Fri; 11am-5pm Sat. Closed Sat in Aug. **Credit** AmEx, MC, V. **Map** p275 J8.

CONSUME

THE BEST PRINTED WORDS

Brookline Booksmith
A touring-author favorite. *See p159.*

Grolier Poetry Book Shop
Local poets' hangout. *See p159.*

Harvard Book Store
New and used. *See p159.*

Trident Booksellers
Bibliophiles and beers. *See p123.*

With tomes on everyone from Henri Matisse to David Hockney, this sprawling store is a haven for art-history buffs. Set on the outskirts of the South End, Ars Libri specialises in rare and out-of-print books on fine art. Check the website for details of the latest art exhibition at the store's Mario Diacono Gallery.
▶ *Ars Libri is just a few buildings down from a cluster of contemporary galleries at 450 Harrison Avenue; see p196.*

★ **Brattle Book Shop**
9 West Street, at Washington Street, Downtown (1-617 542 0210, www.brattlebookshop.com). Downtown Crossing or Park St T. **Open** 9am-5.30pm Mon-Sat. **Credit** AmEx, MC, V. **Map** p272 K5.

Grolier Poetry Book Shop. *See p159.*

Established in 1825, this highly regarded antiquarian bookshop in the heart of downtown has amassed around 250,000 books, maps, prints and other collectible items; the abundant stock spills over into a substantial outdoor space, so you can browse alfresco.

CHILDREN
Fashion

Pixie Stix
131 Charles Street, between Mount Vernon & Pinckney Streets, Beacon Hill (1-617 523 3211, www.pixiestixboston.com). Charles/MGH T. **Open** 10am-7pm Mon-Sat; 11am-6pm Sun. **Credit** AmEx, MC, V. **Map** p272 H3.
Sister store to Red Wagon, Pixie Stix caters to 'tween' girls (sizes 7-16) with casual and semi-formal clothes in lollipop colors. The classic styles won't embarrass parents (or daughters), and there are Lemony Snicket and Beacon Street Girls books available for tweens' reading pleasure.

Red Wagon
69 Charles Street, at Mount Vernon Street, Beacon Hill (1-617 523 9402, www.theredwagon. com). Charles/MGH T. **Open** 10am-7pm Mon-Sat; 11am-6pm Sun. **Credit** AmEx, MC, V. **Map** p272 H3.
This place is the perfect bribe for children who are being dragged unwillingly to Beacon Hill's charming antique shops. Here you'll find mid range designer kids' clothes and shoes for boys and girls, in sizes from newborn to 6/7. Brands include Catamini, Marimekko and Room Seven, and pieces range from charming little smocked dresses to cotton sweaters with pirate skulls on the front. It also stocks picture books and toys, card games for travel play and bright things for babies to chew.

Tadpole
37 Clarendon Street, South End (1-617 778 1788, www.shoptadpole.com). Back Bay T. **Open** 10am-6pm Tue-Sat; noon-5pm Sun. **Credit** AmEx, MC, V. **Map** p275 H7.
The offspring of women's boutique Turtle, Tadpole is designed for the thoroughly modern child. From Dwell crib sets and posh print T-shirts to play tents and spy gear, it will outfit your little darling for life in the city with clothes and toys you'll be hard-pressed to find elsewhere.

Toys

You'll also find toys at children's clothing shops (*see above*) and at the bookshop **Curious George Goes to WordsWorth** (*see p159*).

★ **Magic Beans**
312 Harvard Street, at Babcock Street, Brookline (1-617 264 2326, www.mbeans.com). Coolidge

Tadpole.

Corner T. **Open** 10am-7pm Mon-Wed; 10am-8pm Thur-Sat; 10am-6pm Sun. **Credit** AmEx, MC, V.
Hands-down the best toy store in town, Magic Beans also carries books for kids and parents, and has a large range of baby and nursing gear. Plunk your offspring in the fenced play area in the back and shop for board games, Lego, Playmobil, Thomas the Tank Engine trains, Groovy Girls and art supplies.
▶ *Teen siblings can stroll over to New England Comics next door, or to Eureka Puzzles & Games around the corner at 1349 Beacon Street.*

Stellabella Toys
1360 Cambridge Street, Inman Square, Cambridge (1-617 491 6290, www.stellabella toys.com). Central T then bus 83. **Open** 9.30am-7pm Mon-Sat; 10am-5pm Sun. **Credit** AmEx, MC, V. **Map** p276 C2.
This Cambridge favorite, selling a wide array of traditional and educational toys, now has a second branch near Porter Square that visitors may find more convenient than its original tucked-away Inman Square location. However, only the original offers the popular program of activities such as singalongs and playgroups.
Other locations 1967 Massachusetts Avenue, Porter Square, Cambridge (1-617 864 6290).

ELECTRONICS & PHOTOGRAPHY
General

All-purpose electronics/communications chain **Radio Shack** has branches throughout the city, including one at Downtown Crossing (13 School Street, at Washington Street, 1-617 367 5885, www.radioshack.com).

Specialist

There are three branches of the **Apple Store** serving Boston: one in the CambridgeSide Galleria mall, one in the Mall at Chestnut Hill (for both, *see p158* **Malls**) and the newest, a massive Boylston Street location (no.815, at Fairfield Street, 1-617 385 9400, www.apple. com). All have Genius Bars offering technical support for the technologically confused.

Calumet Photographic
65 Bent Street, at First Street, Kendall Square, Cambridge (1-617 576 2600, www.calumet photo.com). Kendall/MIT or Lechmere T. **Open** 8.30am-5.30pm Mon-Fri; 9am-5.30pm Sat. **Credit** AmEx, MC, V.
This is where local photojournalists buy their gear – the *Boston Globe* has an account here. It has an extensive range of professional photographic equipment for sale or to rent, along with an impressive digital department. Friendly and knowledgeable salespeople round out the experience, making it a friendly place for budding photogs as well.

FASHION

Newbury Street is, among other things, the epicenter of fashion, where you'll find everything from impeccably hip designer wear (**Marc Jacobs** is at no.81, between Berkeley & Clarendon Streets, 1-617 425 0707, www.marcjacobs.com) to preppy standards at **Brooks Brothers** (no.46, at Berkeley Street, 1-617 267 2600, www.brooksbrothers.com) and one-stop style shop **Urban Outfitters** (no.361, at Massachusetts Avenue, 1-617 236 0088, www.urbanoutfitters.com). A branch of laid-back women's clothing and interiors store **Anthropologie** also has a nearby location (799 Boylston Street, at Fairfield Street, 1-617 262 0545, www.anthropologie.com).

Designer

★ Alan Bilzerian
34 Newbury Street, between Arlington & Berkeley Streets, Back Bay (1-617 536 1001, www.alan bilzerian.com). Arlington T. **Open** 10am-6pm Mon-Wed, Fri, Sat; 10am-7pm Thur. **Credit** AmEx, MC, V. **Map** p275 H5.
For 40 years, this trailblazing boutique has been bringing cutting-edge European fashion to Boston. The eclectic mix for men and women includes Lanvin, Yohji Yamamoto, Ann Demeulemeester and Italian line Carpe Diem.

Flock
274 Shawmut Avenue, between Hanson & Milford Streets, South End (1-617 391 0222, www.flock boston.com). Silver Line Washington St to Union Park St. **Open** 11am-7pm Tue-Sat; noon-5pm Sun. **Credit** AmEx, MC, V. **Map** p275 J7.
Opened by a mother-daughter duo, this South End boutique is the perfect place for ladies of all ages to try on girly wares from hard-to-find designers, with an emphasis on proprietor favorite Lauren Moffatt. Tucked away just off the main drag of Tremont Street, the shop's rustic, whimsical decor is positively enthralling.

Holiday
53 Charles Street, between Mount Vernon & Chestnut Streets, Beacon Hill (1-617 973 9730, www.holidayboutique.net). Charles/MGH T. **Open** 11am-7pm Mon-Thur; 11am-6pm Fri; 10am-6pm Sat; noon-5pm Sun. **Credit** AmEx, MC, V. **Map** p275 J4.
Set up by two friends (one a British expat), this women's boutique also has a branch in LA. The vibe is fashionably laid-back, with clothes by youthful American and Europan designers (3.1 Phillip Lim, Paul & Joe, Tart, J Brand), displayed in white-painted armoires in the small but airy space.

★ Stel's
334 Newbury Street, between Hereford Street & Massachusetts Avenue, Back Bay (1-617 262 3348, www.shopstels.com). Hynes T. **Open** 11am-7pm Mon-Sat; noon-6pm Sun. **Credit** AmEx, MC, V. **Map** p274 F6.
It may be one of the hippest designer emporiums in Boston, but there's nothing flashy about Stel's. In fact, its subterranean premises are easily missed. The clothes for men and women, displayed on industrial rails and beat-up wooden tables, are similarly understated but no less achingly cool – deluxe basics by APC, plus jeans by Acne and designs by Maine-based sportswear company Rogues Gallery. *Photo p165.*

Turtle
619 Tremont Street, at Dartmouth Street, South End (1-617 266 2610, www.turtleboston.com). Back Bay T. **Open** 11am-7pm Mon, Wed-Fri; 10am-6pm Tue, Sat; noon-5pm Sun. **Credit** AmEx, MC, V. **Map** p275 H8.
The look is more individualistic than catwalk-led at this boutique stocking womenswear by emerging designers, both local and from further afield. Norwood-based Cheng Lin makes beautifully simple basics, such as wrap dresses, in high quality fabrics, while twin silversmiths Kerry Alice and Heather Collins's lovely twig jewelry is handcrafted.

Wish
49 Charles Street, at Mount Vernon Street, Beacon Hill (1-617 227 4441). Charles/MGH T. **Open** 10am-7pm Mon-Wed, Fri; 10am-8pm Thur; 10am-6pm Sat; noon-6pm Sun. **Credit** AmEx, MC, V. **Map** p272 J4.
Looking for the perfect retro-styled dress? This jam-packed boutique is a good bet, with an almost overwhelming array of frocks in various prints and cuts by Milly, Nanette Lepore, Rebecca Taylor and Tibi, as well as separates, jeans and T-shirts from Vince, Velvet and Splendid. The house style lies between well-groomed preppy and urban sophisticate.

Discount

Downtown Crossing has a concentrated cache of discount stores. The fabled **Filene's Basement** (*see p164* **The Basement Goes**

Flock.

Upmarket?) is in an indefinite holding pattern, so devotees have to get their fix at the Back Bay outpost. **TJ Maxx** (350 Washington Street, 1-617 695 2424) provides fertile bargain-hunting ground for mid-range brand-name and designer clothing (Liz Claiborne, Polo, Tommy Hilfiger) for men, women and children, plus gifts, homewares and accessories. In the same building, **Marshalls** (1-617 338 6205) offers similar fare. Reductions at both range from around 20 to 50 per cent. Across the street, **DSW** (385 Washington Street, 1-617 556 0052) has a huge range of branded shoes at discounts of up to 50 per cent.

Filene's Basement

497 Boylston Street, at Berkeley Street, Back Bay (1-617 424 5520, www.filenesbasement.com). Arlington T. **Open** 9am-9pm Mon-Sat; 11am-7pm Sun. **Credit** AmEx, MC, V. **Map** p275 H6.
See p164 **The Basement Goes Upmarket?**

General

Jean Therapy

524 Commonwealth Avenue, at Brookline Avenue, Kenmore, Back Bay (1-617 266 6555, www.jean-therapy.com). Kenmore Square T. **Open** 11am-7pm Mon-Sat; noon-6pm Sun. **Credit** MC, V. **Map** p274 D6.
Finding the perfect pair of jeans can be stressful – but this specialist store claims to provide a 'therapeutic' approach. Certainly, staff are friendly and helpful, and the selection is impressive, with denim from such old favorites and new discoveries as Earnest Sewn, Grass, Rich & Skinny and Denim for Immortality.

Johnny Cupcakes

279 Newbury Street, at Gloucester Street, Back Bay (1-617 375 0100, www.johnnycupcakes.com). Copley or Hynes T. **Open** 11am-8pm Mon-Thur, Sun; 10am-9pm Fri, Sat. **Credit** AmEx, MC, V. **Map** p274 F6.
Former metal/hardcore keyboard player Johnny Earle started selling his sweetly subversive T-shirt designs while working at a local record store. It was only a matter of time before they were selling like – cupcakes! Choose from a classic cupcake and cross-bones or such slogans as 'Make cupcakes not war'. Shirts are sold in plastic cake boxes and displayed in 'fridges' and on bakery trolleys – and the store doles out free cupcakes on occasional weekends.

Karmaloop

301 Newbury Street, at Hereford Street, Back Bay (1-617 369 0100, www.karmaloopboston. com). Hynes T. **Open** noon-8pm Mon-Thur; 11am-9pm Fri, Sat; noon-7pm Sun. **Credit** AmEx, MC, V. **Map** p274 F6.
What began as a modest online fashion boutique based in Boston has graduated to a trendy flagship

INSIDE TRACK
GETTING INTO THE OUTLETS

If your travel plans include renting a car, take advantage of discounted deals on brand names at outlet-shopping destinations outside the city. Heading south, check out **Wrentham Village Premium Outlets** (www.premiumoutlets. com); with 170 stores, this accessible outdoor mall is the closest to the city. North of Boston are the **Kittery Outlets** (www.thekitteryoutlets.com). At just over an hour, the trip to Kittery, Maine, is scenic and offers off-the-path attractions as a bribe for those in your party who aren't keen on trundling around the endless shops. The **Lee Outlets** (www.primeoutlets.com), 125 miles west of Boston, are a bit out of the way for a day trip, but are a great option if you plan on staying overnight in the Berkshires.

on Newbury Street. With clients such as hip hop superstar Kanye West, Karmaloop is a good place to funk up your wardrobe with its unrivaled selection of hoodies, bags, shoes and denim for both sexes from around 100 brands, from anarchic T-shirts by Fuct, Obey and Manifest Worldwide to exclusive, limited-editon footwear collaborations with the likes of Puma.
▶ *Karmaloop also hosts nightlife events; see their website for what's coming up.*

Mint Julep

6 Church Street, at Harvard Square, Cambridge (1-617 576 6468, www.shopmintjulep.com). Harvard T. **Open** 10am-7pm Mon-Wed; 10am-8pm Thur-Sat; 11am-6pm Sun. **Credit** AmEx, MC, V. **Map** p276 A2.
The first branch of this women's boutique was launched by two Harvard graduates in Brookline in 2004, swiftly followed by this larger Harvard Square shop. Mint Julep offers an appealing melange of labels (both European and American), styles, prints and prices – the only unifying factor is an underlying postmodern country-club aura. You'll find lots of retro-influenced dresses, cool T-shirts and colorful accessories by the likes of Tibi, Milly, Orla Kiely and Kenzie, as well as less expensive brands.
Other locations 1302 Beacon Street, at Coolidge Corner, Brookline (1-617 232 3600).

★ Uniform

511 Tremont Street, at Dwight Street, South End (1-617 247 2360, www.uniformboston.com). Back Bay T. **Open** 11am-7pm Tue, Wed; 11am-8pm Thur-Sat; noon-5pm Sun. **Credit** AmEx, MC, V. **Map** p275 J7.

The Basement Goes Upmarket?

Plans for a rebirth of the iconic store remain in limbo.

In 2007, bargain-loving Bostonians suffered a terrible blow when **Filene's Basement** (*see p163*) shut its doors. However, fans of the city's landmark discount store were placated knowing it would reopen in just two years, after extensive refurbishment. A tower housing a luxury hotel, a restaurant, condos and new shops was set to replace the topside companion department store, Filene's. The plan was to usher in a new era of retail in Downtown Crossing, an area that, like other downtown shopping districts in cities across America, had lost its luster.

That was four years ago. The bad economy coupled with development deals gone sour have left a bombed-out crater where Filene's Basement was, and Downtown Crossing is still little more than a Macy's, an antiquated mall and a series of mobile-phone stores.

A Boston legend, the Basement was founded by Edward A Filene in 1908 to sell excess merchandise from his father's department store (the stores were completely separate from 1987). Soon, other retailers were offloading their unsold goods on Filene – and so the 'off-price' store was born. There are now 25 branches across the country, including an (above-ground) branch in Back Bay (*see p163*), which offers great discounts on designer merchandise from the likes of Barneys New York and Neiman Marcus.

The good news is that the famous wedding gown sale, the 'Running of the Brides', still happens at the Hynes Convention Center. Instituted in 1947, the biannual event is traditionally held on the Friday after Valentine's Day and in mid August. Gowns retail from $249 to $699, but some are worth $10,000.

There are many tales about the Basement. One woman wrote about how she found a bridal gown with 'Maria' mysteriously written on the lining. It happened to fit her daughter Maria perfectly. Another bought a wedding dress for $12 in 1946. Subsequently, five of her friends also wore 'the buy of her life' when it was their turn to walk down the aisle. Before the addition of dressing rooms, the store's central staircase was a prime spot for peeping Toms watching women change in their lunch hour. In 1972, an escalator was installed, spoiling their furtive fun. Although the store introduced dressing rooms in 1991, some people continued to change in the open.

Wily bargain-seekers have been known to try to beat the system, squirrelling away items such as brassieres in men's shoes, so they could retrieve them when they were further marked down. It is rumored that former Massachusetts governor Michael Dukakis hid clothing – a fruitless ploy as a crew was employed overnight to put things back. One man even wrote 'hole in leg' on the tags of suits to discourage other shoppers. There were skirmishes over items, but the Basement also had its share of love stories. In 1958, one man let a woman have a shirt if she would have coffee with him. She said yes, and yes again – six months later they were married.

When the Downtown Crossing store will reopen is uncertain. In 2010, a scaled-back plan was pitched that didn't include the tower of condos, but that summer Mayor Thomas Menino spoke out against the idea, saying it would only generate revenue for the developer. Until a consensus is reached, residents will shake their heads at the bombed out building and shoppers will have to head to the Back Bay location.

A one-stop shop for the fashion-conscious male, with a good selection of smart shirts, casual jackets, shoes and cheeky belt buckles. Uniform also stocks a line of Freitag messenger bags and wallets, made from recycled truck tires, and selected shaving products (from the Art of Shaving and Jack Black).

Velvet Fly
28 Parmenter Street, between Hanover & Salem Streets, North End (1-617 557 4359, www.the velvetfly.com). Haymarket T. **Open** 11am-6pm Mon; 11am-7pm Tue, Wed; 11am-8pm Thur, Fri; 10am-8pm Sat; noon-6pm Sun. **Credit** AmEx, MC, V. **Map** p273 L3.

This North End boutique has garnered lots of local attention for its impeccably edited selection of new and vintage wares, not to mention nods in *Lucky* and *Marie Claire* magazines. Sandwiched between the districts' two main thoroughfares, the stylish space offers the perfect atmosphere to browse their selection of dresses, shoes, bags and jewelry.

Used & vintage

Artifaktori
Suite A, 22 College Avenue, at Winslow Avenue, Davis Square, Somerville (1-617 776 3708, www.artifaktori.blogspot.com). Davis T. **Open** noon-8pm Tue-Fri; noon-6pm Sat, Sun. **Credit** AmEx, MC, V.

This crowded nook in Davis Square looks like it could almost be the well-curated closet of the shop's eccentric owner. The glass counter houses an epic assemblage of costume jewelry, while the walls are covered in the shop's brightest dresses and blouses. Quirky homewares, such as a selection of antique barware, are scattered throughout the store, which has plenty to choose from for both men and women. *Photo p166.*

★ Bobby from Boston
19 Thayer Street, at Harrison Avenue, South End (1-617 423 9299). Back Bay T, or Silver Line Washington St to E Berkeley St. **Open** noon-6pm Tue-Sat. **No credit cards. Map** p275 J8.

Bobby Garnett's fabulous vintage emporium in the SoWa warehouse gallery complex is well known to Japanese denim aficionados, movie wardrobe professionals and local rockers. The pristine stock spans the 1930s to the '70s and, although women's clothes are sold, the focus is on menswear. Here you'll find $25 pairs of 501s and three-figure vintage versions, American sportswear and lots of cool suits, including English labels from the 1960s.
▶ *For more about SoWa, see p158.*

Dame
68 South Street, at Carolina Avenue, Jamaica Plain (1-617 935 6971, www.jpdame.com). Green Street T. **Open** noon-7pm Wed-Fri; 11am-7pm Sat; 11am-6pm Sun. **Credit** MC, V.

Stel's. *See p162.*

This JP boutique stocks tons of high-end vintage and vintage-inspired wares such as refashioned clothing and jewelry from decades past, upcycled accessories and new pieces sewn from vintage patterns. Despite the feminine leanings of the name, Dame does sell a small but swanky collection of menswear.

Garment District & Dollar-a-Pound+
200 Broadway, at Davis Street, Kendall Square, Cambridge (1-617 876 5230, www.garment-district.com). Kendall/MIT T. **Open** 11am-8pm Mon-Fri, Sun; 9am-8pm Sat. **Credit** AmEx, MC, V.

A source of second-hand and vintage threads for cash-strapped students and rockers since the 1980s, Garment District shares its crumbling warehouse premises with a costume shop – the perfect combination if you're off to a fancy-dress party. On the ground floor is the fabled Dollar-a-Pound – literally a pile of clothes, shoes, belts, bags and assorted junk dumped in a pile on the floor. It's a rummager's dream, but due to inflation, you'll actually pay $1.50 a pound. Head upstairs for a vast array of second-hand jeans, branded clothing and vintage attire, some of it unworn – we loved the immaculate 1950s PJs.

Great Eastern Trading Co
49 River Street, at Auburn Street, Central Square, Cambridge (1-617 354 5279). Central Square T. **Open** noon-7pm Mon-Fri; noon-6.30pm Sat. **Credit** AmEx, MC, V. **Map** p276 C3.

This fun, friendly vintage shop on River Street was one of the first in the city, and it still maintains a high

CONSUME

THE BEST VINTAGE WEAR

Artifaktori
A well-curated collection for all. *See p165.*

Bobby from Boston
Top choice for men. *See p165.*

Dame
First lady of JP. *See p165.*

Velvet Fly
Budget-conscious boutique style.
See p165.

standard of second-hand clothing and accessories –
expect an enticing melange of western shirts, belly-
dancing outfits, DJs and glittery platform boots.

Poor Little Rich Girl

*166 Newbury Street, between Dartmouth &
Exeter Streets, Back Bay (1-617 425 4874).
Copely T.* **Open** noon-6pm Mon-Fri, Sun; 11am-
7pm Sat. **Credit** AmEx, MC, V. **Map** p275 G6.
The bulk of the merchandise at this second-hand
emporium is modern consignment stock from mainstream labels such as Anthropologie and J Crew at
snap-uppable prices (skirts start at around $10,
dresses from $25), but there are also pieces from the
1940s to the '80s. Well-preserved handbags, shoes
and jewelry add to the appeal. *Photo p168.*
Other locations 121 Hampshire Street, at
Columbia Street, Cambridge (1-617 873 0809).

FASHION ACCESSORIES & SERVICES

Cleaning & repairs

Ares Shoe Repair

*84 Charles Street, between Pinckney & Mount
Vernon Streets, Beacon Hill (1-617 720 1583).
Charles/MGH T.* **Open** 8.30am-5.30pm Mon-
Fri; 8.30pm-3pm Sat. **No credit cards**.
Map p272 H4.
Don't expect much small talk, but if you're after
expert, reasonably priced shoe repairs, this tradi-
tional workshop below street level is a rare find.

Bush Quality Cleaners

*219 Newbury Street, between Fairfield & Exeter
Streets, Back Bay (1-617 236 1774, www.bush
qualitycleaners.com). Copley T.* **Open** 7am-7pm
Mon-Fri; 8am-6pm Sat; 10am-5pm Sun. **Credit**
AmEx, MC, V. **Map** p275 G6.
This environmentally friendly dry cleaners uses the
silicone-based GreenEarth Cleaning solvent, and has
several locations around town.
Other locations Prudential Center, Lower
Level, 800 Boylston Street, Back Bay (1-617 266
1388); 75-101 Federal Street, Downtown (1-617
261 0611); One International Place, Downtown
(1-617 261 0113).

Hillside Cleaners

*49A Brattle Street, at Farwell Place, Harvard
Square, Cambridge (1-617 354 1872). Harvard
T.* **Open** 7.30am-6pm Mon-Sat. **Credit** AmEx,
MC, V. **Map** p276 A2.

Artifaktori. *See p165.*

The 'Sudden Service' at this trusted Cambridge dry cleaners is remarkably speedy: get it in by 11am and collect at 5pm.

Clothing hire

★ Keezer's

140 River Street, at Kinnaird Street, Central Square, Cambridge (1-617 547 2455, www.keezers.com). Central T. **Open** 10am-6pm Mon-Sat. **Credit** AmEx, MC, V. **Map** p276 B3.

Established in 1895, Keezer's is the oldest second-hand clothing store in the country and a cherished local resource. Max Keezer started the company by going into Harvard dorms in order to buy barely worn fine clothing from allowance-starved heirs. As well as renting out formalwear (they outfit the Boston Symphony Orchestra), the shop sells second-hand and end-of-the-line men's suits, sports coats, overcoats and casualwear, all in good or mint condition, and with at least 75% off. Since stock comes from Neiman's, Louis and Saks, you may find Armani and Zegna among the labels.

Jewelry

20th Century Limited

73 Charles Street, at Mount Vernon Street, Beacon Hill (1-617 742 1031, www.boston vintagejewelry.com). Charles/MGH T. **Open** 11am-6pm Mon-Sat; noon-5pm Sun. **Credit** AmEx, MC, V. **Map** p275 H4.

This tiny sub-street-level shop is an Aladdin's cave, packed with glittering vintage and costume jewellery, hats, handbags and accessories for men and for women, including a massive selection of vintage cufflinks. The stock draws fur-coated Beacon Hill Brahmins as well as retro-styled hipsters. Prices start at around $50 for a pair of flashy, fabulous diamanté earrings.

Lazuli Jewelry

Suite 805, 581 Boylston Street, Back Bay (1-617 375 7879, www.lazulijewelry.com). Copley T. **Open** 10.30am-6.30pm Mon-Fri; noon-6pm Sat. **Credit** AmEx, MC, V. **Map** p275 G6.

Lana Barakat's wonderfully sleek, minimalist designs incorporate copper, gold, silver and finely braided silk ropes, with bold splashes of colorful resins and stones. The men's range, meanwhile, includes elegant matching geometric cufflinks, rings and bangles. Price tags are moderate.

Persona

Shops at Hotel Commonwealth, 504 Commonwealth Avenue, at Kenmore Street, Back Bay (1-617 266 3003, www.personastyle. com). Kenmore T. **Open** 11am-6pm Mon-Wed; 11am-7pm Thur-Sat; noon-5pm. Closed Sun in summer. **Credit** AmEx, MC, V. **Map** p274 D6.

With outposts in three upscale hotel lobbies in town, Persona showcases contemporary designer jewelry collections from the likes of Gurhan, Alexis Bittar, Coomi Jewels and Alex Soldier. The stock is unusual and varied, so there should be something to suit most tastes. Prices run from down-to-earth to stratospheric. A custom design service, courtesy of co-owner and in-house designer Gary Shteyman, is offered, but you'll pay for the privilege – a gorgeous multicolored sapphire and white gold bracelet will set you back a princely $23,585.

Other locations Ritz-Carlton Boston Common, 10 Avery Street, Downtown (1-617 574 7172; Taj Boston, 15 Arlington Street, at Newbury Street, Back Bay (1-617 912 3443).

Shreve, Crump & Low

440 Boylston Street, at Berkeley Street, Back Bay (1-617 267 9100, www.shrevecrump andlow.com). Arlington T. **Open** 10am-6pm Mon-Wed, Fri; 10am-7pm Thur; 10am-5pm Sat; noon-5pm Sun. **Credit** AmEx, MC, V. **Map** p275 H6.

This traditional jewelry and luxury gift shop, established in 1796, is the oldest in North America, though the current Back Bay premises date from the 1920s. Antique pieces are sold alongside the classic diamonds, silver and gold.

▶ *The shop's illustrious customers have included the Kennedy family and Winston Churchill.*

Lingerie & underwear

French Dressing

49 River Street, at Lime Street, Beacon Hill (1-617 723 4968, www.frenchdressinglingerie. com). Charles/MGH T. **Open** 11am-7pm Mon-Fri; 11am-6pm Sat; noon-5pm Sun. **Credit** AmEx, MC, V. **Map** p272 H4.

Underwear rails are color-coded at this delightfully pretty little lingerie boutique, tucked away in a Beacon Hill backstreet, making the barely-there offerings by Hanky Panky, Eberjay and Cosabella even more enticing. Hip night- and loungewear is provided by Skin and Loungerie.

Luggage

Kate Spade

117 Newbury Street, between Clarendon & Dartmouth Streets, Back Bay (1-617 262 2632, www.katespade.com). Copley T. **Open** 10am-6pm Mon-Sat; 11am-5pm Sun. **Credit** AmEx, MC, V. **Map** p275 G6.

Alongside the ladylike handbags by the queen of American modern-classic accessories are retro-styled rollers and cabin bags – but the prices are anything but economy. Clothes, shoes, sunglasses and other accessories are also sold, along with the Jack Spade collection – a line of men's bags designed by Kate's husband Andy.

CONSUME

Poor Little Rich Girl. *See p166.*

CONSUME

Shoes

Posh department stores (*see p156*), including **Barneys**, **Louis**, **Neiman Marcus**, and **Saks Fifth Avenue**, are good sources of designer shoes. Boston's only outpost of quirky Mallorcan company **Camper** is in Back Bay (139B Newbury Street, at Dartmouth Street, 1-617 267 4554, www.camper.com).

For some big-name brands at knock-down prices, *see p163* **DSW**.

At the Buzzer

81 Harvard Avenue, at Gardner Street, Allston (1-617 783 2899, www.atbboston.com). Harvard Ave T. **Open** noon-8pm Mon-Sat; noon-6pm Sun. **Credit** AmEx, MC, V.

This shoe consignment shop caters to sneaker-heads and collectors looking for something beyond general releases. It carries a wide selection of vintage Air Jordans, Nike SBs and Reeboks, among others. Be warned: you can expect to drop a lot of cash for these rarities.

★ Bodega

6 Clearway Street, at Massachusetts Avenue, Back Bay (no phone, www.bdgastore.com). Hynes T. **Open** 11am-6pm Mon, Wed; 11am-7pm Thur, Sat; 11am-8pm Fri; noon-5pm Sun. **Credit** MC, V. **Map** p274 F7.

At first glance, it looks like any other convenience store, the window lined with faded bleach bottles and paper towels. Something's odd though – the kid behind the counter is a little too stylish, the water stains on the ceiling are too perfect, the horse race on the TV seems to be caught in a loop and none of

the bottles of detergent seem to have moved in months. Step in front of the faux Snapple vending machine, to activate the hidden sliding door and reveal the secret store within a store. Inside is the ultra-modern interior of Boston's flyest sneaker shop – carrying rare kicks from Nike Tier Zero and Adidas Consortium, as well as deluxe streetwear and books on art and design.

▶ *For an interview with one of the owners, see left Faces & Places.*

Laced

569 Columbus Avenue, at Massachusetts Avenue, South End (1-617 262 5223, www.lacedboston. com). Mass Ave T. **Open** 11am-7pm Mon-Sat. **Credit** MC, V. **Map** p275 G8.

On the South End-Roxbury border, this 'lifestyle skate boutique' has serious street cred; local sports stars such as the Red Sox's David Ortiz come here to stock up on bling-tastic limited-edition trainers by the likes of Nike SB, Adidas and DC, plus T-shirts, sweatshirts, caps and spectacularly decorated boards.

Moxie

51 Charles Street, between Mount Vernon & Chestnut Streets, Beacon Hill (1-617 557 9991, www.moxieboston.com). Charles/MGH T. **Open** 10am-7pm Mon-Fri; 10am-6pm Sat; 11am-6pm Sun. **Credit** AmEx, MC, V. **Map** p275 J4.

It's not all antiques shops round these parts. This stylish little boutique stocks a tempting mix of shoes, bags, jewelry and accessories from popular designers such as Marc Jacobs, Hollywould, Tory Birch and Taryn Rose. The general style leans towards colorful and girly, and prices are mid range to high.

Faces & Places Oliver Mak

A Boston insider opens up.

Oliver Mak opened Bodega (*see left*) – a deluxe sneaker and streetwear emporium secreted away, Prohibition-style, behind an ersatz shopfront – in 2006 with co-owners Jay Gordon and Dan Natola. Over the years, Mak has been involved in every aspect of local hip hop culture: promoting young graffiti talent, hosting shows, DJing at parties and spearheading the shop that's got everyone in Boston talking – and acting all sneaky in a certain modest little variety store.

Time Out: What inspired Bodega?
Oliver Mak: It was basically a physical manifestation of the old-school sneaker game, which before websites and blogs was just knowledge passed from one head to another. For example, for a while Nike Air Force Ones weren't available outside of this one tiny shop in Baltimore. The culture has expanded, but the physical layout of Bodega is a metaphor for all of that: it's about the hunt. It's not about exclusivity and being cool enough. It's about knowledge, not status. Bodega is a New York name, so it's some respect towards the originators of the culture. But it's also a metaphor for the product we carry out back: immediate, disposable consumer goods, which is what fashion is.

TO: What's a store like this doing in Boston?
OM: Well, we didn't really think of the place in terms of Boston, even though we're all from here. There's actually some gritty urban culture here. I don't see much difference between, say, Central Square in Cambridge and certain parts of Brooklyn. We don't see ourselves in relation to other

shops in Boston, but those trying to lead things globally. We just try to keep our heads down and do our thing.

TO: What other shops do you rate?
OM: Stel's (*see p162*) sells sophisticated, upscale lines like APC and Nom de Guerre and the owners have a laid-back approach.

TO: Where do you hang out in the city?
OM: It's hard not to be a film buff here, with all the good indie houses in the area. The Harvard Film Archive (*see p193*) shows a lot of weird experimental films, and Coolidge Corner (*see p193*) has midnight movies and events with filmmakers. I live in Central Square, which is where all the really good nightlife stuff happens now in intimate spaces like Enormous Room (*see p149 and p213*) and Middlesex (*see p150 and p214*), which book forward-thinking DJs. The Otherside Café (*see p146*) is a beer garden/café around the corner from the shop that we frequent for the good beer selection, and it's run by our friends who are mostly vagrant artist types. It's beyond funky – not safe for families.

TO: And what do you hate?
OM: Boston is transient; there's a gigantic college population but a lack of creative and media jobs, so everyone has to move to New York or LA if they want to work in those industries. Those of us who want to stick around have had to build our own culture.

CONSUME

THE BEST FOR STREET CRED

At the Buzzer
Specializing in vintage kicks. *See p168.*

Bodega
One of Boston's most infamous
backrooms. *See p168.*

Laced
Caters to South End sneakerheads.
See p168.

FOOD & DRINK
Bakeries & confectioners

Athan's
*1621 Beacon Street, at Washington Street,
Brookline (1-617 734 7028, www.athans
bakery.com). Washington Sq T.* **Open** 8am-
10pm Mon-Thur, Sun; 8am-11pm Fri, Sat.
Credit AmEx, MC, V.
Fanciful cakelets, tender baklava diamonds, handmade, gold-foiled chocolates stacked in pyramids,
real-deal gelato (try the fig flavor) – this wood-
planked corner surprise in Washington Square over-
lays the quaintness of an old-fashioned penny candy
shop with the elegance of a European boutique. Late
opening hours are another bonus.
Other locations 407 Washington Street,
between Leicester & Parsons Streets, Brighton
(1-617 783 0313).

Ho Yuen Bakery
*54 Beach Street, at Tyler Street, Chinatown,
Downtown (1-617 426 8320). Chinatown T.*
Open 8am-7pm daily. **No credit cards.**
Bewilderment is bliss at this wee Chinatowner.
Make your way through the glassed-in proliferation
of buns and tarts to a fresh, flaky snack of pastry-
encased barbecued pork, lotus-seed paste or luscious, not-too-sweet egg custard.

★ Lulu's Bake Shoppe
*227 Hanover Street, between Cross & Richmond
Streets, North End (1-617 720 2200). Haymarket
T.* **Open** 10am-10pm Mon-Thur, Sun; 10am-
11pm Fri; 10am-midnight Sat. **Credit** MC, V.
Map p273 L3.
All dolled up like a heartland kitchen circa 1948, this
little cutie stacks its pastel buttercream-frosted cupcakes on display trees, and lines its case with fluffy
muffins, mini-cheesecakes, eclairs and definitive
peanut-butter brownies.

★ Maria's Pastry Shop
*46 Cross Street, at Salem Street, North End
(1-617 523 1196). Haymarket T.* **Open** 7am-7pm

Mon-Sat; 7am-5pm Sun. **Credit** AmEx, MC, V.
Map p273 L3.
Its homeliness overlooked by most tourists, this
long-timer fills the freshest *cannoli* in the 'hood.
Actually, most of its Italian sweets deserve superlatives for their adherence to tradition, from *torrone* and
marzipane to holiday favorites such as ricotta pie.

Drinks

★ Bauer Wine & Spirits
*330 Newbury Street, between Hereford Street
& Massachusetts Avenue, Back Bay (1-617 262
0363, www.bauerwines.com). Hynes T.* **Open**
10am-11pm Mon-Sat; noon-8pm Sun. **Credit**
AmEx, MC, V. **Map** p274 F6.
Between its smart Back Bay address and the renown
of its resident expert and co-owner, Howie Rubin,
this long-established liquor store could easily get
away with catering exclusively to its monied neighbors – a fact that makes its across-the-board accessibility all the more admirable. With one of the most
extensive selections in the city, this is an excellent
and centrally located place to source that hard to
find craft beer or Viognet.

Brix Wine Shop
*1284 Washington Street, at Savoy Street, South
End (1-617 542 2749, www.brixwineshop.com).
Back Bay T then 20min walk, or Silver Line
Washington St to Union Park St.* **Open** 11am-9pm
Mon-Sat. **Credit** AmEx, MC, V. **Map** p275 J8.
Displaying an impressive sense of style and a flair
for hospitality, this lovely cork-floored wine 'bou-
tique' is known for its weekend wine tastings,
which showcase the smaller producers (from both
Europe and the New World) its buyers specialize
in seeking out.

Central Bottle Wine & Provisions
*196 Massachusetts Avenue, at Albany Street,
Central Square, Cambridge (1-617 225 0040,
www.centralbottle.com). Central T or bus 1.*
Open 11am-8pm Mon-Wed, Sat; 11am-9pm
Thur, Fri; noon-6pm Sun. **Credit** AmEx,
MC, V. **Map** p276 C4.
This glass-fronted newcomer was opened by four
friends so enamored with the enotecas of Venice that
they just had to open their own similarly intimate
gathering place when they returned to the States.
Much more than just a wine store, the Bottle also
stocks a variety of cheeses, *salumi, torta,* craft beer
and traditional Venetian *cicchetti. Photo p172.*
▶ *Swing by on a Thursday Wine Bar evening for
wine appreciation events ranging from extolling
the virtues of the screw cap to discussing which
whites to pair with $1 Island Creek oysters.*

★ Wine Bottega
*341 Hanover Street, between Prince & North
Bennet Streets, North End (1-617 227 6607,*

CONSUME

Lulu's Bake Shoppe.

www.thewinebottega.com). Haymarket T. **Open**
11am-10pm Mon-Wed; 11am-11pm Thur; 10am-
11pm Fri, Sat; noon-8pm Sun. **Credit** AmEx,
MC, V. **Map** p273 L2.
Inch for inch, this is arguably Boston's best – not to
mention most eclectic – wine shop. An articulate
staff with a passion for the innovative and the undis-
covered guarantees that the range of its inventory
surpasses expectations for a shop this size.

Farmers' markets

Longevity and location (bordering Faneuil
Hall, on Blackstone Street between Hanover
& North Streets) are on high-profile
Haymarket's side, as are its year-round
accessibility (5am-dusk Fri, Sat) and
consistently low pricing. Fealty to sustainable
practices and organic products, however, is
not. If that's your criteria, try the small but
handsome **Copley Square Market** (St
James Avenue, in front of Trinity Church,
mid May-late Nov, 11am-6pm Tue, Fri) or
the **Boston Public Market** in downtown
Dewey Square (late May-late Nov, 11.30am-
6.30pm Mon, Tue, Thur).
   If you're willing to travel outside Boston
proper, both of Somerville's markets – in **Union
Square** (early June-late Oct, 9am-1pm Sat) and
Davis Square (at Day & Herbert Streets, late
May-Nov, noon-6pm Wed) – are especially
green and gourmet-friendly.

Specialist shops

★ Cardullo's Gourmet Shop
*6 Brattle Street, at Harvard Square, Cambridge
(1-617 491 8888, www.cardullos.com). Harvard
T.* **Open** 7am-9pm Mon-Sat; 9am-7pm Sun.
Credit AmEx, MC, V. **Map** p276 B2.
Call it a novelty shop for foodies. Negotiating
Cardullo's riotous aisles, you'll encounter chai truffles and white chocolate ants; cans of spotted dick
and jars of cassoulet; pecan vinegar and piña colada
jam; wines from Cape Cod and caviar from the
Mississippi River. You can score some fine sandwiches from the deli counter too. Brits abroad will
find store-cupboard standbys such as McVitie's bis-
cuits and Marmite – at a price.

★ Formaggio Kitchen
*244 Huron Avenue, at Appleton Street,
Huron Village, Cambridge (1-617 354 4750,
www.formaggiokitchen.com). Harvard T then
bus 72.* **Open** 9am-7pm Mon-Fri; 9am-6pm Sat;
10am-4pm Sun. **Credit** AmEx, MC, V.
When he kitted it out with a groundbreaking cheese
cave, Ihsan Gurdal landed his flagship among the
nation's top gourmet shops. Today, Formaggio
Kitchen continues to dazzle connoisseurs with its vast
collection of artisanal cheeses from the world over –
as well as its cornucopia of accoutrements. Here you'll
find condiments, charcuterie, confectionery and specialty ingredients, ranging from flowering teas and
heirloom cattle beans to Hawaiian red sea salt and
Piedmontese chickpea flour.
Other locations 268 Shawmut Avenue,
between Milford & Hanson Streets, South End
(1-617 350 6996, www.southendformaggio.com).

★ Savenor's Market
*160 Charles Street, at Cambridge Street, Beacon
Hill (1-617 723 6328, www.savenorsmarket.com).
Charles/MGH T.* **Open** 11am-8pm Mon-Fri;
10am-8pm Sat; noon-7pm Sun. **Credit** AmEx,
MC, V. **Map** p272 H3.
If you can't cook like Julia Child, at least you can
shop like her – this butcher's most celebrated customer regularly praised its meats on her TV show.

CONSUME

THE BEST FOR FOODIES

Cardullo's Gourmet Shop
International standbys and quirky new
favorites. *See above.*

Formaggio Kitchen
Iconic local deli. *See above.*

Wine Bottega
Boston's finest wine shop.
See left.

In addition to sterling traditional cuts, it carries exotic game and a select array of gourmet groceries. **Other locations** 92 Kirkland Street, at Myrtle Avenue, Cambridge (1-617 576 6328).

Supermarkets

Location, location, location: for visitors, the most convenient supermarket is likely to be the behemoth branch of **Shaw's** that sits a block off Copley Square (53 Huntington Avenue, 1-617 262 4688, www.shaws.com). For natural and organic products, your best bets in Boston proper are **Whole Foods'** two stores in Back Bay (15 Westland Avenue, at Massachusetts Avenue, 1-617 375 1010, www.wholefoods.com) and the West End (181 Cambridge Street, at Joy Street, 1-617 723 0004). We're partial to the ardently local **Harvest Co-Op** (www.harvest coop.com), with branches in Cambridge (581 Massachusetts Avenue, at Pearl Street, Central Square, 1-617 661 1580) and Jamaica Plain (57 South Street, 1-617 524 1667).

GIFTS & SOUVENIRS

★ Aunt Sadie's General Store

18 Union Park Street, at Washington Street, South End (1-617 357 7117, www.auntsadiesinc. com). Back Bay T, or Silver Line Washington St to Union Park St. **Open** 10am-5pm Mon; 10am-6pm Tue-Sat. **Credit** AmEx, MC, V. **Map** p275 J8.

A stylish, slightly camp shop selling everything from houndstooth-print napkins to watches with

Salvador Dali's moustache instead of hands. The shop always smells fantastic, as a popular line of scented candles is made on the premises, with some unusual fragrances (fresh-cut grass is nice, and even the 'Divorce Candle' smells sweeter than it should). A side room features wares from local artists and designers, plus an adorable line of children's items.

★ Black Ink

5 Brattle Street, at Harvard Square, Cambridge (1-617 497 1221, www.blackinkboston.com). Harvard T. **Open** 10am-8pm Mon-Sat; 11am-7pm Sun. **Credit** AmEx, MC, V. **Map** p276 B2.

It's wall-to-wall fun at the Cambridge outpost of a Beacon Hill original, where the eclectic stock – everything from Tintin T-shirts and Japanese toys to colorful melamine tableware, hip stationery and strikingly packaged toiletries – is arrayed on floor-to-ceiling shelves for easy browsing. **Other locations** 101 Charles Street, at Pinckney Street, Beacon Hill (1-617 723 3883).

★ Buckaroo's Mercantile

5 Brookline Avenue, at Massachusetts Avenue, Central Square, Cambridge (1-617 492 4792, www.buckmerc.com). Central T. **Open** noon-10pm Mon-Sat; noon-7pm Sun. **Credit** AmEx, MC, V. **Map** p276 C3.

A kitsch-lover's paradise, this quirky variety store sells a mix of wonderfully cheesy novelties, such as Last Supper lunchboxes and a robed 'Elvis, King of Kings' in a flashing dome. Vintage items include 1940s aprons, pulp fiction paperbacks and fruit crate stickers with unintentionally fruity brand names, along the lines of 'Blushing Melons'. Owner Brooks Morris also makes a range of retro homewares, including fabulously decorated lampshades (around $40), coasters ($14 for four) and wall clocks ($25).

★ Grand

374 Somerville Avenue, at Bow Street, Union Square, Somerville (1-617 623 2429, www.grandthestore.com). Porter T then bus 87. **Open** noon-7pm Tue-Fri; 11am-7pm Sat; noon-5pm Sun. **Credit** AmEx, MC, V. **Map** p276 C1.

The creation of three locals with an eye for design, this retail space houses contemporary home furnishings, vintage and new apparel, design books and other odds and ends from independent designers. The Union Square building was formerly a classic nickelodeon-style theater, and the owners use the interior and surrounding space to host enticingly named events, such as their monthly Sip & Shop and the annual Ice Cream Showdown.

★ Magpie

416 Highland Avenue, at Grove Street, Davis Square, Somerville (1-617 623 3330, www.magpie-store.com). Davis T. **Open** 11am-6pm Mon-Wed, Fri, Sun; 11am-8pm Thur; 11am-7pm Sat. **Credit** MC, V.

Central Bottle Wine & Provisions. *See p170.*

Crafts are cool again – as Magpie proves. Owned by four young creatives, it showcases handmade gifts, art, homewares and clothes by independent designers (some of whom live in hip Somerville), at reasonable prices. The displays are as unique as the wares: arty magnets are stuck to an old, wall-mounted fridge door, and notebooks and cards lean on a vintage typewriter. Adorable chenille cupcake pin cushions by Cape Cod-based Crazy Cakes, jewelry made from recycled cutlery and Supermaggie screen-printed T-shirts are just a few examples of the stock.

Motley
623A Tremont Street, between Dartmouth & West Canton Streets, Beacon Hill (1-617 247 6969, www.shopmotley.com). Back Bay T. **Open** 11am-7pm Mon-Sat; 11am-6pm Sun. **Credit** AmEx, MC, V. **Map** p272 H4.
Looking for a gift for the man who has everything? Head for this compact repository of cool stuff: a wide selection of arty and anarchic T-shirts, gadgets such as funky, limited-edition artist-designed USB devices, stylish coffee table tomes and retro-styled grooming products by Sharps Barber and Shop.

★ Shake the Tree
95 Salem Street, at Morton Street, North End (1-617 742 0484, www.shakethetreeboston.com). Haymarket T. **Open** 11am-8pm Tue-Thur; 11am-9pm Fri; 10am-9pm Sat; noon-6pm Sun. **Credit** MC, V. **Map** p273 L3.
A highly browsable combination of casual clothing from the likes of Ella Moss and Velvet, jewelry and accessories, unusual toiletries, stationery, and decorative homewares such as picture frames and ceramics. Some of the items, such as hip jewelry by Flauxy and Wardmaps' mousepads, printed with 19th- and early 20th-century maps of Boston, are locally made.

HEALTH & BEAUTY
Hairdressers & barbers

★ Judy Jetson
1765 Massachusetts Avenue, at Forest Street, Porter Square, Cambridge (1-617 354 2628, www.judyjetson.com). Porter T. **Open** 9am-7pm Mon-Sat; 11am-7pm Sun. **Credit** MC, V. **Map** p276 B1.

You'll be inclined to request the haircut of your stylist at this fashionable salon, named for the futuristic cartoon character. That is, if you're looking for a mohawk, faux-hawk or Technicolor tresses. The sassy yet down-to-earth staff have a good reputation for color and cater to both men and women.

Mario Russo
3rd Floor, 9 Newbury Street, at Arlington Street, Back Bay (1-617 424 6676, www.mariorusso.com). Arlington T. **Open** 10am-6pm Mon-Thur; 10am-8pm Fri; 10am-7pm Sat; 10am-5pm Sun. **Credit** AmEx, MC, V. **Map** p275 H5.
Mario Russo's salon, catering to fashionable, well-heeled Bostonians and visiting celebs alike, is often voted best in the city in the local press. Its own line of olive-based products is luscious.
Other locations Louis, Fan Pier, 60 Northern Avenue, Waterfront (1-857 350 3139).

Shag Salon
840 Summer Street, at East First Street, South Boston (1-617 268 2500, www.shagboston.com). **Open** noon-7pm Tue, Wed, Fri; 1-8pm Thur; 10am-4pm Sat. **Credit** AmEx, MC, V.
Promising 'rock star haircuts by Sandy Poirier', this hip salon in gritty South Boston is a little out of the way, but it's still your best bet for that coveted Joan Jett circa 1982 look. A far cry from the beauty parlors of Newbury Street, Shag has featured in fashion magazine spreads and a segment on MTV, and perhaps that's why you can expect to pay so much for a cut. High ceilings, stripped-down decor, and a funky clientele add to the salon's air of relaxed, self-assured cool.

State Street Barbers
1313 Washington Street, at Waltham Street, South End (1-617 753 9990, www.statestreetbarbers.com). Arlington T. **Open** 10am-9pm Mon-Thur; 10am-7pm Fri; 8am-5pm Sat; 9am-5pm Sun. **Credit** AmEx, MC, V. **Map** p275 J8.
With its dark wood interior and an old-fashioned barbershop pole beckoning, State Street Barbers looks every inch a throwback to the 1920s. But this isn't your grandfather's local barbershop, where you leave with a basic buzz cut (well, you could, but the staff are just as happy to give you a contemporary style). A standard haircut includes a shampoo and condition, a straight-razor neck shave, a shoulder massage and a drink (which, sadly, doesn't extend to granddad's Manhattans or gin and tonics). Walk-ins are welcome, and the salon also offers hot lather shaves, beard trims and exfoliating facials – another departure from the old days.

Opticians

Eye Q Optical
12 Eliot Street, at Bennett Street, Harvard Square, Cambridge (1-617 354 3303, www.eye-q-optical.com). **Open** 10am-6pm Mon-Wed,

Fri, Sat; 10am-7pm Thur; noon-4pm Sun.
Credit AmEx, MC, V. **Map** p276 A2.
Calling themselves 'fashion consultants', this mini optician's chain aims to make wearing glasses fun, with its own range of cool specs that runs from minimalist styles to striking retro looks. High-tech eye examinations, same day service and contact lenses are offered.
Other locations 544 Tremont Street, South End (1-617 542 9600); 7 Pond Street, Jamaica Plain (1-617 983 3937).

Pharmacies

Several branches of chain **CVS** are open 24 hours. The store at 587 Boylston Street, at Dartmouth Street (1-617 437 8414, www.cvs.com) also offers photo developing services.

Colonial Drug
49 Brattle Street, at Harvard Square, Cambridge (1-617 864 2222, www.colonialdrug.com). Harvard T. **Open** 8am-7pm Mon-Fri; 8am-6pm Sat. **Credit** AmEx, MC, V. **Map** p276 A2.
A family-run business, this pharmacy has not changed in appearance for decades. These days, though, the emphasis is more on luxurious scents and unguents than bromide and hot-water bottles. In particular, it specialises in hard-to-find perfumes (stocking more than 1,000 fragrances, including Guerlain and Patou), and beautifully packaged scented soaps.

Shops

The Prudential Center mall contains a branch of make-up and skincare supermarket **Sephora**, while Copley Place has an offshoot of cool New York apothecary **CO Bigelow**, which sells a variety of niche brands. As well as having a stand-alone store, cult skincare line **Kiehl's** (112 Newbury Street, between Clarendon & Dartmouth Streets, Back Bay, 1-617 247 1777, www.kiehls.com) is stocked at Neiman Marcus and Saks Fifth Avenue.

Beauty Mark
33 Charles Street, at Chestnut Street, Beacon Hill (1-617 720 1555, www.thebeautymark.com). Charles/MGH T. **Open** 11am-7pm Mon-Fri; 10am-6pm Sat; noon-5pm Sun. **Credit** AmEx, MC, V. **Map** p272 J4.
This sweet little white and blue shop sells a well-edited collection of products by, among others, Bumble and Bumble (hair), Chantecaille (make-up), SkinCeuticals (skincare) and L'Artisan Parfumeur (fragrance). Manicures, pedicures and make-up consultations are also offered.

Fresh
121 Newbury Street, between Clarendon & Dartmouth Streets, Back Bay (1-617 421 1212,

www.fresh.com). Copley T. **Open** 10am-7pm Mon-Sat; noon-6pm Sun. **Credit** AmEx, MC, V. **Map** p275 H6.
This natural cosmetics and skincare line, made from ingredients such as rice, soy and milk, was born in Boston, but now has branches throughout the US and beyond. Employees are friendly and knowledgeable, and the store occasionally transforms into a sleek space for beauty-related events after dark.

Spas & salons

Beauty spots are scattered throughout the city, but Newbury Street is the capital of preening and pampering – on this eight-block stretch alone, there are around 130 spas and salons.

★ Emerge
275 Newbury Street, between Fairfield & Gloucester Streets, Back Bay (1-617 437 0006, www.emergespasalon.com). Copley or Hynes T. **Open** 8am-8pm Mon-Wed; 8am-9pm Thur, Fri; 8am-6pm Sat; 10am-6pm Sun. **Credit** AmEx, MC, V. **Map** p274 F6.
The mother of all Newbury Street spas, the palatial multistory Emerge, which opened in 2006, really does offer everything: from cosmetic fillers (by appointment) to caviar facials and classic manicures. There's a dedicated Men's Club too; a whole floor of segregated guy heaven with plasma screen TVs. For a complete day of self-indulgence, try the seven-hour top-to-toe Ultimate Emerge Experience, which includes a LaStone massage, aromatherapy, a moor mud pedicure, caviar facial and more.

★ Exhale
28 Arlington Street, at St James Avenue, Back Bay (1-617 532 7000, www.exhalespa.com). Arlington T. **Open** 6am-9pm Mon-Fri; 9am-8pm Sat, Sun. **Credit** AmEx, MC, V. **Map** p275 H6.
Located in the upscale Heritage on the Garden complex, Exhale is a wellness-oriented spa with extensive services, including an excellent fitness and yoga program. Alongside top-notch facials, massage and the usual beautifying services, alternative therapies such as acupuncture are available. The Fusion Pedicure Plus is possibly the best tootsie treat around.

Melt
172 Newbury Street, between Dartmouth & Exeter Streets, Back Bay (1-617 262 1116, www.meltboston.com). Copley T. **Open** 10am-7pm Tue, Wed, Fri; 10am-8pm Thur; 9am-6pm Sat; 10am-4pm Sun. **Credit** AmEx, MC, V. **Map** p275 G6.
This jewel-box-like Newbury Street salon and spa features satin robes and sheets, and products by Luzern, a chemical-free Swiss skincare line that uses organic botanicals. The high-tech HydraFacial is a super-speedy but high-performance treatment – 30 minutes is all it takes to deeply cleanse the skin

CONSUME

via serums and suction, and pump in nutrients that promise to cure all skin evils.

OMBE
551 Boylston Street, at Clarendon Street, Back Bay (1-617 447 2222, www.ombe center.com). Copley T. **Open** 6am-8pm Mon-Thur; 6am-6pm Fri-Sun. **Credit** AmEx, MC, V. **Map** p275 H6.
At One Mind Body Earth Center, or OMBE, what's good for the body is good for the soul – and what's good for the planet is good for you. This holistic health spot provides massage, naturopathy, acupuncture, Pilates and more; services are delivered with organic massage oils and cotton linens, and even the yoga mats are PVC-free.

Pyara Spa & Salon
104 Mount Auburn Street, at John F Kennedy Street, Harvard Square, Cambridge (1-617 497 9300, www.pyaraaveda.com). Harvard T. **Open** 8am-10pm Mon-Fri; 8am-8pm Sat; 10am-6pm Sun. **Credit** AmEx, MC, V. **Map** p276 A2.
This chic Harvard Square establishment uses Aveda's excellent natural, eco-conscious products. For the cleanest, softest skin ever, the Caribbean Therapy Body Treatment is a relaxing ritual that exfoliates, then detoxifies and nourishes with a warm seaweed mask and body wrap, before a Vichy shower water massage and restorative face, scalp and body massage leaves you floating on a cloud.

Tattoos & piercings

★ Fat Ram's Pumpkin Tattoo
380 Centre Street, at Sheridan Street, Jamaica Plain (1-617 522 6444, www.fatramtattoo.com). Stonybrook T. **Open** 10am-10pm Mon-Sat; noon-8pm Sun. **Credit** MC, V.
About as far away from 'Mom' as you can get, the artworks created by the five tattooists here run from baby portraits to colorful abstracts. The staff is friendly, knowledgeable and certain to turn your dream ink into a reality.

HOUSE & HOME
Antiques

No hunt for antiques in Boston is complete without a trip to Charles Street, the city's unofficial 'antiques row', concentrated along a couple of blocks in picturesque Beacon Hill. Spend an afternoon here, stopping every few doors for a different selection of jewelry, silverware, clothing and furniture. **Devonia Antiques** (no.43, 1-617 523 8313, www. devonia-antiques.com) overwhelms with its gorgeous inventory of antique English porcelain and American and European

dinnerware and stemware (circa 1880-1920). **Antiques at 80 Charles** (no.80, 1-617 742 8006) is notorious for sending you away with an extra bag of items you hadn't expected, thanks to its tempting stock and helpful staff.

Abodeon
1731 Massachusetts Avenue, at Prentiss Street, Porter Square, Cambridge (1-617 497 0137, www.abodeon.com). Porter T. **Open** 10am-6pm Mon-Sat; noon-5pm Sun. **Credit** AmEx, MC, V. **Map** p276 B1.
Mid 20th-century modern style is the specialty of this fabulous vintage home store; as well as furniture, there's classic tableware, kitchen appliances and quirky knick-knacks. If you like the Peggy Lee tune you hear on the soundtrack, chances are you can find it (on vinyl, of course) among the large collection of records for sale.

★ Brodney Antiques & Jewelry
145 Newbury Street, at Dartmouth Street, Back Bay (1-617 536 0500, www.brodney.com). Copley T. **Open** 10am-6pm Mon-Sat. **Credit** AmEx, MC, V. **Map** p275 G6.
This refined treasure trove, established in 1939, sells an impressive range of antiques and curiosities. Its shelves hold an alluring mixture of pieces, from art deco jewelry, Victorian oil lamps and sterling silver punch bowls to French clocks, glassware and Asian art (including erotic Japanese watercolors). While the shop is a favorite with serious connoisseurs, casual browsers are welcome. Charm bracelet lovers take note: this place has the best collection of vintage gold charms – from tiny jeweled typewriters to cocktail glasses and dice – we've ever seen, but be prepared to pay over $100.

★ Cambridge Antique Market
201 Monsignor O'Brien Highway, at Third Street, Lechmere, Cambridge (1-617 868 9655, www.marketantique.com). Lechmere T. **Open** 11am-6pm Tue-Sun. **Credit** MC, V.
Akin to wandering through someone's attic, this five-story warehouse features more than 150 antiques dealers, peddling everything from antique furniture, homewares and dolls to clothing, lighting fixtures, books and vintage bikes. Word to the wise: the highest prices are on the more accessible floors; it's worth your while to wander up and down that slightly tilted staircase to its extremeties.

General

Hudson
312 Shawmut Avenue, at Union Park Street, South End (1-617 292 0900, www.hudsonboston. com). Back Bay T then 15min walk, or Silver Line Washington St to Union Park St. **Open** 10am-6pm Mon-Wed, Fri, Sat; 11am-7pm Thur; 11am-5pm Sun. **Credit** AmEx, MC, V. **Map** p275 H8.

CONSUME

Former actress and interior designer Jill Goldberg combines her native New England aesthetic with a laid-back Californian style. Among the creamy, plump armchairs and retro side tables is an array of tempting, unusual items such as locally designed contemporary quilts, pillows made out of vintage feed bags, antique signs and brightly colored glass soda syphons from Argentina.

Lekker
1317 Washington Street, at Rollins Street, South End (1-617 542 6464, www.lekkerhome. com). Back Bay T. **Open** 10am-7pm Tue-Sat; noon-6pm Sun. **Credit** AmEx, MC, V. **Map** p275 J8.
'Lekker' is the Dutch word for tasty and enticing, and it sums up this store's stock of well-designed, affordable merchandise. Expect an East-meets-West melange of Chinese antiques, Dutch furniture and kitchen utensils, including candy-colored tumblers and high-end knife sets. For children, there are cro-cheted toys and rattles by Anne-Claire Petit.

MUSIC & ENTERTAINMENT
CDs, records & DVDs

★ Cheapo Records
645 Massachusetts Avenue, at Prospect Street, Central Square, Cambridge (1-617 354 4455, www.cheaporecords.com). Central T. **Open** 11am-7pm Mon-Wed, Sat; 11am-9pm Thur, Fri; 11am-5pm Sun. **Credit** MC, V. **Map** p276 C3.
When Skippy White's – the fabled store for serious connoisseurs of old-school R&B, jazz, gospel and hip-hop – closed in 2006, the equally legendary Cheapo Records moved into the space. It still stocks some of the best vinyl in the area, with good prices and solid sections for pop/rock, folk, oldies, jazz and country, along with CDs and hard-to-find box sets.

Twisted Village Records
12B Eliot Street, at Bennett Street, Harvard Square, Cambridge (1-617 354 6898, www. twistedvillage.com). Harvard T. **Open** noon-8pm Mon-Fri; 11am-8pm Sat; noon-6pm Sun. **Credit** MC, V. **Map** p276 A2.
A subterranean Harvard Square music store, trea-sured for its selection of indie-rock rarities, psyche-delic 1960s reissues, avant-garde composers, obscure soul and world music, plus a smattering of used vinyl. As a bonus, you won't find a better or more knowledgeable crew of music clerks in the city.

Musical instruments

First Act Guitar Studio
745 Boylston Street, at Ring Road, Back Bay (1-617 226 7899, www.firstact.com). **Open** 11am-8pm Mon-Fri; 10am-8pm Sat. **Credit** AmEx, MC, V. **Map** p275 G6.

If it's good enough for Rufus Wainwright, Keane and KT Tunstall, it's good enough for you. They're just a few of the musicians who have played inti-mate in-store concerts at this Back Bay shop, full of brightly colored guitars mounted on the walls. Even if you're not a rock star, you can buy custom-made guitars (electric and acoustic), or at least test a few models out in the showroom.

SPORT & FITNESS
City Sports
11 Bromfield Street, at Washington Street, Downtown (1-617 423 2015, www.citysports.com). Downtown Crossing or Park St T. **Open** 10am-8.30pm Mon-Fri; 10am-8pm Sat; noon-7pm Sun. **Credit** AmEx, DC, MC, V. **Map** p272 K5.
This branch of the area's ubiquitous, all-purpose sporting goods chain has the company's only bar-gain basement, with goods at half price or less. Its convenient location in Downtown Crossing makes it a great place to swing by for a deal.

TICKETS
TeleCharge (1-800 432 7250, www.telecharge. com), **Ticketmaster** (1-617 931 2000, www. ticketmaster.com) and **TicketWeb** (1-866 468 7619, ticketweb.com) all sell tickets to a variety of shows and events, although booking fees can be on the high side.

BosTix
Faneuil Hall Marketplace, Downtown (1-617 262 8632, www.bostix.org). Gov't Center T. **Open** 10am-6pm Tue-Sat; 11am-4pm Sun. **No credit cards. Map** p273 L4.
Selling cut-price tickets to theater, music and dance performances, Boston's answer to New York's TKTS is located in Faneuil Hall Marketplace (with a sister location in Copley Square). These last-minute tickets are half price and available only on the day of the performance; for the day's shows, check the website in advance. Bear in mind that this is a cash-only deal.

TRAVELERS' NEEDS
If you need to ship things home, the **UPS Store** (1-800 789 4623, www.theupsstore.com) has numerous branches dotted around Boston and Cambridge, including Beacon Hill and Downtown Crossing.

You can rent mobile phones on a weekly or daily basis from **Roberts Rent-a-Phone** (1-800 964 2468, www.roberts-rent-a-phone.com), which delivers to any US address within 24 hours. But it may be cheaper to buy a phone (for as little as $40) and a pay-as-you-go card from one of the main cell-phone service providers (*see p259*).

Arts & Entertainment

Boston Red Sox at Fenway Park. *See p216.*

Calendar

Revels, rebels and a spot of culture.

Everyone knows that Boston's got the wildest tea parties around, but there's more to the city's festive spirit than mere cargo chucking. Given its revolutionary pedigree, it's hardly surprising that Boston's calendar features its fair share of historical re-enactments.

But Boston's rebels aren't confined to the 18th century. Alongside such traditional local celebrations as the annual **Boston Tea Party Re-enactment** and the **Boston Pops Fourth of July Concert** are such controversial events as the **Massachusetts Cannabis Reform Coalition's Freedom Rally** on Boston Common and **The Slutcracker** burlesque of the popular holiday ballet, which gives new meaning to 'boughs of Holly'. This cultured metropolis is also known for its arts events – notably the alcohol-free New Year's Eve program, **First Night**, which has become a model for more than 100 cities worldwide.

SCHEDULING

Unless otherwise specified, the festivals and events listed below take place annually. Precise dates are difficult to pin down in advance, as they're often weather-dependent. The best way to confirm the specifics is by phoning the **City of Boston Special Events Line** (1-617 635 3911), visiting www.cityof boston.gov/arts, or through the individual contacts provided.

We've listed two of the most prominent Boston film festivals here; for more, including those on the coast, *see p194*. For artists' open-studio events, *see p183* **Inside Track**.

SPRING

Together (*see p215* **Inside Track**) is a week-long electronic music fest in mid/late April, while the biennial **Boston Cyberarts Festival** (*see p197* **Inside Track**), hot on its heels, celebrates the area's long tradition of technological and artistic innovation.

Boston Massacre Re-enactment

Old State House, State Street, at Washington Street, Downtown (1-617 720 1713, www. bostonhistory.org). State T. **Admission** free. **Date** 5 Mar. **Map** p273 L4.

Witness the unruly scene that took place beneath the Old State House one winter night in 1770, when a group of 'cowardly' Redcoats emptied their muskets on a mob of malcontent colonists. Costumes, muskets and – let's hope – blanks are supplied courtesy of the Massachusetts Council of Minutemen and Militia.

Restaurant Week Boston

Various locations (www.bostonusa.com/ restaurantweek). **Date** mid Mar & mid Aug.
While some bemoan the conveyor-belt quality, there's no other way you can get into so many high-end restaurants for such a low overhead. With more than 200 establishments participating, the hungry masses can sample the cuisine and enjoy the ambiance normally restricted to special occasions or the well-heeled during this two-week prix fixe event. The prices – $15-$20 for a two- or three-course lunch, $33 for a three-course dinner – exclude beverages, tax and tips.

New England Spring Flower Show

Seaport World Trade Center Boston, 200 Seaport Boulevard, at World Trade Center Avenue, South Boston (1-617 385 5000, www.masshort.org). Silver Line Waterfront to World Trade Center. **Admission** $10-$20. **Date** 16-20 Mar.
After a one-year hiatus stemming from funding woes, this century-old event celebrating flora, bushes and blossoms returned in 2010 at a new location. The Massachusetts Horticultural Society sponsors six

acres of landscaped gardens, flower arrangements and horticultural displays. Lately, the focus has been on environmentally friendly gardening.

St Patrick's Day Parade

Dorchester Street & Broadway, South Boston (1-617 536 4100, www.bostonusa.com). Broadway T. **Admission** free. **Date** 17 Mar.
Boston is the undisputed capital of Irish America, and Southie is the Irish capital of Boston. Everyone and their dog wears a shamrock at the parade, making this both the best and worst place to be. The day kicks off with a time-honored traditional breakfast where politicians sing limericks roasting their peers and opponents, setting the jovial stage for one of the largest St Patrick's Day parades in the US, complete with floats, marching bagpipers and, of course, waving politicians. Pubs along the route and throughout Boston overflow with green beer and ample merrymaking. Later on, the downtown streets are so full of soused pedestrians that hailing a taxi is tantamount to catching a fly ball at Fenway Park.

Boston Underground Film Festival

Various cinemas (www.bostonunderground.org). **Admission** varies. **Date** late Mar.
Launched in 1999, Boston's fringiest film festival gives venues and voices to local and national auteurs with little money and big dreams. Screenings at indie cinemas throughout the area culminate in an awards show where winners receive a Bacchus, the festival's coveted demonic bunny trophy. Past attendees of the BUFF include legendary Troma founder Lloyd Kaufman and zombie-film pioneer George A Romero.

PAX East

Boston Convention & Exposition Center, Waterfront (1-617 720 1713, www.paxsite.com/paxeast). Silver Line Waterfront to World Trade Center. **Admission** $35-$55. **Date** late Mar.
Gamers flock to the East Coast version of this festival celebrating first-person shooters and RPGs, with tournaments, free play and unreleased titles. The 2010 festival was such a resounding success – with over 60,000 attendees – organizers are moving the three-day event to this new, larger location.

Boston Marathon

Finishes at Copley Square, Back Bay (1-617 236 1652, www.bostonmarathon.org). Copley T. **Admission** free. **Date** 3rd Mon in Apr. **Map** p275 G6.
These days, Patriot's Day in Boston has less to do with national pride and more to do with thousands of feet pounding 26 miles of pavement. The race begins in Hopkinton (south-west of Boston), wraps around the campus of Boston College and finishes in Copley – and you can be sure at least one jogging Batman will make the trek. Thousands of spectators come out to soak up the adrenaline and cheer on friends along the route; the best – and most crowded – spot is near the finish line.

Boston Pops Fourth of July Concert. *See p181.*

ARTS & ENTERTAINMENT

Patriot's Day Re-enactments

Lexington Green, Lexington (1-781 862 1450, www.libertyride.us, www.lexingtonminutemen.com). **Admission** free. **Date** 3rd Mon in Apr.
Stick around the city to see Paul Revere gallop past, shouting his warning – 'the British are coming!' – to the colonists. Later, on Lexington Green, you can watch a full-scale re-enactment of the skirmish that produced the 'shot heard round the world'.
► *For more about what happens on Patriot's Day, see p219 Inside Track.*

James Joyce Ramble

Start/finish at Endicott Estate, 656 East Street, Dedham (1-781 329 9744, www.ramble.org). **Admission** free (race registration $20). **Date** last Sun in Apr or 1st Sun in May.
The brainchild of a local runner and Joyce fan, who realized that struggling through *Finnegans Wake* was akin to running a particularly arduous race, this six-mile run/walk stampedes through suburban Dedham every spring. The Ramble pays tribute to its namesake by punctuating the road race with an ensemble of Joyce-reading actors dressed in period costume. Mile one features *Finnegans Wake*, mile three *A Portrait of the Artist as a Young Man* and mile six, appropriately enough, *The Dead*.

Lilac Sunday

Arnold Arboretum, 125 Arborway, at Centre Street, Jamaica Plain (1-617 524 1718, www.arboretum.harvard.edu). Forest Hills T. **Admission** free. **Date** 2nd Sun in May.

**INSIDE TRACK
SAINTLY LOVE, ITALIAN STYLE**

St Anthony's Feast (*see p182*) may be the most famous of the North End events celebrating Catholic saints, delectable dining and gondolier-style balladeers, but whether or not it is the best is up for debate. Every weekend in August, Boston's most charming neighbourhood hosts a century-old carnival-style *festa* honoring a patron saint by cooking up *arancini*, pasta and panini. It starts with **St Agrippina's Feast**, on Hanover Street, on the first weekend of August. That's followed by the **Madonna della Cava North End Feast Celebration** (Hanover & Battery Streets) and the **Fisherman's Feast of the Madonna del Soccorso di Sciacca North End Festival** (North, Fleet & Lewis Streets) on the second and third weekends. If you can make it through to **St Lucy's Feast** (Endicott Street), following St Anthony's Feast, it's probably time to go on a diet.

The name says it all – float through the Arboretum on the spring breeze, when over 400 deliciously fragrant lilac plants, of nearly 200 different varieties, are in bloom. Come for the flowers, stay for the Morris dancing – groups from all over the Northeast show up to jingle and jangle their way through sword blade tangles in honor of May Day. Refreshments are available, but Lilac Sunday is perfect for a picnic.

SUMMER

The second helping of **Restaurant Week** Boston (*see p178*) takes place in mid August.

Boston Pride

Throughout Boston (1-617 262 9405, www.bostonpride.org). **Admission** free. **Date** 1st wk in June.
Toast Gay Pride in the first state in America to legalize same-sex marriage. Although unofficial festivities extend throughout the month of June, the main event is a week-long line-up of everything from club nights and book signings to an AIDS awareness walk. The festival culminates with a riotous parade through Boston's own gay central, the South End, on Saturday, and further revels on Sunday.
► *For background, see p201 A Colorful History.*

Bunker Hill Day Celebrations

Various locations in Charlestown (1-617 242 5642, www.nps.gov/bost). Community College T. **Admission** free. **Date** wknd in mid June.
A weekend of historical talks and re-enactments of the infamous battle of Bunker Hill (which actually took place on neighboring Breed's Hill) – complete with period costumes and muskets. Though British forces won the skirmish, they suffered such heavy casualties that they were forced to abandon their first major siege of Boston. The celebration finishes with a grand parade through hilly Charlestown.
► *For more about Bunker Hill, see p74.*

River Festival

Along the Charles River, Cambridge (1-617 349 4380, www.cambridgema.gov/cac). Harvard T. **Admission** free. **Date** mid June.
If crowding along the Charles on the Fourth of July isn't your bag, come for this earlier celebration, which takes place on the section of riverbank between John F Kennedy Street and Western Avenue. Sponsored by the Cambridge Arts Council, the riverside festival features an arts bazaar, concerts, children's events and plenty of dancing.

Boston Harborfest

Various locations in Boston (1-617 227 1528, www.bostonharborfest.com). **Admission** varies. **Date** 4th wk in June.
The annual maritime- and colonial-themed festival of fireworks, open-air concerts and (yet more) historical re-enactments in the run up to the Fourth of July now has 200-plus events taking place in more

What the Fluff? Festival. *See p183.*

than 30 harborside venues. The Chowderfest (a celebration of New England's traditional bivalve soup, in which top restaurants vie for the title of 'Boston's Best Clam Chowder') is the high point.

Boston Pops Fourth of July Concert

Hatch Shell, Charles River Esplanade, Back Bay (1-888 484 7677, www.july4th.org). Charles/MGH T. **Admission** free. **Date** 4 July. **Map** p272 H4.

Not surprisingly, the Fourth of July attracts hundreds of thousands of visitors to the birthplace of American independence – most of whom plant themselves along the banks of the Charles River to watch the fireworks. The Boston Pops are an American institution, and this concert is the center of the universe for fans. Frantically territorial families show up at dawn to claim their grassy patch for the day. Technically, the event is non-alcoholic, but that doesn't stop savvy regulars from slipping drinks into plastic cups. In the early evening – after everyone is tuckered out from a sweaty day of guarding blankets (and hiding beer) – the Pops play in the Hatch Shell. The accompanying fireworks display, set off from a barge on the Charles, is not to be missed. *Photo p179.*

Turning of the USS Constitution

Viewing along Boston Harbor (1-617 426 1812, www.ussconstitutionmuseum.org). **Admission** free. **Date** 4 July.

Still a commissioned naval vessel, 'Old Ironsides' makes her stately annual sail around Boston Harbor to turn and re-dock in the opposite direction at the Charlestown Naval Yard. This is done not for the tourists, but to ensure that the ship weathers evenly. ▶ *You can board the ship at other times; see p74.*

Bastille Day

French Library & Cultural Center, 53 Marlborough Street, at Berkeley Street (1-617 912 0400, www. frenchlib.org). Arlington or Copley T. **Admission** $28-$35. **Date** mid July. **Map** p275 H5.

This 60-year-old non-profit organization throws a street party on an evening before or after Bastille Day, with French cuisine, Francophone musicians, children's activities and plenty of joie de vivre.

Lantern Festival

95 Forest Hills Avenue, Jamaica Plain (1-617 524 0128, www.foresthillstrust.org). Forest Hills T then 10min walk. **Admission** free ($10 for lanterns). **Date** mid July.

A party in a graveyard? Sounds a tad morbid – but the Forest Hills Cemetery, full of lush gardens and intriguing sculpture, is one of the most gorgeous green spaces in the Boston area. Never is it more beautiful than during the annual Buddhist ritual-inspired Lantern Festival. An afternoon filled with performances from local artists (including taiko drummers and gospel choirs) prefaces the main event: after sunset, visitors set little lanterns adrift in Lake Hibiscus, until they form a shimmering flotilla of light.

ArtBeat

Davis Square, Somerville (1-617 625 6600 ext 2985, www.somervilleartscouncil.org). Davis Square T. **Admission** $3. **Date** 3rd wknd in July.

Davis Square is a breeding ground for artists, writers, musicians, performers and sundry other Bohemian types, not to mention a funky place to spend an afternoon people watching on a summer afternoon. Every year, Somerville exalts its creative geniuses with a weekend-long celebration of all

First Night. *See p184.*

ARTS & ENTERTAINMENT

that's artsy. The revelries include concerts by local indie, blues and folk bands, theatrical performances, readings and a street art market.

Caribbean Carnival
Franklin Park, at Blue Hill Avenue, Dorchester (1-617 512 7803, www.bostoncarnivalvillage. com). Forest Hills T then 10min walk. **Admission** free. **Date** late Aug.
Franklin Park, in the Dorchester end of Roxbury, hosts this lively weekend celebration of Caribbean culture. Expect ethnic food, music, dance and a colorful parade. The feathered costumes and sun-drenched festivities offer a vibrant counterpoint to Boston's buttoned-up re-enactments, and celebrate an entirely different strand of colonial history.

St Anthony's Feast
Endicott, Thacher & North Margin Streets, North End (1-617 723 8669, www.stanthonys feast.com). Haymarket T. **Date** late Aug.
There's no better neighborhood for a stroll than the North End, and no better time to do it than during this annual Catholic shindig. For one weekend, the winding streets of Boston's Italian district are lined with vendors of delectable Mediterranean fare and effigies of weeping saints. A parade and performances by Italian crooners round out the bustling weekend.
▶ *For more saints' feasts, see p180 Inside Track.*

AUTUMN

Boston Ahts Festival
Christopher Columbus Park, North End (1-617 635 3911, bostonahtsfestival.com). Haymarket T. **Admission** free. **Date** 1st wknd in Sept. **Map** p273 M3.
Poking fun at the Boston accent, this festival features visual and performance artists coming together on two stages in Christopher Columbus Park (*see p75*), one of Boston's best. Over 60 artists – including performers from the Boston Ballet to the Blue Man Group – showcase their wares and strut their stuff. You might even discover the next Edward Hoppah…
▶ *For more about language quirks, see p262.*

Boston Tattoo Convention
Back Bay Sheraton Hotel, 39 Dalton Street, Back Bay (1-978 744 9393, www.bostontattoo convention.com). Hynes T. **Admission** $20-$70. **Date** wknd in Sept. **Map** p274 F7.
Until 2001, Massachusetts residents had to cross the state line in order to get a tattoo. Once it was legalized, though, it didn't take long for Boston to establish itself as a hub for body art – as the Tattoo Convention proves. Over 100 tattoo artists converge at the Sheraton for the four-day event, which includes contests, vendors, galleries and performances, plus numerous ink-slingers setting up shop.

Boston Film Festival

Stuart Street Playhouse, 200 Stuart Street, Downtown (1-617 523 8388, www.bostonfilm festival.org). Chinatown T. **Admission** varies. **Date** 2nd wk in Sept. **Map** p275 J6.

This annual festival of lectures, panels and screenings showcases feature-length films, shorts and independent works. There's a strong local contingent of participants, many from nearby colleges. Past entries include the Oscar-winning *American Beauty* and Billy Ray's directorial debut, *Shattered Glass*.

What the Fluff? Festival

Union Square, Somerville (1-617 623 1392 ext 119, www.unionsquaremain.org). Harvard T then bus 86, or Lechmere T then bus 87. **Admission** free. **Date** late Sept.

There's more to Boston's history than the fight for independence. In 1917, for example, the entrepreneur Archibald Query invented Marshmallow Fluff – the beloved confectionary spread – right here in Somerville. Union Square celebrates its favorite son with a day-long festival that includes a tug of war over a tub of Fluff, erupting Fluff volcanoes and Fluff-based nibbles aplenty. *Photo p181.*

Massachusetts Cannabis Reform Coalition's Freedom Rally

Boston Common, Downtown (1-781 944 2266, www.masscann.org). Park St T. **Admission** free. **Date** mid Sept. **Map** p272 J5.

Every year, the city of Boston broods over issuing permits to this annual ganja-fest. Regardless, the rally always goes down, with thousands of proud stoners sneaking spliffs on to the Common. A handful of local bands play, which in former years has included Letters to Cleo and the Dresden Dolls. Booths manned by left-leaning activist groups preach to the converted. It goes without saying, but people inevitably end up getting arrested.

Beantown Jazz Festival

Various locations in Boston (1-617 747 2260, www.beantownjazz.org). **Admission** varies. **Date** Last wknd in Sept.

Boston's lively jazz scene steals the limelight at this yearly festival, which brings hot talents to Boston's various venues. The festival includes performances at Sculler's Jazz Club, Berklee Performance Center and the Beehive. Vendors and musicians also take to the streets in the South End.

▶ *For more about Boston's jazz scene, see p210.*

Lowell Celebrates Kerouac! Festival

Various locations in Lowell (1-978 970 4257, www.lowellcelebrateskerouac.org). Commuter rail to Lowell. **Admission** varies. **Date** 1st wk in Oct.

Most famous for his seminal 1957 novel *On the Road* – an American traveler's ode to wanderlust, amphetamines and boisterous adventure – Jack Kerouac was born and buried in Lowell, a former mill town

north-west of Boston. While he never claimed to have taken much from the place, it still celebrates his legacy. Every year, the town commemorates its legendary tie to the Beat Generation with a three-day festival of open mics, jazz and poetry readings.

Harvard Square Oktoberfest

Harvard Square, Cambridge (1-617 491 3434, www.harvardsquare.com). Harvard T. **Admission** free. **Date** early Oct. **Map** p276 B2.

Celebrate all things frothy and boozy as Harvard Square transforms itself for a weekend into a Bavarian township. Bands, dancers, ethnic food and beer gardens line the streets, and some 200 regional artisans and merchants display their wares.

Head of the Charles Regatta

Charles River, between the Boston University Bridge and the Eliot Bridge (1-617 868 6200, www.hocr.org). Central or Harvard T then 10min walk. **Admission** free. **Date** wknd in mid Oct.

This is one of the most spectacular boat races anywhere. The hundreds of thousands of spectators lining the bridges and riverbanks along the Charles are a sight to be seen, as are the thousands of rowers who converge on Cambridge for this world-class regatta. Supporters bring blankets and picnic baskets to the banks of the Charles to cheer on the teams.

Salem's Haunted Happenings

Various locations in Salem (1-978 744 3663, 1-877 725 3662, www.hauntedhappenings.org). **Admission** varies. **Date** throughout Oct.

As you'd expect from a place that's on the map for executing witches, spooky Salem hosts a wicked Halloween. The town is also a haven for present-day pagans. A huge costumed parade kicks off a month of jack-o'-lantern carving, haunted-house tours, candlelit vigils, modern witchcraft ceremonies, magic shows and a psychics' fair. Leave your skepticism at home – but bring your wallet and the most fabulous costume you can dream up.

▶ *For excursions to Salem, see p236.*

INSIDE TRACK
OPEN-DOOR POLICY

Just missed the Ahts Festival? Not to worry, on weekends from September to December you can be on the insiders' list at artists' studios in neighborhoods across town. The **Boston Open Studios Coalition** (www.cityofboston.gov/arts) allows the public a first-hand look at the creative process, and you can get steep discounts on the artwork. The **Fort Point Arts Community** (www.fortpointarts.org) hosts a particularly impressive list of artists, with doors open in mid October.

ARTS & ENTERTAINMENT

WINTER

For new twists to that classic holiday favorite, *see p228* **The Nutcracker Variations**.

Boston Common Tree Lighting

Boston Common, Downtown (1-617 635 4505, www.cityofboston.gov). Park St T. **Admission** free. **Date** late Nov or early Dec. **Map** p272 J5.
The behind-the-scenes legwork for this annual holiday tree-lighting tradition is just as captivating as the ceremony itself, as a Boston tree scout treks to Nova Scotia to select a shapely 50ft spruce. (Ever since 1917, Nova Scotia has donated its trees as a gift, out of gratitude for Boston's fast response to a devastating fire in Halifax.) A local dignitary (often the mayor) flicks the switch. The rest of the Common's trees are strung with lights as well, while an illuminated Nativity scene and menorah grace the grounds near the Park Street T station.

Christmas Revels

Sanders Theatre, Memorial Hall, 45 Quincy Street, at Cambridge Street, Cambridge (1-617 972 8300, www.revels.org). Harvard T. **Admission** $20-$45; $15-$35 reductions. **Date** mid-late Dec.
Put on by a local non-profit performance troupe, the Revels have practically become an institution come the winter solstice. Each year focuses on a different theme – based on culture and time period – of Christmas pageantry. Performances include dances, plays and plenty of audience-participatory carol-singing. This is Christmas, old-school style.

Boston Tea Party Re-enactment

Old South Meeting House, 310 Washington Street, Boston (1-617 482 6439, www.oldsouth meetinghouse.org). State House T. **Admission** $8. **Date** mid Dec. **Map** p273 L4.
Patriots gather for a town meeting at the Old South Meeting House to condemn the crimes of nasty old King George III. Fife and drum in hand, the excitable mob then marches to a replica tea ship on the waterfront and does the dirty deed.
   The Boston Tea Party Ships & Museum (Congress Street Bridge, 1-800 868 7482, www.bostonteaparty. com), where another tea party re-enactment used to take place, is undergoing major renovations. Due to open in 2011, the new museum (twice as large as the old one, and with three traditional tall ships) will then resume its own annual tea-tossing ceremony.

First Night

Throughout the city (1-617 542 1399, www.first night.org). **Admission** $15-$18. **Date** 31 Dec.
Boston was the first city in the country to offer this alcohol-free alternative to ringing in the New Year. Launched in 1976, First Night is celebrated citywide, with over 1,000 artists and 200 exhibitions at nearly 40 venues. Events range from poetry readings to rock concerts. There are activities from noon, but the fun really starts in the early evening with the carnival-style Grand Procession in Back Bay, culminating in a midnight fireworks display at the harbor. The massive ice sculptures in Copley Square and on the Common are another signature feature. *Photo p182.*

Arisia

Westin Boston Waterfront Hotel, 425 Summer Street (no phone, www.arisia.org). Silver Line Waterfront to World Trade Center. **Admission** $25-$60. **Date** wknd in mid Jan.
You don't have to be a *Star Wars*-quoting, Asimov-obsessed über-nerd to have fun at Arisia (though that certainly doesn't hurt). For this annual convention, the largest of its kind in New England, the science fiction-loving hordes (often with kids in tow) flock to Boston for futuristic speaker panels, workshops, art exhibits and movie marathons. The gala event is the masquerade ball, where professional and amateur costumiers show off their mind-blowing handiwork.

Boston Wine Expo

Seaport World Trade Center Boston, 200 Seaport Boulevard, at World Trade Center Avenue, South Boston (1-877-946-3976, www. wine-expos.com/boston). Silver Line Waterfront to World Trade Center. **Admission** $65-$85 1 day; $95-$105 2 days. **Date** wknd in Feb.
Every year, oenophiles storm the harborside World Trade Center for the country's largest consumer wine event. The festival features tastings from over 450 domestic and international wineries, celebrity-chef demonstrations, and educational seminars.

Chinese New Year

Beach & Tyler Streets, Chinatown (1-888 733 2678, www.bostonusa.com). Boylston or Chinatown T. **Admission** free. **Date** late Jan or early Feb.
Dragons dance and fireworks explode in a swirl of color and sound at one of the nation's largest celebrations of the first day of the Chinese calendar. Traditionally, festivities last 15 days, and much of the action takes place in and around Beach and Tyler Streets in Boston's Chinatown. Expect plenty of fireworks and tantalizing Asian cuisine.

Beanpot Hockey Tournament

TD Garden, Causeway Street, at Friend Street (1-617 624 1000, www.beanpothockey.com). North Station T. **Admission** varies. **Date** 1st & 2nd Mon in Feb. **Map** p272 K2.
Players from Harvard, Northeastern and Boston Universities and Boston College go head-to-head in this annual ice hockey clash. It's a welcome reprieve from the Bruins' often disappointing performances, as an audience of rival college students assault one another with fusillades of jeers and cheers. The winning team gets a trophy shaped like a bean pot.
▶ *For Boston Bruins hockey games, see p219.*

ARTS & ENTERTAINMENT

Children

Pirate ships, puppet shows and posh playgrounds for little people.

Boston is rich in history, but children only have so much patience for standing in old buildings and listening to a guide, even one dressed in a funny-looking costume. Still, the **USS Constitution Museum** (*see p74*) rarely fails to fire young imaginations, and **Georges Island** (*see p76*), has a 19th-century fort where they can romp around.

The city's green spaces and harbor are great for families to explore but rainy days can be more of a challenge. The **Boston Children's Museum** has plenty to do for active kids, and they might learn something at the fun **Museum of Science**.

SIGHTSEEING & ACTIVITIES

If you're here during the February or April school holidays, you'll find daily kids' activities at every museum and library in town. For more ideas, try the Calendar section of Thursday's edition of the *Boston Globe*, which has a broad list of activities for the coming week. Or check out the *Parents' Paper*, available at newsstands, street boxes and, more reliably, online at www.boston.parenthood.com. Boston's web-savvy parents also rely on www.gocitykids.com and www.bostoncentral.com. Another good resource is the Greater Boston Convention & Visitors Bureau's *Kids Love Boston*; full of useful tips (1-888 733 2678, www.bostonusa.com).

Animals & nature

The **New England Aquarium** (*see p75*) enthralls kids with its noisy penguins, three-story tank filled with sea turtles and sharks, and hands-on tidal basin, where you can reach in and touch starfish and hermit crabs. Quieter tykes will enjoy the Curious George Discovery Corner, which explores the ocean and its inhabitants through toys and videos. To spot bigger marine creatures, book a place on one of the Aquarium's summer Whale Watch trips. A catamaran takes you out to Stellwagen Bank, accompanied by trained naturalists who can tell you the names of all the humpbacks you see.

Paddling around Boston's waterways can offer a fresh perspective on the city. **Charles River Canoe & Kayak** (*see p220*) rents boats by the hour or day in Boston during the summer, and in Newton for an extended season.

Franklin Park Zoo

1 Franklin Park Road, Dorchester (1-617 541 5466, www.franklinparkzoo.org). Forest Hills T then bus 16. **Open** *Apr-Sept* 10am-5pm Mon-Fri; 10am-6pm Sat, Sun. *Oct-Mar* 10am-4pm daily. **Admission** $14; $8-$11 reductions; free under-2s. **Credit** AmEx, MC, V.

Kids can walk right up to the glass enclosures at Franklin Park Zoo and make faces at young gorillas or take a peek at stalking lions, and can actually pet the sheep and goats at the Contact Corral. Brilliantly colored birds dart through the Tropical Forest over the heads of pygmy hippos and capybaras (and visitors), while butterflies will flutter on to outstretched hands at the Butterfly Landing (June-Sept). Some children will happily ignore the animals altogether, and tackle the zoo-themed playground equipment instead. *Photo p186.*

★ Swan Boats

Public Garden, entrance on Arlington Street, Back Bay (1-617 522 1966, www.swanboats. com). Arlington T. **Open** *Apr-mid June* 10am-4pm daily. *Mid June-Aug* 10am-5pm daily. *Sept* noon-4pm Mon-Fri; 10am-4pm Sat, Sun. **Admission** $2.75; $1.50 reductions. **No credit cards. Map** p272 H5.

What child could resist sitting in a swan? A part of Boston's touristic history, these odd watercraft were created by designer Robert Paget in 1877, when the swan-drawn boat in the opera *Lohengrin* was a tad more familiar. Contemporary kids are more likely to know about Robert McCloskey's classic book *Make Way for Ducklings*, in which the Mallard family decides to move to Boston Pond, lured by the peanuts tossed by swan boat riders. You'll spend 15 minutes cruising around the small

Franklin Park Zoo. *See p185.*

lagoon, amid the ducks and willow trees, as your children play at being swashbuckling pirates.

▶ *The Mallards also feature in an annual Duckling Day parade in mid May; for details, see www.friendsofthepublicgarden.org.*

Museums & attractions

In addition to the excellent **Boston Children's Museum** (*see p188* **Profile**), most of the city's grown-up institutions run excellent children's programs at weekends. The **Museum of Fine Arts** (*see p65*) hosts Family Art Cart programs (on weekends between October and May, and some weekdays in July and August), which send children out into the galleries, with activities that encourage them to take a closer look at art. The **Institute for Contemporary Art** (*see p79*) hosts a 'Play Date' on the last Saturday of the month, featuring hands-on art activities and free admission for two adults and children aged 12 and under. It also has a great outside deck overlooking the harbor – perfect for running after seagulls.

★ Boston Children's Museum
308 Congress Street, at Children's Wharf, Fort Point, Waterfront (1-617 426 6500, www.bostonkids.org). South Station T. **Open** 10am-5pm Mon-Thur, Sat, Sun; 10am-9pm Fri. **Admission** $12; $8 reductions. $6 for all 4-5pm Mon-Thur, Sat, Sun; $1 for all 5-9pm Fri. **Credit** AmEx, MC, V. **Map** p273 M5.
See p188 **Profile**.

Harvard Museum of Natural History
26 Oxford Street, at Harvard Square, Cambridge (1-617 495 3045, www.hmnh.harvard.edu). Harvard T. **Open** 9am-5pm daily. **Admission** $9; $6-$7 reductions; free under-3s. **Credit** AmEx, MC, V. **Map** p276 B2.

This historic museum has a vast and slightly creepy collection of stuffed, mounted and glass-encased creatures from around the globe, from beady-eyed llamas to coelacanths and butterflies. Fossil-mad children can gawk at dinosaur skeletons and admire the 42ft kronosaurus, a prehistoric marine reptile, while rock fans head straight for the meteorites and gemstones.

▶ *Entry includes admission to the Peabody Museum of Archaeology & Ethnology; see p85.*

Museum of Science & Charles Hayden Planetarium
For listings, see p57.

Although not exclusively a children's domain, the Museum of Science – visited by more than 250,000 students in school groups each year – is largely geared towards youngsters. Its 700-plus hands-on displays and straightforward explanations aim to make science fun. All areas are covered, from the natural world to the latest high-tech inventions. Disciplines such as physics are explored in terms of everyday life, such as a Science in the Park exhibit with fully functional swings and seesaws. There is much to excite, from dinosaurs and the new Butterfly Garden conservatory to space capsules and steam engines. In the Discovery Center, babies and toddlers can crawl safely while their older siblings put together animal skeletons or perform simple experiments. The domed Mugar Omni Theater shows a changing programme of IMAX movies, and the multimedia Charles Hayden Planetarium is a treat for small star-gazers.

Tall Ship Formidable
Meet at the Boston Waterboat Marina, Long Wharf, Waterfront (1-617 262 1119, www.tallshipformidable.com). Aquarium T. **Tours** June-Sept times vary. **Tickets** $25; $10 reductions. **Credit** MC, V. **Map** p273 M3.

The whole family can have a peaceful tour of Boston Harbor on this traditional, square-rigged sailing ship, or, on Saturdays, experience a dramatic harbor battle, when the *Formidable* is ambushed by privateers on the tall ship *Poincare*. Pirate-obsessed tots will swoon, and adults will appreciate attempts to relate the goings-on to historical naval warfare.

▶ *For more nautical kids' adventures, visit the USS Constitution Museum; see p74.*

Playgrounds

Christopher Columbus Waterfront Park

Atlantic Avenue, adjacent to Commercial Wharf, Waterfront (www.bostonharborwalk.com). Aquarium T. **Open** dawn-dusk daily. **Map** p273 M3.

Ahoy land-lubbers! Kids can wave at the ferries cruising to the Harbor Islands from this nautical-themed park, a short walk away from Faneuil Hall and the North End. There's a big blue and white climbing structure and a beach-sized sandpit, plus spray showers to play in on hot days. The flat ground means easy access for strollers.

Clarendon Street Playground

Corner of Clarendon Street & Commonwealth Avenue, Back Bay (1-617 247 3961, www.nabbonline.com/playground.htm). Copley T. **Open** dawn-dusk daily. **Map** p275 H5.

Set amid Back Bay's Victorian townhouses, Clarendon Street Playground provides a shaded urban oasis. It's sunk slightly below street level, muffling street noise – but you'll hear plenty of happy shrieks from the swings, slides, climbing frames and large open area for plain old romping. Local folk leave riding toys out for anyone to use.

Christopher Columbus Waterfront Park.

Tadpole Playground

Boston Common, Downtown (www.tadpoleplayground.org). Park St T. **Open** dawn-dusk daily. **Map** p272 K4.

Bronze frogs, fish and lily pads adorn this gated playground by Boston Common's Frog Pond skating rink/sprinkler wading pool. The park has climbing frames and slides to occupy the kids, and plenty of benches where weary parents can find respite.

▶ *For more about Boston Common, see p43.*

Tours

For the child-friendly **Boston Old Town Trolley Tours** and the amphibious **Boston Duck Tours**, *see p252.*

Boston by Little Feet

Meet at the Samuel Adams statue on Congress Street (1-617 367 2345, www.bostonbyfoot.com). State T. **Tours** 10am Mon, Sat; 2pm Sun. **Tickets** $8. **Credit** MC, V.

This hour-long tour for kids aged six to 12 (accompanied by a grown-up) is organized by the acclaimed Boston by Foot (*see p252*) tour group. It provides a child's-eye view of sites along the Freedom Trail.

Theater

Where theaters keep regular opening and performance times, we've listed them. Where no opening times are given, please contact the venue or check online for details.

Artbarn Community Theater

50 Sewall Avenue, Coolidge Corner, Brookline (1-617 975 0050, www.artbarn.org). Coolidge Corner T. **Tickets** $10. **No credit cards**.

Founded in 1999, this not-for-profit establishment provides affordable opportunities for kids to get involved in theater, building their confidence and self-esteem as well as honing their acting talents. If there's not enough time to commit to a term's classes, drop in for one of the performances.

Boston Children's Theatre

Various locations (1-617 424 6634, www.bostonchildrenstheatre.org). Mass Ave or Northeastern T. **Tickets** prices vary. No under-3s. **Credit** MC, V.

One of the country's oldest theater organizations, the BCT puts on three main stage shows a year in venues around the city. Productions – by kids, for kids – coincide with the school holidays.

Once Upon a Time at the Lyric Stage

YWCA Building, 140 Clarendon Street, at Copley Square, Back Bay (1-617 585 5678, www.lyricstage.com). Back Bay or Copley T. **Box office** noon-5pm Tue, Sun; noon-8pm Wed-Sat. **Tickets** $8; free under-2s. **Credit** AmEx, MC, V. **Map** p275 H6.

ARTS & ENTERTAINMENT

Profile Boston Children's Museum

Keeping youngsters entertained – and educated – for decades.

Founded in 1913 by a well-meaning group of local science teachers, the **Boston Children's Museum** (*see p186*) was just another collection of things to look at until director Michael Spock arrived in 1961. The son of the late American pediatrician and childcare guru Benjamin Spock, he took out the glass cases of dusty taxidermy and rocks, and turned the museum into a joyously interactive hands-on experience. In 1979, it moved from Jamaica Plain to new premises – a handsome 19th-century brick warehouse overlooking Boston Harbor's Fort Point Channel.

After nearly three decades of little feet trotting through its hallowed halls (it now attracts more than 400,000 visitors each year), the museum was outgrowing its building, and starting to show its age. But a $47 million restoration project, completed in spring 2007, including a glass-walled extension and a landscaped outdoor space, transformed the cramped, confusing layout into a series of light spacious open areas, with plenty of room for energetic kids. To children, it's

like a vast indoor playground – little do they know how much they're learning in the process.

The centerpiece of the new-look museum is the New Balance Climb, a twisty, turning three-storey climbing structure made of serpentine wires and curved plywood sails. (The third-floor exit is guarded by museum staff, who compel fast-footed children to wait for their puffing parents to catch up.) On the ground floor, the Kid Power exhibit explores health and fitness, complete with climbing wall, bikes and an interactive light-up dance floor to stomp on. It's also home to the ever-popular Science Playground, where young researchers can sit under a glass-bottomed turtle tank, create walls of bubbles or make a maze for rolling golf balls down the wall.

If the kids ever get past ground level (and there's a good chance they won't), they can learn about currents by steering boats through a 28-foot reproduction of the Fort Point Channel in Boats Afloat. Young pilots may prefer climbing into the model cockpit in the *Arthur and Friends* exhibit, hosted by television's most charismatic aardvark, before a story in the reading corner. Creative kids can make a mess at the Art Studio, or visit the Recycle Shop to buy odd pieces of plastic, papers, and string for their sculptural masterpieces.

Watching kids in the know make a beeline for their favorite exhibits is part of the fun for adults. One particularly popular area, the Construction Zone, includes a real Bobcat vehicle for tykes to climb into, vests and hard hats to wear and tunnels to climb through.

In the 3,000-square-foot space called the Common, families can regroup and debate

WHERE TO REFUEL

The museum has indoor and outdoor picnic areas, as well as bakery-café **Au Bon Pain**. In summer, the **Hood Milk Bottle** opens up for ice-cream and snacks.

what to visit next – or try out the electronic musical chairs, play a giant game of chess and swat at virtual marbles projected on a wall. For under-threes, meanwhile, there's the smaller, gentler Playspace, which has toddler-friendly amusements such as toy trains and an aquarium, as well as a special room for nursing babies.

Themes range from global to locally oriented; on the top floor, the Boston Black area explores the city's ethnic diversity – kids can play steel drums for an Afro-Caribbean parade or go shopping in a Dominican grocery store. Next to it is a 100-year-old Japanese house from Kyoto, which they can explore as long as they first respectfully remove their shoes. There are also a number of performances that take place throughout the day at the Kidstage. Many of the plays incorporate lessons such as healthy food and lifestyle choices while others are

interactive, re-imagining traditional tales such as *The Three Little Pigs* with the help of the audience.

The exhibits are changed or updated frequently, so you might still see one that focuses on the various scientific properties of air in a fun, hands-on way or perhaps the temporary exhibit portraying Curious George's neighborhood.

Even the giant Hood Milk Bottle outside, which dispenses sandwiches and ice-cream in summer, has been given a refurb along with the grounds. The 77-year-old, 40-foot-high structure, which started life as a drive-in fast-food joint on Route 44, is a well-loved Boston landmark.

Visit the museum on a Friday night after 5pm and you'll only pay $1 admission, courtesy of a corporate sponsor. Beware, though: throngs of kids come for the discount and the exhibits can be quite packed.

Children

INSIDE TRACK PARK THE KIDS

All that sightseeing starting to bore your toddler? Take the MBTA commuter boat for $1.70 from Long Wharf by the New England Aquarium to the Charlestown Navy Yard. **Shipyard Park**, a short walk from where the ferry docks, has a great water park for kids looking for a break from the museums and walks, and the park itself, usually not too crowded, is a nice place to relax for an afternoon. (For more playgrounds, *see p187*.)

The Once Upon a Time theater company stages interactive renditions of such classic children's stories as *The Princess and the Pea*. Two professionals start the story, then ten to 15 children from the audience are called up on stage to play supporting roles. Tales are geared towards two- to eight-year-olds.

Puppet Showplace Theatre
32 Station Street, at Washington Street, Brookline (1-617 731 6400, www.puppet showplace.org). Brookline Village T. **Box office** 10am-4pm Tue-Sun. **Tickets** $10. **Credit** AmEx, MC, V.
Traditional fairy tales, from *Cinderella* to *Jack and the Beanstalk*, are brought to life by the theater's puppeteers, along with more contemporary stories. On Wednesday and Thursday mornings, the theater hosts special 'tot shows' for kids aged three to six.

Wheelock Family Theatre
200 The Riverway, at Short Street, Fenway, Back Bay (1-617 879 2300, www.wheelock.edu/wft). Fenway T. **Box office** noon-5.30pm Mon-Fri. **Tickets** $15-$23. **No credit cards**.
This professional theater company has been staging children's shows at Wheelock College since 1982. Productions range from the preschool-friendly classic *Winnie the Pooh*, to *Holes*, a tale for the over-eights based on Louis Sachar's 1998 novel.

RESTAURANTS & CAFES

The city is strong on eateries that are familiar enough to keep children happy, yet with enough interest to appeal to adults. Pizzerias such as **Antico Forno** (*see p128*) always appeal, as do the marvelous flavors at **Christina's Homemade Ice Cream** (*see p133*).

Fire + Ice
50 Church Street, at Harvard Square, Cambridge (1-617 547 9007, www.fire-ice.com). Harvard T. **Open** 11.30am-10pm Mon-Thur; 11.30am-11pm Fri, Sat; 10am-10pm Sun. **Main courses** $17. **Credit** AmEx, DC, MC, V. **Map** p276 A2.

Don't let the sleek, trendy interior fool you – this is a child-friendly place. Picky eaters can choose their own ingredients, then watch their meal being cooked on the grill right before their eyes. It's an all-you-can-eat establishment, with reduced rates for younger kids. **Other locations** 205 Berkeley Street, at St James Street, Back Bay (1-617 482 3473).

Full Moon
344 Huron Avenue, between Lake View Avenue & Fayerweather Street, Huron Village, Cambridge (1-617 354 6699, www.fullmoonrestaurant.com). Harvard T then bus 72. **Open** 11.30am-2.30pm, 5-9pm Mon-Sat; 9am-2.30pm, 5-9pm Sun. **Main courses** $6-$20. **Credit** MC, V.
The Full Moon is stocked with baskets of toys, books, a chalkboard and a dolls' house to keep the children sweet. While the kids play, you can sample the Moroccan chicken stew or grilled shrimp skewers, washed down with a glass of Chianti. The children's menu ranges from hot dogs and fries to cheesy quesadillas. Book ahead as it's popular with families.

Hard Rock Cafe
22-24 Clinton Street, at Faneuil Hall, Downtown (1-617 424 7625, www.hardrock.com). Haymarket T. **Open** 11am-midnight Mon-Thur; Sun; 11am-2am Fri, Sat. **Main courses** $15-$25. **Credit** AmEx, DC, MC, V. **Map** p273 L3.
Noisy, boisterous and filled with memorabilia from the golden age of rock. Kids can be as raucous as they want in one of the most popular burger joints in town and nobody will get angry.

★ Jasper White's Summer Shack
50 Dalton Street, at Scotia Street, Back Bay (1-617 867 9955, www.summershackrestaurant.com). Hynes T. **Open** 11.30am-10pm Mon-Thur, Sun; 11.30am-1.30am Fri, Sat. **Main courses** $15-$25. **Credit** AmEx, MC, V. **Map** p274 F7.
If you don't have time for a clam bake on the beach, head here. Its cheery, colorful decor and friendly vibe make it great for families. Kids can try corn dogs, clam chowder or chicken wings, while you savor wood-grilled lobster or oysters from the raw bar. **Other locations** 149 Alewife Parkway, Cambridge (1-617 520 9500).

BABYSITTING

Nanny Poppins *Suite 272, 165 U New Boston Street, Woburn (1-617 697 0052, www.nanny poppins.com). Washington St T.* **Open** *Office* 9am-5pm Mon-Fri. **Rates** placement fee $30; plus sitter salary $10-$18/hr. **Credit** AmEx, MC, V.
Parents in a Pinch *45 Bartlett Crescent, at Washington Street, Brookline (1-617 739 5437, www.parentsinapinch.com). Washington St T.* **Open** *Office* 8am-5pm Mon-Fri. **Rates** placement fee $45; plus sitter salary $15/hr. **Credit** AmEx, MC, V.

Film

A top location for film buffs and, increasingly, filmmakers.

As a result of tax breaks, more and more movies and television shows are being filmed in-state, so much so that entrepreneurs in Plymouth are trying to establish local studios with a Hollywood East tagline. Things may not be quite there yet, but seeing the likes of Tom Cruise or Leonardo DiCaprio on location isn't as rare as it once was.

If you're more interested in seeing stars on the big screen than on the streets, Boston has a wide array of cinemas, from multiplexes to arthouses. There are also a number of film festivals appealing to movie buffs throughout the year.

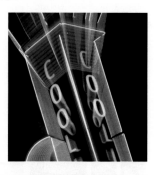

CINEMAS

Boston's screening venues ranges from glitzy stadium theaters showing the latest budget-busting Hollywood releases, such as the giant **Regal Fenway**, to funky repertory houses, which are among the nation's best for arthouse fare. Opened in 1933, the oldest of Boston's arthouse cinemas is the **Coolidge Corner Theatre**, a historic art deco venue in Brookline. Across the river in Cambridge, the single-screen **Brattle Theatre** continues to project restored classics, world cinema and imaginative double bills, earning it a loyal following.

For newer independent releases and foreign films, Boston cinephiles flock to the Landmark chain's Cambridge outpost, the **Kendall Square Cinema**, and to **Loews Harvard Square**. If you don't mind waiting a week or two before seeing new releases, the **Somerville Theatre** (*see p208*), and the **Capitol Theatre** in Arlington (204 Massachusetts Avenue, 1-781 648 6022), screen second-run films for about half the price of regular cinemas ($5-$7).

INFORMATION AND TICKETS

For the location of your nearest cinema or information on films currently showing, visit www.timeoutboston.com or check local listings in the *Boston Globe* or the free weekly papers.

Arthouse & revival

AMC Loews Harvard Square

10 Church Street, at Massachusetts Avenue, Harvard Square, Cambridge (1-617 864 4581, www.amctheatres.com). Harvard T.

Tickets $7.25-$9.25; $6.25-$8.25 reductions.
Credit AmEx, MC, V. **Map** p276 B2.
This Loews outpost blends arty fare with the hottest hits – and runs high-spirited screenings of *The Rocky Horror Picture Show* on Saturday nights. While the main screen is huge, the other four are small and somewhat oddly configured.

★ Brattle Theatre

40 Brattle Street, at Harvard Square, Cambridge (1-617 876 6837, www.brattlefilm. org). Harvard T. **Tickets** $9.50; $6.50-$7.50 reductions. **Credit** MC, V. **Map** p276 A2.
Built as a theater in 1890 by the Cambridge Social Union, the slightly ragged Brattle became a movie house in the 1950s, when it offered Humphrey Bogart marathons as a stress reliever for students

---

INSIDE TRACK
GOOD WILL DRINKING

Woody's L Street Tavern (658A East 8th Street, South Boston, 1-617 268 4335) doesn't have the trappings of a tourist hotspot, but fans of *Good Will Hunting* regularly venture deep into the residential neighbourhood for a drink on location of the quintessential Boston film. Now a stop on the **Boston Movie Tours** (www.boston movietours.net) – they even give patrons enough time for a round – the L Street's regular denizens tell stories of J-Lo popping in with then paramour Ben Affleck, and of Robin Williams gleefully buying drinks for the house.

1000s of
things to do...

during exam weeks. In the half century since then, it has kept Bogart in the annual line-up – which includes a Valentine's Day screening of *Casablanca*. The theater also celebrates such influential directors as David Lynch (who showed up for a special screening of his film *Inland Empire*), brings back short-lived cult hits and offers repertory series with themes such as 'Blondes Have More Fun' and 'Truman Capote on Screen'. Lately, the Brattle has expanded into experimental, arthouse and documentary territory – even throwing in the occasional concert. Its versatility (and newly minted license to serve wine and beer) make it a welcome independent powerhouse in the heart of Harvard Square.

★ Coolidge Corner Theatre

290 Harvard Street, at Green Street, Brookline (1-617 734 2500, www.coolidge.org). Coolidge Corner T. **Tickets** $7.50-$9.50; $6-$7.50 reductions. **Credit** MC, V.

Once the Beacon Universalists Church, the Coolidge was transformed into an art deco movie palace in 1933, but fell into disrepair. After putting up with shabby seats and dim lighting for years, Coolidge fans were rewarded in 2006 with new seats and beautifully restored fixtures, following major renovations. Local filmmakers get exposure in the new screening room upstairs, while the best indie films grace the balcony and ground-floor theaters. Children's matinées and special shows add to the appeal.

★ Harvard Film Archive

Carpenter Center for the Visual Arts, 24 Quincy Street, at Harvard University, Cambridge (1-617 495 4700, www.hcl.harvard.edu/hfa). Harvard T. **Tickets** $9; $7 reductions. **No credit cards.** **Map** p276 B2.

One of Cambridge's best-kept secrets, the Harvard Film Archive is a great place to see everything from obscure European films and hard-to-find experimental works to cinematic classics by the likes of Fassbinder and Truffaut. With its sleek, modern contours and 210-seat state-of-the-art Cinematheque, it provides a great viewing experience for everyone from serious-minded filmgoers to hip art kids.

Kendall Square Cinema

1 Kendall Square, at Cardinal Medeiros Avenue, Cambridge (1-617 333 3456, www.landmark theatres.com). Kendall/MIT T. **Tickets** $9.25; $7 reductions. **Credit** AmEx, MC, V.

Gourmet goodies, knowledgeable staff and nine screens showing arthouse offerings. Conveniently located a stone's throw from such up and coming eateries as Hungry Mother, the Blue Room, Emma's Pizza and the Friendly Toast, dinner and a movie in Cambridge has rarely looked so hot.

► *For our reviews of restaurants and cafés around Kendall Square, see pp132-135.*

Museum of Fine Arts

465 Huntington Avenue, at Museum Road, Fenway, Back Bay (1-617 369 3907, www.mfa.org). Museum of Fine Arts T. **Tickets** $7-$9; $6-$8 reductions. **Credit** AmEx, MC, V. **Map** p274 E9.

The MFA's Remis Auditorium screens an intellectually stimulating programme of films, with a focus on local and foreign features and documentaries. Annual French, Jewish and international film festivals draw an arty crowd.

► *For exhibitions at the MFA, see p65.*

Mainstream & first-run

AMC Loews Boston Common

175 Tremont Street, at Boylston Street, Downtown (1-617 423 5801, www.amctheatres.com). Boylston or Chinatown T. **Tickets** $8-$10; $7-$9 reductions. **Credit** AmEx, MC, V. **Map** p272 K5.

This state-of-the-art complex, in a convenient central location, features 19 screens, all with stadium-style seating. With that many screens, it's a safe bet that the latest blockbuster is showing here.

Regal Fenway

Landmark Center, 401 Park Drive, at Brookline Avenue, Fenway, Back Bay (1-617 424 6111, www.regalcinemas.com). Fenway T. **Tickets** $10; $6-$8 reductions. **Credit** AmEx, MC, V.

This is where moviegoers head for mindless fun: things that go boom; lighter-than-air romance; and

ARTS & ENTERTAINMENT

Coolidge Corner Theatre.

predictable schmaltz. With fast food, comfy chairs and 13 huge screens, it's all about entertainment.

FILM FESTIVALS

Although it's a long way from becoming the home of the next Sundance, Boston has a fine array of film festivals in its cultural calendar. AMC Loews Theatres sponsor and host the **Boston Film Festival** (*see p183*). The week-long event in mid September shows a substantial roster of shorts and feature films. The **Boston Underground Film Festival** (*see p179*) screens bizarre and provocative cinematic fare, while spring's **Independent Film Festival of Boston** (1-617 697 8511, www.iffboston.org) has premières of indie films

heading for general release. The **Museum of Fine Arts** (*see p193*) hosts various annual festivals, ranging from the African Film Festival to the Human Rights Watch International Film Festival.

A couple of highly regarded out-of-town summer festivals allow you to combine sun, sand and screenings. Down on the Cape, the **Provincetown Film Festival** (1-508 487 3456, www.ptownfilmfest.org) blends indie and queer sensibilities in a packed June weekend, while the **Nantucket Film Festival** (1-508 325 6274, www.nantucketfilmfestival.org), also held in June, is a favorite excursion for Boston film-lovers, who take in shorts, documentaries and staged readings of scripts by emerging talents and celebrated screenwriters.

Faces & Places Tom Perrotta

The novelist and screenwriter has a few words to say about his city.

Novelist Tom Perrotta moved to the Boston area to take up a Harvard teaching post in 1994. He lives with his wife Mary and two children in the leafy suburb of Belmont, which helped to shape the fictional setting of his critically acclaimed novel *Little Children*. Perrotta (also the author of book-to-big-screen adaptation, *Election*) co-wrote the screenplay and made a cameo appearance in the 2006 film, which starred Kate Winslet and Jennifer Connelly. His latest novel is *The Abstinence Teacher*.

TO: Why do you live in the Boston area?
TP: This is really where my cultural life is oriented. Cambridge is the ultimate college town, and I always thought when I was young that I'd like to live in a college town. I'm a bus or bike ride away from Cambridge – I'll go to Harvard Square if I just want to be around people.

TO: So what's your favorite place around Harvard Square?
TP: Café Gato Rojo (Dudley House, Harvard Yard, 1-617 496 4658, open during term time) on the Harvard Campus, a little coffee shop run by students. I used to go there when I taught, so it's one of my old haunts. I like the atmosphere and the music and feeling like I'm back in college. I've got a bit of the permanent student in me.

TO: Where else in town do you enjoy spending time?
TP: I also like Central Square, and Davis Square in Somerville is one of the most happening places right now. I'm always happy to see music at the Lizard Lounge (*see p208*) or Toad (*see p209*). I go for the great local bands – Bill Janovitz and Crown Victoria, Dennis Brennan, the Gentlemen, the Rudds.

TO: Are you involved in the local film scene, and where do you go to view?
TP: I've participated in the Belmont World Film Festival (www.belmontworldfilm.org) and am a big fan of the theater where it takes place: the Belmont Studio Cinema (376 Trapelo Road, 1-617 484 1706). I also love the Coolidge Corner Theatre in Brookline (*see p193*).

TO: What inspires you about the city?
TP: It's one of those intangible things. Maybe I'd be the same writer if I lived somewhere else, but there's an energy here that works for me. It's a smart place – hopefully that keeps you sharp.

TO: And what annoys you?
TP: Trying to park my car in Cambridge. And the roads are terrible – too many potholes!

Galleries

Creatively and geographically, the art scene is pushing the boundaries.

Independent galleries and arts spaces are springing up all over the map – until recently, they tended to be clustered on a single street, block or locale. The expansion has been driven in part by the growing popularity and accessibility of video, digital and abstract art, and by initiatives such as the ongoing open-studio events that have brought fresh attention to thriving artistic communities in sometimes unexpected parts of the city.

While the increasingly swanky South End art scene continues to see the greatest growth, and the more established Newbury Street remains a vital destination, there are now must-see spaces all over Cambridge, Somerville and Jamaica Plain, as well as in longtime artists' live-work district Fort Point Channel.

BACK BAY

Although the South End has given its more conservative neighbor Back Bay a run for its money with a cluster of contemporary galleries, Newbury Street is still the centre of Boston's commercial art scene (as well as its main upscale retail drag). Here you'll find the cream of the crop and the bottom of the barrel: blue-chip art emporiums and groundbreaking galleries share stylish brownstones with tourist traps selling hotel-lobby art. Listed here is our pick of the best.

★ Barbara Krakow Gallery

10 Newbury Street, at Arlington Street (1-617 262 4490, www.barbarakrakowgallery.com). Arlington T. **Open** 10am-5.30pm Tue-Sat. **Map** p275 H5.

This is one of the most prestigious, long-standing galleries in the city, and Barbara Krakow is the reason why. Her continued enthusiasm for new talent – both local and international – along with her excellent taste in well-established contemporary artists guarantee that there's always plenty to engage with and appreciate here. Past exhibitions have included the dark drawings of Louise Bourgeois, and political art on the theme of censorship from Jenny Holzer.

Chase Gallery

129 Newbury Street, between Clarendon & Dartmouth Streets (1-617 859 7222, www. chasegallery.com). Copley T. **Open** 10.30am-6pm Mon-Fri; 10am-5.30pm Sat. **Map** p275 G6.

An expansive picture window gives artists a stunning showcase for bustling foot traffic to peer in at. Best known for showing work in a variety of media by renowned national artists, the Chase Gallery also prides itself on helping up-and-coming artists from the local area, such as Melora Kuhn and Steve Hollinger, to gain a foothold on the aspirational strip.

THE SOUTH END

Before the high-rise condos, style-conscious boutiques and ever-expanding slew of restaurants changed the character of this formerly edgy district, an enclave of galleries set up shop near one of the city's main homeless shelters. Now the South End is one of the top destinations for art in the city. In the area

INSIDE TRACK
MARKETING ARTISTS

The vibrant **SoWa Open Market** (*see p158*), held every Sunday – except holiday weekends – from May to October, offers Boston's best chance to find a new artist, uncover eclectic antiques, buy artisanal and locally grown food or sift through vintage and handmade clothes. The weekly event has been compared to West London's Portobello Market and is teeming with chances to bring home one-of-a-kind artworks at decent prices.

Out of the Blue Gallery.

rebranded, to the irritation of locals, as SoWa (south of Washington Street), a varied collection of studios, commercial and experimental spaces is housed in the old warehouse on the corner of Thayer Street and Harrison Avenue.

The South End galleries and artists' studios co-ordinate their schedules so that all openings are held on the first Friday evening of every month – making for an unmissable open-house bash. See www.sowaartistsguild.com for more information on the next event.

Howard Yezerski Gallery

460 Harrison Avenue, at Thayer Street (1-617 262 0550, www.howardyezerskigallery.com). Back Bay T then 10min walk, or Silver Line Washington St to East Berkeley St. **Open** 10am-5.30pm Tue-Sat. **Map** p275 H5.

A fixture on the Back Bay scene for decades, Yezerski managed to embody the upscale milieu of the area while still presenting some of the most provocative and resolutely non-commercial work to be found anywhere in the city. And now he's entered new territory in the culturally fertile SoWa area. He's also willing to devote shows to younger groups such as Coach TV, who combine performance art with photography and painting, as well as showcasing established local names such as video artist Denise Marika.

★ Mills Gallery

Boston Center for the Arts, 539 Tremont Street, at Clarendon Street, South End (1-617 426 8835, www.bcaonline.org). Back Bay T. **Open** noon-5pm Wed, Sun; noon-9pm Thur-Sat. **Map** p275 H7.

One of the most experimental galleries in town, the BCA's exhibition space is best known for hosting unusual collaborative group shows. Past exhibitions have explored such subjects as obsessive-compulsive disorder; another project brought together six artists from Iran, Belgium and the Netherlands to create artwork on the theme of totalitarian regimes using the internet, video, sound and graphic design.

Samson Projects

450 Harrison Avenue, at Thayer Street, South End (1-617 357 7177, www.samsonprojects. com). Back Bay T then 10min walk, or Silver Line Washington St to East Berkeley St. **Open** noon-5pm Wed-Sat. **Map** 275 J8.

A commercial gallery with a very experimental attitude, Samson Projects represents a group of edgy artists that includes Suzannah Sinclair, whose simple line drawings of young women explode with sensuality; and Taylor Davis, a sculptor of strangely mundane items – his work *Cage for a Bale of Hay* is on the surface exactly that, but holds a deeper meaning.
► *For more on the SoWa area, see p66.*

CAMBRIDGE

It's also worth checking out MIT's **List Visual Arts Center** (*see p86*), known for its challenging contemporary exhibitions.

Cambridge Multicultural Arts Center

41 Second Street, at Otis Street, Lechmere (1-617 577 1400, www.cmacusa.org). Lechmere T. **Open** 10am-6pm Mon-Fri.

The CMAC is a huge performing arts space that features two galleries, dedicated almost exclusively to visual arts. Exhibitions represent cultures from around the globe: here you'll find intense, thought-provoking exhibitions, such as drawings by war-scarred children in Sierra Leone and photographs of shanty towns in Buenos Aires.

Out of the Blue Gallery

106 Prospect Street, between Harvard & St Paul Streets, Central Square (1-617 354 5287, www.outoftheblueartgallery.com). Central T. **Open** 10.30am-8pm most days (staff are volunteers, so call ahead).

Completely dedicated to the local arts scene, this gallery focuses exclusively on homegrown talent. Artists with even the most minimal amount of experience can show at the space, which handles 40 to 60 artists a month and features everything from painting to pottery. Out of the Blue also provides artwork for the walls of many of the coffee shops, clubs, restaurants and other venues in town.

ELSEWHERE

Although the developers have moved in, several artists' studios have survived in the Fort Point Channel area of the waterfront. There are also interesting arty enclaves worth investigating in Jamaica Plain and Somerville.

Axiom

141 Green Street, at Armory Street, Jamaica Plain (1-617 676 5904, www.axiomart.org). Green St T. **Open** 2-5pm Tue; 6-9pm Wed; 2-9pm Thur.
This spunky little gallery, which shares its premises with the Green Street T station, is one of the biggest promoters of innovative new media and video art in Boston. The shows almost always have an element of anarchic fun to them, like the Interactive Cake exhibition, in which artists used baked goods as a medium, and the iArt show, during which an artist who had transmitted a video blog from his car then drove it into the gallery.

Brickbottom Gallery

1 Fitchburg Street, off McGrath Highway, Lechmere, Somerville (1-617 776 3410, www.brickbottomartists.com). Lechmere T then 10min walk. **Open** noon-5pm Thur-Sat.
The denizens of this bustling artists' colony live and work in their own studio spaces. The on-site gallery shows only the work of Brickbottom artists, which ranges from painting to sculpture and conceptual art.

Fort Point Arts Community Gallery

300 Summer Street, at A Street, Waterfront (1-617 423 4299, www.fortpointarts.org). South Station T. **Open** 9am-3.30pm Mon-Wed, Fri; 9am-6pm Thur.
On the ground floor of a live/work studio building, the FPAC Gallery specialises in challenging video art, such as the work of Michael Sheridan, who projected sensual close-up films of vegetables being cut on to a bed of white rice, and strange metaphysical visual art, such as the Metamorphosis Chamber show, which featured mutated oddball pen and ink drawings by John Casey and the automatic drawing of Basil El Halwagy.
▶ *Check the website for details of the annual autumn open studios, when more than 200 artists in the Fort Point area open to the public.*

JP Art Market

36 South Street, at Sedgwick Street, Jamaica Plain (1-617 522 1729, www.jpartmarket.com). Bus 39. **Open** 1.30-8.30pm Wed-Fri; 11am-8.30pm Sat; 11am-5pm Sun.

In 1992, artist/curator Patti Hudson opened this tiny space, similar to one she'd run in NYC in the '80s. It's best known for exclusive showings of the visual artwork of Hudson's friend, rock poetess Patti Smith, as well as a long list of local artists associated with the Boston music scene, such as photographer Liz Linder.

★ Photographic Resource Center

832 Commonwealth Avenue, at Amory Street, Allston (1-617 975 0600, www.bu.edu/prc). BU West T. **Open** 10am-6pm Tue-Fri; 10am-8pm Thur; noon-5pm Sat, Sun. **Admission** $4; $2 reductions. **Map** p276 B5.
Although exclusively devoted to photography, this space manages to present some of the most varied and scintillating shows in the city. Past exhibitions have included the photographic efforts of rock stars (including Lou Reed) and a show featuring work that was made using the technology of early optical and cinematic devices. A non-profit organization located on the campus of Boston University, the PRC also offers regular workshops and lectures, plus the occasional photography-related film screening.

Studio Soto

Thompson Design Group, 35 Channel Center Street, at Iron Street, Waterfront (1-617 426 7686, www.studiosoto.com). South Station T. **Open** 5-9pm Thur, Fri; noon-5pm Sat, Sun.
Calling itself 'a space for ideas', Studio Soto is one of the most versatile and innovative galleries in town. Previous exhibitions here have included works by visual artist Reuben Moore, who renders taut, emotional black and white drawings; and the curious modular wooden tube installations of sculptor Tim Murdock; as well as musical performances by such eclectic groups as the Metal and Glass Ensemble and the Gang Clan Mafia. The debut of the documentary *Radical Jesters*, by local filmmaker Tim Jackson, also took place here. In short, anything goes.

INSIDE TRACK
THE ART OF SCIENCE

Encompassing indoor and outdoor spaces across town, the biennial **Boston Cyberarts Festival** (1-617 524 8495, www.bostoncyberarts.org) brings together arty types and science boffins in a glorious fusion of aesthetics and technology. The two-week festival is held in odd-numbered years and includes art exhibitions at small galleries, futuristic dance concerts, talks and readings. Past years have featured everything from robot orchestras to motion-triggered sound installations, and it seems to get more out-there every time. An unmissable spectacle if you happen to find yourself here in late April.

ARTS & ENTERTAINMENT

Gay & Lesbian

Welcome to the US capital of same-sex marriage.

Although some neighborhoods are more welcoming than others, Boston is generally the kind of place where you can walk downtown hand in hand with your same-sex paramour and no one will bat an eyelid. The city's gay and lesbian population is one of the largest in the United States, and one of the most integrated.

But while the strict social and religious mores of its founders may have long since given way to laissez-faire liberalism, Boston has inherited from its Puritan ancestry a tendency toward aloofness – and the city is infamous among gay travelers for its 'attitude' problem. Still, many gay and lesbian residents, most of whom are from somewhere else to begin with, adopt a frosty demeanor only because it's the local custom – given half a chance, they'll lower their guard soon enough.

THE SCENE

The South End is no longer the magnet it once was for young men wanting to get their first taste of living in a 'gay ghetto'. But even if straight people are buying into the area far more than they once did, the South End has by far the largest concentration of gay-owned businesses in Boston. Most shops are adorned with rainbow-striped flags, signaling their gay-friendliness. The streets are lined with little shops that mix kitsch with quality in equal measure. Gay men set the tone on Tremont Street: flirting with a waiter or salesperson of the same sex will not always get you better service, but it's still a no-risk strategy.

A few adjacent neighborhoods also have a large gay presence. To the north, Bay Village is a tiny enclave of small brick houses; to the west, the Fens is a notorious cruising area (be warned, it can be risky after dark).

Jamaica Plain – Boston's answer to New York's Brooklyn – is home to an ever-growing lesbian population, and across the river, Cambridge and Somerville are especially queer-friendly. Meanwhile, unexpectedly gay neighborhoods seem to be sprouting up in historically conservative Dorchester.

INFORMATION & MEDIA

Bay Windows (www.baywindows.com) is the city's main paper for the gay and lesbian community, covering local and national news

in a fairly straightforward fashion. The weekly is distributed on Thursdays in bookstores, cafés and gay bars throughout Boston, Cambridge and Somerville, and is also available online. Boston's *Weekly Dig* (*see p256*) and *Boston Phoenix* (*see p256*), two free alternative papers, also feature plenty of articles related to gay and lesbian issues in their pages. Finally, the local glossy magazine *Boston Spirit* is published every other month.

BARS & CLUBS

Perhaps it's simply a sign of just how integrated the scene here is, but for its size, Boston has surprisingly few gay bars. The problem doesn't seem to be rooted in any kind of homophobia; rather, the city's powerful neighborhood groups make it downright difficult to open any establishment that might lead to nocturnal sidewalk loitering. Boston isn't a late-night town: the city's legally mandated 2am closing time shuts the party down early, and the T stops running at 12.30am, forcing club-goers to either cab it or compete for scarce parking spots. Lesbian nightlife options are particularly sparse, and the lack of a seven-day-a-week bar for the ladies is a perennial complaint. After-hours culture does exist, but you need to know where to look – for starters, check out the members-only **Rise**. Once one of the biggest gay clubs in town, **Venu** (*see p215*) is more mixed these days.

Boston's bar scene might not compete with the likes of New York or Montreal, but there are plenty of places to see and be seen, chat up the locals or just sit back and enjoy a nice quiet pint.

Alley

275 Washington Street, at School Street, Downtown (1-617 263 1449, www.thealleybar. com). Gov't Center or State St T. **Open** 2pm-2am daily. **No credit cards. Map** p272 K4.

This unmarked two-level haunt for bears, cubs and leatherfolk (and the twinks who dig them) is the unofficial torch-bearer of its equally cruisey antecedent, 119 Merrimack. It's a good place to ogle Red Sox players (games are shown on a huge screen), shoot some pool, ignore the bad house music and shake paws with the generally friendly ursine community. Saturday nights are the big 'uns.

Club Café

209 Columbus Avenue, at Berkeley Street, South End (1-617 536 0966, www.clubcafe.com). Back Bay T. **Open** 1pm-1am Mon; 1pm-2am Tue-Sat; 11am-1am Sun. **Credit** AmEx, DC, MC, V. **Map** p275 H6.

A sprawling bar/restaurant complex, and one of gay Boston's mainstays, Club Café hasn't changed much over the years. At the front lingers an older, professional crowd of cruisey gay men and a few business-suited lesbians. Out back is the men's video bar, the Moonshine Room – a crowded, preppy, collegiate version of the posh scene at the front. It peaks at about midnight, after which people drift toward the clubs – or, you know, wherever.
▶ *For the restaurant 209 at Club Café, see p202.*

Dbar

1236 Dorchester Avenue, at Hancock Street, Dorchester (1-617 265 4490, www.dbarboston. com). Savin Hill T. **Open** 5pm-midnight Sun-Wed; 5pm-2am Thur-Sat. *Food served* 5-10pm daily. **Main courses** $16-$19. **Credit** AmEx, MC, V.

The owners of Dbar took over a grubby little Irish pub and installed a dark wood interior, a lengthy martini list and an upscale menu that rivals most of its downtown cousins. After 10pm on weekends, the smoke machines, lights and rib-shaking subwoofers come on, and suddenly the night belongs to Mariah.

Eagle

520 Tremont Street, at Berkeley Street, South End (1-617 542 4494, www.clubcafe.com). Back Bay T. **Open** 3pm-2am Mon-Fri; 1pm-2am Sat; noon-2am Sun. **No credit cards. Map** p275 J7.

While it seems that the Eagle in every other major city ends up, by default, serving as the hub of the leather-and-Levi's scene, Boston's Eagle has slowly become a divey, neighborhood cruise bar; perhaps thanks to the high-speed yuppification of its cushy South End environs. Either way, it's a classic – especially the 2am 'sidewalk sale' that takes place along Tremont Street.

Fritz

Chandler Inn, 26 Chandler Street, at Berkeley Street, South End (1-617 482 4428, www.fritz boston.com). Back Bay T. **Open** noon-2am Mon-Fri; 11am-2am Sat, Sun. **No credit cards. Map** p275 H7.

ARTS & ENTERTAINMENT

Club Café.

A low-key neighborhood bar that attracts all types, including out-of-towners staying upstairs at the Chandler Inn (see *p108*). When people complain about Boston gays being unfriendly, take them here for an Amstel and a ballgame, and prove them wrong by chatting with the regulars. Brunch is served until 3pm on weekends.

Jacque's Cabaret

79 Broadway, between Piedmont & Winchester Streets, Back Bay (1-617 426 8902, www.jacques cabaret.com). Arlington T. **Open** noon-midnight daily. **Admission** $6-$10. **No credit cards. Map** p275 J6.

The oldest – and easily the most rocking – gay bar in town, Jacque's features drag queen shows from Tuesday to Saturday, fringe rock 'n' roll from Friday to Monday and cheap beer all the time. It's hardly glamorous, but the filthy banter and all the discount-store outfits add up to an entertaining evening, and once in a while there's a performer who's shockingly good.

Machine

1254 Boylston Street, between Ipswich Street & Yawkey Way, Fenway, Back Bay (1-617 536 1950, www.machine-boston.com). Kenmore T. **Open** 10pm-2am Mon, Tue, Fri, Sat. **Admission** $5-$6. **No credit cards. Map** p274 D7.

Jacque's Cabaret.

This popular, glitzy club beneath the Ramrod (see *below*) features a dancefloor with state-of-the-art lighting (which equals fun), a video lounge (which equals porn) and a separate room with pool tables.

Midway Café

3496 Washington Street, at McBride Street, Jamaica Plain (1-617 524 9038, www.midway cafe.com). Green St T. **Open** 4pm-2am daily. **Admission** free-$5. **No credit cards.**

Though not officially gay, this tiny, noisy, divey Jamaica Plain rock bar has always been popular with local queer folk. On Thursdays, a rowdy, dykey crowd takes over the bumping dancefloor and postage-stamp stage for Queeraoke.

Paradise

180 Massachusetts Avenue, at Albany Street, Kendall, Cambridge (1-617 868 3000, www. paradisecambridge.com). Central T then 10min walk, or bus 1. **Open** 9pm-2am Mon-Wed, Sun; 9pm-2am Thur; 7pm-2am Fri, Sat. **Admission** free-$4. **No credit cards. Map** p276 C4.

It's just on the other side of the Charles River from Boston, but Paradise has the feel of the only gay bar in a small town. The crowd is racially mixed and includes all age groups. Upstairs, there are porn videos and often-shirtless bartenders. Admittedly hot go-go dancers circulate among the customers, cheap drinks flow and, downstairs, the dancefloor fills to the sound of power diva vocals.

Precinct

70 Union Square, at Washington Street, Somerville (1-617 623 9211, www.precinctbar. com). Davis T then bus 87. **Open** 4pm-1am Mon-Thur; 4pm-2am Fri; 11am-2am Sat; 11am-1am Sun. **Admission** $5. **Credit** AmEx, MC, V.

It's easy to miss the entrance to Precinct, tucked away below sidewalk level on Union Square. But once inside, you'll see the lounge is upscale without being too pretentious, and big enough (with several different rooms) to offer variety while retaining an intimate feel. Irish music evenings from Sunday to Wednesday are free, while themed nights held during the rest of the week require a small cover charge.

Ramrod

1254 Boylston Street, between Ipswich Street & Yawkey Way, Fenway, Back Bay (1-617 266 2986, www.ramrod-boston.com). Kenmore T. **Open** noon-2am daily. **No credit cards. Map** p274 D7.

This Boylston Street bar is the HQ of Boston's leather scene, and home to such master-and-slave groups as the Leather Knights. On the weekend, the backroom is restricted to men who are bare-chested or wearing leather gear. Because the Ramrod also serves as a neighborhood bar, the front area isn't so intimidating.
▶ *For something different, head downstairs to Machine; see above.*

A Colorful History

Four centuries of gay and lesbian life.

Back in 2003, the eyes of the nation turned to the gay community in Massachusetts, as a local lesbian couple, Julie and Hillary Goodridge, became the lead plaintiffs in a historic legal victory for gay civil rights. The Massachusetts Supreme Judicial Court ruled that preventing gay couples from marrying violated the state constitution. The Goodridges were among the first same-sex couples to wed in May 2004 when gay marriage became legal in Massachusetts. Despite spirited opposition from conservatives, same-sex marriage has been upheld by the state legislature and remains the law of the land, although gay couples who marry here cannot get federal recognition of their marriages.

Leading the nation on gay rights is a Massachusetts tradition that stretches back decades. Back in 1972, Bostonian Elaine Noble became the first openly gay or lesbian person to win a seat in any state legislature. Some 15 years later, the first two openly gay members of the US Congress (Gerry Studds and Barney Frank) represented suburban Boston. In 1990, Massachusetts became one of the first states to pass a comprehensive gay rights law; more recently, it has developed programs to protect gay youth from harassment in schools.

While Boston's gay community can often feel transient and somewhat youth-oriented, it's rooted in 400 years of history. The first governor of the fledgling state of Massachusetts, John Winthrop, wrote love letters to a man he had left behind in England. Later, at least one lesbian from Boston, Deborah Sampson, fought for Independence alongside the Minutemen. Using the name Robert Shurtleff, Sampson wooed many a maiden, and no one discovered that she was in fact a woman until she was wounded in battle.

In the 19th century, the 'Athens of America' is said to have been rife with men-loving literary men. Much has been read into Herman Melville's dedication of *Moby-Dick* to Nathaniel Hawthorne, and Ralph Waldo Emerson's diary chronicles an obsession with a Harvard classmate. Better documented are the so-called 'Boston Marriages' – socially sanctioned relationships between women. Writer Sarah Orne Jewett and poet Amy Lowell, among

others, took female partners. By the end of the century, Boston's art scene also included a strong queer presence. Isabella Stewart Gardner, the widow who founded the museum that bears her name (*see p64*), surrounded herself with a posse of gay admirers, including architect Ralph Adams Cram and the painter John Singer Sargent.

Still, gay culture in town remained underground until after World War II, when Boston's first gay bars began springing up among the strip joints and burlesque houses of Scollay Square (sadly, this teeming, saucy neighborhood is no more; it's now the sterile Government Center). In a reference to the sleazy area of New York City, lower Washington Street became known as 'Gay Times Square', while Bay Village – sandwiched between Chinatown and the South End – became a haven for gay Bostonians. Most of these areas were razed in a neo-Puritan attempt at 'urban renewal' back in the 1960s – although by then, Boston's homosexual network was well established.

The gay community took to the streets after the infamous 1969 Stonewall riots in New York kicked off gay emancipation across the country, and organized what became one of the country's first annual Gay Pride parades in 1971. For the first few years, the parade involved only a few hundred people and had a somewhat militant tone. These days, however, **Boston Pride** (*see p180*) is a giant party that lasts an entire week in June, including everything from *Idol*-style singing competitions to art exhibitions and Boston Harbor party cruises. The event regularly draws crowds in excess of 100,000 from all over New England, and corporate sponsors vie for space at the post-march fair.

ARTS & ENTERTAINMENT

Rise

*306 Stuart Street, at Arlington Street, Back Bay
(1-617 423 7473, www.riseclub.us). Arlington T.*
Open 2am-6.30am Fri; 1.30am-6.30am Sat.
Admission $10 members; $20 guests.
Credit MC, V. **Map** p275 J6.
Saturday nights at Boston's only sanctioned after-hours club offer an enticing mix of gay boys who just can't go to bed yet. The beat goes on until 6.30am, however there is a catch: the club is members only, and entry can only be secured via the sponsorship of a current member. Something to bear in mind when you're meeting guys earlier in the evening, perhaps.

RESTAURANTS & CAFES

Any restaurants or cafés in the South End are, by virtue of their location, gay-friendly. The eateries listed below are particularly popular with queer patrons.

209 at Club Café

*209 Columbus Avenue, at Berkeley Street,
South End (1-617 536 0966, www.clubcafe.com).
Back Bay T.* **Open** 1pm-1am Mon; 1pm-2am
Tue-Sat; 11am-1am Sun. **Main courses**
$10-$23. **Credit** AmEx, DC, MC, V.
Map p275 H6.
209 had long been a cruisey standby on the lounge scene, with a contemporary American restaurant that was mostly incidental to the action at the bar in Club Café. That's changed, though: thanks to a new chef and an updated menu, the restaurant has earned its place in the spotlight. It's also one of the

few places in town where you'll see both gay men and lesbians congregating on a regular basis.
▶ *For our review of the Club Café bar, see p199.*

City Girl Café

*204 Hampshire Street, at Inman Street, Inman
Square, Cambridge (1-617 864 2809, www.
citygirlcafe.com). Central T then 15min walk.*
Open 11am-9pm Tue-Fri; 10am-9pm Sat; 11am-4pm Sun. **Main courses** $7-$14. **Credit** MC, V.
Map p276 C2.
A tiny, friendly, funky lesbian-owned café in the heart of Inman Square. Drop by for freshly made pizza, pasta, sandwiches and salads, and a decent cup of coffee. They also serve wine and beer.

Diesel Café

*257 Elm Street, at Chester Street, Davis Square,
Somerville (1-617 629 8717, www.diesel-café.com).
Davis T.* **Open** 7am-11.30pm Mon-Fri; 8am-11.30pm Sat, Sun. **Credit** MC, V.
There's always a sizeable hipster contingent at the Diesel – drawn, no doubt, by the posse of cute, androgynous baristas (or is it the vegan cake?). Whatever the attraction, this popular coffee and lunch spot is usually packed with Davis Square locals, fuelling up on high-octane espresso, giggling in the instant photo booth or lining up shots at one of the pool tables. Wi-Fi is available.

Francesca's Café & Espresso Bar

*564 Tremont Street, at Clarendon Street, South
End (1-617 482 9026). Back Bay T.* **Open** 8am-11pm daily. **Main courses** $4-$10. **No credit
cards**. **Map** p275 H7.

Diesel Café.

A Perfect Day in Ptown

The gay coastal destination of first resort.

New England's answer to Miami's South Beach or San Francisco's Castro area, **Provincetown** is the definitive gay summer destination on the East Coast, even more so than New York's Fire Island. The coastal resort on the outermost tip of Cape Cod has long been a destination for gay and lesbian visitors, with roots going back to 1899, when Charles Hawthorne started an artists' colony there. It became a Bohemian enclave, isolated by its geography – and alluring for that very reason.

Out of season, it's a sleepy seaside hamlet, but in summer it throngs with hip gay and lesbian pleasure-seekers, drag queens, artists and heterosexual tourists. Served by a 90-minute high-speed ferry (*see p246*), it makes an easy weekend jaunt. Follow our insiders' itinerary so you don't waste a minute.

MORNING
A morning in Ptown doesn't begin until you've dropped by **Wired Puppy** (379 Commercial Street, 1-508 487 0017) for a potent espresso, checking your email for free while you wait.

Next, to the sea. There's no need to worry about finding the best spot for cruising – every beach here is prime hunting ground. For a little exercise, trek over the town's harbor to **Long Point Beach**. It's at least 45 minutes each way, but the relatively sparse crowds and views of the nearby lighthouses are worth the walk.

AFTERNOON
With its shops, galleries, bars and restaurants, Commercial Street is the epicenter of Ptown. For a chic lunch on the cheap, **Frappo66** (214 Commercial Street, 1-508 487 9066) serves posh salads, soups and sandwiches. Next door, at no.212, is **Muir Music** (1-508 487 5777), whose wares represent a potted history of gay music and film.

By 5pm, you'll see a steady stream of visitors flocking to the **Boatslip** (*see p244*) for a summer tradition: the afternoon tea dance. For the uninitiated, there's no tea involved (unless it's of the Long Island iced variety) and the techno-thumping scene is anything but sedate.

EVENING
Keep that buzz with a pre-dinner cocktail on the porch at the unpretentious **Gifford House** (9 Carver Street, 1-508 487 0688). Beware: the bartenders pour with a heavy hand, and a single manhattan will send you stumbling into the night. For a little bit of romance, catch the $1 Provincetown Shuttle from MacMillan Pier or outside the Provincetown Inn (1 Commercial Street), which runs every half-hour to **Herring Cove Beach**; kick off your shoes and admire a panorama awash in sunset reds and oranges.

For dinner, try **Lorraine's** (133 Commercial Street, 1-508 487 6074), which offers upmarket Mexican dishes and an eye-popping tequila menu.

If playwright/actor Ryan Landry (*see p229*) is performing at the **Crown & Anchor** (247 Commercial Street, 1-508 487 1430), his show is a must. A local treasure, Landry is famed for his whip-smart Tennessee Williams parodies (*Pussy on the House*, anyone?) and weekly Showgirls nightlife revue in summer.

After a waterside stroll, it's time to dance – if you can move at the packed **A-House** (*see p244*), the town's vanguard gay bar. Ladies, meanwhile, should check out low-key **Vixen** (336 Commercial Street, 1-508 487 6424) for drinks and a game of pool.

A casual hangout for posh South Enders, coffee purists and – most importantly – gossiping gay neighbors, with a fantastic streetside view. Service isn't fast, but it is friendly, and they know how to pick the music. Grab a pastry and coffee to go, or cozy up to the counter for a light lunch and a scoop of ice-cream while you read the gay news.

▶ *For more South End eateries, see pp124-128.*

SHOPS & SERVICES

Blade Barber Shop
603 Tremont Street, at Dartmouth Street, South End (1-617 267 2200, www.bladebarbershop. com). Back Bay T. **Open** 10am-7pm Mon; 11am-8pm Tue, Wed; 10am-8pm Thur, Fri; 9am-5pm Sat. **Credit** MC, V. **Map** p275 H7.
It might seem a mite on the pricey side for a plain ol' barbershop (a haircut costs $25) – but the fellas at Blade pay special attention to detail, and the gossip you'll overhear is worth the price alone. Everyone likes a clean-cut boy, so call ahead and book an appointment.

★ Boomerangs
716 Centre Street, at Harris Avenue, Jamaica Plain (1-617 524 5120, www.shopboomerangs. com). Green St T then 10min walk, or bus 39. **Open** 10am-7pm Mon-Wed, Fri, Sat; 10am-8pm Thur; 11am-6pm Sun. **Credit** AmEx, MC, V.
A resale store run by the AIDS Action Committee, Boomerangs has a great variety of used clothes, furniture and household items. Quality is usually a cut above the norm, and the eye to detail and love of the odd (1950s retractable projection screen, anyone?) make this a delightful place to lose an hour or two. **Other locations** Boomerangs Special Edition, 1407 Washington Street, at Union Park Street, South End (1-617 456 0996).

Calamus Bookstore
92B South Street, at East Street, Downtown (1-617 338 1931, www.calamusbooks.com). South Station T. **Open** 9am-7pm Mon-Sat; noon-6pm Sun. **Credit** AmEx, MC, V. **Map** p273 L5.
A replacement for proprietor John Mitzel's former venture, Glad Day Bookshop (a victim of rising rents in Back Bay), this spacious shop has all the books, magazines and videos you'll need. But the out of the way location has prevented a re-creation of the original's entertaining, cruisey atmosphere.

Eros
581A Tremont Street, at Union Park Street, South End (1-617 425 0345, www.erosboutique. com). Back Bay T. **Open** 10am-10pm daily. **Credit** AmEx, MC, V. **Map** p275 H7.
This Tremont Street sex shop caters mostly to the fetish crowd. Despite the shop's small square footage, there's an impressive variety of leather, latex and black rubber goods.

Good Vibrations
308A Harvard Street, at Coolidge Corner, Brookline (1-617 264 4400, www.goodvibes.com). Coolidge Corner T. **Open** 10am-7pm Mon-Wed, Sun; 10am-8pm Thur; 10am-9pm Fri, Sat. **Credit** AmEx, MC, V.
Boston's friendliest sex shop isn't as much fun or as independent-minded as its predecessor (Grand Opening!), but it's still a nice, brightly lit, women-centered place to pick up a few toys. As a bonus, there's a (somewhat terrifying) museum of antique vibrators in the back.

Liquid Hair Studios
640 Tremont Street, at Canton Street, South End (1-617 425 4848, www.liquidhairstudios.com). Back Bay T. **Open** 11am-8pm Tue, Thur, Fri; 11am-6pm Wed; 10am-6pm Sat. **Credit** AmEx, MC, V. **Map** p275 H8.
Elvis lives on at this fashion-forward salon. The tattooed and well-coiffed staff dispense Newbury Street pampering at Tremont Street prices; styles range from mildly trendy to all-out punk.

Marquis Leathers
92 South Street, at Tufts Street, Downtown (1-617 426 2120). South Station T. **Open** 10am-11pm daily. **Credit** AmEx, MC, V. **Map** p273 L5.
Marquis Leathers' store is, appropriately enough, found in the loft apartment-laden Leather District. In addition to renting and selling pretty much every video known to male homodom, Marquis keeps the neighborhood well supplied with magazines, toys, leather accessories and lube.

Revolution Fitness
209 Columbus Avenue, at Berkeley Street, Back Bay (1-617 536 3006, www.revfitboston.com). Back Bay T. **Open** 5am-10pm Mon-Fri; 8am-8pm Sat, Sun. **Rates** $20 day pass. **Credit** AmEx, MC, V. **Map** p275 H6.
Where the South End boys with attitude work out. Revolution has the latest weight-training and cardio equipment and very good aerobics staff. It's best at off-peak hours if you're the type who just wants to get the workout over with. Otherwise, it can be a little like a gay bar with weights.

▶ *For more gyms, see p222.*

Teddy Shoes
548 Massachusetts Avenue, at Brookline Street, Central Square, Cambridge (1-617 547 0443, www.teddyshoes.com). Central T. **Open** 10am-6pm Mon-Thur, Sat; 10am-7pm Fri. **Credit** AmEx, MC, V. **Map** p276 C3.
At Teddy's Shoes, drag-worthy PVC thigh-highs go toe-to-toe with ballet slippers and serious ballroom-dancing gear. Behind the unprepossessing storefront lies a massive collection of fetish shoes, platforms, and stilettos, in sizes up to a rather manly 16.

Music

Listen up: there's always a glut of gigs, both rockin' and refined.

Boston is a city built on rock 'n' roll, best known for its gritty clubs, which served as a breeding ground for well-known rock acts spanning four decades. However, the city also has a rich history of fostering classical, folk and jazz performances. And it's an up-and-coming destination for electronic music, evident in the success of the first New England electronic music festival, **Together** (*see p215* **Inside Track**), which sold out clubs around the city during its 2010 debut.

Home of one of the premier music schools in the country, **Berklee College of Music**, Boston's musical tastes are panoramic, and acts worth seeing can be found on any day of the week at one of the many clubs, concert halls and arena-sized venues that populate the city.

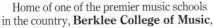

Classical & Opera

Boston's classical music scene is in good health, thanks, in part, to the presence of the **New England Conservatory** (www.newenglandconservatory.edu), which continues to bring a steady stream of musical talent to the city.

Founded in 1881, the highbrow **Boston Symphony Orchestra** (www.bso.org) remains a world-class institution. Its more mainstream offshoot, the **Boston Pops Orchestra** (www.bostonpops.org) pushes for the popular vote, reaching for a younger audience by pairing up with artists such as Ben Folds and My Morning Jacket. There's also the feisty young BPO – the **Boston Philharmonic Orchestra** (www.bostonphil.org) – formed in 1979.

And it doesn't end there; the renowned **Boston Lyric Opera** (BLO; www.blo.org) celebrated its 30th anniversary in 2007. Then there's **Opera Boston** (www.operaboston.com), which takes a more innovative approach, staging modern and rarely performed works. In 2007, it also launched the **Boston Opera Underground**, which performs 'opera cabaret' in clubs and other non-classical settings.

On the more traditional side of things, **Emmanuel Music** (www.emmanuelmusic.org) continues its tradition of presenting Bach's cantatas, along with large-scale works and

chamber music from a pantheon of greats. The melodious **Boston Cecilia** (www.bostoncecilia.org), one of America's oldest musical institutions, presents choral works ancient and modern in venues around the city, while the **Boston Musica Viva** (www.bmv.org) ensemble dedicates itself to contemporary music. Finally, there's **Boston's Early Music Festival** (www.bemf.org), whose mission is to revive medieval, Renaissance and Baroque works.

In addition to the venues listed below, the **Wang Theatre** and **Shubert Theatre**, both part of the **Citi Performing Arts Center** (*see p225*), host the occasional concert, featuring artists from all over the globe. Summer brings free concerts at the **Hatch Shell** (*see p212*

INSIDE TRACK
ORCHESTRAL MOVEMENTS

The **Boston Symphony Orchestra**'s home, Symphony Hall (*see p206*), is one of the finest concert halls in the world. But in July and August, the BSO packs up and moves to **Tanglewood** (1-413 637 1600, www.tanglewood.org), in the Berkshires, in Western Massachusetts – a venue more conducive to picnicking. It also hosts the Festival of Contemporary Music and the Tanglewood Jazz Festival.

ARTS & ENTERTAINMENT

Inside Track) on the Charles River Esplanade, where the Boston Pops Fourth of July Concert (*see p181*) is an annual must-see for locals.

TICKETS AND INFORMATION

Weekly music listings can be found in the city's major daily newspapers, the *Boston Globe* (www.boston.com) and the *Boston Herald* (www.boston herald.com), as well as alternative weeklies, the *Boston Phoenix* (www.thephoenix.com) and the *Weekly Dig* (www.weeklydig.com) – although the latter has more of a rock focus.

Ticketmaster (*see p176*) makes buying tickets for most major events simple, but you'll pay extra for the privilege. Dealing directly with venues, either by phone or online, may cut out the 'convenience charge'. Tickets are also sold through **TicketWeb** (*see p176*).

VENUES

Cutler Majestic Theatre at Emerson College

For listings, *see p230*.
Dating from 1903, this jewel-box Beaux Arts opera house was the first venue in Boston designed without pillars or other obstructions to visibility and sound. Nowadays, it hosts opera from the Teatro Lirico d'Europa, Opera Boston and the New England Conservatory, along with comedy performances and pop concerts.

Jordan Hall

30 Gainsborough Street, at Huntington Avenue, Back Bay (1-617 585 1260, www.newengland conservatory.edu/jordanhall). Mass Ave or Symphony T. **Box office** 10am-6pm Mon-Fri; noon-6pm Sat. **Tickets** prices vary. **Credit** MC, V. **Map** p274 F8.
The New England Conservatory's 1,013-capacity venue opened in 1903, providing another option for the city's classical music lovers, as well as an auditorium and lecture room for the faculty and its students. The program incorporates visits from world-class classical artists in addition to regular performances from NEC students.

Sanders Theatre.

Sanders Theatre

Memorial Hall, 45 Quincy Street, at Cambridge Street, Harvard Square, Cambridge (1-617 496 2222, www.boxoffice.harvard.edu). Harvard T. **Box office** (1350 Massachusetts Avenue, at Holyoke Street) noon-6pm Mon-Sat. **Tickets** prices vary. **Credit** AmEx, MC, V. **Map** p276 B2.
Its unusual semi-circular design, church-like wooden interior and wonderful acoustics make Harvard's main concert hall worth a visit. Apart from the university's major lectures (Winston Churchill and Martin Luther King Jr have stepped up to the stage), it hosts concerts by the Boston Philharmonic and Boston Chamber Music Society, plus the occasional folk, world and rock artist.

★ Symphony Hall

301 Massachusetts Avenue, at Huntington Avenue, Back Bay (1-617 266 1492, www.bso.org). Mass Ave or Symphony T. **Box office** 10am-6pm Mon-Fri; noon-6pm Sat. **Tickets** $17-$108. **Credit** AmEx, MC, V. **Map** p274 F8.
Symphony Hall opened its doors in 1900 as the home of the Boston Symphony Orchestra and the Boston Pops Orchestra. Extended in 1990 to add the Cohen Wing, it continues to update its facilities with new audio reproduction technology. Still, it's the all-important acoustics of the original interior design that have made it one the world's top auditoriums.
▶ *In summer, the BSO decamps to Tanglewood (see p205 Inside Track), while the Boston Pops wows with its Fourth of July Concert; see p181.*

Rock, Pop & Roots

The breeding ground of such greats as the Pixies, Aerosmith and the Mighty Mighty Bosstones, Boston has an impressive – and eclectic – musical heritage. However, most of the best-known clubs are actually across the river in Cambridge and Somerville. Central Square institutions such as the **Middle East**, **TT the Bear's Place** and the **Plough & Stars** attract a hip, music-savvy crowd of all ages.

The legendary downtown dives, jumping from the late 1970s through to the early '90s are all but gone. These days, the scene south of the river – aside from a cluster of rock clubs in or around hipster haven Allston – largely consists of major venues, hosting national and international touring acts. The trend seems to be moving towards mega-clubs such as the **House of Blues** (15 Lansdowne Street, Fenway, 1-888 693 2583, www.houseofblues. com), which rose from the ashes of two major Lansdowne Street clubs, Avalon and Axis, in 2009 and sold more tickets (314,597) in its inaugural year than any other club in the world. With a capacity of nearly 2,500, the kitsch Southern-inspired music hall and restaurant is one of Boston proper's only viable options for bands that are too large for the regular club scene, but not quite **TD Garden** material, which hosts acts such as Aerosmith and Madonna.

TICKETS AND INFORMATION

Local papers run extensive weekly listings for gigs and concerts (*see p255*). For tips on what's coming up and who's worth seeing, keep an eye on Boston's well-informed music blogs too (*see p211* **Sites & Sounds**).

For tickets to smaller concert, your best course of action is to check the venue websites. Tickets for bigger events are sold through **Ticketmaster**, **TicketWeb** or **TeleCharge** (for more about tickets, see *p176*). For sold-out events, **Craigslist** may come up with the goods (www.boston.craigslist.org). It's illegal to sell tickets for more than $2 above face value in Massachusetts – which isn't to say that it doesn't happen all the time. Forgeries aren't uncommon either.

VENUES

Arenas & stages

High-priced beer and wine are available at most large venues. In addition to those listed below, the Remis Auditorium at the **Museum of Fine Arts** (*see p65*) offers a great music program, with an emphasis on cool jazz, pop and indie rock acts, as well as classical offerings. With its fine acoustics and line-up, it's one of the best places to sit back and listen to music that taps into the head and not just the toes. Also look out for the MFA's summer series of live music, from indie rock to Latin, in the courtyard.

Bank of America Pavilion

290 Northern Avenue, at D Street, Waterfront (1-617 728 1600, www.livenation.com). Silver Line Waterfront to Silver Line Way. **Box office** 11am-4pm Mon-Fri. **Credit** AmEx, MC, V.
Boston's major outdoor venue (4,994 capacity) is pleasantly located in the South Boston waterfront area. It operates from May to September, featuring mainly mainstream rock, pop and R&B oldies, with a sprinkling of more contemporary acts. The Pavilion is basically a large tent, usually all seated, with an extensive concourse at the rear. Many gig-goers prefer to buy the cheaper concourse tickets, so they can party at the back.
► *Want to make a day of it, like the locals do? See p78 Inside Track.*

Berklee Performance Center

136 Massachusetts Avenue, at Boylston Street, Back Bay (1-617 747 2261, www. berkleebpc.com). Hynes T. **Box office** 10am-6pm Mon-Sat. **Tickets** $2-$10. **Credit** MC, V. **Map** p274 F7.
The line-up at Berklee School of Music's concert hall features an impressive roster of big-name artists, as well as student and faculty performances. All kinds of music are showcased here, from hip hop and rock to jazz and folk. The venue is modern, low-key and offers good views of the stage. It is, however, somewhat bland in design, the notable exception being the cool retro circular molded plastic seating (think Austin Powers psychedelic '60s pop) that forms the centerpiece of the second-floor lobby area.

Comcast Center for the Performing Arts

885 South Main Street, Mansfield (no phone, www.livenation.com). **Open** 1-5pm Mon-Sat. **Credit** AmEx, MC, V.
Some 35 miles south of Boston, the Comcast Center is Massachusetts' largest outdoor amphitheater, with a capacity of 19,000. It offers an all-American arena concert experience, featuring massively popular country, pop and rock acts – not to mention car park tailgating parties, in which concertgoers can cook up barbecues and sink a few beers before the show. Lawn seats at the back of the venue offer a cheaper and more mellow experience – but you'll need to take your binoculars.

Orpheum Theatre

1 Hamilton Place, at Tremont Street, Downtown (1-617 679 0810, www.laorpheum. com). Park St T. **Box office** 10am-5pm Mon-Sat. **Credit** AmEx, MC, V. **Map** p272 K4.

Originally named the Boston Music Hall, the now somewhat shabby Orpheum was built in 1852. It's hard to imagine that it was once a state-of-the-art venue that housed the New England Conservatory and the Boston Symphony Orchestra. These days, on more gregarious evenings, the lobby is packed wall to wall with drinkers, and the toilets develop unsavory puddles. But for all its down-at-heel feel, it remains a great medium-sized venue which manages to maintain a cozy ambiance, and attracts some great bands (the Pogues, Arcade Fire and the Fray have all played sell-out shows).

★ Somerville Theatre
55 Davis Square, Somerville (1-617 625 5700, www.somervilletheatreonline.com). Davis T.
Box office 3-8pm daily. **No credit cards**.
Once a thriving theatre (Busby Berkeley directed here in the 1920s), the Somerville is now a hip indie and second-run multiplex cinema. But the 900-seat main theater also hosts eclectic rock and pop artists, as well as world music acts. Ryan Adams, Billy Bragg and Bright Eyes are among the acts who've taken to the stage over the years.

TD Garden
100 Legends Way, at Causeway Street, West End (1-617 624 1000, www.tdgarden.com). North Station T. **Box office** 10am-5pm Mon-Fri.
No credit cards. **Map** p272 K2.
Home to the Celtics (basketball) and the Bruins (ice hockey), the 19,600-capacity Garden also plays host to such top-drawer touring acts as the Rolling Stones and U2, whose multiple-night tenures dominate local newspaper headlines and news broadcasts. Tickets are available in person from the box office, or from Ticketmaster (*see p176*). You can often pick up tickets on concert nights from the hard-bitten scalpers to be found circling the venue like starved vultures.

Clubs

The Hub's lively music scene also stretches into its neighborhood clubs and bars, including the **Baseball Tavern** (*see p145*), a new haunt for old scenesters; **Precinct** (*see p154*), in Somerville's Union Square; and in Cambridge the divey **Cantab Lounge** (738 Massachusetts Avenue, at Inman Street, 1-617 354 2685), which runs entertaining soul and blues cover nights.

Bill's Bar
5.5 Lansdowne Street, at Ipswich Street, Fenway, Back Bay (1-617 421 9678, www.billsbar.com). Kenmore T. **Open** 9pm-2am Mon, Wed-Fri; 10pm-2am Tue, Sat, Sun. **Admission** $10-$30.
Credit AmEx, MC, V. **Map** p274 D7.
The exterior sign of Bill's Bar famously featured in a scene in the film *Fever Pitch*, as the place where a group of Red Sox players are dining. But Bill's doesn't actually have a restaurant; it's just a nice,

cosy bar with a good stage – with hit and miss musical performances. The booker here can't seem to decide whether to be hip, or just stick with the cover and reggae bands that draw crowds of students.

Great Scott
1222 Commonwealth Avenue, at Harvard Avenue, Allston (1-617 566 9014, www.great scottboston.com). Harvard Ave T. **Open** noon-2am daily. **Admission** $5-$10. **No credit cards**. **Map** p276 A5.
The efforts of a savvy booking team have transformed this once dull neighborhood sports bar into one of Boston's most important – though still intimate – indie rock venues. Along with national and international touring bands, it features the best and brightest (or sometimes simply the trendiest) local bands on the scene. It's worth hopping the T out to Allston – or Rock City, as the local musos would have it.

Harpers Ferry
158 Brighton Avenue, at Harvard Avenue, Allston (1-617 254 9743, www.harpersferry boston.com). Harvard Ave T or bus 57.
Open 8pm-2am daily. **Admission** $5-$10.
No credit cards.
Although Harpers Ferry has one of the city's best stages and a superior sound system, you might not find much variety or innovation on its jam and tribute band-heavy schedule. Its student-friendly location in Allston and the added attraction of a pool hall to the rear mean that this place can feel more like a sports bar than a bona fide rock club.

★ Lizard Lounge
1667 Massachusetts Avenue, at Wendell Street, Porter Square, Cambridge (1-617 547 0759, www.lizardloungeclub.com). Porter T. **Open** times vary. **Admission** $5-$10. **Credit** AmEx, MC, V. **Map** p276 B1.
A short walk from Harvard Square, this diminutive basement bar puts on a jam-packed program of shows. The beauty of the Lizard Lounge is that there is no stage. Instead, bands perform on a well-worn rug – the only delineation between audience and performer. The musical fare runs the gamut from rock and folk to Americana – along with the odd Boston

---

THE BEST INTIMATE VENUES

Precinct
Underground and intimate. *See p154.*

Toad
Nightly jazz, folk and Americana.
See right.

Wally's
A real hole in the, er, wall. *See p212.*

Great Scott.

Opera Underground performance. There's great food too, served in the Lounge early on, then all night up in the Cambridge Common restaurant.

★ Middle East

472 & 480 Massachusetts Avenue, at Brookline Street, Central Square, Cambridge (1-617 864 3278, www.mideastclub.com). Central T. **Open** 11am-12.30am Mon-Wed, Sun; 11am-1.30am Thur-Sat. **Admission** free-$10. **Credit** AmEx, MC, V. **Map** p276 C3.

This sprawling venue is one of America's leading rock clubs, and a major player on the national and local music scenes. A Middle Eastern restaurant as well as a club, it was the nurturing ground for Boston's alternative and indie music scenes, beginning in the mid 1980s in the smaller Upstairs room. 'Downstairs' was added later and, like many of Boston's basement clubs, was once a bowling alley. In the restaurant, musicians play the Corner without a cover charge, and in keeping with the Middle Eastern theme, there are also belly-dancers. ZuZu sits in-between Upstairs and Downstairs, offering food, hip DJ nights and bands.
▶ *For more about ZuZu, see p152.*

PA's Lounge

345 Somerville Avenue, at Hawkins Street, Union Square, Somerville (1-617 776 1557, www.paslounge.com). Porter Square T then bus 87. **Open** 5pm-1am daily. **Admission** $6-$8. **No credit cards. Map** p276 C1.

It might not have the clout of Great Scott (*see left*), but this Somerville bar offers a broad spectrum of great local bands and eclectic, often experimental out-of-town artists. Like its Allston counterpart, PA's (originally the Portuguese-American Club) owes its success to a dedicated booker and an ownership that's willing to take a few risks.
▶ *If you ask nicely in the adjacent bar, they might make you a delicious Fluffatini (named after the marshmallow spread Fluff, created in Somerville).*

Paradise Rock Club

967-969 Commonwealth Avenue, at Pleasant Street, Allston (1-617 562 8800, www.thedise. com). Pleasant St T. **Open** *Back room* 7pm-2am Mon-Wed, Sun; Thur-Sat 8pm-2am. *Lounge* 6pm-2am daily. **Admission** *Back room* $10-$20. *Lounge* free-$10. **No credit cards. Map** 276 B5.

The lounge area at this much-loved rock 'n' roll club generally features local bands, with the occasional showcase by up-and-coming major label signings. It also exhibits work by local artists, and serves pizzas, salads and sandwiches. But the larger, two-tiered back room is where the real action happens. The view-blocking support pillar bang in front of the stage? Well, that's now gone (*see p210* **Inside Track**). Given the caliber of bands performing – from Coldplay to Kings of Leon – this is one of Boston's must-visit rock haunts.

Plough & Stars

912 Massachusetts Avenue, at Hancock Street, Cambridge (1-617 576 0032, www.plough andstars.com). Central T. **Open** 11.30am-2am daily. **Admission** free-$3. **Credit** AmEx, MC, V. **Map** p276 B3.

This tiny Irish bar is a Cambridge institution – just ask the bartender for a potted history. Live music and more ear-friendly poetry readings bring the scenesters crowding in to the small, convivial space, where you'll often find local legends performing. The atmosphere is magical – even if it's a bit of a squeeze to get to the loo.

Toad

1912 Massachusetts Avenue, at Porter Square, Porter Square, Cambridge (1-617 497 4950, www.toadcambridge.com). Porter T. **Open** 5pm-1am Mon-Wed; 5pm-2am Thur-Sat; 6pm-1am Sun. **Admission** free. **No credit cards. Map** p276 B1.

The tiny Toad, which shares the same ownership as the Lizard Lounge (*see left*), is a true neighborhood pub. Here you'll find local Americana and rock acts both in the audience and knocking out a tune or two. There are two performances from different artists on most nights, generally at 8pm and 10pm. Just don't expect a night of quiet conversation – you'll be sitting within ear-splitting range of the performers.

ARTS & ENTERTAINMENT

ARTS & ENTERTAINMENT

★ TT the Bear's Place

10 Brookline Street, at Massachusetts Avenue, Central Square, Cambridge (1-866 468 7619, www.ttthebears.com). Central T. **Open** 6pm-1am daily. **Admission** $3-$15. **Credit** AmEx, MC, V. **Map** p276 C3.

Named after the owner's pet hamster, TT's is a world-class venue in miniature (275 capacity). Its reputation as one of the city's most happening rock joints is richly deserved, with a packed nightly schedule that features hotly tipped national and international acts as well as local bands. The bar area allows for socializing and there's a small pool room too.

▶ *TT's and Middle East (see p209) sometimes offer joint club-hopping tickets on weekends.*

Western Front

343 Western Avenue, at Putnam Avenue, Cambridgeport, Cambridge (1-617 492 7772, www.thewesternfront.com). Central T. **Open** 8pm-1am Wed-Thur; 10pm-1am Fri, Sat. **Admission** $3-$10. **No credit cards**. **Map** p276 B3.

The area's best venue for reggae, Western Front also features Caribbean and Latin music, plus jazz. It attracts a racially mixed crowd, including a good proportion of students and jam band fans – no surprise there – grooving to syncopated soul sounds from both bands and DJs.

Jazz, Blues, Folk & World

Jazz aficionados should make for the South End, where a handful of longstanding haunts includes the splendid **Wally's Café**. Founded in 1947, it's still run by the original owner's

grandsons. Also in the area, the bohemian **Beehive** (*see p124*) is the classy antithesis of a rock club, both intimate and eclectic, the small restaurant by day and venue by night hosts diverse acts, from bluegrass to burlesque.

The Harvard Square folk scene of the '60s has since been whittled down, though acoustic guitars and beret-clad intellectuals can still be found at one classic venue, **Club Passim**. Known as Club 47 in the 1960s, Passim was a mainstay for Joan Baez, Bob Dylan and Joni Mitchell; it even turned down an early Bruce Springsteen performance, as legend has it.

Located in Rhode Island, an-hour-and-a-half's drive from Boston, the **Newport Jazz Festival** (www.festivalproductions.net) and **Newport Folk Festival** (www.newportfolk.com), held on consecutive weekends in August, are worth the trip (*see p241* **Jazz Tunes & Tycoons**). In 1965, Bob Dylan was famously booed for performing with an electric guitar and a similarly tuned band at the latter. These days, the musical palette has broadened to include more pop and indie folk acts; likewise, the Jazz Festival's offerings run from experimental to easy listening. The setting for both is sublime: Fort Adams is by a quiet marina with lovely views over the bay to the Newport Bridge.

Thanks to the efforts of the non-profit organization **CrashArts** (www.worldmusic. org), and a diverse multi-racial society, world music is less of a rarity around Boston these days. **Ryles Jazz Club** also runs regular Latin dance party nights, and showcases a global array of artists.

TICKETS AND INFORMATION

Tickets for events with big-name headliners may appear through ticket agencies (*see p176*), but generally your best bet is contacting the venue direct. Advance booking is recommended for well-known artists and at weekends, even in the smaller clubs.

VENUES

Club Passim

47 Palmer Street, at Church Street, Harvard Square, Cambridge (1-617 492 7679, www.club passim.org). Harvard T. **Open** 11.30am-1am daily. **Box office** 6.30-10pm daily. **Admission** $5-$40. **Credit** AmEx, MC, V. **Map** p276 A2.

This small, not-for-profit venue was once at the vanguard of the 1960s folk scene, and regularly welcomed the likes of Joan Baez and Bob Dylan. The club retains its relaxed, hippie-ish vibe, with plenty of singer-songwriters on the bill.

▶ *The club's popular restaurant, Veggie Planet, packs in the denizens of the Square but remains in keeping with those progressive '60s ethics – and serves a mean vegetarian pizza.*

Sites & Sounds

The local buzz about the local noise.

It can seem as if every second person you meet in Boston is in a band. Due to sheer numbers if nothing else, chances are that the city will regularly turn out, if not the Next Big Rock Thing, acts that will make an impact beyond the local scene. The Boston area has already produced a stellar line-up of rock legends: the eponymous rock band Boston, of course, along with other '70s greats Aerosmith and Jonathan Richman and the Modern Lovers; '80s stars and innovators the Cars, Mission of Burma, Dinosaur Jr and the Pixies; and artists of all stripes in the '90s and '00s: Throwing Muses, the Lemonheads, Belly, Morphine, Staind and Dropkick Murphys…

The list goes on, with the new crop of potential stars including up-and-coming indie rock duo Drug Rug; and Passion Pit, which (so the story goes) got its start when its lead singer, then an Emerson College student, was discovered after performing a bunch of songs he'd haphazardly written as a Valentine's Day present for his girlfriend.

This fecundity is largely the result of the many local colleges – and not just the renowned Berklee School of Music, whose talented alumni include Aimee Mann and Quincy Jones – as they draw thousands of young people eager to hit the clubs. It's this phenomenally plentiful supply of gig-goers that creates the symbiotic relationship between thriving venues and keen young musicians.

For newcomers and short-term visitors to Boston, navigating the array of interesting acts can be a little overwhelming. Help is at hand from a new breed of local band bloggers, tweeters and web all-stars.

Ashley Willard, Michael Epstein, Sophia Cacciola and a host of rockin' contributors keep up on the local music scene with the fervor of a teenage romance on **Boston Band Crush** (www.bostonbandcrush.com) a blog that touts itself as 'focused on Boston music and the people who make it.' The bands featured range from townie favorites to the next big things. The website is a great resource for those about to rock, but can't find the best place to do so.

Long before the word 'blog' had entered the common lexicon, Vermont-born, Allston-based Brad Searles was compiling his personal diary, **Bradley's Almanac** (www.bradleysalmanac.com), with his

Drug Rug.

comments on Boston's rock scene. He covered his favorite bands, often recording performances and posting MP3s. Launched in 2001, the 'Nac, as Searles fondly calls it, now receives between 4,000 and 5,000 hits a day. It provides a gig guide as well as a 'try before you buy a ticket' listening gallery and, because there's no sponsorship or ads, the only bias is his personal taste. He's a fan – albeit a well-informed one – and he also happens to be a drummer.

Over in Somerville, Andy Guthrie and Jen Kelley produce **Band in Boston** (www.bandinbostonpodcast.com), which aims to provide a weekly podcast of who's playing where. The site compiles the now-extensive 'Flophouse Sessions', a series of recordings of local bands playing in the couple's living room. **Tourfilter** (www.tourfilter.com), which began as a tool to keep up with the astonishing number of gigs happening around Boston, now provides one-stop rock and pop gig browsing in over 70 cities, and, according to *Rolling Stone*, 'could become the Craigslist of the concert-info world'. Although it's by no means definitive – there's too much going on.

ARTS & ENTERTAINMENT

ARTS & ENTERTAINMENT

Johnny D's Uptown Restaurant & Music Club

17 Holland Street, at Davis Square, Somerville (1-617 776 2004, www.johnnyds.com). Davis T. **Open** 3pm-1am Mon; 11am-1am Tue-Fri; 8.30am-1am Sat, Sun. **Admission** $8-$15. **Credit** AmEx, MC, V.

Situated just off Davis Square, Johnny D's Uptown features blues, jazz, folk and alt-country artists, both local and national. During the 1970s this was one of the area's most important country and western clubs, and it remains one of the best places to hear Americana. Until 9.30pm, JD's, as it's affectionately known, serves as a popular local restaurant and neighborhood bar. After that, the music kicks in.

Lily Pad

1353 Cambridge Street, at Springfield Street, Inman Square, Cambridge (1-617 395 1393, www.lily-pad.net). Central T then 15min walk or bus 83, 91. **Open** times vary. **Tickets** $10 suggested donation. **Credit** AmEx. **Map** p276 C2.

When it opened in 2006, this charming little storefront venue in Inman Square had a troubled start due to noise complaints. Luckily, it was given a reprieve and now regularly hosts jazz, folk, indie rock and even classical performances – usually of an improv, experimental or otherwise outsider nature. Artists basically rent out the small room and promote their own shows – which means that members of the audience usually know one another. It's all very cozy; seating is on wooden chairs, placed right in front of the performers. There is no alcohol license, but people often bring in drinks.

Regattabar

Charles Hotel, 1 Bennett Street, at Eliot Street, Harvard Square, Cambridge (1-617 661 5000,

www.regattabarjazz.com). Harvard T. **Open** 7.30pm-2am Tue-Sat. **Tickets** $15-$36. **Credit** AmEx, MC, V. **Map** p276 A2.

Situated in the lovely Charles Hotel in Harvard Square, this sleek modern club serves up jazz, blues, gospel and R&B. It seats around 225 and is smarter than many of the city's other jazz venues, which tend to be quite casual. The annual Regattabar Jazz Festival runs from midwinter through to spring, while the Regattabar Summer Kids Music Series takes place in July and August.

Ryles Jazz Club

212 Hampshire Street, at Inman Street, Inman Square, Cambridge (1-617 876 9330, www.rylesjazz.com). Central T then bus 83, 91. **Open** 5pm-2am daily. **Tickets** $6-$15. **Credit** AmEx, MC, V. **Map** p276 C2.

Ryles has become a local institution, and a hopping Inman Square haunt for jazz fans. Split into two levels, it has live music from Tuesday to Sunday. The ground floor features national and local jazz artists, interspersed with world music, blues and comedy. Upstairs is the dance hall, where spicy salsa and merengue are often the order of the night. Mitch's Barbecue adds more Southern heat to a night out at Ryles.

Scullers Jazz Club

Doubletree Guest Suites Hotel, 400 Soldiers Field Road, at River Street, Allston (1-617 562 4111, www.scullersjazz.com). Pleasant Street T. **Open** 11am-2am daily. *Shows* times vary. **Tickets** $10-$30. **Credit** AmEx, MC, V. **Map** p276 B4.

Housed in the Doubletree hotel, overlooking the Charles River, Scullers features big-name artists (the likes of Jamie Cullum, Michael Bublé and Tony Bennett), as well as rising stars on the jazz, R&B and Latin music scenes. The dimly lit, mahogany paneled lounge has a sophisticated but relaxed atmosphere.

▶ *Scullers offers special three-course dinner packages, as well as 'Jazz Overnighter' deals for stays at the Doubletree Hotel.*

★ Wally's

427 Massachusetts Avenue, at Columbus Avenue, South End (1-617 424 1408, www.wallyscafe. com). Mass Ave T. **Open** 11am-2am Mon-Sat; noon-2am Sun. *Shows* 9pm-2am Mon-Sat; 3.30-7.30pm Sun. **Admission** free. **No credit cards.** **Map** p275 G8.

One visit to this bohemian jazz den seems to hook music fans of all persuasions into becoming lifelong devotees. It's a no-nonsense, non-expense-account jazz club known for its stellar jams – during which students from Berklee and the New England Conservatory are sometimes joined by visiting hotshots. Still owned by the family that founded it, Wally's rode the second wave of American jazz in the late 1940s, and remains a joyous breeding ground for uninhibited musical innovation.

INSIDE TRACK
SOMETHING IN
THE AIR TONIGHT

One of the best places to rock out outdoors in Boston is the **Bank of America Pavilion** (*see p207*). Interesting architecturally, it's absolutely stunning when the sun sets over Boston Harbor and your favorite band is playing your favorite song. If the stars align, it can be Boston's most unforgettable venue. Another al fresco treat is the **Hatch Shell** (www.hatchshell.com). Classical and classic rock concerts are held at this iconic spot along the Charles River all summer long. Pack a picnic and settle on the lawn; it's the perfect way to spend an evening without spending much money – concerts are free.

Nightlife

What the dance scene lacks in size, it makes up for in enthusiasm.

Maybe it's the 2am closing time, maybe it's because live music has always been more popular here than dancing. Or maybe, just maybe, people simply don't enjoy dancing among throngs of tipsy college kids doing the 'running man'. Whatever the reason, Boston is not a city known for its dance clubs.

However, what Boston lacks in dancefloor square footage, it makes up for with sheer variety. Hip hop is perhaps the most prominent genre, but a burgeoning house and techno scene is emerging. Of course, the club scene isn't immune to Beantown's dorky streak – DJs often spin eclectic mixes of Italo disco, wild mashups, Northern Soul, Latin sounds and whatever else ends up in the crate on a given night.

THE SCENE

While Lansdowne Street was once the hub of Boston's nightlife scene, the Theatre District has stepped up its game of late. Tucked between Chinatown and Back Bay, it's the headquarters for the Prada-clad international set. Here you'll find a high concentration of seemingly perfect-looking people with money to burn. If that's your scene, this is your place.

Nearby, Boylston Place (known as 'the Alley') is lined with bars, restaurants and clubs, and drunken twentysomethings wobble from one spot to the next most weekend nights. In Cambridge and Somerville, a number of bars feature DJs playing non-commercial music. Central Square in particular is a hotbed of underground sounds. Collectives of DJs and producers have been known to throw parties in offbeat locations – but that's the sort of info you can squeeze out of the locals once you find your niche.

The sole after-hours club in town is **Rise** (306 Stuart Street, 1-617 423 7473, www.rise club.us), which stays open until the sun comes up, but only admits members and their guests – although if you strike up a conversation with the right person, then you just might be able to wangle your way in.

Clubs nights change at a rapid rate in this town, so call ahead to check that that low-key spot still plays sleek downtempo instead of the latest tracks from the Black Eyed Peas.

Credit cards are only accepted at the bar in all the places listed below – admission at the door is cash only.

THE CODE

Because of all sorts of collegiate shenanigans, the vast majority of nightclubs in town sport a '21 and over' entry policy – though the occasional '18 and over' night springs up every now and then. Dress codes are looser than they used to be, and tend to be enforced at the discretion of large, stoic doormen. As a general rule, avoid caps, trainers and athletic wear of all kinds – basically, anything that might identify you as a potential meathead.

Enormous Room

567 Massachusetts Avenue, at Pearl Street, Central Square, Cambridge (1-617 491 5550, www.enormous.tv). Central T. **Open** 5.30pm-1am

---

THE BEST
FOR DANCING THE NIGHT AWAY

Rise
The city's only afterhours club. *See left.*

Royale
Recently revamped. *See p215.*

Saint
Be seen. *See p215.*

Enormous Room.

Given the substantial student population in the Allston/Brighton area, it was only a matter of time before a bar that mingled the local pick-up scene with Euro accents would take over. The ground-floor Met Lounge features a DJ playing mainly Top 40 hits, R&B and hip hop, with the occasional commercial house tune. The spacious loft-style top level is for chilling out and catching a game, with a 70ft oval bar, TVs and decent food.

Middlesex
315 Massachusetts Avenue, between State & Village Streets, Central Square, Cambridge (1-617 868 6739, www.middlesexlounge.com). Central T. **Open** 5pm-1am daily. **Admission** free-$5. **Credit** AmEx, MC, V. **Map** p276 C4.
Tucked between the hullabaloo of Central Square and the relative peace and quiet of the MIT campus, the low-profile Middlesex has quickly asserted itself as one of the best clubs in Cambridge. Sophisticated techno, obscure R&B and sporadic sets from visiting international electronic luminaries fit perfectly with Middlesex's spacious and artfully designed environs.

★ Phoenix Landing
512 Massachusetts Avenue, at Brookline Street, Central Square, Cambridge (1-617 576 6260). Central T. **Open** 11am-1am Mon-Wed; 11am-2am Thur, Fri; 10am-2am Sat; 10am-1am Sun. **Admission** free-$5. **Credit** AmEx, DC, MC, V. **Map** p276 C3.
Deep house and Guinness may not seem like the most natural match in the world, but the Phoenix Landing pulls off the hybrid pub/club marvelously. The decor is unremarkable, but the no-frills atmosphere fits well with the gritty underground sounds that find their way through the speakers. The floor is tiny, but the variety is huge: hip hop, reggae, house, drum 'n' bass, techno, new wave and dubstep all have a home here.

Mon-Wed, Sun; 5.30pm-2am Thur-Sat.
Credit AmEx, MC, V. **Map** p276 C3.
The door, marked only by the silhouette of a pachyderm, is the only low-key thing about the Enormous Room. Early evenings find the after-work crowd lounging on carpeted platforms enjoying platters of North African food; but come nightfall, a host of DJs spin the city's most progressive mix of classy house, breakbeats, classic soul, techno and local talent. The line forms early – so it's a good idea to go for an early evening snack to claim your spot.

Estate
One Boylston Place, at Boylston Street, Downtown (1-617 351 7000, www.theestateboston.com). Boylston T. **Open** 10pm-2am Fri; 9pm-2am Sat. **Credit** AmEx, MC, V. **Map** p275 J5.
The name has changed, but the song remains the same. The cul-de-sac of clubbery that is Boylston Place is a reliable hot spot on weekends, and the Estate is the latest moniker of the strip's largest space. Hip hop and mashups make up the bulk of the playlist, and the interior features lots of leather, fireplaces and balconies.

Joshua Tree
1316 Commonwealth Avenue, at Redford Street, Allston (1-617 566 6699, www.joshuatreeallston.com). Griggs St/Long Avenue T. **Open** 5pm-1am Mon-Wed; 5pm-2am Thur, Fri; 10.30am-2am Sat; 10.30am-1am Sun. **Admission** $5 Thur-Sat. **Credit** AmEx, MC, V.

Precinct
70 Union Square, at Washington Street, Somerville (1-617 623 9211, www.precinct.com).

THE BEST FOR DANCING TO A DIFFERENT BEAT

Enormous Room
Boston's best DJs in a shockingly small space. *See p213.*

Phoenix Landing
Hip-hop and pints of hops. *See above.*

ZuZu
Eclectic music to move to. *See p152.*

Davis T, then bus 87. **Open** 9pm-2am daily.
Credit AmEx, MC, V.

A lounge that doubles as a dance club, the tiny, intimate Precinct screams 'swanky New York hot spot' – despite its sleepy location in Union Square. Precinct offers a diverse mix of international sounds and occasional live music. There's no set dress code, but dress down too much and you may feel out of place.

Redline

59 John F Kennedy Street, at Eliot Street,
Harvard Square, Cambridge (1-617 491 9851,
www.redlinecambridge.com). Harvard T. **Open**
5pm-1am Mon-Wed, Sun; 5pm-2am Thur-Sat.
Admission free-$5. **Credit** AmEx, DC, MC, V.
Map p276 A3.

It's a bit on the small side, and generally packed with Harvard students attempting to bust a move, yet Redline still comes out on top in Harvard Square thanks to its constantly changing roster of DJs. The sound system alone separates it from similar lounge hybrids. For a good time, check out the Saturday night Soul Shack.

Royale

279 Tremont Street, at Stuart Street,
Downtown (1-617 338 7699, www.royaleboston.
com). Boylston or Tufts Medical Center T. **Open**
Club nights 10pm-2am Fri, Sat. *Live music* days
& times vary. **Admission** $15-$20. **Credit**
AmEx, MC, V. **Map** p275 J6.

Middlesex.

When the Roxy's shabby sort of elegance became just plain shabbiness, new ownership took over to revamp the entire interior, renaming the space the Royale. The massive room has a grand stage, an elegant marble foyer, cushy seating nooks, a fantastic sound system, a festive light show and more hotties than you can shake a glowstick at. There are VIP balconies if you feel like getting away from it all – but Boston clubs rarely reach the size of this place, so why not take the opportunity to get lost? The DJ spins house/dance on weekend nights, while hipper-than-thou promoters Bowery Boston (yes, the Hub's own branch of the much-loved Bowery group in NYC) bring in a diverse range of indie and mainstream rock, pop and hip hop acts throughout the week.
▶ *For upcoming concerts promoted by the Bowery Presents, visit www.boweryboston.com.*

Saint

90 Exeter Street, at Huntington Avenue, Back
Bay (1-617 236 1134, www.saintboston.com).
Copley T. **Open** 10pm-2am Thur, Sun; 9pm-2am
Fri, Sat. **Admission** $20. **Credit** AmEx, MC, V.
Map p275 G6.

Billed as a 'nitery', Saint has a mix of dining, drinking and dancing that's made it a favorite among velvet rope types, who reserve VIP tables for prime posing opportunities and line up each night in the hope of spotting some Red Sox players or the occasional Patriot. Don't go wearing your sneakers – this is a hive of fashionistas (which means you don't really have to be a good dancer to fit in, either).

Venu

100 Warrenton Street, at Stuart Street,
Downtown (1-617 338 8061, www.venuboston.
com). Boylston or Tufts Medical Center T.
Open 11pm-2am Tue, Thur-Sat. **Admission**
$20; $15 guests. **Credit** AmEx, MC, V.
Map p275 J6.

Once one of Boston's biggest gay clubs, the scene at Venu is now much more mixed (but just as fun). House and techno are tempered with a healthy dose of Latin, and the result is a packed floor. Get a hotel close by – you're not going to want to join the mass cab hunt that starts around 2am. Trust us.

ARTS & ENTERTAINMENT

Sport & Fitness

Whether it's baseball or biking, locals love to get in on the action.

Depending on who you ask, Boston has the best or the worst sports fans in the country. Their allegiance to the 'Big Four' – the **Boston Bruins**, **Celtics** and **Red Sox**, and the **New England Patriots** – is borderline psychotic and has been the subject matter for a number of books and films.

However, the dangers of wearing New York Yankees paraphernalia and the hysterically serious cult of sports talk radio also make Boston one of the best places to get wrapped up in home town pride at a professional sporting event. You can either poke fun at it or embrace it, but there is no way to get around sports in Boston, even at Symphony Hall, where arts patroness and namesake for the Back Bay museum, Isabella Stewart Gardner, once wore a headband with the words, 'Oh you Red Sox!' hand-written upon it.

SPECTATOR SPORTS

In addition to the 'Big Four' teams, Boston (Foxborough, to be exact, about 20 miles south-west of the city) is also home to a professional soccer team, the **New England Revolution**, which shares Gillette Stadium with the Patriots. Locals haven't entirely embraced the most popular sport in the world, but interest has remained steady since the team was founded in 1996. College sports are very popular too, especially Boston College football and basketball, and Boston University hockey games. **The Beanpot** ice hockey tournament has pitted the BU, BC, Northeastern and Harvard puck teams against each other every winter since 1953. The **Head of the Charles Regatta** (*see p183*) in October is another big event, attracting international crowds since 1965. But for sheer longevity, the Harvard-Yale football game has 'em both beat: it's been drawing a rowdy crowd, mostly alumni, since 1875.

For local sporting information, look no further than the two daily newspapers, the *Boston Globe* and the *Boston Herald*. Both have nationally recognized sports sections that report on professional goings-on in great detail. The *Globe* also publishes daily listings of local and national television and radio coverage. Sports radio is also popular, particularly WEEI on 850 AM.

Baseball

In Boston, there are the **Red Sox** and then there's everything else. True, the Patriots are the main event for 16 Sundays during the colder months (and if they tack on a few more Sundays for the post-season, as they have several times in recent years, all the better),

ARTS & ENTERTAINMENT

but the Red Sox rule this city, and this region. They are more than a baseball team. From Fort Kent, Maine to Newport, Rhode Island, the Sox are a lynchpin of New England's identity, a shared currency for its 14 million residents.

And it's not just for the 162 games every spring, summer and (hopefully) autumn. This is a year-round obsession. In recent years, the excitement surrounding the team has reached – to crib the name of the Red Sox rom-com adapted from Nick Hornby's book – *Fever Pitch*. There was the epic heartbreak of 2003, of course, then the utter euphoria of 2004. It saw the Red Sox hanging on by their fingertips, only to fight their way back from the brink of elimination to beat their arch-rivals, the New York Yankees, and go on to win their first World Series in nearly a century. The signing of ace Japanese pitcher Daisuke Matsuzaka in 2006 added a new dimension to the hype surrounding the team. Now, Red Sox Nation has gone international, with millions of people in Tokyo and Yokohama getting up at 3am to watch him pitch. Seeing a game at **Fenway Park** is a near-religious experience for many people. The catch? As charming as the oldest ballpark in the Majors is (it dates from 1912), it's also the smallest (with about 38,000 seats), so tickets are hard to come by.

★ Fenway Park

4 Yawkey Way, Fenway, Back Bay (1-877 733 7699, www.redsox.com). Kenmore T. **Box office** 9am-5pm Mon-Fri & game days. **Open** *Tours* 9am-4pm daily; game days from 9am until 3hrs before game. **Tickets** *Games* $12-$90. *Tours* $10-$12. **Credit** AmEx, MC, V. **Map** p274 D7. *Photos p218.*

Basketball

There was a time in the not-too-distant past when the **Celtics** were in a major slump. An especially rough year, 2006-07 was marked by a poor record, numerous injuries and the deaths of team patriarch Red Auerbach and Dennis Johnson, a veteran of the mid 1980s squad. But some key moves during the 2007 off-season by former player and current team president Danny Ainge brought new life to the C's in the form of Kevin Garnett and Ray Allen, who, along with Paul Pierce, came to be known as the Big Three.

Under coach Doc Rivers, the Big Three led Boston to its first NBA Championship in over 20 years and also compiled the sixth-best season record in history. The Celtics would make it to the playoffs and then the finals in the next two years respectively, but despite their successful seasons, the older, injury-prone players fell short of the championship.

While players' ages have brought the Celtics longevity into question, even with the 2010 off-season signing of Shaquille O'Neal, who has also been around for a while, a crop of younger stars, led by the stunning Rajon Rondo, have given die-hard Gang Green fans hope for the upcoming seasons.

For years, obtaining Celtics tickets was not a problem, but recently, they have been consistently selling out home games at the **TD Garden**. While you might have to pay a little extra, scoring tickets to a game is well worth it for basketball aficionados. Having won more championships than any other NBA team, the Celtics are the most successful of the Big Four teams, with some of the best players in history. For many, a peek at Larry Bird's No.33 jersey hanging from the rafters alone covers the price of admission.

TD Garden

100 Legends Way, West End (1-617 624 1000, www.tdgarden.com). North Station T. **Box office** 10am-5pm Mon-Fri. **Tickets** $10-$150. **Credit** AmEx, DC, MC, V. **Map** p272 K2.

Cricket

Perhaps unsurprisingly, cricket is not very big in the States. For those yearning to catch some innings, the best bet for watching a match is the **Massachusetts State Cricket League,**

ARTS & ENTERTAINMENT

Fenway Park. *See p217.*

whose teams play several games a week between May and September around the city. Visit www.mscl.org for schedule and locations.

Football

For a long, long time, the **New England Patriots** were simply not a very good football team. Then in 2001, all that changed. Led by golden boy quarterback Tom Brady and gnomic genius coach Bill Belichick, the Pats rattled off three Super Bowl championships within four years – and made it look easy. But what at first looked like a sure-fire dynasty has stumbled slightly in recent seasons, especially after an injured Brady sat out the 2008 season.

Nonetheless, the team, as always, remains very competitive, and as long as Brady and Belichick remain with the squad, more Super Bowl rings are always a very real possibility. As such, tickets at **Gillette Stadium** are hard to snag. But you can catch the action in a lively sports bars (one of the best is **Champion's Sports Bar**, 110 Huntington Avenue, at Belvidere Street, Back Bay, 1-617 279 6996).

Gillette Stadium
1 Patriot Place at Route 1, Foxborough (1-508 543 1032, www.gillettestadium.com). **Box office** 9am-5pm Mon-Fri. **Tickets** $59-$125. **Credit** V.

Horse racing

Rockingham Park
Rockingham Park Boulevard, Salem, New Hampshire (1-603 898 2311, www.rockinghampark.com). **Open** *late May-early Sept* post time 1.05pm Wed, Fri, Sat, Sun; simulcast noon-midnight daily. **Admission** $2.50; simulcast $1. **No credit cards.**
Although it's just across the state line in New Hampshire, Rockingham Park is only a half-hour drive from Boston. Once host to Seabiscuit, the park offers simulcast horse racing from around the country as well as live races.

Suffolk Downs
111 Waldemar Avenue, at junction of routes 1A & 145, East Boston (1-617 567 3900, www.suffolkdowns.com). **Suffolk Downs T. Open** *May-Nov* post time 12.45pm Sun, Mon, Wed, Sat; simulcast noon-midnight daily. **Admission** $2. **No credit cards.**
Live racing takes place on a seasonal basis on selected days. The track is open daily for simulcast racing.

Ice hockey

Once known as the 'Big Bad **Bruins**', this team had a rough, fearless style of play that struck fear into the hearts of all who entered

the rink. That was then – oh, about 30 years ago – but the Bruins have at last shown signs of improvement: if not steady, then at least promising. Some aggrieved fans once accused owner Jeremy Jacobs of putting profit before success; a website selling bumper stickers, www.pleasesellthebruins.com, is a visible manifestation of the discontent.

However, others argue that what success the Bruins have recently seen, namely retaining the second-best record in the NHL during the 2008-09 season, is the result of off-the-ice moves made by Jacobs and the new management he instituted. That said, the Bruins have yet to bring home another Stanley Cup, and the 2009-10 playoff choke after leading the Philadelphia Flyers 3-0 in the 7 game series was just heart-breaking. Ticket prices for games at the **TD Garden** (*see p217*) range from $10 to $180; visit www.bostonbruins.com for details.

Rugby

The **Boston Rugby Club** has been playing high-level rugby against other American city teams since 1961. Call 1-617 566 2732 or visit www.brfc.org for information about game times and locations. Another option is the **Boston Irish Wolfhounds**, who play the game with an Irish accent (not to mention Welsh, Scottish, English, Australian and French). All games take

INSIDE TRACK
BEST DAY OF THE YEAR

One of the greatest days on the sporting calendar in this sports-crazy town is the quintessentially New England holiday of **Patriot's Day**. (It's celebrated in Massachusetts on the third Monday of every April, to commemorate the battles of Lexington and Concord; *see also p180*.) On Patriot's Day, the **Red Sox** (*see p217*) stride into the stadium at Fenway for a rare morning game. Then, about an hour after the first pitch, 26.2 miles to the west in Hopkinton, another 20,000 or so people tighten their shoelaces as the starting pistol is fired for the running of the venerable **Boston Marathon** (*see p179*). By the time the Red Sox game is over, fans are spilling from the park towards Kenmore Square, where scores of weary runners are making their way down Commonwealth Avenue towards the finish line in Copley Square. This occasion sees a joyous confluence marking two of the city's greatest – and longest-standing – athletic traditions.

place at the **Irish Cultural Centre** in Canton (1-617 254 9732, www.biwrfc.com). Alternatively, Boston's major universities – Boston University, Boston College, Northeastern, Harvard, MIT, Tufts – all have rugby teams that are either sanctioned or club league; check the college websites for game information.

Soccer

The **New England Revolution** share a stadium (**Gillette Stadium**; *see p219*) and an owner (the Kraft family) with the New England Patriots, but the Revs don't enjoy anything close to the popularity of the US football team. In the United States, despite a recent wave of interest among younger sports fans, soccer still lags behind many other sports in its following. Despite an influx of young, dynamic talent – and holding the distinction of being the only original MLS team to have every one of its games televised – the Revs have a long way to go before changing the Big Four to the Big Five. You can almost always get a ticket ($18-$34); phone the stadium for details or check out the Revolution's website: www.revolutionsoccer.net.

ACTIVE SPORTS & FITNESS

One of New England's charms is that it enjoys four distinct seasons every year. During the frigid winters, locals head north to ski slopes in Maine and Vermont, while in spring the sidewalks are clogged with runners and skaters exulting in the warm weather. Summer and autumn, meanwhile, are perfect times for mountain biking in the western hills. Boston itself offers sports for all seasons, from rowing on the Charles River in summer to ice-skating on the Common's Frog Pond in winter.

The *Boston Globe* publishes activities listings on Saturdays, but it's not a comprehensive directory of weekend events.

Boating & sailing

Boston Harbor Sailing Club

Rowes Wharf, at Atlantic Avenue, Waterfront (1-617 720 0049, www.bostonharborsailing.com). Aquarium T. **Open** *May-Oct* 9am-9pm daily. **Rates** *Rental* $92-$531/day. *Lessons* $769-$3,000. *Skippered charter* $55/hr plus boat rental. **Credit** MC, V. **Map** p273 M4.
The BHSC is popular with locals, particularly college students, as it offers boat rentals for qualified sailors and one-on-one lessons for beginners.

Boston Sailing Center

54 Lewis Wharf, at Atlantic Avenue, Waterfront (1-617 227 4198, www.boston sailingcenter.com). Aquarium or Haymarket T.

Open *May-Oct* 9am-sunset daily. *Nov-Apr* 10am-5pm Mon-Fri. **Rates** *Lessons* $275-$1,925. *Skippered charters* $120-$190/hr. **Credit** MC, V. **Map** p273 M3.
Offers boat rentals, lessons or charters in which you can lean back and let someone else do the work. This is a great deal on sailing in the city, and the view of Boston and its environs from the river is one that cannot be beat.

Charles River Canoe & Kayak

2401 Commonwealth Avenue, Newton (1-617 965 5110, www.ski-paddle.com). Riverside T. **Open** *Mar-Nov* 10am-8pm Mon-Fri; 9am-8pm Sat, Sun. **Rentals** $7-$20/hr; $28-$80/day. **Credit** MC, V.
To join the hordes on the river in summer, rent a slim boat from the company's boathouse in Newton or, between May and October, from its kiosk in Boston (Soldiers Field Road, upstream from the Eliot Bridge) or Cambridge (Kendall Square). Phone or visit the website for kiosk opening times.

★ Community Boating

On the banks of the Charles River, between the Hatch Shell & the Longfellow Bridge, Back Bay (1-617 523 1038, www.community-boating.org). Charles/MGH T. **Open** *Apr-Oct* 1pm-sunset Mon-Fri; 9am-sunset Sat, Sun. **Rates** (2-day pass) $50 kayak; $100 sailboat. **Credit** MC, V. **Map** p272 H4.
This not-for-profit company was established in 1936 to keep local kids off the streets. It offers boat rentals to non-members, but requires that customers have some level of boating experience.

Bowling

Massachusetts (and New England, for that matter) is famous for **candlepin bowling**, a variation of the game characterized by smaller, hole-less balls and scaled-down, harder to knock over pins, invented in Worcester in the late 19th century. Try it here, unless you're planning to visit New Brunswick, Nova Scotia or the town of Wyoming, Ohio, any time soon – the only other places where candlepin is played. With most candlepin venues serving food, drink and other entertainment, it makes for a good, clean, fun night out. There are plenty of ten-pin places around town too.

Boston Bowl

820 Morrissey Boulevard, Dorchester (1-617 825 3800, www.bostonbowl.com). JFK/UMass T. **Open** 24hrs daily. **Rates** $3.30-$5 per person per game; shoes $4.25. **Credit** MC, V.
Greater Boston's largest ten-pin venue (30 lanes) also has 14 candlepin lanes, and a goodly number of pool tables and video games. Poor players take note – all 44 lanes are equipped with optional

Sacco's Bowl Haven

45 Day Street, at Herbert Street, Davis Square, Somerville (1-617 776 0552, www. saccosbowlhaven.com). Davis T. **Open** 10am-11pm Mon-Thur, Sun; 10am-midnight Fri, Sat. **Rates** $3 per person per game; shoes $1.50. **No credit cards**.

Sacco's Bowl Haven attracts a mix of blue-collar types and urban hipsters to its 15 candlepin lanes. There's no alcohol here, just a couple of soda vending machines. But with an interior that looks like it hasn't changed since before World War II, the faded charm more than makes up for that.

Cycling & mountain biking

Anyone who's tried to navigate Boston's narrow city streets by car can confirm that cyclists – especially those who don't follow traffic laws – can often make the experience that much more nerve-wracking. However, a recent surge of interest, spearheaded by biking enthusiast Mayor Thomas Menino, has led to new bike lanes on some of Boston's busiest streets. While the culture shift, especially for notoriously bad New England drivers, will take a while, the city is steadily improving its reputation for cycling.

Designated trails in and around Boston keep cyclists off the road and also provide an escape route from the city's congestion. **Pierre Lallement Bike Path** runs parallel to the Orange Line. The four-mile stretch runs through the Southwest Corridor Park from Copley Place to Franklin Park. The **Paul Dudley White Charles River Bike Path** is an 18-mile stretch running between the Science Museum and Watertown. The **Minuteman Bikeway** (www.minute manbikeway.org) offers cyclists an 11-mile ride from Alewife or Davis T to Lexington and Bedford along a former rail line.

Mountain-bikers should make for the lush and lovely **Blue Hills Reservation** – 7,000 acres spread through Quincy, Dedham, Milton and Randolph, south of the city. There are 125 miles of trails, some designated for mountain biking, others for walkers only. Stop at the park office at 695 Hillside Street, Milton (1-617 698 1802) for mountain-bike maps. For more information on all of the paths listed above, visit www.mass.gov.

The MBTA allows bikes on Blue, Orange and Red lines, as well as rail, at no extra cost in off-peak hours. See www.mbta.com for the rules.

For bike rentals in Boston, try either of **Community Bicycle Supply** in the South End (496 Tremont Street, 1-617 542 8623, www.communitybicycle.com), or **Back Bay Bicycles** (362 Commonwealth Avenue, 1-617 247 2336, www.backbaybicycles.com).

bumpers 'to keep your frustrations low and scores high!' It's also open around the clock – so if you fancy a late-night game, then let 'em roll. Ten-pin games cost more than candlepin.

Kings

50 Dalton Street, at Scotia Street, Back Bay (1-617 266 2695, www.backbaykings.com). Hynes T. **Open** 5pm-2am Mon; 11.30am-2am Tue-Sun. **Rates** $6.50 per person per game ($5.50 before 6pm); shoes $4. **Credit** AmEx, MC, V. **Map** p274 F7.

Be it bowling, billiards, or simply lots and lots of glowing neon, this Back Bay establishment has it all. The drinks and food aren't bad either, all in a slick nightclub setting. Just come early and expect to wait in line – and it won't be exactly cheap.

Lucky Strike Lanes at Jillian's

145 Ipswich Street, at Lansdowne Street, Fenway, Back Bay (1-617 437 0300, www. luckystrikeboston.com). Kenmore T. **Open** 11am-2am Mon-Sat; noon-2am Sun. **Rates** $6 per person per game; shoes $3.50. **Credit** AmEx, MC, V. **Map** p274 E7.

This ten-pin bowling alley – or self-styled 'upscale bowling lounge' – is located within the Jillian's entertainment complex. As if bowling weren't entertainment enough, there's also a wall-to-wall video screen showing the day's must-see sporting event. Food is also available.

Across the river, there's **Cambridge Bicycle** (259 Massachusetts Avenue, Cambridge, 1-617 876 6555, www.cambridgebicycle.com).

Fitness centers & gyms

There's no shortage of fitness centers and gyms in the city, but most operate solely on a membership basis. Here are a few places that allow walk-ins.

Boston Body

6th Floor, 8 Newbury Street, at Arlington Street, Back Bay (1-617 262 3333, www.bostonbody.com). Arlington T. **Open** 8am-8pm Mon-Thur; 8am-2pm Fri, Sat. **Rates** $89/mth; $20/day. **Credit** AmEx, MC, V. **Map** p275 H5.

With four locations in the metropolitan area, Boston Body is the city's best Pilates, yoga and healing arts center, offering both private training and group classes. If you prefer to chill out rather than work out, book in for a Thai massage or acupuncture session. **Other locations** 46 Austin Street, Newtonville (1-617 969 2673).

Dance Complex

536 Massachusetts Avenue, Central Square, Cambridge (1-617 547 9363, www.dance complex.org). Central T. **Open** classes daily; check website for schedule. **Rates** $8-$14/class. **No credit cards**.

The Dance Complex is not a gym per se, but a non-profit arts organisation that offers workshops and classes in ballet, salsa, tango, belly dancing and hip hop, plus capoeira, the intense Brazilian fusion of dance and martial arts.

Healthworks Fitness Center for Women

441 Stuart Street, at Dartmouth Street, Back Bay (1-617 859 7700, www.healthworksfitness.com). Back Bay or Copley T. **Open** 5.30am-10pm Mon-Fri; 7.30am-8pm Sat, Sun. **Rates** $20/day. **Credit** MC, V. **Map** p275 H6.

For women who'd rather exercise and chill out in an all-female environment, Healthworks offers several locations throughout Boston with spas and daycare spaces, as well as the usual workout facilities, classes and personal training.

Other locations 920 Commonwealth Avenue, Brookline (1-617 731 3030); 35 White Street, Porter Square, Cambridge (1-617 497 4454); 1300 Boylston Street, Chestnut Hill (1-617 383 6100).

Revolution Fitness

209 Columbus Avenue, at Berkeley Street, Back Bay (1-617 536 3006, www.revfitboston.com). Back Bay T. **Open** 5.30am-10pm Mon-Fri; 8am-8pm Sat; 9am-8pm Sun. **Rates** $20/day. **Credit** AmEx, MC, V. **Map** p275 H6.

Revolution offers a wide variety of workout options, including yoga and kick-boxing classes as well as a full gym with new cardio and resistance equipment.

Golf

The following public courses are located in, or close to, the city. If you're looking for a course with elevation changes and a variety of hole types, look no further than the **Brookline Golf Club**; weather can be an issue though (there is little drainage, so steer clear after a heavy rain).

Brookline Golf Club at Putterham *1281 West Roxbury Parkway, at Newton Street, Chestnut Hill (1-617 730 2078, www.brooklinegolf.com). Chestnut Hill T.* **Open** *Apr-Nov* dawn-dusk daily. **Rates** $22-$48; clubs $25. **Credit** AmEx, MC, V.

Franklin Park Golf Course *Franklin Park, 1 Circuit Drive, Dorchester (1-617 265 4084, www.sterlinggolf.com/franklin). Forest Hills T then bus 16.* **Open** 5am-dusk daily. **Rates** $16-$26 Mon-Fri; $18-$34 Sat, Sun; clubs $10-$12. **Credit** AmEx, MC, V.

Fresh Pond Golf Course *691 Huron Avenue, at Fresh Pond Parkway, Cambridge (1-617 349 6282, www.freshpondgolf.com). Alewife T.* **Open** *Apr-Nov* dawn-dusk daily. **Rates** $21-$37; $16-$27 off season; clubs $20. **Credit** MC, V.

George Wright Golf Course *420 West Street, Hyde Park, Dorchester (1-617 364 2300, www.georgewrightgolfcourse.com).* **Open** 6am-dusk daily. **Rates** $28 Mon-Fri; $40 Sat, Sun; clubs $10-$18. **Credit** MC, V.

Leo J Martin Memorial Golf Course *190 Park Road, Weston (1-781 891 1119).* **Open** *Apr-Nov* 8am-dusk Mon; 6am-dusk Tue-Sun. **Rates** $17-$22 Mon-Fri; $25 Sat, Sun; clubs $10. **Credit** MC, V.

Newton Commonwealth Golf Course *212 Kenrick Street, Newton (1-617 630 1971, www.sterlinggolf.com/newton). Boston College T.* **Open** *Apr-Nov* dawn-dusk daily. **Rates** $19-$30 Mon-Thur; $30-$37 Fri-Sun; clubs $12-$16. **Credit** AmEx, MC, V.

In-line skating

Boston and nearby cities offer a plethora of open paved trails and safe roadways for the passionate eight-wheeler. Both novices and experienced skaters should check out the **Paul Dudley White Charles River Bike Path** and the **Minuteman Bikeway** (*see p221*). If you want to get a good workout in on sunny weekend mornings, hit the trail before 10am – otherwise you'll run into major traffic in the form of all the other runners, walkers, skaters and bikers with the same idea. Visit the **InLine Club of Boston**'s website (www.sk8net.com) for details of the best and most popular skating locations, plus races and special events.

To hire or buy blades, try the **Beacon Hill Skate Shop** (135 South Charles Street, at Stuart Street, 1-617 482 7400), which, despite its name, is actually in the South End.

Pool & billiards

It's getting harder and harder, it seems, to find a pool table in a regular old Boston bar. One of our favorites is the red felt tabletop at the Central Square's the **Field** (*see p149*), even if its proximity to the back wall necessitates

using a sawn-off cue. But it's easier than ever for serious players to find bars devoted solely to pool. Aspiring Fast Eddie Felsons can cue up at **Big City** (138 Brighton Avenue, at Harvard Avenue, Allston, 1-617 782 2020, www.allstons finest.com), the **Boston Billiard Club** (126 Brookline Avenue, at Park Drive, Fenway, 1-617 536 7665, www.bostonbilliardclub.com) and **Flat Top Johnny's** in Cambridge (1 Kendall Square, at Broadway, 1-617 494 9565, www.flattopjohnnys.com).

The more fashion-conscious might prefer to head to **Felt** (533 Washington Street, at Delafayette Avenue, Downtown 1-617 350 5555, www.feltclubboston.com), a club/restaurant where black-clad NYC-wannabes rack 'em up after enjoying roasted sea bass or lobster ravioli.

Running

Downtown Boston, a winding warren of narrow roadways, isn't always the most amenable part of the city for joggers. But there are numerous opportunities if you know where to look and are willing to venture a bit outside city limits. Many runners flock to the **Minuteman Bike Path** and the **Paul Dudley White Charles River Bike Path** on the weekend for long runs (*see p221*). A bonus of the Minuteman is that miles are marked on the path. **Memorial Drive**, the major road along the river in Cambridge, is closed to traffic between 11am

ARTS & ENTERTAINMENT

and 6pm on Sundays from mid April to mid November, making it a great place to run, skate or cycle. Check out www.cambridgerunning.org for information on paths and the opportunity to meet up with others for Saturday runs.

Further afield, there are running trails in the beautiful **Middlesex Fells Reservation** (off Route 28 in Malden, Medford, Stoneham, Melrose and Winchester, 1-617 727 1199, www.mass.gov/dcr/parks/metroboston/fells.htm).

For the **Boston Marathon**, *see p179.*

Skateboarding

With its winding cobblestone streets, cracked sidewalks and numerous handrails, stairways, curb cuts and molded concrete ledges, Boston is a great place to skateboard. Unfortunately, officers of the law often look askance at skating in unauthorized areas. Always keep an eye peeled for signs indicating where it might be forbidden.

The **Christian Science Plaza** (*see p62*) in Back Bay and the area fronting the **Boston Medical Center** (near the intersection of Massachusetts and Harrison Avenues) in the South End, with its enormous curved brick banks, are two popular spots.

The completion date for the long-awaited **Charles River Skate Park** (www.charles riverconservancy.org) remains an unknown. The multimillion-dollar project aims to create one of the biggest skateboard parks on the East Coast, with all the pipes, bowls, stairs, railings, ledges and ramps that everyone from beginners to experts can handle – but the big question is when. Check the website for the latest updates.

Harborside Community Center/ Skateboard Park

312 Border Street, East Boston (1-617 635-5114). Blue Line to Maverick. **Open** 24hrs daily. Established in 1976, Boston's oldest skate park offers assorted ramps and rails, along with a commanding view of downtown.

Messina Brothers Skateboard Park

John LeRoy Drive, at Braintree High School, off Route 37, Braintree (1-781 794 8910). Braintree T then bus 236. **Open** 24hrs daily. For an old-school experience, hit Messina Brothers' 5,000 square feet of asphalt and its concrete ramps. You'll need to be dedicated though, as it's not the easiest (or quickest) place to get to.

Skiing

New England skiing, with its rocky trails and slushy snow, can sometimes be hit or miss. Seldom will you find the plumes of feather-light white powder they kick up out west. All the same, there's some good downhill action to be had in the northern states. In the last decade most New England resorts – including **Sugarloaf** and **Sunday River** in Maine and **Killington** and **Sugarbush** in Vermont – have taken the art of snow-making to a new level. As long as the temperature co-operates, there will be snow to ski on, regardless of snowfall. Or, for a day's (or, better, a weekend's) excursion, zip up Route 93 North to Loon Mountain on the Kancamagus Highway or to Cannon Mountain in the Franconia Notch Parkway, both in nearby New Hampshire.

Those who can't afford to stray far from the city should try the **Blue Hills** (4001 Washington Street, at Green Street, Canton, 1-781 828 5090). It's not the most challenging terrain and snow conditions are entirely dependent on the weather, but it's just a 20-minute drive from Boston. For non-drivers, the recently launched **Ski Train** on the MBTA's commuter rail offers a service to **Wachusett Mountain**, in Princeton, west of Boston (499 Mountain Road, 1-978-464-2300, www.wachusett.com). The train leaves North Station every Saturday and Sunday at 8.35am for the commuter rail stop about an hour and a half away in Fitchburg, where a complimentary shuttle bus awaits to take skiers and boarders to the resort. Return trips leave Fitchburg at 5.35pm, pulling into the city around 7pm. Tickets cost $15.50 return.

Swimming

Boston public pools vary widely in quality and accessibility – visitors who are keen swimmers may do better to book into a hotel with facilities. The Boston Department of Conservation & Recreation operates all the public pools in the area. Most are open daily from late June to mid August. Call 1-617 727 1300 to find the location of your nearest pool, or go to www.mass.gov/dcr/recreate/swimming.htm.

Tennis

Although most tennis games in town take place in members-only clubs, there are more than 25 public courts in the Boston area. Most are available on a first-come, first-served basis, and there's an unspoken understanding that players shouldn't monopolize courts for more than an hour. The Boston Department of Conservation and Recreation oversees the majority of these courts, the most centrally located of which is on **Boston Common**, at Beacon Street. For a list of other courts (be warned: some of them are quite a trek from the city centre), visit www.mass.gov/dcr/recreate/tennis.htm.

Theater & Dance

Catch a Broadway hit or some edgy local fringe.

Boston's performing arts scene is more intriguing than meets the eye. A quick search unearths all the big names – the **Huntington**, the **American Repertory Theatre**, the distinctive **Blue Man Group** – and various touring Broadway shows.

But a closer look reveals that some of the Bean's best theater bubbles up from its extensive fringe theater scene. Innovative companies break new ground, while venues such as the **Devanaughn Theatre** and **Charlestown Working Theater** put on ambitious productions, despite tiny budgets.

Boston is also home to a small but eclectic dance community, ranging from the world-class **Boston Ballet** to progressive local companies that perform everything from classical ballet to Japanese butoh dance.

TICKETS AND INFORMATION

Getting tickets usually means either hoofing it to a venue's box office, or shelling out extra cash to buy them over the phone or on the web. Ticket agencies (*see p176*) range from all-encompassing event giants such as **Ticketmaster**, **TeleCharge** and the specialist **TheaterMania** (1-866 811 4111, www.theatermania.com) to the smaller, more local **Boston Theatre Scene** (1-617 933 8600, www.bostontheatrescene.com). If the search for seats becomes unbearable but you don't want to resort to scalpers, try **BosTix**, where you can buy cut-price tickets on the day.

THEATER

Boston's Theater District, where opulent playhouses stage touring shows and big productions, runs south along Tremont Street from the Boylston T stop to the Mass Pike. But don't be fooled – the town's performing arts scene is scattered all over the map, from Cambridge to the South End.

Major venues

Charles Playhouse
74 Warrenton Street, at Stuart Street, Downtown (1-617 426 6912, www.charles-playhouse.com). Boylston or Tufts Medical Center T. **Box office** 10am-6pm Mon, Tue, Fri; 10am-7pm Wed, Thur; 10am-9pm Sat;

11am-4pm Sun. **Tickets** $43-$53. **Credit** AmEx, MC, V. **Map** p275 J6.
If it ain't broke, don't fix it. That's the rule at the Charles Playhouse, which has kept its two crowd-pleasing acts running for years – *Shear Madness* since 1980, and the Blue Man Group since 1995. See Blue Man for a wild, noisy, paint-splattered evening, or *Shear Madness* for a comic whodunit fix.

Citi Performing Arts Center (Shubert Theatre & Wang Theatre)
265 & 270 Tremont Street, at Stuart Street, Downtown (1-617 482 9393, www.citicenter.org). Boylston or Tufts Medical Center T. **Box office** 10am-6pm Mon-Sat. **Tickets** $15-$100. **Credit** AmEx, MC, V. **Map** p275 J6.
The Citi Center complex is the big daddy of Boston theaters, encompassing the 3,600-seat Wang Theatre and the smaller Shubert opposite. Originally known as the Metropolitan Theatre, the Wang opened in 1925. The theater's gilt-trimmed interior was restored to its former glory a few years ago; today it hosts everything from Broadway hits to Shakespeare, plus opera, ballet and the occasional pop concert. The 1,600-seat Shubert Theatre opened in 1910, but the Theater District's 'Little Princess' was given a multi-million dollar facelift in the mid 1990s. These days, the bill is divided between theater, music, dance and opera – it's home to the Boston Lyric Opera. *Photo p229.*

Colonial Theatre
106 Boylston Street, at Tremont Street, Downtown (1-617 426 9366, www. bostonscolonialtheatre.com). Boylston T.

Opera House

Box office 10am-6pm Mon-Sat; noon-6pm Sun (call to check). **Tickets** $25-$100. **Credit** AmEx, MC, V. **Map** p275 J5.
A solid venue for big musicals, the Colonial was built in 1900 and is the oldest continuously operating theater in Boston. The fan-shaped auditorium means there's not a bad seat in the house.

Opera House

539 Washington Street, at Avenue de Lafayette, Downtown (1-617 259 3400, www.bostonopera houseonline.com). Downtown Crossing T. **Box office** (at Colonial Theatre; *see p225*) 10am-6pm Mon-Sat. **Tickets** prices vary. **Credit** AmEx, MC, V. **Map** p272 K5.
Once a vaudeville theater, and revamped in 2004, the breathakingly elegant Opera House plays host to everything from Broadway touring shows to concerts, plus the Boston Ballet's annual *Nutcracker* performance – though oddly enough, no actual operas.
▶ *For more on the festive season favorite, see p228 The Nutcracker Variations.*

Other theaters & companies

★ American Repertory Theatre

Loeb Drama Center, Harvard University, 64 Brattle Street, at Hilliard Street, Cambridge (1-617 547 8300, www.amrep.org). Harvard T. **Box office** noon-5pm Tue-Sun. **Tickets** $35-$69. **Credit** AmEx, MC, V. **Map** p276 A2.
One of the country's top regional theaters, the ART has been making waves on the international scene since its inception in 1980. Luminaries such as Philip Glass, Anne Bogart and David Mamet have all worked with the company to produce decidedly edgy world premières. In 2005, the troupe opened a second venue, the Zero Arrow Theatre. This intimate space plays host to even more experimental

works from local alt-luminaries, traveling monologuists and the like. Tickets are available through the main ART box office.

★ Boston Center for the Arts

539 Tremont Street, at Berkeley Street, South End (1-617 426 5000, www.bcaonline.org). Back Bay or Copley T. **Box office** times vary. **Tickets** $10-$35. **Credit** AmEx, MC, V. **Map** p275 J7.
After expanding in 2004 to include the Stanford Calderwood Pavilion, the much-loved BCA has become a veritable cultural haven. Dominating the South End, the complex comprises four theaters which play host to companies large and small. Resident groups Company One, SpeakEasy Stage Company and the Theater Offensive have been joined by the Publick Theatre and Up You Mighty Race Performing Arts Company, but most of the city's small and medium companies have trodden these boards at some point or another.

Huntington (Boston University Theatre)

264 Huntington Avenue, at Massachusetts Avenue, Back Bay (1-617 266 0800, www. huntingtontheatre.org). Symphony T. **Box office** noon-6pm Mon; noon-7.30pm Tue-Fri; noon-8pm Sat; noon-4pm Sun. **Tickets** $38-$64. **Credit** AmEx, MC, V. **Map** p274 F8.
Having transformed from a theater into an arthouse cinema, and back into a theater once again, this venue is now owned by Boston University. It's home to the Huntington Theatre Company, an accomplished, ambitious troupe that brings big names to the little city. Consistently top-notch, Huntington productions often go on to Broadway glory, and have won a clutch of Elliot Norton Awards in recent years. Tell your friends you saw it here first.

Lyric Stage

YWCA Building, 140 Clarendon Street, at Copley Square, Back Bay (1-617 585 5678, www.lyric stage.com). Back Bay or Copley T. **Box office** noon-5pm Tue, Sun; noon-8pm Wed-Sat. **Tickets** $35-$50. **Credit** AmEx, MC, V. **Map** p275 H6.
Under the inspired leadership of artistic director Spiro Veloudos, the once middling Lyric Stage Company has risen to challenge companies such as the Huntington and SpeakEasy for hometown supremacy. Look for moderately priced stagings of classics and recent New York exports. The delightful Once upon a Time children's theater company also performs here.
▶ *For children's theater, see p187.*

New Repertory Theatre at Arsenal Center for the Arts

321 Arsenal Street, at School Street, Watertown (1-617 923 8487, www.newrep. org). Central Square T then bus 70, 70A. **Box office** noon-6pm Tue-Fri. **Tickets** $40-$60. **Credit** AmEx, MC, V.

One of Boston's most respected repertory companies, the New Rep has garnered numerous Elliot Norton Awards over the past decade or so. The troupe mounts challenging productions of contemporary plays and musicals, including its fair share of New England premières.

Alternative theater

Venues are relatively scarce in Boston, so the city's smaller theater groups often rent out performance space in less mainstream locations. The result is a vibrant, varied subculture of intermingling companies such as the **Zeitgeist Stage Company**

(www.zeitgeiststage.com), the **Nora** (www.thenora.org) and **Company One** (www.companyone.org).

Boston Playwrights' Theatre

949 Commonwealth Avenue, at Harry Agganis Way, Allston (1-866 811 4111, www.bu.edu/bpt). Pleasant Street T. **Box office** 1hr before showtime. **Tickets** $5-$15. **Credit** AmEx, MC, V. **Map** p276 B5.
It's easy to miss the BPT, tucked away in an alley between McDonald's and Store 24. The search is worth it, though: as an incubator for emerging playwrights, the theater is home to some of the city's fringiest fringe.

Faces & Places The Dresden Dolls

A dynamic duo spill the beans on Boston.

The theatrical rock duo the Dresden Dolls – pianist/singer/songwriter Amanda Palmer and drummer/background vocalist Brian Viglione – have been a dynamic force on the city's arts scene since they brought their self-styled 'Brechtian punk cabaret' to Boston's small clubs and art spaces in 2001. Although still based in Boston (Viglione lives in Jamaica Plain, Palmer in an artists' collective in the South End), they're now an international touring act, and Palmer has appeared as a solo artist in the Edinburgh Fringe Festival.

The Dolls recently diversified into theater, when Palmer co-wrote *The Onion Cellar* in collaboration with the American Repertory Theatre. Although she had envisaged it as a riskier production, the play – which featured the duo's music and transformed the Zero Arrow Theatre into a 1930s-style nightclub – was a hit. Palmer also went back home to Lexington to work with her old high school to produce *With the Needle That Sings in Her Heart*, a stage interpretation of indie rock band Neutral Milk Hotel's classic album *In the Aeroplane Over the Sea*.

TO: Describe your perfect day in Boston.
BV: I'd have an amazing breakfast at Zaftigs (*see p138*) in Brookline, then take a long walk in the Arnold Arboretum in Jamaica Plain. Then maybe I'd go over to the Lily Pad (*see p212*) in Inman Square. It's a great showcase for alternative styles of music, whether it's jazz, experimental, avant-garde or classical. Afterwards, I might head down to Central Square to see if anyone good is playing at the Middle East (*see p209*).

AP: I would probably take a jog to Boston Common, then eat at Whole Foods in Back Bay – it has the best salad bar in the city. After that I'd go to Harvard Square and read at Café Pamplona [it featured in the duo's song 'Truce'; *see p132*] for a while. Then I'd head back to the South End and go to the Columbus Café (535 Columbus Avenue, 1-617 247 9001) for dinner and drinking. I also really like the Otherside Café (*see p146*).

TO: What inspires you about Boston?
AP: You can call me hokey and sentimental, but I'm really inspired by the history of the city itself. I'm one of those dorky people who will take a walk downtown to the Old South Meeting House and get nostalgic. It's easy to lose sight of what is here because it can seem so touristy and typical, but when you really think about it, the history is mind-blowing. Plus I grew up in Lexington, so it's kind of in my blood.
BV: I'm inspired by the concertgoers who are willing to get behind a band they love no matter what the genre is. There's a supportive and energized left-wing music scene that never completely faded out, although we've unfortunately seen a lot of performance art spaces and all-ages punk clubs shut down over the last ten years.

TO: And what annoys you?
BV: The music scene is great, but it can get petty and catty sometimes.
AP: I don't like how unfriendly everyone is. There is a pervasive air of suspicion here that you don't start to notice until you've spent a lot of time in other places.

ARTS & ENTERTAINMENT

The Nutcracker Variations

The holiday classic gets a few new twists.

Visiting Boston when the cobbled streets shimmer with a fresh coat of snow and Christmas lights twinkle in the windows of Back Bay brownstones can truly be an unforgettable experience. Should you find your cup runneth over with holiday spirit, seeing a production of *The Nutcracker* is a fine way to embrace this magical time of the year. However, in Boston, you may be surprised to find it's also a nice way to see girls brandish their assets while singing randy songs about sexual promiscuity.

Annually, three adaptations of the holiday classic are performed in the city of Boston: one a faithful reiteration of the ballet, another is seen through an African-American lens and finally there's the red-light district version, a burlesque of the original where Clara has grown up and discovered her feminine wiles.

Graceful choreography and a beautifully set stage have come to be expected from the Boston Ballet's faithful rendition of **The Nutcracker** (1-617 695 6950, www.boston ballet.org). Their production of the ETA Hoffmann fairy tale is staged annually at the Opera House (*see p226*) and tickets start at around $35 and increase to over $160.

BalletRox's presentation of Tony Williams' **Urban Nutcracker** (John Hancock Hall, 180 Berkeley Street, at Stuart Street, Back Bay, 1-617 524 3066, www.ballet rox.org, $20-$55) embraces inner-city multiculturalism by weaving classical, modern Russian, Chinese and African dance into the familiar tale, utilizing Duke Ellington's and Billy Strayhorn's jazz version of the *Nutcracker Suite* as a springboard.

And then there is **The Slutcracker: A Burlesque** (www.theslutcracker.com, $20-$25). By only its second year, this irreverent spin on the ballet had become a new tradition at the Somerville Theatre (*see p208*). Sit back with a glass of wine or beer to watch this loose adaptation, in which the protagonist Clara is dating Fritz – instead of being his older sister. And while everything seems to be perfect in their relationship, Fritz's lack of prowess between the sheets is ultimately leaving her unsatisfied. That's where Herr Drosselmeyer – traditionally Clara's mysterious gift-giving godfather and purveyor of the Nutcracker toy – steps in, and you can pretty much figure out what happens from there.

ARTS & ENTERTAINMENT

Charlestown Working Theater
442 Bunker Hill Street, at Main Street,
Charlestown (1-617 242 3285, www.charlestown
workingtheater.org). Sullivan Square T. **Box**
office 2hrs before showtime. **Tickets** $10-$20.
Credit AmEx, MC, V.
Housed in a converted Victorian fire station, the
Charlestown Working Theater radiates a deeper
sense of history than any of its big brothers on
Tremont Street. Its versatile staging area means the
theater never looks the same twice, while oodles of
community support means tickets are dirt cheap.

Devanaughn Theatre
Piano Factory, 791 Tremont Street,
at Northampton Street, Roxbury (1-617 247
9777, www.devtheatre.com). Mass Ave T. **Box**
office 1hr before showtime. **Tickets** $10-$20.
No credit cards. Map p274 G8.
The Devanaughn is the little theater with the big
heart. Opened in 2001, it hosts various fringe troupes
while maintaining its own fast-evolving resident
company. Each summer, hordes of actors crowd into
the space for the Dragonfly Festival, a showcase of
new plays by local writers.

Oberon
2 Arrow Street, at Massachusetts Avenue,
Harvard Square, Cambridge (1-617 496 8004,
www.cluboberon.com). Harvard T. **Box office**
1hr before showtime. **Tickets** $15-$50. **Credit**
MC, V. **Map** p276 B3.
Oberon is the quirky stepchild of Boston theater. Half
disco, half dinner-theater, every experience within
their walls is different. But you can always count on
being entertained – and possibly doused in glitter.

★ Theater Machine
1256 Boylston Street, Fenway, Back Bay
(1-617 265 6222, www.golddustorphans.com).
Kenmore T. **Box office** times vary. **Tickets**
$28. **No credit cards. Map** p274 D7.
This makeshift theater is in the basement of
Ramrod, a much-loved gay bar behind Fenway
Park. You can depend on Theater Machine residents
Ryan Landry and the Gold Dust Orphans to put on
consistently hilarious, original plays, performed in
drag. Productions have included the likes of *Death
of a Saleslady* and *A T Stop Named Denial.*
▶ *For more about the Ramrod, see p200.*

COMEDY

Although small, Boston's comedy scene is
thriving. Plenty of big names have tried out
their acts here on their way to the top, including
Denis Leary, Steven Wright and Conan O'Brien.
The laughs keep coming, with popular comedy
venues on both sides of the river. Touring
comedy acts occasionally grace the **Berklee
Performance Center** (*see p207*) too.

Comedy Connection
2nd Level, Quincy Market Building, Faneuil
Hall Marketplace, Downtown (1-617 248 9700,
www.comedyconnectionboston.com). Gov't Center
or State T. **Box office** 9am-10pm Mon-Fri;
10am-10pm Sat; noon-showtime Sun. **Shows**
days & times vary. **Admission** $15-$35. **Credit**
AmEx, MC, V. **Map** p273 L4.
Familiar names from TV shows and sitcoms, and
up-and-coming hopefuls, take their turn on the bill
at this Faneuil Hall Marketplace institution. There
are shows most nights, usually at 8pm or 8.30pm,
with second shows on Fridays and Saturdays.
▶ *For more about Faneuil Hall, see p47.*

Comedy Studio
Hong Kong Restaurant, 1236 Massachusetts
Avenue, at Bow Street, Harvard Square,
Cambridge (1-617 661 6507, www.thecomedy
studio.com). Harvard T. **Shows** 8pm Tue-Sun.
Admission $8-$10. **No credit cards.**
Map p276 B3.
Tucked away on the top floor of a Chinese restau-
rant, this place is a haven for alternative comedy.
It offers a huge variety of stand-up and sketch rou-
tines, with a slew of new acts performing most
nights of the week. *Photo p230.*
▶ *For our review of Hong Kong, see p150.*

★ Improv Asylum
216 Hanover Street, at Cross Street, North End
(1-617 263 6887, www.improvasylum.com).
Haymarket T. **Box office** 2-5pm Tue; 1-9pm
Wed, Thur; 1-11pm Fri; noon-11pm Sat. **Shows**
Wed-Sat; times vary. **Admission** $15-$20.
Credit MC, V. **Map** p273 L3.

Shubert Theatre. *See p225.*

Improv Asylum now has shows in both New York and LA, but it all started here. The main stage show is arguably the hottest comedy ticket in town, while the ASS (after show series) includes the popular Midnight Show on Saturday nights.

ImprovBoston
40 Prospect Street, at Bishop Allen Drive, Central Square, Cambridge (1-617 576 1253, www.improvboston.com). Central T. **Shows** Wed-Sat, Sun; times vary. **Admission** $5-$15. **No credit cards. Map** p276 C3.
In the heart of Central Square, surrounded by some great dining options, ImprovBoston hosts an ever-changing line-up of improv and sketch shows. Times vary, but there are usually two shows a night Wednesday through Friday (at 8pm and 10pm), plus an extra 'family show' at 6pm on Saturday and one show on Sunday at 7pm.

DANCE

In addition to the venues listed below, it's worth checking what's on at the **Institute of Contemporary Art** (*see p79*). An assortment of world-class choreographers and troupes take their turn in the gorgeous theater, with its two windowed walls providing a panoramic view of the harbor. The multi-talented **Citi Performing Arts Center** (*see p225*) also fits contemporary dance and ballet performances into its vibrant schedule at both the Shubert and the Wang theaters. The latter is also the stage for the **Boston**

Comedy Studio. See p229.

Ballet (1-617 695 6955, www.bostonballet.org), which has its HQ at the Boston Center for the Arts (*see p226*) in the South End and continues to reign as one of the top companies in the US. Its productions range from contemporary gems to old favorites – including its annual *Nutcracker* performance (*see p228*).

Cutler Majestic Theatre at Emerson College
219 Tremont Street, at Boylston Street, Downtown (1-617 824 8000, www.maj.org). Boylston T. **Box office** 10am-6pm daily. **Tickets** $15-$85. **Credit** AmEx, MC, V. **Map** p275 J5.
After a $10 million renovation, the 1,200-seat Cutler Majestic Theatre at Emerson College reopened in 2003, a century after it first flung wide its doors as the more simply named Majestic. These days, it's one of Boston's busiest venues. Its stage is occupied by a steady stream of ballets and operas from the prestigious Teatro Lirico d'Europa, and shows by the college's students, as well as an array of visiting comedians and theater troupes.

Dance Complex
536 Massachusetts Avenue, at Brookline Street, Central Square, Cambridge (1-617 547 9363, www.dancecomplex.org). Central T. **Open** 9am-9pm Mon-Fri; 9am-6pm Sat; 10am-5pm Sun. **Tickets** $10-$30. **No credit cards. Map** p276 C3.
This volunteer-based, non-profit organisation hosts artists-in-residence, who teach classes and perform for the masses. Local choreographers première new and unusual work that's a world away from the classical repertory. If you feel like taking a class, just drop in with a little cash and your sweats.

Green Street Studios
185 Green Street, at Brookline Street, Central Square, Cambridge (1-617 864 3191, www.greenstreetstudios.org). Central T. **Box office** 1hr before showtime. **Tickets** $10-$15. **No credit cards. Map** p276 C3.
This choreographer-run center is a hotbed of new dance talent. In addition to community outreach through classes and programs, Green Street offers a slew of collaborative dance concerts each month. Phone the venue to reserve tickets (leave a message if no one answers).

Sanctuary Theatre
400 Harvard Street, at Remington Street, Harvard Square, Cambridge (1-617 354 7467, www.balletthreatre.org). Harvard T. **Box office** 10am-6pm Mon-Fri. **Tickets** prices vary. **Credit** MC, V. **Map** p276 B3.
José Mateo's innovative modern dance company finally has a home of its own, after years of renting local venues. The historic Old Cambridge Baptist Church serves as both a studio space for instruction and as a performance space.

ARTS & ENTERTAINMENT

Escapes & Excursions

Cape Cod. *See p243.*

Escapes & Excursions

History, blue collars and blue bloods.

Along the rocky coastline of Massachusetts you'll find seagulls, sand dunes and salty sea air. You'll also discover lonely lighthouses, rattletrap clam shacks and gruff seafaring charm. There's lowlife too – if you know where to look. Many of the communities along the Massachusetts shoreline still rely on the Atlantic for their livelihood. This is what people are talking about when they refer to the 'real' New England.

It was this coast that drew the early settlers to Plymouth, and then further inland, where you'll find a host of charming, sleepy towns. It won't take you long, however, to be awoken by the impact of the Revolutionary War, or to observe the reverence and pride modern residents of colonial villages have for their shared memories – keeping a turbulent history alive for 300 years. From literary forefathers to battle scenes to fresh seafood, each of these locations has its own character, but goes a long way in further defining New England.

ESCAPES & EXCURSIONS

One if by Land…

CONCORD, LEXINGTON & LINCOLN

Concord and Lexington, neighboring towns about half an hour's drive west of Boston, are known as the battleground of American independence. The villages enjoy a friendly rivalry over who hosted the first rumblings of revolution; Lexington can claim the first shot, but Concord entertained the first fight. In fact, the first true battle in the American Revolution started in Lexington and ended in Concord, thus forever combining the two in the minds of many.

It all began in 1774, when the Provincial Congress delegated a division of elite militia soldiers known as the Minutemen. They were authorized to form 'for defense only'. But the Minutemen, in anticipation of future battles, had begun stockpiling weapons in the village of Concord. British generals caught word of the arsenal and sent 700 troops to make the 25-mile journey from Boston to Concord. Alerted by a trio of rebels (Paul Revere among them) sent on horseback, 70 Minutemen met the troops at Lexington Green. When the British soldiers arrived they ordered the Americans to drop their weapons. The colonists refused – and a battle began. During that first struggle, 18 Minutemen were killed or wounded, while not a single British soldier was injured. Emboldened by their victory, the British didn't stop to rest, but marched on to Concord where, unknown to them, more militia were marshalling. As the American troops awaited the Redcoats' arrival outside Concord, they spotted smoke rising from the town. Convinced that the British were

INSIDE TRACK HOUSE DEALS

A three-house package tour covering the **Buckman Tavern**, **Hancock-Clarke House** and **Munroe Tavern** (*for all, see right*) is available from any of them for $10 ($6 reductions) and is valid for a year.

burning their homes, they attacked a British patrol sent out to hold the Old North Bridge (*pictured p234*). It is said that the colonial troops were so enraged that Captain John Parker told the militia: 'Stand your ground. Don't fire unless fired upon, but if they mean to have a war, let it begin here!' And so it did. Two Americans and 11 British soldiers were killed there. With that, the war began in earnest (*see p19*).

Lexington

All the major sights of **Lexington** center on **Lexington Green**, the triangular plot upon which the battle occurred. Today, it is anchored by the **Minuteman Statue** and dotted with other markers and memorials. The statue is of Captain Parker, his famous quote engraved below his feet. Turning right as you come out of the green you'll see the yellow colonial house known as **Buckman Tavern**. Here, the Minutemen assembled to await the arrival of British troops; they later used it as a field hospital. The tavern, one of the oldest buildings in the area, was already 85 years old at the time of the battle. These days it is staffed by guides in period costume. The high bar counter is said to have been set at this level to prevent under-age drinking: if a boy's chin wasn't above the bar, he couldn't buy a beer. The tavern keepers tracked the sales of pints and quarts by chalking them up behind the bar, giving rise to the expression 'mind your Ps and Qs'.

Just behind the tavern is the small but perfectly informed **Lexington Visitors' Center**, which has a diorama illustrating the particulars of the battle. It also offers tours of the town's historically significant houses.

North of the green, on Hancock Street, sits the **Hancock-Clarke House**. On the night of the battle, largely by coincidence, rebels Samuel Adams and John Hancock were spending the night here, as guests of the owner, Rev Jonas Clarke. In the end, Revere awoke them in time, and they were hustled out of town to safety. He did not, however, warn the soldiers at Concord, as he was captured by the British. The Hancock-Clarke house now contains a permanent collection of the furnishings and paintings owned by the two families, as well as relics of that night in April 1775.

About a mile east of the green is the **Munroe Tavern**. It was here that the British troops retreating from Concord stopped to rest and treat their injured, shooting the bartender who tried to flee after serving them. George Washington tried to redeem the bar's reputation by visiting it after the war, and several artifacts relating to his stay are kept here today. Further along, at the intersection of Massachusetts Avenue and Marrett Road, is the modern brick building that houses the **National Heritage Museum**. Colonial farm tools and Freemason propaganda mingle with rock concert posters and baseball memorabilia, making the museum a breezy respite from the rest of the area's emphatically colonial history.

Concord

Four miles from Lexington down Route 62 is the village of **Concord**. As well as playing a major role in the War of Independence, Concord is distinguished by its place in American letters. Ralph Waldo Emerson, Henry David Thoreau, Louisa May Alcott and Nathaniel Hawthorne all lived here at various times, and within a few short blocks you'll find a group of houses that once contained an unparalleled flowering of American literary genius. But the first sites most visitors feel obliged to see are tied in to the country's earliest days. The most significant is the **Minute Man National Historical Park**, which marks the spot where the Battle of Concord took place after the British marched on victorious from Lexington. Every April, on Patriots' Day Weekend (*see also p219* **Inside Track**), thousands of people in traditional Minuteman and Redcoat garb hold a historical re-enactment of the opening events of the Revolutionary War.

Once inside the park, it's best to start at the **North Bridge Visitors' Center**, set on a hill

Minuteman Statue.

overlooking the bridge and the Concord River. Inside is a diorama, alongside a collection of Revolutionary War memorabilia, including uniforms and weapons from both sides. The helpful park rangers at the center provide guided tours of the site. From there, it's just a short walk to the reconstruction of the North Bridge, where the 'shot heard around the world' was fired. It's worth stopping along the way to listen to recordings that tell the story of the battle and the area. The **Battle Road Trail** is a five-mile stretch that connects many of the park's points of interest.

Essayist and philosopher Ralph Waldo Emerson lived in two houses in town, but his primary residence was at what is now known as the **Ralph Waldo Emerson House**. He lived here with his family from 1835 until his death in 1882; while he was on tour in Europe, his friend and fellow Transcendentalist Henry David Thoreau kept house. The house contains some of the original furnishings, and many of Emerson's personal belongings.

Another Emerson residence is the **Old Manse**, built by his grandfather in 1770. Both Emerson and Nathaniel Hawthorne lived here at different times; Emerson with his wife from 1842 to 1847, and many of their personal effects are on display. Hawthorne's stories inspired by his time here brought him his earliest fame. Not far away is **Orchard House**, once home to the educator Bronson Alcott, another prominent Transcendentalist. However, its best-known resident was his daughter, Louisa May Alcott. Her *Little Women* was both written about and set at Orchard House. The house, filled with the family's belongings, attracts thousands of fans

of the book every year. A ticket includes a highly detailed tour. Alcott also lived at **The Wayside**, a neighboring residence where, coincidentally, Hawthorne later came to spend his final years. The **Concord Museum**, built on the site of Emerson's orchard, contains a tidy collection of local relics, including a number of Thoreau's effects But the museum's most famous item is one of the lanterns that was hung in the Old North Church on the night of Paul Revere's famous ride, to signal the approach of British troops.

From the nearby town square, you can catch a glimpse of the steep embankment of **Sleepy Hollow Cemetery** (*see p45* **Six Feet Under**) on Bedford Street, the eternal home of Concord's most celebrated writers-in-residence. At the top of a hill, under the shade of enormous maple trees, lie the graves of Emerson, Thoreau, Alcott and Hawthorne. It's an especially apt tableau for naturalists Thoreau and Emerson, who drew inspiration for their work from the serenity of Concord's landscape. Concord's best-known muse, though, lies just south of town. At **Walden Pond**, in a one-room cabin off Route 126, he lived in rustic meditation for a year or so from 1846. He wrote the ground-breaking essay *Walden* about the experience, but fame only came with *Civil Disobedience* three years later. The house in which Thoreau sought his simple life is long since gone – a pile of stones marks the spot – but the well-preserved **Walden Pond State Reservation** affords the kind of swimming and hiking the native seer advocated. A full-size replica of the original cabin, with painstakingly reproduced furnishings, is open to visitors. In summer, the

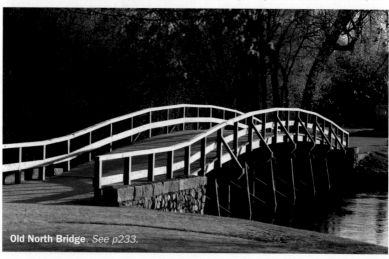

Old North Bridge. *See p233.*

pond's wooded banks can become quite crowded with Bostonians hoping to cool off.

Lincoln

Lincoln was originally part of Concord, but became a separate town in 1754, nipping off a few bits of other surrounding towns in the process. (Its piecemeal geography earned it the nickname 'Niptown'.) Like its neighbors, Lincoln boasts Revolutionary history aplenty. Just off Route 2A, in the Minute Man National Historical Park, is the site where Paul Revere was captured by British soldiers on his way to Concord.

Nearby, just off Route 128, is the stunning **DeCordova Museum and Sculpture Park**. The castle-like premises (the former estate of Boston entrepreneur Julian de Cordova, 1850-1945) are home to the largest contemporary art museum in the region, and New England's only permanent sculpture park. Devoted to living New England talent, the DeCordova holds annual shows of accomplished regional artists. A varied and ever-changing array of enormous sculptures bespeckle the 35-acre park, where visitors can wander or picnic.

Tucked into the farmlands and forests along Baker Bridge Road is the spare, minimalist **Gropius House** (*see p237 Profile*), the family home of acclaimed mid 20th-century German architect Walter Gropius. A half-hour's walk through the woods will bring you to the much more Colonial-looking **Codman House**. The grand, Federal-style estate of the Codman family, it dates back to 1735. The grounds are home to extensive gardens, as well as the **Codman Community Farm**, a working, educational vegetable and livestock farm that's open to visitors.

Buckman Tavern *1 Bedford Street, Lexington (1-781 862 5598, www.lexingtonhistory.org).* **Open** *Apr-Oct* 10am-4pm Mon-Sun. **Admission** $5; $3 reductions. **Credit** MC, V.

Codman Community Farm *58 Codman Road, Lincoln (1-781 259 0456, www.codmanfarm. org).* **Open** 9am-6pm Tue-Sun. **Admission** $1. **No credit cards.**

Codman House *The Grange, Codman Road, Lincoln (1-781 259 8843).* **Open** *June-mid Oct* 11am-4pm 1st & 3rd Sat of mth. **Admission** $5. **Credit** AmEx, MC, V.

Concord Museum *200 Lexington Road, Concord (1-978 369 9763, www.concordmuseum.org).* **Open** *Jan-Mar* 11am-4pm Mon-Sat; 1-4pm Sun. *Apr, May, Sept-Dec* 9am-5pm Mon-Sat; noon-5pm Sun. *June-Aug* 9am-5pm daily. **Admission** $10; $5-$8 reductions. **Credit** AmEx, MC, V.

DeCordova Museum & Sculpture Park *51 Sandy Pond Road, off Route 2 or 128, Lincoln (1-781 259 8355, www.decordova.org).*

DeCordova Sculpture Park.

Open 11am-5pm Tue-Sun. **Admission** $9; $6 reductions; free under-5s. **Credit** AmEx, MC, V.

Hancock-Clarke House *36 Hancock Street, Lexington (1-781 862 1703, www.lexington history.org).* **Open** *Apr-mid June* 11am-2pm Sat, Sun. *Mid June-Oct* 11am-2pm daily. **Admission** $5; $3 reductions. **Credit** MC, V.

Gropius House *68 Baker Bridge Road, Lincoln (1-781 259 8098, www.historicnewengland.org).* **Tours** (hourly) *June-mid Oct* 11am-4pm Wed-Sun. *Mid Oct-May* 11am-4pm Sat, Sun. **Admission** $10; $5-$9 reductions; free under-5s. **Credit** MC, V. *See p237* **Profile**.

Minute Man National Historical Park Visitors' Center *174 Liberty Street, Concord (1-978 369 6993, www.nps.gov/mima).* **Open** *Apr-Oct* 9am-5pm daily (phone for winter hours). **Admission** free.

Munroe Tavern *1332 Massachusetts Avenue, Lexington (1-781 862 1703, www.lexington history.org).* **Open** *Apr-mid June* 1.30-3pm Sat, Sun. *Mid June-Oct* 1.30-3pm daily. **Admission** $5; $3 reductions. **No credit cards.**

Old Manse *269 Monument Street, Concord (1-978 369 3909).* **Open** *Mid Apr-Oct* 10am-5pm (last tour 4.30pm) Mon-Sat; noon-5pm Sun. **Admission** $8; $5-$7 reductions. **Credit** AmEx, MC, V.

Orchard House *399 Lexington Road, Concord (1-978 369 4118).* **Open** *Apr-Oct* 10am-4.30pm Mon-Sat; 1-4.30pm Sun. *Nov-Mar* 11am-3pm

Mon-Fri; 10am-4.30pm Sat; 1-4.30pm Sun.
Admission $8; $5-$7 reductions.
Credit AmEx, MC, V.
Ralph Waldo Emerson House *28 Cambridge Turnpike, Concord (1-978 369 2236)*. **Open** *Apr-Oct* 10am-4.30pm Thur-Sat; 1-4.30pm Sun. **Admission** $7; $5 reductions; free under-8s.
Credit MC, V.
Walden Pond State Reservation *915 Walden Street, Concord (1-978 369 3254, www.mass.gov/dcr)*. **Open** 7am-8pm daily.
Admission free.
Wayside *455 Lexington Road, Concord (1-978 318 7863, www.nps.gov/mima/wayside)*. **Open** *late May-Oct* 9.30am-5.30pm Fri-Sun. **Admission** $5; free under-16s. **No credit cards**.

Where to stay

Concord has two historic inns: the 19th-century **Hawthorne** (462 Lexington Road, 1-978 369 5610, www.concordmass.com, $135-$315 double) and the 18th-century **Colonial Inn** (48 Monument Square, 1-978 369 9200, www. concordscolonialinn.com, $165-$269 double), which occupies a prime spot on the square and houses a highly regarded restaurant. For something a little more intimate, the **North Bridge Inn** (21 Monument Square, 1-978 371 0014, www.northbridgeinn.com, $165-$250 double) has six suites of various sizes.

Where to eat & drink

Concord isn't known for its fine dining, but there are a few decent options in the area. **Serafina** (195 Sudbury Road, 1-978 371 9050, www.serafinaristorante.com) features Tuscan-style Italian cuisine and live music at the weekend. In nearby Bedford, **Dalya's Restaurant** (20 North Road, 1-781 275 0700, www.dalyas.com) offers pricey but tasty American and Mediterranean food.

Getting there

By car Lexington is nine miles north-west of Boston on Route 128 (I-95). Concord is 18 miles north-west of Boston and six miles west of Lexington. Take Route 2A from Lexington, or Route 2 from Boston. Lincoln is 12 miles north-west of Boston and just a few miles south-east of Concord. Take Route 2 from Boston or Concord.
By bus or rail The MBTA Commuter Rail (*see p251*) has services to Concord and Lincoln from North Station. Buses 62 and 76 go to Lexington from Alewife T station in Cambridge. Awkwardly, there is no direct public transport connection between Lexington and Concord or Lincoln.

Tourist information

For the **Minute Man National Historical Park Visitors' Center** , *see p235*.

Lexington Visitors' Center *Lexington Green, 1875 Massachusetts Avenue, Lexington (1-781 862 1450)*. **Open** *Apr-Nov* 9am-5pm daily. *Dec-Mar* 10am-4pm daily.

SALEM

There are few American towns with reputations as dark as **Salem**. While there is more to its history than the notorious Witch Trials of 1692, the mass hysteria that consumed the town during those seven months still casts a pall on its name. According to local lore, Tituba, an Arawak maid who practiced voodoo, turned the interest of a group of repressed young Puritan girls towards magic, with devastating results; other stories attribute their behavior to adolescent hysteria, or even ergot poisoning. The tragic conclusion of it all, the executions of more than 20 people – mostly elderly women – means the town will be forever linked with madness.

Black magic associations aside, Salem is a lovely place. It has a slightly split personality: one side of it is darkly colonial, with red-brick buildings and cemeteries dating back to its earliest days, but it's also a beach town, with a brisk fishing trade and colorful summer houses by the coast. The colonial section makes a good starting point in terms of chronology, because you move towards the more modern buildings as you get closer to the water.

Though Salem is small, it is sprawling enough to make getting from one end to the other a bit of a hike – but walking really is the best way to get around. Not surprisingly, the town is overrun with witchcraft-related attractions, many of them closer to Halloween spectacles than actual historical points of interest. The few sites worth investigating are mostly scattered around **Salem Common**, a scenic park in the middle of the oldest section of town. The **Witch House**, also known as the Jonathan Corwin House after the former inhabitant and witch trial judge, was where the 200 or more unfortunates suspected of witchcraft were questioned. The house is truly spooky, though probably more for its dearth of windows than for its ominous pedigree. The **Salem Wax Museum** displays re-creations of the characters involved in the trials. Nearby, and the best of the lot, the **Salem Witch Museum** features a very thorough (and somewhat scary) mixed-media re-enactment of the Puritan hysteria. There's also a refreshingly enlightened exhibit on modern-day 'witches', including pagans and Wiccans.

Profile Gropius House

A Bauhaus in the country.

Walter Gropius arrived in Cambridge in 1937 to teach at Harvard's Graduate School of Design after the Nazis closed the Bauhaus, the innovative German design school he'd founded 18 years earlier. Offered a hillside site in rural Lincoln by a wealthy patron to build a home for himself and his family, he turned it into a laboratory of sorts where he and his colleagues could explore new forms and materials, and a new way of life.

Completed in 1939, **Gropius House** (*see p235*) is a sculptural tour de force, inventively engaging its hilltop site. Its boxy white form may have grown out of 1920s European modernism, but its fieldstone foundation, screened porch and colonnade tie it to the traditions of the region.

A white wooden box dominates the composition, a familiar New England icon stripped of the pitched roof, vertical windows and traditional ornamental features. Instead, there are horizontal ribbons of windows and a series of projecting elements and sculptural cutouts that open it up to the pastoral setting.

An angular, steel-and-glass block entrance entices visitors inside; next to it, a staircase spirals upwards to a sheltered terrace (which gave Gropius and his wife Ise a surreptitious view from inside of their precocious teenage daughter's late-night comings and goings). To the rear, a wafer-thin roof hovers on slender columns above a terrace wrapped in a taut skin of screening. The interior comprises interconnected spaces that are cool and serene. A floating glass dividing wall, steel framed windows and sleek black counters echo the aesthetic of the exterior. The

sensuously curving central stairway is a lovingly designed piece of sculpture with its cascade of metal, wood and unpainted plaster.

The house is furnished with pieces collected or designed by Gropius. The dining room chairs by collaborator Marcel Breuer are icons of modern design, and the Miró hanging in the entrance was a gift from the artist. Hour-long tours take visitors around the entire property and site, putting the aspirations and innovations of its designer into the context of their time and place.

MORE MODERNISM
Le Corbusier also made his mark in New England; *see p85* **Carpenter Center for the Visual Arts**.

Old downtown Salem is a National Historic District and site of architectural interest. Along Chestnut Street, Samuel McIntyre, a native of Salem and a pioneer of the American Federal style, designed a number of houses. In the heart of the area is the **Peabody Essex Museum**, an exceptional resource for international art and culture. Founded by the East India Maritime Company in the late 18th century, when Salem was prominent in the shipping trade to China, the Peabody collection documents the history of whaling and merchant shipping, and features an extensive collection of exhibits from sailors' travels. Renovations have brought several new galleries and exhibits, including Yin Yu Tang, a spectacular Qing dynasty merchant's house that was shipped over and reassembled in partnership with the Chinese government.

Salem's seafaring past is on display aboard the **Friendship**, a full-scale replica of a three-masted 1797 East India merchant ship. It is docked at the end of Derby Street, amid the nine-acre **Salem Maritime National Historic Site**, which offers tours of reconstructions of wharves, warehouses and stores, as well as the old Customs House where Nathaniel Hawthorne worked before he wrote *The Scarlet Letter*. Salem's most famous son, Hawthorne took the inspiration for his other great novel from his cousin's home, the **House of the Seven Gables**. It's an extraordinary building, large and gloomy, with a peaked roof and turrets. Built in 1668, it is filled with period furniture, much of which is described in Hawthorne's novel. Tours also take in the modest house where Hawthorne was born, which was moved to the grounds from its original site on nearby Union Street in 1958.

House of the Seven Gables *54 Turner Street, at Derby Street, Salem (1-978 744 0991, www.7gables.org)*. **Open** *Jan-June, Nov, Dec* 10am-5pm daily. *July-Sept* 10am-7pm daily. *Oct* 10am-7pm Sun-Thur; 10am-11pm Fri, Sat. **Admission** $12; $7.25-$11 reductions. **Credit** AmEx, MC, V.

Peabody Essex Museum *East India Square, at Liberty Street, Salem (1-978 745 9500, 1-866 745 1876, www.pem.org)*. **Open** 10am-5pm daily. **Admission** $13; $9-$11 reductions. **Credit** AmEx, MC, V.

Salem Maritime National Historic Site *174 Derby Street (1-978 740 1660, www.nps.gov/sama)*. **Open** 9am-5pm daily. **Admission** *Tours* $5; $3 reductions. **Credit** AmEx, MC, V.

Salem Wax Museum *288 Derby Street (1-978 740 2929, www.salemwaxmuseum.com)*. **Open** *Jan-Mar* 11am-4pm daily. *Apr-June, Sept* 10am-6pm daily. *July, Aug* 10am-midnight daily. *Nov, Dec* 10am-5pm daily. **Admission** $6; $4 reductions. **Credit** MC, V.

Salem Witch Museum *19½ Washington Square North, at Route 1A (1-978 744 1692, www.salemwitchmuseum.com)*. **Open** *Jan-June, Sept, Dec* 10am-5pm daily. *July, Aug* 10am-7pm daily. **Admission** $7.50; $5-$6.50 reductions. **Credit** MC, V.

Witch House *310 Essex Street, at North Street (1-978 744 8815, www.salemweb.com/witchhouse)*. **Open** *May, June* 10am-5pm Tue-Sun. *July-Nov* 10am-5pm daily. **Admission** $8; $4-$6 reductions. **Credit** MC, V.

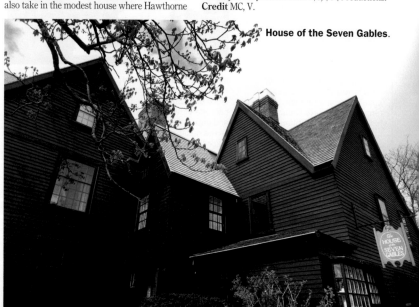

House of the Seven Gables.

INSIDE TRACK PROFITING FROM THE DARK ARTS

Salem's residents have turned the black mark of the infamous 17th-century witch trials into both a local industry and a curious point of pride – or at least an identity. The city's police cars and local newspaper sport caricatures of a witch's profile as their logos, while the local high school calls its football team the Witches. And there's nowhere spookier to spend Halloween than at **Salem's Haunted Happenings** (see p183).

Where to stay

Aside from the usual chains, there are several more colorful options in town. One is the **Salem Inn** (7 Summer Street, 1-800 446 2995, www.saleminnma.com, $119-$235 double), a complex of three 19th-century houses, all on the National Register of Historic Places. Another is the **Hawthorne Hotel** (18 Washington Square West, 1-978 744 4080, www.hawthornehotel.com, $109-$315 double), which is nicely furnished, close to the sights and reasonably priced – although it's not as old as its name would suggest. More reasonable still, though a little further off the common, the **Amelia Payson B&B** (16 Winter Street, 1-978 744 8304, www.amelia paysonhouse.com, $95-$155 double) is an 1845 Greek Revival house with a piano in the parlor. The **Coach House Inn** (284 Lafayette Street, 1-800 688 8689, www.coach housesalem.com, $105-$185 double), a 19th-century captain's mansion, is another elegant yet inexpensive choice.

Where to eat & drink

Salem offers fairly extensive dining options; the best bet is **Grapevine** (26 Congress Street, 1-978 745 9335), a funky, well-priced New American bistro facing Pickering Wharf. For something more upscale, try **Lyceum Bar & Grill** (43 Church Street, 1-978 745 7665); housed in the building where Alexander Graham Bell conducted his early telephone experiments, it offers contemporary American cuisine in refined surroundings.

Getting there

By car Salem is 16 miles north of Boston. Take Route I-95 North to Route 128 North, then Route 114 East into Salem. The drive should take around 30 minutes.

By rail The journey by rail takes 30 minutes by MBTA Commuter Rail (see p251) out of Boston's North Station.

Tourist information

Salem Visitors' Center 2 New Liberty Street, Salem (1-978 740 1650). **Open** 9am-5pm daily.

PLYMOUTH

As you head south along the scenic coast between Quincy and Cape Cod, aka the **South Shore**, you come into the heart of colonial New England. Near Plymouth, the roadside retailers adopt faux 'Olde English' signage to emphasize the local heritage, and there are lots of 'towne shoppes'. In addition to the glut of historical attractions clustered near the old Pilgrim settlement, the lovely South Shore is home to old colonial trails and parks that remain, for the most part, uncorrupted by the tourist trade.

Famously, this is the spot where the Pilgrims landed in 1620 after their harrowing voyage from England. The landmark in these parts is **Plymouth Rock**, where, according to lore, they first stepped (see p240 **Inside Track**). A replica of the ship in which the Pilgrims made their epic journey is docked close by. The **Mayflower II** is a full-scale version of the original, staffed by performers in 17th-century garb who recount the tale of the Pilgrims' struggles. The boat seems tiny, and it's hard to imagine how the settlers spent months aboard it, much of that time amid violent storms.

Plymouth itself is charming, its narrow streets lined with 17th- and 18th-century houses, many of which are open to the public. But the main attraction is the **Plimoth Plantation**, a huge, surreal re-creation of the 1627 settlement, developed by historians and archaeologists. The village is populated by actors who speak, work, play, eat and breathe 17th-century life. The project pays painstaking – some might say obsessive – attention to detail, and visitors can watch the 'settlers' stocking firewood, stuffing sausages and plucking geese. The effect is like entering a time warp and it's extremely entertaining. Also worth seeing are the **Pilgrim Hall Museum**, with its *Mayflower*-era artifacts and exhibits on the native Wampanoag tribe, and the epitaphs on **Burial Hill**, on Carver Street, one of the oldest cemeteries in America and resting place of many of the first settlers.

Just south of the town center is **Plymouth Long Beach**, a pretty three-mile stretch of coastline. **Morton Park**, near Summer Street, is another peaceful retreat, with its swimming holes and woodland hiking trails.

Other towns around Plymouth Bay include Hull, Cohasset and Hingham. **Hull** was evacuated during the Revolution after a military fort was constructed on one of its hills. Today, its beaches do a brisk tourist trade, while the **Hull Lifesaving Museum** tells the tale of local superhuman shipwreck rescues.

Close by, **Cohasset** is a picture-perfect colonial village with none of the tourist trade of Plymouth or Hull. The century-old **Minot's Ledge Lighthouse** in Cohasset is a classic piece of New England scenery. At 4 Elm Street, the small, seasonally open **Maritime Museum** commemorates local early American heritage; its neighbor, the **Captain John Wilson House** at no.2, is also worth a look (1-781 383 1434, www.cohassethistoricalsociety.org for both).

Peaceful and bucolic **Hingham**, the next hamlet over, is a good place to while away a few peaceful hours. **Cove Park** is great for a stroll, and the clapboard-clad **Old Ordinary** (21 Lincoln Street, 1-781 749 0013) is a 14-room museum with period furniture and a tap room.

Hull Lifesaving Museum *1117 Nantasket Avenue, Hull (1-781 925 5433, www.lifesaving museum.org).* **Open** 10am-4pm daily. **Admission** $5; $3 reductions; free under-18s. **Credit** MC, V.
Mayflower II *State Pier, Water Street, Plymouth (1-508 746 1622, www.plimoth.org).* **Open** *Apr-Nov* 9am-5pm daily. **Admission** $8; $6-$7 reductions. **Credit** DC, MC, V.
Pilgrim Hall Museum *75 Court Street, Plymouth (1-508 746 1620, www.pilgrimhall.org).* **Open** *Feb-Dec* 9.30am-4.30pm daily. **Admission** $6; $3-$5 reductions. **Credit** AmEx, MC, V.
Plimoth Plantation *137 Warren Avenue, off Route 3A South at Exit 4, outside Plymouth (1-508 746 1622, www.plimoth.org).* **Open** *Apr-Nov* 9am-5pm daily. **Admission** $21; $12-$19 reductions. *Combined ticket with Mayflower II* $25; $16-$22 reductions. **Credit** DC, MC, V.

INSIDE TRACK
SOLID AS A ROCK?

While there's no evidence that the Pilgrims ever saw the rock that folks around Plymouth (*see p239*) make such a big fuss of – much less set foot on it – the legend alone almost makes it worth a look. The rock has been moved several times and was once even broken in two, and only came to rest at its present location, in a landscaped park on Water Street, near the harbour, in 1867. The thing itself is rather unimpressive, especially compared to the neoclassical monument that both girds and dwarfs it. It is, after all, just a rock.

Where to stay

Plymouth has a number of serviceable, if undistinguished, motels within convenient reach of downtown. A more pleasant choice, and one with its own private beach, is the **Pilgrim Sands Motel** (150 Warren Avenue, 1-800 729 7263, www.pilgrimsands.com, $84-$195 double), a few miles out of town. The **Auberge Gladstone B&B** (8 Vernon Street, 1-508 830 1890, 1-866 722 1890, www.auberge gladstone.com, $110-$140 double), a colonial mansion with modern furnishings, is another good option.

If you're looking for water views, check out the **Cohasset Harbor Inn** (124 Elm Street, 1-781 383 6650, www.cohassetharbor resort.com, $109-$259 double), a low-key hotel with two on-site restaurants.

Where to eat & drink

Dining around Plymouth is a briny business. Top-notch fish and shellfish at the self-service **Lobster Hut** (Town Wharf, 1-508 746 2270) are inexpensive and come with a view. The more upmarket **Isaac's** (114 Water Street, 1-508 830 0001) offers another great ocean vista and more elaborate seafood.

In nearby Hull, locals swear by the lobster at **Jake's** (50 George Washington Boulevard, 1-781 925 1024), an award-winning eatery that overlooks the bay. Hingham has a number of good restaurants, including the Italian-inspired **Tosca** (14 North Street, 1-781 740 0080, www.toscahingham.com) and **Stars on Hingham Harbor** (4 Otis Street, 1-781 749 3200).

Getting there

By car Plymouth is 40 miles south-east of Boston on the I-93 (Southeast Expressway) to Route 3. Take Exit 6. It's roughly 45 minutes' drive from Boston.
By bus or rail Plymouth & Brockton Street Railway and MBTA Commuter Rail run services from Boston's South Station (*see p251*). The journey is about an hour.

Tourist information

Plymouth Chamber of Commerce *15 Caswell Lane, Plymouth (1-508 830 1620, www.plymouthchamber.com).* **Open** 9am-5pm Mon-Fri.
Plymouth Visitor Information Center *130 Water Street, Plymouth (1-508 747 7533, 1-800 872 1620, www.visit-plymouth.com).* **Open** *Apr, May, Sept-Nov* 9am-4pm daily. *June-Aug* 8am-8pm daily.

Jazz Tunes & Tycoons

A wealth of music amid the mansions of the wealthy.

Although it's across the border in Rhode Island, Newport is a favorite summer seaside excursion for Bostonians. A relatively short drive from Boston, the town has two main lures: its magnificent architecture and its Jazz Festival.

Newport was once the summer playground of America's wealthiest industrialists. The Rockefellers and the Vanderbilts came here and built what they called 'cottages'. The size of English stately homes, the sweeping mansions along Bellevue Avenue – each in a different style – are opulent testimony to the wealth of their owners. Some, most notably the **Breakers** – a 70-room Italian Renaissance-style pile built in 1895 for Cornelius Vanderbilt – are open to the public. Roam room after room of imported marble, gold leaf, precious antiques and art. Other tourable mansions in the vicinity include the **Elms**, **Rosecliff** and **Marble House**. Individual or combination tickets are available; for more information, phone 1-401 847 1000 or visit www.newportmansions.org.

The history of the **Newport Jazz Festival** is equally lofty, boasting such musical royalty as Ella Fitzgerald, Dizzy Gillespie and Billie Holiday – and that was just its inaugural year. Miles Davis also performed in Newport, as did Nina Simone and BB

Breakers.

King. But it's not all scatting and saxophones: in 1959, the granddaddy of jazz festivals (it celebrated its 50th anniversary in 2004) spawned the **Newport Folk Festival**. Bob Dylan, Joan Baez, Joni Mitchell and, more recently, Billy Bragg, Emmylou Harris and Lyle Lovett have all taken to the Newport stage as well as such fringe indie rockers as Jim James from My Morning Jacket, Calexico and Andrew Bird. Both events are held in August. Call 1-401 848 5055 or visit www.newportfolkfest.net for details.

Newport is about 90 minutes by car from Boston. Take the I-93 South to Route 24 South, then on to Route 114 South. Peter Pan Bus Lines (*see p250*) runs daily services from Boston's South Station.

Newport Folk Festival.

ESCAPES & EXCURSIONS

…Two if by Sea

Cape Ann is the less frequently visited of the Bay State's two capes, and has managed to survive the past 200 years with minimal commercial interruption. Its pride, personality and picturesque panoramas are fully intact, unlike the holiday hotspot and significantly more tourist-clogged **Cape Cod**. This wedge of New England is an area of extremes, and asserts a rough loveliness all of its own: regal schooners are moored next to rickety old row boats, while grand, multi-tiered homes are flanked by ramshackle cottages and shacks with the stability of card castles.

CAPE ANN

Cape Ann includes Gloucester, Essex, Rockport and Manchester-by-the-Sea. These towns all started off with post-Pilgrim seafaring histories: shipbuilding, shipwrecks, intrepid sailors crossing the Atlantic, tragedy and heroism, captured by poets and artists such as Winslow Homer and Henry Wadsworth Longfellow.

Gloucester, the largest of the towns, has been a center of the fishing industry since 1623, and some 10,000 locals are said to have perished at sea over the years (Sebastian Junger's book *The Perfect Storm*, and the subsequent film of the same name, documented a 1991 tragedy). The town's tribute to these men, a bronze statue known as 'The Man at the Wheel', stands sentinel on the harbor promenade, just off Western Avenue.

Further down the street is the more recent – and equally poignant – Fishermen's Wives Memorial, dedicated to the families of the men who risk their lives at sea. **Rocky Neck**, in East Gloucester, is the country's oldest working artists colony. Here, **Hammond Castle** is a full-scale stone replica of a medieval castle, built between 1926 and 1929 by John Jays Hammond Jr. You'll also find ample opportunity for whale-watching excursions and day-long fishing trips around these parts.

Essex relies on clamming as one of its principal industries, and the sweet, tender Essex clam is about as famous as a clam can get. In 1914, a clam-digging local named Lawrence 'Chubby' Woodman, opened a clam shack here, **Woodman's** (*see right*). Whether Chubby actually 'invented' the fried clam is not important. What really matters is that the ones at Woodman's, where the motto is 'Eat in the rough', are some of the best on the coast.

The main strip in Essex, known as the Causeway, is lined with antique shops – the most famous of which is the White Elephant.

Some look like cluttered, chaotic junk shops, while others resemble mini museums, and are priced accordingly.

Shipbuilding began in Essex in the mid 1600s, and by the 1850s the town was reknowned as the North American center for schooner building. Craftsmen still build ships by hand here today, and you can learn about the history of the industry at the **Essex Shipbuilding Museum**.

In **Rockport**, visitors poke around its narrow streets, lined with little gift shops and galleries. Bear Skin Neck, a small peninsula that juts into the harbor, has a profusion of tiny storefronts and cafés, though don't expect any alcoholic revelry – Rockport has been dry since 1856, when 75-year-old resident Hannah Jumper was so outraged by the rampant boozing that she led 200 women, armed with hatchets and hammers, to smash every bottle and keg in the town's bars.

Manchester-by-the-Sea is the most sleepy and residential of the four towns. Nonetheless, its **Singing Beach**, named in honor of the rare 'singing' sand that chirps when you step on it, is lovely. Other notable Cape Ann beaches include **Long Beach** in Rockport, and **Wingaersheek** and **Good Harbor**, both in Gloucester. South of Gloucester, at **Rafe's Chasm Reservation**, the granite ledges open on to a 200-foot-long and 60-foot-deep chasm, where the tides often produce some striking

Essex Shipbuilding Museum.

sights and sounds. East of town, **Pebble Beach** has an unusual shoreline of timeworn stones stretching into the horizon.

Although not in Cape Ann proper, **Ipswich** (www.ipswichma.com), to the north of Essex, boasts **Castle Hill**, the **Crane Wildlife Refuge** and **Crane Beach** (Argilla Road, 1-978 356 4354), all once part of the expansive estate of Chicago plumbing magnate Richard T Crane Jr. Crane Beach is a four-mile stretch of sand that's home to the threatened piping plover. The funding for wildlife preservation in this conservation area is raised by hiring out the regal Great House on Castle Hill. It's set in 165 acres, with the Grand Alleé path running from its porches down to the bluffs overlooking Crane Beach.

Essex Shipbuilding Museum *66 Main Street, Essex (1-978 768 7541, www.essexshipbuilding museum.org).* **Open** *June-Oct* 10am-5pm Wed-Sun. *Nov-May* 10am-5pm Sat, Sun. **Admission** $7, $5-$6 reductions. **Credit** MC, V.
Hammond Castle *80 Hesperus Avenue, Gloucester (1-978 283 7673, www.hammond castle.org).* **Open** *Sept-mid June* 10am-4pm Sat, Sun. *Mid June-early Sept* 10am-4pm daily. **Admission** $9; $6-$7 reductions. **Credit** MC, V.

Where to stay & eat

The most interesting choices for a bed for the night include the **Addison Choate Inn** in Rockport (49 Broadway, 1-800 245 7543, www.addisonchoateinn.com, $120-$179 double), a Greek Revival house from the 1850s, and the **Inn on Cove Hill** (37 Mount Pleasant Street, 1-978 546 2701, www.innoncovehill.com, $110-$165 double), which was reputedly built with funds from a cache of pirate loot. **Cape Ann Chamber of Commerce** runs a hotel reservation service on 1-800 321 0133.

For dining, of course there's the famous **Woodman's** (121 Main Street, Essex, 1-800 649 1773, www.woodmans.com). In Gloucester, the **Rudder** (73 Rocky Neck Avenue, 1-978 283 7967, www.rudderrestaurant.com, closed winter), in the heart of the Rocky Neck Art Colony, has a well-priced, eclectic menu, quirky decor and a festive atmosphere. The **Franklin Café** (118 Main Street, 1-978 283 7888, www.franklincafe. com), sibling to the venue in Boston's South End (*see p126*), serves funky comfort food.

Getting there

By car Gloucester is 30 miles north-east of Boston on I-93 to Route 128 North; Rockport is 40 miles from Boston, and seven miles north of Gloucester on Routes 127 or 127A. Ipswich

INSIDE TRACK MOTIF NO.1

The entrance to Rockport's main harbour, an old red building with rows of colorful buoys hanging off the outer wall and rugged jetties in the background, has been painted so often it's known by locals as 'Motif Number 1'.

is 25 miles north-east of Boston. Take Route I-95 North to Route 1 North.
By bus or rail MBTA Commuter Rail (*see p251*) runs trains to Gloucester and Ipswich from Boston's North Station. The bus service on the Cape Ann peninsula is run by the Cape Ann Transportation Authority (1-978 283 7278, www.canntran.com).

Tourist information

Cape Ann Chamber of Commerce
33 Commercial Street, Gloucester (1-978 283 1601, www.capeannvacations.com). **Open** 8am-5pm Mon-Fri (call for extended summer & weekend hours).

CAPE COD

Order a Cape Codder at the bar, and you'll get a vodka and cranberry juice with a wedge of lime – a cosmopolitan without the Cointreau. And that's the Cape right there: sharp, strong and a splash away from being something fancy. It's a mix of swarthy, fisher-folk year-rounders and the summer crowd in their khaki shorts and Polo button-downs; of sweeping Cape estates and quaint old clapboard cottages. In summer, ask a Bostonian what they're up to for the weekend and invariably the answer will be: 'I'm heading to the Cape.'

Cape Cod was named after the fish found there in 1605 by English explorer Bartholomew Gosnold. These days, cranberry-growing and tourism provide the region's economic support, rather than the traditional industries of fishing, whaling, shipping and salt-making. This area is the nation's largest producer of the red berries (hence the name of the cocktail), and the burgundy bogs add swathes of color to the often austere landscape. As for tourism, you can expect the summer weekend traffic over Sagamore Bridge – the gateway to the Cape – to be backed up for miles.

The Cape is made up of 16 towns, organized into three chunks: Upper (Wareham, Bourne, Sagamore, Sandwich, Falmouth and Mashpee); Mid (Barnstable, Dennis, Yarmouth, Brewster and Harwich); and Lower, or Outer (Chatham, Orleans, Eastham, Wellfleet, Truro and

Provincetown). Within these larger towns are settlements such as Hyannis in Barnstable. The **Cape Cod National Seashore** boasts 43,685 acres of beaches, sand dunes, heathlands, marshes and freshwater ponds, along with a number of historic sites.

Sandwich was the first of the Pilgrims' Cape towns. In the 19th century, the town became a center of American glass-making, its plentiful scrub brush fuelling the artisans' ovens. Today, its **Glass Museum** contains a wealth of examples of the work produced here. Meanwhile, at the restored 17th-century **Dexter Grist Mill** on the corner of Main and Water Streets, you can still buy a bag of freshly ground cornmeal. The nearby 76-acre **Heritage Plantation** is home to a hotchpotch of objects, ranging from vintage cars to Currier & Ives prints. It includes several museums and a Shaker barn, and offers children rides on a 19th-century carousel.

Provincetown was the place where Miles Standish and his *Mayflower* boatload of Pilgrims first landed on American soil on 11 November 1620 – they quickly decided against the site, and moved on to that famous rock in Plymouth (*see p239*).

Today, Provincetown supports a booming tourist trade and a notorious nightlife, based around its three-and-a-half miles of beach. In summer, it becomes the queer community's Disneyland destination, and an anything-goes

Hyannis.

attitude pervades the scene (*see p203* **A Perfect Day in Ptown**). Tea dancing at the **Boatslip** (161 Commercial Street, 1-508 487 1669, www.boatslipresort.com), a midnight boogie at **A-House** (4-6 Masonic Place, 1-508 487 3821, www.ahouse.com) and a late-night dinner at **Spiritus Pizza** (190 Commercial Street, 1-508 487 2808, www.spirituspizza.com) are all part of the seasonal routine.

A year-round local artist community has long been established here. The **Provincetown Art Association & Museum** has been offering exhibitions, lectures and classes since 1914, while **DNA**, a well-respected local gallery, shows daring contemporary work.

Woods Hole, on the Cape's south-west tip, is one of the world's great centers of maritime research. The **Woods Hole Oceanographic Institute**, which assembled the team that located the remains of the *Titanic* in 1985, has exhibitions on undersea exploration. The more visitor-friendly **Marine Biological Laboratory** gives guided tours on weekends.

Hyannis, halfway out on the Upper Cape, is the transport hub of the area, with rail and airport services and ferries to **Nantucket** and **Martha's Vineyard** (*see p246*). Famously the location for the Kennedys' summer home, it remains inseparably linked to visions of a suntanned JFK at the helm of a skiff. The family's compound is walled off south of town in Hyannisport, but there's an extensive photographic display to admire at the **JFK Hyannis Museum**.

Chatham is a chic little town that has been continuously settled since the mid 17th century. In its earliest days, Chatham's perch on the shipping lanes made it a favorite location for 'moon-cussers' – bands of pirate wreckers who roamed the beaches with false lights that led boats aground to be pillaged. But the most prominent landmark today is one that guides sailors safely back to shore: the **Chatham Light** lighthouse. Fishing is still a major industry here, along with the tourist trade – which the town accommodates in genteel style with its downtown crafts and antique shops.

For a glimpse of a more primal New England, head south of town and past the Chatham Light to **Morris Island**, and take the ferry out to the **Monomoy Island National Wildlife Refuge** (www.fws.gov/northeast/monomoy). This barrier island serves as a stopover point for bird migration in the Atlantic Flyway, and became a designated wildlife sanctuary in 1944. You might spot a grey seal or two here as well.

Along the sandy Cape Cod National Seashore you'll find some of Massachusetts' loveliest beaches. **Nauset Beach**, at the southern tip outside East Orleans, has the best surf and draws the youngest, liveliest crowd.

Wellfleet Harbor.

This last, narrow stretch of the Cape has managed to escape most of the horrors of commercialization. **Wellfleet Harbor**, on the bay side, encloses the 1,000 acres of the **Wellfleet Bay Wildlife Sanctuary**. Here the Massachusetts Audubon Society (www.massaudubon.org) sponsors tours and lectures and allows camping (for a fee, and for Audubon members only).

Wellfleet and nearby **Truro** have long been known as artists' and writers' retreats. Edna St Vincent Millay and Edmund Wilson lived in Wellfleet in the 1920s, while Edward Hopper admired the bleak light and beauty of the high dunes outside Truro.

DNA *288 Bradford Street, Provincetown (1-508 487 7700, www.dnagallery.com).* **Open** *Summer* 11am-6pm daily (call for off-season hours). **Admission** free.

Glass Museum *129 Main Street, Sandwich (1-508 888 0251, www.sandwichglassmuseum. org).* **Open** *Feb, Mar* 9.30am-4pm Wed-Sun. *Apr-Dec* 9.30am-5pm daily. Closed Jan. **Admission** $4.75; $1 reductions. **Credit** MC, V.

Heritage Plantation *67 Grove Street, Sandwich (1-508 888 3300, www.heritage museumsandgardens.org).* **Open** *Apr-Oct* 10am-5pm daily. *Nov-Dec* 10am-4pm Fri-Sun. **Admission** $12; $6-$10 reductions. **Credit** AmEx, MC, V.

JFK Hyannis Museum *397 Main Street, Hyannis (1-508 790 3077, www.jfkhyannis museum.com).* **Open** *mid Apr-May, Oct* 10am-4pm Mon-Sat; noon-4pm Sun. *June-Sept* 9am-5pm Mon-Sat; noon-5pm Sun. *Nov-mid Apr* 10am-4pm

Thur-Sat; noon-4pm Sun. **Admission** $5; $2.50 reductions. **Credit** AmEx, MC, V.

Marine Biological Laboratory *100 Water Street, Woods Hole (1-508 548 3705, www.mbl. edu).* **Tours** *late June-Aug* 1pm & 2pm, Mon-Fri. **Admission** free.

Provincetown Art Association & Museum *460 Commercial Street, Provincetown (1-508 487 1750, www.paam.org).* **Open** *June-Sept* 11am-8pm Mon-Thur; 11am-10pm Fri; 11am-5pm Sat, Sun. *Oct-May* noon-5pm Thur-Sun. **Admission** free. **Credit** AmEx, MC, V.

Wellfleet Bay Wildlife Sanctuary *291 State Highway, Route 6A, Wellfleet Harbor (1-508 349 2615).* **Open** *June-Sept* 8.30am-5pm daily. *Oct-May* 8.30am-5pm Tue-Sun. **Admission** $5; $3 reductions. **Credit** MC, V.

Woods Hole Oceanographic Institute *15 School Street, Woods Hole (1-508 289 2663, www.whoi.edu).* **Open** *May-Oct* 10am-4.30pm Mon-Sat. *Nov, Dec* 10am-4.30pm Tue-Fri. **Admission** free (donation suggested). **No credit cards.**

Where to stay

Lodging is extremely varied the whole length of Cape Cod; as a rule, towns on the Cape Cod Bay side of the peninsula are more interesting and relaxing. Rates tend to drop the further down the Cape you are from Provincetown, though there are bargains there too, if you book well in advance. Off-season rates drop steeply – and the Cape has a wonderful austerity once the tourists have gone.

In Sandwich, the **Belfrey Inne** (8 Jarves Street, 1-800 844 4542, www.belfryinn.com, $115-$275 double) occupies three charming 19th-century buildings, including a converted church with stained-glass windows. In Barnstable, the **Beechwood** (2839 Main Street/Route 6A, 1-800 609 6618, www.beechwoodinn.com, $120-$199 double) nestles among the trees from which it takes its name. The historic district of Chatham has a number of carefully restored 19th-century inns, such as the **Chatham Bars Inn** on Shore Road (1-800 527 4884, www.chathambarsinn. com, $220-$2,200 double), but they can be pricey.

To be in the thick of the action, head to Provincetown's most luxurious lodging, the **Brass Key** (67 Bradford Street, 1-800 842 9858, www.brasskey.com, $100-$485 double). For a free directory of gay- and lesbian-owned hotels, restaurants, bars and services, contact the **Provincetown Business Guild** (3 Freeman Street, no.2, 1-508 487 2313, www.ptown.org).

Where to eat & drink

Dining in Provincetown runs the gamut – but phone ahead wherever you go, as off-season hours are unpredictable and sometimes non-existent. Upmarket interpretations of New American cuisine are the order of the day at **Front Street** (230 Commercial Street, 1-508 487 9715, www.frontstreetrestaurant.com); decent contemporary Italian food can be had at the venerable **Ciro & Sal's** (4 Kiley Court, 1-508 487 6444, www.ciroandsals.com); and stylish light fare is served at **Café Heaven** (199 Commercial Street, 1-508 487 9639). For more, *see p203* **A Perfect Day in Ptown**.

It's worth driving to Wellfleet for dinner at **Winslow's Tavern** (316 Main Street, 1-508 349 6450, closed in winter), a classy bistro with a focus on fresh, light dishes. Provincetown also has a significant Portuguese community, émigrés from the Azores who came to work on the fishing boats. For an afternoon sandwich, *linguiça* concoction or codfish fritters – or a sweet treat after dinner – try the **Provincetown Portuguese Bakery** (299 Commercial Street, 1-508 487 1803), famous for their *malasadas* – a fried dough pastry sometimes filled with cream.

Getting there

By car The Sagamore Bridge, linking Cape Cod to the mainland, is 30 miles south-east of Boston on Route 3, and the most direct route. The entire journey from Boston to Cape Cod is 77 miles, and takes about an hour and a half – though it can be considerably longer if traffic is bad.

By bus The Plymouth & Brockton bus (1-508 746 0378, www.p-b.com) runs several times a day from Boston's South Station to Hyannis and then on to Provincetown. The Cape Cod Regional Transit Authority (1-800 352 7155, www.capecodtransit.org) and Peter Pan Bus Lines (*see p250*) cover the mid-Cape region. Provincetown runs local shuttle bus services in the area in the summer months (see the CCRTA's website for details).

By boat Bay State Cruise Company (1-877 783 3779, www.boston-ptown.com) runs a high-speed ferry from Boston to Provincetown daily throughout the summer season and for the first few weekends in October. The journey from Commonwealth Pier takes 90 minutes.

Tourist information

Cape Cod Chamber of Commerce
Junction of Routes 6 & 122, Hyannis
(1-508 362 3225, www.capecodchamber.org).
Open 9am-5pm daily.

MARTHA'S VINEYARD & NANTUCKET

If locals aren't heading to the Cape, chances are they're off to the islands. Beautiful New England seascapes bring in money by the bucketload, and every summer the beaches, bars, restaurants and air of exclusivity of Martha's Vineyard and Nantucket draw thousands of tourists.

The first recreational use of **Martha's Vineyard** was for Methodist camp meetings in the summer of 1835. Today, summer residents include Spike Lee and Bill Clinton. **Edgartown** is the largest and oldest of the main towns. A walk along the harborside, past the stately captains' mansions on Water Street, reveals the prosperity they brought back from the sea. The **Vineyard Historical Museum** is replete with scrimshaw, model ships and other local artifacts. Nearby **South Beach**, also known as Katama, is the island's largest and most popular strand.

Oak Bluffs buzzes a bit more than the other Vineyard towns. It has a collection of gingerbread cottages and the wonderful 1876 **Flying Horses Carousel** (corner of Oak Bluffs and Circuit Avenue, 1-508 693 9481), reputedly the country's oldest. A prime example of American folk art, it runs every day in summer until 10pm for $2 a ride (15 rides for $10). Stick to Oak Bluffs for the island's liveliest late-night action too. Enjoy a beer on the beach by the harbor at **Menemsha Blues** (6 Circuit Avenue

Extension, 1-508 693 9599), or go celebrity-spotting at **Seasons Eatery & Pub** (19 Circuit Avenue, 1-508 693 7129).

Vineyard Haven (also known as Tisbury), on the north coast, was long the island's chief port and it's where the old colonial atmosphere is best preserved. One of the prettiest spots to visit on the island is the town of **Aquinnah** on the western tip. The public beach there is famous for its dramatic mile-long cliffs of multicolored clay and the panoramic views from the trails above them.

While Martha's Vineyard is only a 45-minute ferry ride away, it takes over two hours on the open seas to get to **Nantucket**, making the 'Faraway Island' an apt nickname. In *Moby-Dick*, Herman Melville calls Nantucket 'a mere hillock, an elbow of sand; all beach without a background'. You can bet there's background now, in the form of eye-poppingly expensive properties – though Nantucket is doing everything it can to control the development of its precious land.

For 150 years, the island was one of the key centers of the whaling industry, and its streets and historic houses are soaked in that history. The **Whaling Museum** (13 Broad Street, 1-508 228 1894, www.nha.org) tells the story – complete with a 46-foot sperm whale skeleton. But in the 19th century, with the rise of the petroleum industry, a devastating fire in 1846 and the onset of the Civil War, the island's economy began to tumble. Between 1840 and 1870, the population decreased from 10,000 to 4,000. Nantucket was revived by tourism.

A sense of history still pervades the island, and in spring and summer, the Nantucket Historical Society runs guided walking tours of the downtown hub. Highlights include the last of the town's 18th-century mills, as well as the **Old Gaol**, a lock-up in which the prisoners were allowed to go home for the night. Also offering guided walking tours is the **Museum of African American History**, headquartered in Boston (*see p55*), which maintains the **African Meeting House** and **Florence Higginbotham House** on Nantucket.

These days, cobblestoned Main Street has fleets of Range Rovers blocking the traffic, women dripping in gold and men in linen trousers and loafers, dangling keys to Lexus SUVs and million-dollar 'cottages'. The streets are lined with smart boutiques, antiques shops and upscale clothing stores. Conspicuous consumption aside, in its beaches, foggy moors and ubiquitous grey clapboard houses, Nantucket has a grace that is missing in mainland Massachusetts.

Bring a bicycle – or rent one at **Young's Bicycle Shop** (6 Broad Street, Steamboat Wharf, 1-508 228 1151). Bike paths thread around the island, and having two-wheeled transport means you won't have to pay the prohibitively expensive car-ferry reservation, imposed to discourage drivers. A ride out to **Madaket** will be rewarded with a long and lovely stretch of beach on the west side of the island. **Cisco Brewery & Triple 8 Vodka Distillery** (5 & 7 Bartlett Farm Road, 1-800 324 5550) is the island's very own oasis of beer,

Provincetown.

wine and spirits. Tucked away out of town, the brewery is open to the public – and worth a stopover for the free samples.

African Meeting House *29 York Street, Nantucket (1-508 228 9833, www.afroam museum.org)*. **Open** *July, Aug* 11am-3pm Tue-Sat; 1pm-3pm Sun. **Admission** free.
Nantucket Historical Association *7 Fair Street, Nantucket (1-508 228 1894, www.nha.org)*. **Walking tours** (every 30min) *mid May-mid Oct* 10am-5pm Mon-Sat; noon-5pm Sun.
Vineyard Historical Museum *59 School Street, Martha's Vineyard (1-508 627 4441, www. marthasvineyardhistory.org)*. **Open** *Jan-Apr* 10am-4pm Sat. *Apr-mid June, Oct-Dec* 1pm-4pm Wed-Fri; 10am-4pm Sat. *Mid June-Sept* 10am-5pm Tue-Sat. **Admission** $6-$7; $4 reductions. **Credit** MC, V.

Where to stay

Good, cheap accommodation can be found on both islands, even in high season, thanks to the youth hostels. **Hostelling International – Nantucket** is at 31 Western Avenue (1-508 228 0433, www.capecodhostels.org, $27-$37 for dorm beds, $119-$145 for private rooms); while **Hostelling International – Martha's Vineyard** is in Edgartown (West Tisbury Road, Box 3158, 1-508 693 2665, www.capecod hostels.org, $27-$35 dorm beds, $75-$150 private rooms). Beyond that, the cost per night is going to be pretty high – if you can even secure a room. In Edgartown, comfort and convenience at relatively modest prices can be found at the pretty, white-painted **Victorian Inn** (24 South Water Street, 1-508 627 4784, www.thevic.com, $140-$385 double), the former home of a whaling captain.

Prices run even higher among the swells of Nantucket, but the local landmark **Jared Coffin House** (29 Broad Street, 1-508 228 2400, www.jaredcoffinhouse.com, $90-$450 double), isn't too exorbitant, and is packed with history. Nantucket also has a wealth of B&Bs, which are listed through services such as **Nantucket Accommodations** (1-508 228 9559, www.nantucketaccomodation.com).

Where to eat & drink

As a result of all the celebrities and other super-rich folk on Martha's Vineyard, and the need to import most produce, dining out on the islands isn't that cheap. If you want to splash out on the Vineyard, **L'Etoile** (27 South Summer Street, 1-508 627 5187, www.letoile.net) is renowned for its contemporary French fare. The always-packed **Black Dog Tavern** (Beach Street Extension, Vineyard Haven,

1-508 693 9223, www.theblackdog.com) is where everyone flocks to load up on a huge breakfast or watch the sunset – and invariably buy the T-shirt.

On Nantucket, pack a picnic with gourmet sandwiches, salads and chocolate brownies from **Something Natural** (50 Cliff Road, 1-508 228 0504, www.somethingnatural.com), or breakfast on a lobster omelet or eggs Benedict at Main Street mainstay **Arno's** (no.41, 1-508 228 7001, www.arnos.net). A decent dinner can be had at the **Brotherhood of Thieves** (23 Broad Street, 1-508 228 2551, www.brotherhoodofthieves.com), followed by live music and more drinks at the **Chicken Box** bar (16 Dave Street, 1-508 228 9717, www.thechickenbox.com).

Getting there

By air Cape Air (1-508 771 6944, www. flycapeair.com) has flights to Hyannis, Provincetown, Martha's Vineyard and Nantucket from Boston.
By car Check with the ferry services about taking cars to the islands, as there are restrictions. However, car rental firms abound and both islands have extensive shuttle bus services for most of the year, run by the Martha's Vineyard Transit Authority (1-508 693 9440, www.vineyardtransit.com) and the Nantucket Regional Transit Authority (1-508 228 7025, www.shuttlenantucket.com).
By boat Martha's Vineyard and Nantucket are served by several ferry companies.

The Massachusetts Steamship Authority (1-508 477 8600, www.steamshipauthority.com) has a year-round service from two Cape Cod locations: the trip from Woods Hole to Martha's Vineyard takes 45 minutes. The trip from Hyannis to Nantucket is two hours and 15 minutes, but a Steamship Authority high-speed ferry from Hyannis only takes about an hour.

In summer, Island Queen (1-508 548 4800, www.islandqueen.com) and Pied Piper (1-508 548 9400, www.falmouthferry.com) ferries run from Falmouth to Martha's Vineyard; Hy-Line (1-508 778 2600, www.hy-linecruises.com) has a summer service that runs to Nantucket.

Tourist information

Martha's Vineyard Chamber of Commerce *Vineyard Haven, Martha's Vineyard (1-508 693 0085, www.mvy.com)*. **Open** 9am-5pm Mon-Fri.
Nantucket Island Chamber of Commerce *48 Main Street, Nantucket (1-508 228 1700, www.nantucketchamber.org)*. **Open** 9am-5pm Mon-Fri.

Directory

Getting Around

ARRIVING & LEAVING

By air

Logan International Airport
1-800 235 6426,
www.massport.com.
On a spit of reclaimed land east
of Boston, the airport is three miles
from downtown. Its four terminals
– A, B, C and E – are connected
by walkways and shuttle buses.
The subway (known as the T;
see p251) is the quickest and
cheapest route to and from the
airport. The **Airport T** station
is on the Blue Line, which runs
to State or Gov't Center, a trip that
takes about 15 minutes. Massport's
airport **shuttle buses** (22, 33
and 55) take passengers from the
airline terminals to the Airport T.
Alternatively, the **Silver Line
Waterfront** route SL1 (*see p251*)
stops at each terminal and goes
to South Station. T maps are
available from information
booths in terminals A, C and E.
The **taxi** rank is outside the
airport's baggage reclaim area. The
fare to downtown Boston is around
$20-$25 ($35-$40 to Cambridge),
with an extra $4.50 toll for traveling
through Sumner Tunnel and Ted
Williams Tunnel from Logan to
Boston, plus a $2 Massport tunnel
fee. On your return, heading into
Logan from Boston, you'll have
to pay a $2.75 toll for traveling
through Callahan Tunnel or Ted
Williams Tunnel. For a list of
reputable taxi firms, *see p251*.
If you want to travel in style,
make a booking with **Carey
Limousine** (1-617 623 8700)
or **Commonwealth Limousine
Worldwide** (1-617 787 5575).
The most pleasant way of
getting to and from the airport
is by boat. **Rowes Wharf Water
Transport** (1-617 406 8584,
www.roweswharfwatertaxi.com)
runs services between Rowes
Wharf and Logan's **Water
Transportation Terminal**
(accessible via the free no.66 airport
shuttle bus). In winter (Nov-Mar),
boats run 7am-7pm daily. For
the rest of the year, services run
7am-10pm Mon-Sat, 7am-8pm
Sun; tickets are $10 one way.
Harbor Express (1-617 222 6999,
www.harborexpress.com) runs a
similar service between the airport,

Quincy and Long Wharf in
downtown Boston. Finally, **City
Water Taxi** (1-617 422 0392,
www.citywatertaxi.com) operates
year-round (7am-10pm Mon-Sat,
7am-8pm Sun), running from the
airport to the World Trade Center,
Congress Street (near South Station)
and other stops. A one-way ticket
costs $10.

Major airlines

Aer Lingus *1-800 474 7427.*
Air Canada *1-888 247 2262.*
Air France *1-800 237 2747.*
AirTran Airways *1-800 247 8726.*
Alitalia *1-800 223 5730.*
American Airlines
1-800 433 7300.
American Eagle *1-800 433 7300.*
British Airways *1-800 247 9297.*
Cape Air *1-800 352 0714.*
Continental *1-800 525 0280.*
Delta Air Lines *1-800 221 1212.*
Iberia *1-800 772 4642.*
Icelandair *1-800 223 5500.*
JetBlue Airways *1-800 538 2583.*
Lufthansa *1-800 645 3880.*
Midwest *1-800 452 2022.*
Porter Airlines *1-888 619 8622.*
SATA *1-800 762 9995.*
Southwest Airlines
1-800 435 9792.
Spirit Airlines *1-800 772 7117.*
Swiss *1-877 359 7947.*
TACV *1-866 359 8228.*
United Airlines *1-800 241 6522.*
US Airways *1-800 428 4322.*
Virgin America *1-877 539 8474.*
Virgin Atlantic *1-800 862 8621.*

By bus

The Chinatown-to-Chinatown
express used to be the cheapest
way to get to New York from
Boston, but the embattled
Fung Wah Bus (1-617 345 8000,
www.fungwahbus.com) servicing
this route has had its share of
accidents and mishaps, allowing
competitors to get in on this
popular mode of transport for the
cash-strapped. These days, you
can also take **Lucky Star** (1-617
426 8801, www.luckystarbus.com),
or ride the double-decker, Wi-Fi
enabled fleets of **Bolt Bus** (1-877
265 8287, www.boltbus.com)
or **MegaBus** (1-877 462 6342,
http://us.megabus.com). All have
regular departures, usually every
hour or half hour, and cost around

$15 or less. The Wi-Fi addition has
given the latter two lines an edge,
and though Fung Wah's rocky
history has given safety-minded
travelers pause, it remains popular.
MegaBus leaves from Back Bay
Station (*see p251*). All of the other
low-cost services arrive at and
depart from the **South Station
Transportation Center**
(700 Atlantic Avenue, at Summer
Street), which is also served by
the following bus companies.

Concord Trailways
1-800 639 3317,
www.concordtrailways.com.
For New Hampshire and Maine.
Greyhound
1-800 231 2222,
www.greyhound.com.
For national services.
Peter Pan
1-800 343 9999,
www.peterpanbus.com.
For New England (including Cape
Cod and Providence), plus New York.
**Plymouth & Brockton
Street Railway**
1-508 746 0378, www.p-b.com.
For Plymouth and Cape Cod.

By car

The three main highways that lead
into town are the **I-95**; the **I-93**,
which runs all the way to Vermont;
and the **I-90** (the Massachusetts
Turnpike, or 'Mass Pike'), which
runs into New York State.

By rail

The national rail service **Amtrak**
(1-800 872 7245, www.amtrak.com)
runs from **South Station**, **North
Station** and **Back Bay Station**
(*see p251*).

PUBLIC TRANSPORT

Local public transport is run by the
**Massachusetts Bay Transport
Authority (MBTA)** and consists
of the subway system (known as
the T), commuter rail, buses and
ferries. For a map of the T and
commuter rail lines, *see p251*.

Fares & tickets

In 2007, the T and buses converted
to a new fare system based on
plastic **CharlieCards** and paper

CharlieTickets. (The name derives from a character from a 1948 Kingston Trio protest song, in which Charlie was doomed to ride the T forever because he couldn't pay the full fare.) Fares are slightly cheaper with a CharlieCard. Ask at the ticket windows at Back Bay, Harvard, Downtown Crossing, North Station or South Station, or order one on MBTA's website. The cards are rechargeable (you add credit using machines in T stations), and work via an embedded microchip and simple touch-in system.

LinkPasses for one day (at $9, not a great deal), one week ($15) or one month ($59) can be used on the T, local buses, ferries across Boston Harbor and local commuter rail. Passes can be bought from fare vending machines at airport terminals and T stations.

Up to two children aged 11 or under can ride for free when accompanied by a paying adult. For other reduced fares, see the MBTA website.

MBTA *1-617 222 3200, 1-800 392 6100, www.mbta.com.*

Subway

Boston's T was America's first subway, and is easy to use, efficient and cheap, though delays often cause grumbles. Rides cost $2 with a CharlieTicket, or $1.70 using a CharlieCard. Transfers between subway lines are free, but transfers from subways to buses are only free with a CharlieCard. Trains run from 5.15am to 12.30am Mon-Sat and from 6am to 12.30am on Sundays. Free T maps are available from the larger stations. Note that some maps may still have NE Medical Center T – which was changed in 2010 to Tufts Medical Center T – and that many Bostonians still use the old name.

'Outbound' and 'Inbound' services sometimes have different subway entrances. Inbound trains will always be heading towards downtown stations Park Street, State, Downtown Crossing and Gov't Center; Outbound trains head away from them.

Although the two Silver Line routes appear on subway maps, they actually use buses. Silver Line Waterfront serves the airport, South Station and the South Boston Waterfront. Silver Line Washington Street serves Downtown Crossing, Washington Street and Dudley Square in Roxbury, and charges a local bus fare.

Not many people know that each branch color was chosen to reflect a characteristic of the area the line covers. The Green Line, for example, was named in honor of the Emerald Necklace, the chain of parks that links Boston and the western suburbs. The Red Line, serving Harvard, pays homage to Harvard Crimson, the university's official color. The Blue Line is supposed to mirror the color of the waterfront, and the Orange Line runs along Washington Street, once known as Orange Street. The newer Silver Line was so named in an effort to convey a sense of speed.

Buses

The MBTA runs around 175 bus routes in Boston and the suburbs. The flat fare is $1.50 if you use a CharlieTicket or pay cash on board, or $1.25 if you use a CharlieCard. Express buses are $2.80-$4. Transfers to the subway are discounted if you use a CharlieCard, and bus-to-bus transfers are free with a CharlieTicket or CharlieCard. If you overpay in cash, you'll get a CharlieTicket with the change on it.

Routes and timetables are available from major T stations or the MBTA central office (10 Park Plaza, 120 Boylston Street); they are also on the MBTA's website. The busiest bus routes run from 5.30am-1am daily.

Rail

Boston has three main train stations: **South Station** (700 Atlantic Avenue, at Summer Street), **North Station** (135 Causeway Street, at Canal Street) and **Back Bay Station** (145 Dartmouth Street, at Stuart Street).

The MBTA Commuter Rail runs from North Station and South Station, serving the Greater Boston area and Massachusetts, as far away as Providence, Rhode Island; fares range from $1.70 to $7.75 a trip. Tickets can be bought on the train, but it's cheaper to buy them at the station.

TAXIS

Taxis can be hailed at any time of day or night, although it becomes difficult after 1am. Taxi ranks can be found near major hotels, big train stations and in Harvard Square in Cambridge. Call ahead for wheelchair-accessible vehicles or vans (for the latter, there may be a surcharge). Normal meter fares cost

$2.60 for the first eighth of a mile, then 40¢ for each seventh of a mile.

If you have a complaint about a taxi, or to report lost property, phone the police department's **Hackney Carriage Unit** at 1-617 343 4475.

The following taxi companies offer a 24-hour service. Most accept major credit cards, but it's always best to phone to check first.

Bay State Taxi *1-617 566 5000.*
Independent Taxi Operators Association *1-617 426 8700.*
Metrocab *1-617 782 5500.*
Town Taxi *1-617 536 5000.*

DRIVING

Thanks to the Big Dig project, driving in Boston isn't the purgatory it used to be. But traffic can still be painfully slow, and tempers often fray.

The speed limit on many major highways is 55mph, going up to 65mph on sections of the Mass Pike. Elsewhere in Boston, speed limits range from 20-50mph. State law requires seat belts to be worn.

The **American Automobile Association** (AAA) provides maps and other information, free if you're a member or belong to an affiliated organization such as the British AA. It also offers a 24-hour breakdown service (except on the privately run Mass Pike, which has its own patrol cars to aid breakdowns). The Boston office (125 High Street, Downtown, 1-617 443 9300, www.aaa.com) is open 9am-5pm Mon-Fri.

Car hire

To rent a car, you'll need a credit card and a driver's license (British licenses are valid, but those from non-English-speaking countries may need to be accompanied by an International Driving Permit). Few firms will rent to under-25s. Rental rarely includes insurance.

Car rental companies

Alamo *1-877 222 9075, www.alamo.com.*
Avis *1-800 331 1212, www.avis.com.*
Budget *1-800 527 0700, www.budget.com.*
Dollar *1-800 800 3665, www.dollar.com.*
Hertz *1-617 654 3131, www.hertz.com.*
National *1-877 222 9058, www.nationalcar.com.*

DIRECTORY

Parking

Despite the city's ample public transportation, Bostonians still have that American love of cars; traffic congestion is dreadful, and parking spaces rare. Many are metered and only available to non-residents for up to two hours between 8am and 6pm.

A fine can cost $20, and retrieving a towed car may be well over $50. If you do get a ticket, call the **Boston Office of the Parking Clerk** (1-617 635 4410) or pay online at www.cityofboston.gov/parking.

Boston's two main car parks are under Boston Common (entrance on Charles Street, directly opposite the Public Garden, 1-617 954 2098) and under the Prudential Center (800 Boylston Street, Back Bay, 1-617 236 3060). Other garages can be found at Government Center (50 New Sudbury Street, Downtown, 1-617 227 0385), the New England Aquarium (70 East India Row, Waterfront, 1-617 367 3847) and Post Office Square (at Congress Street, Downtown, 1-617 423 1500).

CYCLING

Boston was once consistently rated one of the worst cities in America for bikers by cycling magazines, but some newly designated bike lanes have made things much better. Overall, however, the roads are often narrow and hilly and drivers are still getting accustomed to sharing the road. Cambridge is a bit better, but we recommend that all but the most hardened urban cyclists should stick to special bike trails such as the **Paul Dudley White Charles River Bike Path** and the **Minuteman Bikeway**. For details of these and other trails, as well as more information on biking in Boston, *see p221*.

WALKING

Boston is not called 'America's Walking City' for nothing. You can easily cover the city centre on foot, and walking through the different neighborhoods is a pleasurable way to explore.

TOURS

For self-guided walking trails, *see p49* **Trail Blazers**. **Boston Movie Tours** (*see p191*) take cinephiles on location in the city. For child-oriented tours, *see p187*.

Boston Duck Tours

1-617 267 3825, www.boston ducktours.com. Tours leave from the Prudential Center, at Huntington Avenue (Copley, Hynes or Prudential T); or from the Museum of Science, Science Park (Science Park T). **Tours** (every 30-60mins) *Apr-mid June* 9am-5pm. *Mid June-early Aug* 9am-7pm. *Early Aug-mid Sept* 9am-6pm. *Mid Sept-3rd wk in Oct* 9am-5pm. *3rd wk in Oct-late Nov* 9am-3pm. **Rates** $21-$31; $5-$24 reductions. **Credit** AmEx, MC, V. **Map** p275 G7 or p272 H2.

You can travel by land *and* sea – in a restyled World War II amphibious landing craft. Manned by so-called conDUCKtors, the tours are informative and especially fun for kids. Shortened tours are also available, which depart from the New England Aquarium (Aquarium or Haymarket T); check the website for details.

Boston Harbor Cruises

1-617 227 4321, 1-877 733 9425, www.bostonharborcruises.com. Tours leave from Long Wharf, Waterfront. Aquarium T. **Tours** *USS Constitution Cruise: Apr-Nov* every hr, 10.30am-4.30pm daily. *Historic Sightseeing Cruise: May-Aug* 11am, 1pm, 3pm daily. *Sept* 11am, 1pm, 3pm Sat, Sun. *Sunset Cruise: May-Aug* 7pm daily. *Sept* 6pm Thur-Sun. **Rates** $17-$23. **Credit** AmEx, MC, V. **Map** p273 M4.

BHC offers a variety of themed sightseeing, entertainment and meal cruises, as well as whale-watching excursions (call for seasonal schedules).

Urban AdvenTours

1-617 670 0637, www.urban adventours.com. Tours leave from 103 Atlantic Avenue, North End, Aquarium or Haymarket T. **Tours** *Apr-Oct* (weather permitting) 10am, 2pm, 6pm. **Rates** $35-$50. **Credit** AmEx, MC, V. **Map** p273 M4.

A variety of cycling tours around Boston are on offer, with themes such as a tour along the Emerald Necklace (*see p64* **Inside Track**), a waterfront tour that ends at a brewery (they pick up the bikes from there so you don't need to worry about cycling under the influence) and a monthly re-creation of Paul Revere's Midnight Ride. Tours last two to three hours and rates include a bicycle, helmet and water. They also rent hybrid bikes for $75 for 24 hours.

Boston by Foot

1-617 367 2345, www.boston byfoot.com. Tours leave from a variety of locations (phone for details). **Tours** *May-Oct* times vary. **Rates** $8-$15; $8 reductions. **No credit cards**.

A broad array of 90-minute historical and architectural tours, led by volunteer guides who encourage questions. Tours focus on neighborhoods or themes, such as Victorian Back Bay or Literary Landmarks.

Boston Old Town Trolley Tours

1-617 269 7150, www.trolley tours.com. Tours leave from Old Atlantic Avenue, at State Street, Waterfront. Aquarium T. **Tours** *May-Oct* every 15-20mins 9am-5pm daily. *Nov-Apr* every 25-30mins 9am-4pm daily. **Rates** $38; $15-$34 reductions; free under-3s. **Credit** AmEx, MC, V. **Map** p273 M4.

One of these faux trolley cars (they ride on wheels, not rails) always seems to be passing, no matter where you are. You can leave and rejoin the tour at will, which is useful if you want to get a better look at a particular neighborhood. Seasonal tour themes range from chocolate to Ghosts & Gravestones.

Charles Riverboat Company

1-617 621 3001, www.charles riverboat.com. Tours leave from Lechmere Canal, at CambridgeSide Galleria, 100 CambridgeSide Place, Cambridge. Lechmere T. **Tours** *Charles River Tour: May-Oct* 11.30am, 12.45pm, 2pm, 3.15pm, 4.30pm daily (weekends only in early May). *Boston Harbor & Locks Tour: May-Oct* 10am daily (weekends only in early May). *Sunset Cruise: June-Aug* 6pm, 7.30pm daily. **Rates** $14-$16; $10-$14 reductions. **Credit** AmEx, MC, V.

The Charles River tour departs from the Lechmere Canal then cruises the river basin, taking in the sights along the way.

WalkBoston

1-617 367 9255, www.walk boston.org. Tours leave from a variety of locations (phone for details). **Tours** times vary. **Rates** free. **No credit cards**.

This group offers a shifting menu of offbeat tours, including one focusing on George Washington's warpaths. Others focus on areas, including colonial Roxbury and the siege of Boston, as well as the East Boston area.

Resources A-Z

AGE RESTRICTIONS

Buying/drinking alcohol 21. Proper ID is required to buy or be served alcohol: a passport should suffice, an out-of-state driving license might not.
Driving 16.
Sex 16, for consensual heterosexual sex, although the laws regulating gay sex are blurry. Certain wording in the Massachusetts General Laws suggests that the age of consent for 'unnatural acts' is 18. As this guide went to press, the Massachusetts Supreme Judicial Court had not repealed the state's ancient sodomy laws, but it has limited the law to cases that are non-consensual or committed in public places.
Smoking 18. Be warned: to buy cigarettes, ID is required from anyone who looks younger than 30.

BUSINESS

Conventions & conferences

Boston Convention & Exhibition Center 415 Summer Street, at D Street, Waterfront (1-617 954 2000, www.mccahome.com). Silver Line Waterfront to World Trade Center.
John B Hynes Veterans Memorial Convention Center 900 Boylston Street, at Gloucester Street, Back Bay (1-617 954 2000, www.mccahome.com). Hynes T. Map p274 F6.
Seaport World Trade Center 200 Seaport Boulevard, at Seaport Lane, Waterfront (1-617 385 5000, www.wtcb.com). Silver Line Waterfront to World Trade Center.

Couriers & shippers

DHL Worldwide Express 1-800 225 5345, www.dhl.com.

FedEx 1-800 463 3339, www.fedex.com.
Metro Cab 1-617 782 5500, www.metro-cab.com. **Open** 24hrs daily.
New England Courier 1-866 286 4500, www.newenglandcourier.com. **Open** 24hrs daily.
USGround 1-617 523 9500, www.usground.com. **Open** 7am-9pm Mon-Fri; 7am-7pm Sat, Sun.
US Postal Service 1-800 222 1811, www.usps.com.

Office services

Boston Translation Suite 805, 31 St James Avenue, at Arlington Street, Back Bay (1-617 778 0594, www.bostontranslation.us). Arlington T. **Open** 9am-5pm Mon-Fri. **Credit** AmEx, MC, V. **Map** p275 H6.
Translation and interpreting services for all major languages.

FedEx Kinko's 10 Post Office Square, at Congress Street, Downtown (1-617 482 4400, www.fedex.com). State T. **Open** 7am-11pm Mon-Fri; 9am-9pm Sat, Sun. **Map** p273 L4.
On-site computer rental, printing, Wi-Fi, copying, faxing and mailing. **Other locations** 2 Center Plaza, Downtown (1-617 973 9000); 187 Dartmouth Street, Back Bay (1-617 262 6188); 1 Mifflin Place, Cambridge (1-617 497 0125).

Regus 19th Floor, 101 Federal Street, between Franklin & Matthews Streets, Downtown (1-617 342 7000, www.regus.com). South Station T. **Open** 9am-5pm Mon-Fri. **Credit** AmEx, MC, V. **Map** p273 L5.
Meeting rooms and office space for rent.

Sir Speedy 827 Boylston Street, between Fairfield & Gloucester Streets (1-617 267 9711, www.sirspeedy.com). Copley T. **Open** 8.30am-6pm Mon-Fri; 9am-4.30pm Sat. **Credit** AmEx, MC, V. **Map** p274 G6.
Copying, printing, binding and graphic design.
Other locations throughout the city.

TransPerfect Translations 4th Floor, 420 Boylston Street, at Berkeley Street, Back Bay (1-617 523 6936, www.transperfect.com). Arlington T. **Open** 8.30am-6pm Mon-Fri. **Credit** AmEx, MC, V. **Map** p273 L4.
Translation and interpreting, plus a multilingual secretarial service.

CONSUMER

Better Business Bureau 1-508 652 4800, www.bosbbb.org.
Contact the bureau if you wish to file a complaint about a business in the north-eastern US.

Office of Consumer Affairs & Business Regulation 1-617 727 7780, www.state.ma.us/consumer.
If you have a complaint to make regarding your consumer rights, contact the OCABR. It also provides arbitration services for disputes involving home improvement contractors and car sales, and can refer you to mediation or legal services.

CUSTOMS

During your inbound flight, you will be given a customs declaration form to fill in and hand in when you land at the airport.

DIRECTORY

DIRECTORY

US Customs allows visitors to bring in $100 worth of gifts duty free (generally $800 for returning Americans), 200 cigarettes or 100 cigars and one liter of spirits.

Any amount of currency can be brought into the US, but you must fill in a form (available from the airport) for amounts over $10,000. Prescription drugs must be clearly marked; be prepared to produce a written prescription upon request.

No meat or meat products can be taken through customs, while seeds, plants and fruit are heavily restricted. For more information, call Logan Airport's **Customs & Border Protection Office** (1-617 568 1810) or visit the US Customs website (www.cbp.gov).

The UK's **HM Revenue & Customs** allows returning travelers to bring in £145 worth of goods.

DISABLED TRAVELLERS

Boston is generally well equipped for disabled travelers. Hotels must provide accessible rooms; museums and street curbs have ramps; and MBTA buses and certain subways are wheelchair-accessible. That said, it's always best to phone the venues first to double-check facilities and accessibility.

Transportation Access Passes (TAP), entitling disabled passengers to reduced fares on public transport, are available for free from the **MBTA Office for Transportation Access** in Back Bay (1-617 222 5976, www.mbta. com). Applications for passes must be completed by a licensed healthcare professional. The office also supplies a map that shows disabled access points to the T.

For information on access to more than 200 local arts and entertainment facilities contact **VSA Arts** (1-617 350 7713).

Airport Accessible Van
1-617 561 1769.
Runs a service for disabled people between the airport and the Airport T stop. Call for details.
Massachusetts Office on Disability
1-617 727 7440, 1-800 322 2020, www.mass.gov/mod.
This governmental agency provides information on rights enforcement and building access.

ELECTRICITY

The US uses 110-120V, 60-cycle AC voltage. Laptops and most travel appliances are dual voltage

and will work in the US and Europe, but it's a good idea to check with the manufacturer before you plug them in – older computers have been known to blow. Adaptors can be bought at the airport or at pharmacies.

EMBASSIES & CONSULATES

Australia *1601 Massachusetts Avenue NW, Washington, DC (1-202 797 3000, www.usa.embassy.gov.au).*
Canada *Suite 400, 3 Copley Place, at Huntington Avenue, Back Bay (1-617 247 5100, www.boston.gc.ca). Copley T.* Map p275 G6.
New Zealand *37 Observatory Circle NW, Washington, DC (1-202 328 4800, www.nzembassy.com/usa).*
Ireland *3rd Floor, 535 Boylston Street, at Clarendon Street, Back Bay (1-617 267 9330). Copley T.* Map p275 H6.
South Africa *9th Floor, 333 E 38th Street, New York (1-212 213 4880, www.south africa-newyork.net).*
UK *7th Floor, One Broadway, Cambridge (1-617 245 4500, www.britainusa.com/boston). Kendall T.*

EMERGENCIES

For all emergency services, dial **911**. The call is toll free from any payphone. For more information, see *right* **Accident & emergency**, *see p255* **Helplines** and *see p257* **Police**.

GAY & LESBIAN

For more gay and lesbian resources, as well as shops, restaurants and bars catering to the lesbian and gay community, *see pp198-204*. For HIV/AIDS information, *see p255*.

Out in Boston
www.outinboston.com.
Information on the Boston area's gay scene, plus a list of useful gay and lesbian organizations.

HEALTH

Foreign visitors should ensure they have full travel insurance, as treatment can be costly. Contact the emergency number on your insurance policy before seeking treatment, and you'll be directed to a hospital that deals directly with your insurance company.

Accident & emergency

The following hospitals have 24hr emergency rooms:
Brigham & Women's Hospital
75 Francis Street, between Huntington & Brookline Avenues, Brookline (1-617 732 5500, 1-617 732 5636, 1-800 294 9999, www.brighamandwomens.org). Brigham Circle or Longwood T.
Children's Hospital
300 Longwood Avenue, at Binney Street, Brookline (1-617 355 6000, 1-617 355 6611, www.childrens hospital.org). Longwood or Brigham Circle T.
Floating Hospital for Children
755 Washington Street, Downtown (1-617 636 5000, www.tuftsmedical center.org). Tufts Medical Center T. Map p275 J6.
Massachusetts General Hospital (MGH) *55 Fruit Street, at Cambridge Street, West End (1-617 726 2000, www.mass general.org/ed). Charles/MGH T.* Map p272 J3.
Mount Auburn Hospital
330 Mount Auburn Street, at Memorial Drive, Cambridge (1-617 492 3500, 1-800 322 6728, www.mountauburnhospital.org). Harvard T. Map p276 A2.
Tufts Medical Center
800 Washington Street, Downtown (1-617 636 5000, www.tuftsmedical center.org). Tufts Medical Center T. Map p275 J6.

Complementary medicine

Market Street Health
214 Market Street, at North Beacon Street, Brighton (1-617 787 3511, www.marketstreet health.com). Cleveland Circle T then bus 86. **Open** varies. **No credit cards.**
Market Street Health offers a wide variety of complementary medicine and holistic therapies. Services offered include acupuncture, chiropractic therapy, homeopathy, Chinese medicine, massage and psychotherapy.

New England School of Acupuncture *3rd Floor, 150 California Street, Newton (1-617 926 4271, www.nesa.edu). Kenmore T then bus 57.* 8am-8.30pm Mon; 7am-8pm Tue; 7am-8.30pm Wed; 7am-10pm Thur; 8am-6pm Fri; 7.30am-4pm Sat. **Credit** MC, V.
The oldest college of acupuncture and Oriental medicine in the country, this well-known school offers a wide array of treatments.

Contraception & abortion

Planned Parenthood Greater Boston Health Center
1055 Commonwealth Avenue, at Alcorn Street (1-617 616 1617, www.pplm.org). Babcock St T. **Open** 9am-7.15pm Mon; 7.30am-7.15pm Tue, Thur, Fri; 7.30am-3pm Wed; 7.30am-3.30pm Sat.

Dentists

Dental Referral Service
1-800 511 8663. **Open** 24hrs daily.
Massachusetts Dental Society
1-508 480-9797, 1-800 342 8747, www.massdental.org. **Open** 9am-4pm Mon-Fri.
Tufts Dental School *1 Kneeland Street, at Washington Street, South End (1-617 636 6791). Chinatown T.* **Open** *Emergency walk-in clinic* 9am-noon, 1-4pm, 4.30-7pm Mon-Fri. **Map** p275 J6.

Opticians

See p173.

Pharmacies & prescriptions

See p174.

Psychiatric emergency services

Boston Emergency Services Team *1-800-981-4357.*
This 24-hour helpline directs callers to one of several local psychiatric crisis centers.
Massachusetts General Hospital *For listings, see p254 (1-617 724 4100).* **Open** 24hrs daily.
Acute psychiatric treatment is offered by the MGH emergency room.

STDs, HIV & AIDS

AIDS Hotline *1-800 235 2331, www.aac.org.* **Open** 9am-9pm Mon-Thur; 9am-7.30pm Fri.
Advice on emotional issues, testing and insurance, as well as referrals for legal and financial advice.
Fenway Community Health *1340 Boylston Street (1-617 267 0900, 1-888 242 0900, www. fenwayhealth.org). Fenway or Kenmore T.* **Open** 8am-8pm Mon-Fri. **Map** p274 D7.
The clinic offers HIV, hepatitis and STD testing and services.

HELPLINES

Alcoholics Anonymous *1-617 426 9444, www.aaboston.org.* **Open** 9am-9pm Mon-Fri; 1-9pm Sat, Sun.

Child-at-Risk Hotline
1-800 792 5200. **Open** 24hrs daily.
Drug & Alcohol Hotline
1-800 327 5050. **Open** 24hrs daily.
Rape Crisis
1-617 492 8306, 1-800 841 8371. **Open** 24hrs daily.
Samaritans
1-617 247 0220, 1-877 870 4673, www.samaritansofboston.org. **Open** 24hrs daily.

ID

The legal drinking age of 21 is rigorously upheld, and photo ID checks are taken very seriously. Not all forms of out-of-state identification may be accepted, so it's always best to carry your passport with you.

INSURANCE

You should take out comprehensive insurance cover before traveling to the US: it's almost impossible to arrange once you are there. Make sure that you have adequate health cover, since medical expenses can be sky-high. (For a list of hospitals and clinics, *see p254* **Health.**)

INTERNET

Wi-Fi access is generally available for free at chain cafés, such as Starbucks and Au Bon Pain, and at many boutique coffeehouses in the Boston area.
The cybercafé trend never really caught on – there is only one in a central location: **Tech Superpowers CyberCafé** (252 Newbury Street, at Fairfield Street, Back Bay, 1-617 267 9716). It charges a minimum of $3 for 15 minutes, and $5 for an hour.
The main **Boston Public Library** (*see right*), at Copley Square, offers free 'express' internet access (30-minute sessions for non-members). You'll need to drop by the computer desk and make a reservation in advance.
Alternatively, you can pay to use a computer at a copy/office centre (*see p253* **Office services**) – some branches of **FedEx Kinko's** offer high-speed access.
Another option is to swing by the free internet terminals in the **Shops at Prudential Center** (*see p158*), located near the entrance to the Sheraton hotel. But be warned: there are no seats, and there's often a queue.
For a list of useful websites, with information on the city and the local area, *see p262* **Websites**.

LEFT LUGGAGE

At the time this guide went to press, no luggage storage facilities were available at Logan Airport due to FAA restrictions.

LEGAL HELP

If you run into legal trouble, contact your insurers or your embassy or consulate (*see p254*).

LIBRARIES

Boston Public Library
700 Boylston Street, at Copley Square, Back Bay (1-617 536 5400, www.bpl.org). Copley T. **Open** 9am-9pm Mon-Thur; 9am-5pm Fri, Sat; 1-5pm Sun. *Print department, rare books & manuscripts* 9am-5pm Mon-Fri. *Young adults' room* 10am-6pm Mon-Thur; 9am-5pm Fri, Sat; 1-5pm Sun. **Map** p275 G6.
The city's enormous main library.
Other locations 25 Parmenter Street, North End (1-617 227 8135); 685 Tremont Street, South End (1-617 536 8241); 151 Cambridge Street, West End (1-617 523 3957).

LOST PROPERTY

For lost credit cards, *see p257.*

Airport

Logan Airport *1-617 561 1714.*
The Massachusetts State Police also run an airport lost and found office at 2 Service Road (1-617 561 2047), across from the Airport T station.

Public transport

If you lose something on a bus or the subway, phone 1-617 222 5000 (8.30am-5pm Mon-Fri). For property lost on the Commuter Rail from North Station, phone 1-617 222 3600 (7am-11pm daily); for South Station, call 1-617 222 8120 (7.30am-4.30pm Mon-Fri).

Taxis

If you leave something in one of the city's taxis, call the police department's **Hackney Hotline** (1-617 536 8294), open 8.30am-4.30pm Mon-Fri.

MEDIA

Newspapers & magazines

Bay Windows
www.baywindows.com.

Boston's flagship gay newspaper provides exhaustive coverage of the latest gay and lesbian politicking at the State House, but saves some room for solid arts coverage as well. The paper is distributed free in stores and sidewalk dispensers across town.

Boston Globe *www.boston.com.*
The city's oldest and most popular daily newspaper generally takes a cautiously liberal line, covering local politics quite well and regaining its national stride with a growing stable of Pulitzer-winning journalists. 'G', a daily events insert, functions as a fluffy arts and entertainment guide.

Boston Herald
www.bostonherald.com.
A raucous, conservative-leaning tabloid newspaper in the style of the *New York Post*, the *Herald* has a strong following among working-class Bostonians. It has been very successful in unearthing local political scandals, and the sports coverage is extensive.

Boston Magazine
www.bostonmagazine.com.
A general-interest glossy monthly magazine with a mix of lifestyle features and pieces on city issues, catering mostly to an upmarket audience. The annual 'Best of Boston' issue and the restaurant reviews are highly regarded.

Boston Phoenix
www.bostonphoenix.com.
An irreverent free weekly, the *Boston Phoenix* takes an alternative line on the city's politics and culture. The arts section is strong, and the entertainment and events listings are the most comprehensive you'll find. You can pick a copy up at sidewalk dispensers, clubs and cafés around the city.

Community Newspaper Company *www.wickedlocal.com.*
This chain of newspapers caters to particular cities or neighborhoods; publications include the *Cambridge Chronicle* and *Brookline TAB*. Mostly focused on community issues and local arts coverage.

Stuff Boston
www.stuffboston.com.
This bi-monthly arts and lifestyle magazine is published by the owners of the *Boston Phoenix*, and can be found next to it in dispensers across town. The coverage is self-consciously hip, with a focus on fashion and food. Read it for the latest bars and clubs favored by the 'in' crowd.

Weekly Dig *www.weeklydig.com.*
Boston's popular free weekly covers local listings and news

from an indie standpoint. Its columnists have strong political stances and take great pleasure in lashing out at anyone and anything in the Boston scene – from local politicos to other newspapers and their editors (particularly the *Dig*'s older rival, the *Phoenix*). Grab a copy from dispensers around town.

Radio

WBOS *92.9 FM, www.myradio929.com.*
Expect alternative bands – anything from the Offspring to the Crash Kings.

WBUR *90.9 FM, www.wbur.org.*
A public radio station, dedicated almost completely to news and talk – including the flagship NPR (National Public Radio, the US equivalent of the BBC) programs. The nationally syndicated *Car Talk* is produced here.

WBZ-FM *98.5 FM, 985thesportshub.cbslocal.com.*
The Sports Hub, an upstart WEEI competitor with CBS backing, entered the market in 2009 as the new official flagship radio station of the Boston Bruins and the New England Patriots.

WEEI *850 AM, www.weei.com.*
A station for die-hard Red Sox and Celtics fans – just about everyone in Boston, then.

WERS *88.9 FM, www.wers.org.*
A high-quality semi-professional college radio station, run by students at Emerson College. Daily slots are dedicated to folk, rock, jazz, world music, reggae and hip hop, with lots of interviews and live performances thrown into the mix.

WGBH *89.7 FM, www.wgbh.org.*
This public radio station airs the main NPR news shows, including *Morning Edition* and *All Things Considered*, along with classical music, folk, blues and jazz.

WHRB *95.3 FM, www.whrb.org.*
Harvard University's station plays a pleasing combination of classical and jazz during the day. Punk, indie, rock and hip hop take over in the small hours.

WJMN *94.5 FM, www.jamn945.com.*
Mainstream hip hop and R&B.

WRKO *680 AM, www.wrko.com.*
Talk radio and news programs with a predominantly conservative bent.

WTKK *96.9 FM, www.969bostontalks.com.*
More talk radio with a local Boston flavor; you can expect incendiary commentary on local and national hot topics.

Television

Boston's local PBS (Public Broadcasting Service, www.pbs.org) station, **WGBH**, on channels 2 and 44, is one of the best in the country, producing acclaimed shows such as *Nova* and *Frontline*. The local affiliates of national commercial networks are:
WBZ Channel 4 (CBS).
WCVB Channel 5 (ABC).
WHDH Channel 7 (NBC).
WFXT Channel 25 (Fox).

MONEY

The US dollar ($) equals 100 cents (¢). Coins range from copper pennies (1¢) to silver nickels (5¢), dimes (10¢), quarters (25¢) and rarely seen silver dollars ($1). Paper money 'bills' come in denominations of $1, $2 (rare), $5, $10, $20, $50 and $100 – and all, confusingly, are the same size and color.

Since counterfeiting of $50 and $100 bills is a booming business, many small shops will not accept them. On the whole, it's better to restrict your paper money to smaller denominations. Tax is applied to hotels (12.45%), meals (5%) and retail purchases (5%), excluding food bought from supermarkets and clothing under $175; and for a brief period in summer, when the state has a 'tax holiday' (*see p156* **Inside Track**).

ATMs

Automated Teller Machines (ATMs) are easy to find. Most will accept American Express, MasterCard, Visa and selected international debit and cash cards. Most charge a fee. You can get directions to your nearest ATM location by calling the Visa Plus System (1-800 843 7587) or MasterCard (1-800 424 7787). If you have forgotten your PIN or have de-magnetized your card, most banks will dispense cash to cardholders with valid ID. You can also get cash back at supermarkets with a card with the Cirrus or Plus logo.

Banks & bureaux de change

Most banks are open from 9am to 5pm Monday to Friday, and some are open from 9am to noon on Saturday. If you arrive in Boston after 5pm, exchange money at the airport. If you want to cash travelers' checks at a shop, ask first if a minimum purchase is required.

You can obtain cash on a credit card account from certain banks; check with your credit card company before you leave, and be prepared to pay interest rates that vary daily. You will need some kind of photo identification, such as a passport, to cash travelers' checks or obtain cash from a credit card.

American Express Travel Services *1 State Street, Downtown (1-617 723 8400, www.americanexpress.com).* State *T.* **Open** 8.30am-5.30pm Mon-Fri. **Map** p273 L4.
Other locations 39 John F Kennedy Street, Cambridge (1-617 868 2600).

Bank of America *100 Federal Street, at Franklin Street, Downtown (1-617 434 3412, www.bankofamerica.com). Downtown Crossing or South Station T.* **Open** 8am-5.30pm Mon-Fri. **Map** p273 L5.
Other locations throughout the city.

Citizens Bank *28 State Street, at Congress Street, Downtown (1-617 725 5900, www.citizens bank.com). Government Center T.* **Open** 8.30am-5pm Mon-Thur; 8.30am-6pm Fri; 9am-noon Sat. **Map** p273 L4.
Other locations throughout the city.

OneUnited Bank *133 Federal Street, at Summer Street, Downtown (1-617 457 4400, www.oneunited.com). South Station T.* **Open** 9am-5pm Mon-Fri. **Map** p273 L5.

Travelex *Logan Airport (1-800 287 7362, www.travelex.com).* **Open** 7am-8.30pm daily.
The Travelex bureau de change is located in Terminal E of the airport.
Other locations 745 Boylston Street, Back Bay (1-617 266 7560).
Western Union *1-800 325 6000, www.westernunion.com.*

Credit cards

Less disastrous if you're robbed, and accepted almost everywhere, credit (and not debit) cards are required by almost all hotels, car rental agencies and airlines. The cards most widely accepted in the US are American Express, Discover, MasterCard and Visa. If you lose your credit card (or travelers' checks) call the appropriate number:

American Express *1-800 221 7282 cards, 1-800 221 7282 travelers' checks.*

Discover *1-800 347 2683.*
MasterCard *1-800 307 7309.*
Thomas Cook *1-800 223 7373 travelers' checks.*
Visa *1-800 336 8472, 1-800 227 6811 travelers' checks.*

OPENING HOURS

Opening hours vary depending on the type of business and time of year. **Shops** tend to open around 10am and close around 7pm, though many stay open later, especially during the tourist season. **Banks** are usually open 9am to 4pm or 5pm Monday to Friday, and some open from 10am to noon or 1pm on Saturdays. **Post offices** are usually open from 8am to 5pm Monday to Friday, and 8am to noon on Saturdays.

POLICE

For emergencies dial **911**. Otherwise, call the **Boston Police** on 1-617 343 4200. The headquarters are at 40 New Sudbury Street, Downtown, with another outpost at 650 Harrison Avenue, at East Dedham Street, South End (1-617 343 4250). For more information, visit www.cityofboston.gov/police.

POSTAL SERVICES

Post office opening hours in Boston are usually 9am to 5pm Monday to Friday, with limited hours on Saturday. Contact the **US Postal Service** (1-800 275 8777, www.usps.com) for details of your nearest branch and mailing facilities (be ready with a post code or zip code).

Stamps can be bought at any post office, as well as at many hotels, grocery stores and convenience stores. It costs 44¢ to send a one-ounce (28g) letter within the US. Each additional ounce costs 17¢. Postcards mailed within the US cost 28¢; for international postcards it's 75¢ and up depending on the destination (98¢ anywhere outside Canada or Mexico). Airmailed letters to anywhere overseas cost 98¢ for the first ounce and 84¢ for each additional ounce. Express mail costs extra and guarantees 24-hour delivery within the US, and two- to three-day delivery to international destinations with no guarantee. Call 1-800 275-8777 for more information on various deadlines.

For **couriers & shippers**, *see p253.* Also, *see p176* **Travelers' needs**.

Main Post Office *25 Dorchester Avenue, behind South Station, Downtown (1-617 654 5302). South Station T.* **Open** 6am-midnight daily.
Beacon Hill *136 Charles Street, between Cambridge & Revere Streets. Charle/MGH T.* **Open** 8am-5.30pm Mon-Fri; 8am-noon Sat.
Cambridge *Suite 1, 125 Mount Auburn Street, at Harvard Square. Harvard T.* **Open** 7.30am-6.30pm Mon-Fri; 7.30am-3pm Sat.
North End *217 Hanover Street, near Mechanic Street. Haymarket T.* **Open** 8am-6pm Mon-Fri; 8am-2pm Sat.

RELIGION

For more of the many places of worship in and around Boston, check the Yellow Pages.

Baptist

First Baptist Church of Boston *110 Commonwealth Avenue, at Clarendon Street, Back Bay (1-617 267 3148, www.first baptistchurchofboston.org). Copley T.* **Services** 11am Sun. **Map** p275 H5.

Buddhist

Cambridge Zen Center *199 Auburn Street, Cambridge (1-617 576 3229, www.cambridge zen.com). Central T.* **Daily practice** 5.45am, 6.30pm. **Map** p276 C3.

Catholic

Sacred Heart Church *49 Sixth Street, at Otis Street, Cambridge (1-617 547 0399). Harvard T then bus 69.* **Services** 9am Mon, Wed-Fri; 9am, 6pm Tue; 5pm Sat; 7.30am, 9am, 11am Sun.

St Anthony Shrine *100 Arch Street, at Summer Street, Downtown (1-617 542 6440). Downtown Crossing T.* **Services** 6am, 7am, 10am, 11.45am, 12.30pm, 1.15pm, 5.15pm Mon-Fri; 8am, 10am, noon, 4pm, 4.15pm, 5.30pm, Sat; 6am, 7am, 8am, 9am, 10am, 11am, noon, 5.30pm Sun.

Christian Science

Church of Christ, Scientist *175 Huntington Avenue, Back Bay (1-617 450 2000, www.tfccs. com). Symphony T.* **Open** 9am-5pm Mon-Fri. **Services** noon, 7.30pm Wed; 10am, 5pm Sun. **Map** p274 F8.

DIRECTORY

Episcopal

Church of the Advent
*30 Brimmer Street, West End
(1-617 523 2377, www.theadvent.
org). Charles/MGH T.* **Services**
12.15pm Mon, Tue, Thur, Fri; 6pm
Wed; 9am Sat; 8am, 9am, 11.15am
Sun. **Map** p272 H4.

Old North Church (Christ Church)
*193 Salem Street, at Hull Street,
North End (1-617 523 6676, www.
oldnorth.com). Haymarket T.*
Services 9am, 11am Sun.
Map p273 L2.
For information about the church's
history, *see p70* **Profile**.

Jewish

**Jewish Religious Information
Services** *177 Tremont Street,
at Boylston Street, Downtown
(1-617 426 2139). Boylston T.*
Open 9am-4pm Mon-Thur.
Map p272 K5.
Referrals to groups, organizations,
temples and synagogues throughout
the area, as well as advice on kosher
foods and restaurants.

Temple Israel *477 Longwood
Avenue, at Riverway, Brookline
(1-617 566 3960, www.tisrael.org).
Longwood T.* **Services** 5.45pm Fri;
9am, 10.15am Sat.

Methodist

Old West Church
*131 Cambridge Street, at Staniford
Street, Downtown (1-617 227
5088, www.oldwestchurch.org).
Government Center T.* **Services**
11am Sun. **Map** p272 K3.

Muslim

Islamic Society of Boston
*204 Prospect Street, at Broadway,
Cambridge (1-617 876 3546,
www.isboston.org). Central T.*
Services Check online for daily
prayer times. **Map** p276 C3.

Presbyterian

Church of the Covenant
*67 Newbury Street, at Berkeley
Street, Back Bay (1-617 266 7480,
www.churchofthecovenant.org).
Arlington or Copley T.* **Services**
10.30am Sun. **Map** p275 H5.

Quaker

Beacon Hill Friends House
*6 Chestnut Street, at Walnut Street,
Beacon Hill (1-617 227 9118,*

www.bhfh.org). Park St T. **Meetings**
10.30am Sun. **Map** p272 J4.
The Friends House on Beacon
Hill also has rooms for rent (in the
Quaker style) for $70-$95 per night.

SAFETY & SECURITY

Boston is one of the safest cities
in the United States. However,
as in any big city, it's wise to take
basic precautions. Don't fumble
with your map or wallet in public,
and always plan where you're going
and walk with brisk confidence.
Avoid walking alone at night, and
don't park in questionable areas of
town (if in doubt, use valet parking
when you can). Always keep your
car doors locked when parked
and while driving.
    Central Boston is generally
well lit, but pedestrians should
probably avoid Boston Common,
the Public Garden and the
walkways along the Charles River
after dark. Although the old red-
light district, the Combat Zone, is
all but gone bar a couple of clubs,
the section of Washington Street
between Avery and Stuart Streets
still has a slightly rough edge after
night falls. As on all urban mass
transit systems, don't flash your
mobile phones or other valuables
on the MBTA.

SMOKING

Smoking is banned in all indoor
public places statewide, including
bars, clubs and restaurants.
Smokers now have to congregate
out on the pavement to get their
nicotine fix, although some bars
have set up beer gardens equipped
with heaters to help them get
through Boston's brutally cold
winter months.

STUDY

As Boston has the world's
largest number of colleges and
universities per square mile,
the choices for study are plentiful.
The city is a great place to be a
student, with a huge variety of
courses and summer schools and
a jumping social scene.
    Harvard University (1-617
495 1000, www.harvard.edu) is
the oldest and most prestigious
university in America – not to
mention one of the most difficult
colleges in the world to get into.
    Other prominent institutions
include **Boston College** (1-617
552 8800); the massive **Boston
University** (1-617 353 2000,

www.bu.edu); and the renowned
**Massachusetts Institute of
Technology** (MIT; 1-617 253
1000, www.mit.edu), one of the
world's top science and technology
universities.
    Devoted to the arts and
communication, **Emerson
College** (1-617 824 8500, www.
emerson.edu) has a famously
artistic student body and an
award-winning radio station,
WERS (*see p256*).
    In Back Bay there's
Northeastern University
(1-617 373 2000, www.neu.edu),
while **Suffolk University**
(1-617 573 8000, www.suffolk.edu)
sits plum in the heart of Boston,
perched on Beacon Hill.
    North-west of the city, in nearby
Medford, is **Tufts University**
(1-617 628 5000, www.tufts.edu),
founded in 1852. The **University
of Massachusetts at Boston**
(1-617 287 5000, www.umb.edu)
is a branch of the state-wide
university system (commonly
known as UMass). Situated on
the Columbia Point peninsula in
Dorchester, it's blessed with one
of the most dramatic campus
locations in the city.

TELEPHONES
Dialing & codes

The area codes for metropolitan
Boston (including Cambridge,
Somerville and Brookline) are
617 and **857**. The first ring of
suburbs are in the 781 and 339 area
codes, considered a local call from
metropolitan Boston. The northern
suburbs and north coast are served
by 978 and 351, while the western
and southern suburbs (including
Cape Cod and the islands) use 508
and 774. Western Massachusetts
uses area code 413. These are all
long-distance calls from Boston.
    Toll-free calls generally start
with 1-800, 1-888 or 1-877, while
costly pay-per-minute calls usually
start with 1-900 or 1-976. Many
hotels add a surcharge on all calls.

Collect calls To make a collect
(reverse charge) call, dial 0 for the
operator followed by the area code
and phone number. For help, dial 0
for an operator.

Direct dial calls Calls made from
all nine area codes should be dialed
using all ten digits: area code +
seven-digit phone number – even
when calling within the area
code covers. If you are trying to

reach a Boston number from elsewhere within the US, dial 1 + area code + seven-digit number.

International calls When you're calling Boston from abroad, dial the international access code of the country from which you are calling (00 from the UK), followed by the US country code (1), the area code and the number.

To phone abroad from Boston, dial 011 followed by the country code, area code and phone number. For other countries, check the White Pages of the telephone book for a full list of country codes.

Australia 61
New Zealand 64
Republic of Ireland 353
South Africa 27
UK 44

Mobile phones

Whereas in Europe mobile phones work on the GSM network at either 900 or 1800 megahertz, the US does not have a standard mobile phone network that covers the whole country. This means that many European handsets will not work, and travelers may need to rent a handset once they arrive (*see p176* **Travelers' needs**). Check with your service provider before you travel. **AT&T Wireless** (1-888 333 6651) and **T-Mobile** (1-800 937 8997) both offer prepaid services at outlets across the city.

Operator services

Operator assistance 0
Emergency
(police, ambulance, fire) 911
Directory enquiries
1-617 555 1212.

Public phones

A local call costs 50¢; operator, directory and emergency calls are free. Public payphones only accept nickels, dimes and quarters – not ideal for long-distance calls. Pick up the receiver and check for a dial tone before parting with your money; many payphones are broken and battered, and once you put your money in, it's gone. Some phones require you to dial the number first and wait for an operator or recorded message to tell you how much change to deposit.

Phone cards are widely available, ranging in price from $5 to $50, with call costs as low as 3¢ per minute. Read the card information carefully before

buying; some have a 'connection charge'. Alternatively, you can charge calls to your MasterCard with **AT&T** (1-800 225 5288).

TIME & DATES

Massachusetts operates on **Eastern Standard Time**, which is five hours behind Greenwich Mean Time, one hour ahead of Central Time (Manitoba to Texas), two hours ahead of Mountain Time (Alberta to Arizona and New Mexico) and three hours ahead of Pacific Time (California). Daylight Saving Time is observed from the second Sunday in March to the first Sunday in November, when the clocks are put forward one hour.

In the US, dates are written in month, day and year order; so 12/5/04 is 5 December, not 12 May.

TIPPING

Tipping is a way of life in the US, as the service industry is based largely on cheap labor. Waiters and bartenders, in particular, often make little more than $2 per hour outside of tips. That's why Americans tip much more than people in other countries, spawning the myth that US residents throw their money around trying to impress people by tipping heavily.

If service isn't included in your bill, tip waiters 15 to 20 per cent and bartenders around 15 per cent. Leave a 15 to 20 per cent tip for cabbies, hairdressers and food delivery people. In hotels, it's the norm to give bellhops and baggage handlers $1-$2 per bag and to tip housekeepers around $2 a night.

TOILETS

Malls (*see p158*) are your best bet for public toilets. Central locations include the Copley Place and Prudential Center malls, and Faneuil Hall Marketplace.

TOURIST INFORMATION

Boston Common Visitor Information Center *147 Tremont Street, Downtown (1-617 426 3115, 1-888 733 2678 advance information). Park Street T.* **Open** 8.30am-5pm Mon-Fri; 10am-6pm Sat, Sun. **Map** p272 J5.
Boston National Historical Park Visitor Center *15 State Street, at Devonshire Street, Downtown (1-617 242 5642, www.nps.gov/ bost). State T.* **Open** 9am-5pm daily. **Map** p273 L4.

A useful source of information on Boston and New England; there's also a bookshop.
Cambridge Office of Tourism *4 Brattle Street, at John F Kennedy Street, Cambridge (1-617 441 2884, 1-800 862 5678, www.cambridge-usa.org). Harvard T.* **Open** 9am-5pm Mon-Fri. **Map** p276 A2.

Drop in for general enquiries on Cambridge. The office also publishes the *Cambridge Visitor Guide*, which has information on accommodation, sights and attractions as well as maps, a seasonal calendar of events and a walking tour map. The office runs the **Visitor Information Booth** in Harvard Square (open 9am-5pm Mon-Fri, 9am-4pm Sat, 9am-1pm Sun), which has a touch-screen service to help you find your way around Cambridge.
Greater Boston Convention & Visitors Bureau *Suite 105, 2 Copley Place, Back Bay (1-617 536 4100, 1-888 733 2678, www.bostonusa.com).* **Open** *Phone enquiries* 8.30am-5pm Mon-Fri.

The GBCVB provides information on attractions, restaurants, performing arts and nightlife, shopping, and travel services. The main office operates as a telephone information service, but the bureau also runs the visitor centers at Boston Common and the Prudential Center.
Massachusetts Office of Travel & Tourism *1-617 973 8500, 1-800 447 6277 recorded information, www.mass-vacation.com.* **Open** 9am-5pm Mon-Fri. **UK office** *+44 (0)20 7978 7429.* **Open** 9am-5.30pm Mon-Fri.

The Office of Travel & Tourism has a telephone information service and also publishes a free magazine, *Getaway Guide*, which includes information on attractions and lodgings, a map and a seasonal calendar of events in Massachusetts.
Prudential Center Visitor Information Center *Center Court, Prudential Center, 800 Boylston Street, Back Bay (1-617 236 3100, www.prudential center.com). Hynes or Prudential T.* **Open** 10am-9pm Mon-Sat; 11am-6pm Sun. **Map** p275 G6.
Travelers Aid Society *17 East Street, at Atlantic Avenue, Downtown (1-617 542 7286, www.travelersaid.org). South Station T.* **Open** 9am-4.30pm Mon-Fri. **Map** p273 L5.

DIRECTORY

A non-profit social service agency that has been helping travelers since 1920. These days, most of the organization's work is with homeless families, although its volunteers also provide information on Boston and will help stranded travelers (but only those with serious financial problems). **Other locations** Logan Airport, Terminal E (1-617 567 5385).

VISAS & IMMIGRATION

Under the Visa Waiver Program (VWP), citizens of 27 countries (including the UK, Ireland, Australia, New Zealand and Japan) do not need a visa for stays in the United States of less than 90 days (business or pleasure) – as long as they have a passport that is valid for six months past their expected stay in the US, and a return or onward ticket. An open standby ticket is acceptable. Canadians and Mexicans do not need visas. All other travelers must have a visa. For more information, *see below* **Passport regulations** and *see right* **Working in the US**.

Visa applications can be obtained from your nearest US embassy or consulate.

UK travelers should check the US Embassy's website at www.usembassy.org.uk, or call its helpline on 09042 450100 (£1.20 per min) for further information.

Passport regulations

All travelers who enter the US on the VWP must carry their own machine-readable passport, or MRP. All burgundy EU and EU-lookalike passports issued in the UK since 1991 (and still valid) should conform; however, check at your local passport-issuing post

office if in any doubt at all. Further information for UK citizens is available online at www.passport.gov.uk or on 0870 521 0410.

Nationals of other countries should check well in advance of their trip whether their passport meets the requirements for the time of their trip at http://travel.state.gov/visa, and also with the issuing authorities of their home country.

WEIGHTS & MEASURES

The US uses the imperial system. Here are a few basic metric equivalents.
1 foot = 0.305 meter
1 mile = 1.61 kilometer
1 square foot = 0.093 square meter
1 pound = 0.454 kilogram
1 pint (16fl oz) = 0.473 liter

WHEN TO GO

Climate

Weather-wise, the best time of year in Boston is the autumn. Temperatures are generally in the low 70s Fahrenheit (20s Celsius) (*see below* **The Local Climate**) and the skies are clear for days. Of course, this also means that the city is packed to bursting-point, prices soar, and booking a hotel room becomes difficult. It's the time when students of over 60 colleges are returning to town; many professional conventions take place, and autumn foliage sightseers arrive by the busload. In other words, it is the best of times and the worst of times to find yourself in Boston.

Summer is much quieter, Bostonians are more relaxed and it's easier to get around town. But the downside is that temperatures

can soar, with almost 100 per cent humidity. This can make sightseeing arduous and sleeping difficult. It's worth making sure your hotel has air-conditioning.

Spring is also a quieter time of year, when blossoms appear and the city is quite beautiful. But the weather can be very unpredictable, and it also tends to be rainy; bring an umbrella.

Winter is often grey, cold and dreary, which is why hotel rates drop. The city is lovely after a light dusting of snow, but there can be debilitating blizzards in January and February, during which the city comes to a standstill.

Whichever season you visit Boston, pack plenty of layers of clothing. The old saying – 'If you don't like the Boston weather, wait ten minutes' – holds true. Hat, gloves and scarf are essential in winter, and an umbrella or waterproof gear is a good idea at any time of year. Call 1-617 936 1234 for free daily weather information, or check the forecast online.

Public holidays

New Year's Day 1 Jan.
Martin Luther King Day 3rd Mon in Jan.
Presidents' Day 3rd Mon in Feb.
Memorial Day Last Mon in May.
Independence Day 4 July.
Labor Day 1st Mon in Sept.
Columbus Day 2nd Mon in Oct.
Veterans Day 11 Nov.
Thanksgiving Day Last Thur in Nov.
Christmas Day 25 Dec.

WOMEN

Boston is a safe city for women, but visitors should use common sense and avoid deserted streets at night. One nuisance is the loutish frat boys roaming the streets after the bars close. They're generally harmless, but sometimes enjoy shooting their mouths off after a dozen pints.

WORKING IN THE US

Non-nationals seeking work in the US must be sponsored by a US company and get an H-1B visa, which permits the holder to work in the US for up to six years. For the visa to be approved, your prospective employer must convince the Immigration Department that no American could do the job.

THE LOCAL CLIMATE

Average temperatures and monthly rainfall

	High (°C/°F)	Low (°C/°F)	Rainfall (mm/in)
Jan	2 / 36	-5 / 23	92 / 3.6
Feb	3 / 38	-4 / 24	86 / 3.4
Mar	7 / 45	0 / 32	98 / 3.9
Apr	14 / 57	5 / 41	92 / 3.6
May	20 / 67	10 / 50	82 / 3.2
June	25 / 77	15 / 59	80 / 3.1
July	28 / 82	18 / 65	80 / 3.1
Aug	27 / 80	18 / 64	91 / 3.6
Sept	22 / 72	14 / 57	81 / 3.2
Oct	17 / 63	8 / 47	84 / 3.3
Nov	11 / 52	4 / 39	99 / 3.9
Dec	4 / 40	-3 / 27	93 / 3.7

Further Reference

BOOKS

Fiction

Nathan Aldyne
Canary; Cobalt; Slate; Vermilion
Four tongue-in-cheek mystery
novels set in the gay communities
of Boston and Provincetown, c.1980.
Margaret Atwood
The Handmaid's Tale
Dystopian, post-nuclear fallout
set in Cambridge.
Edward Bellamy
Looking Backward: 2000-1887
A socialist Rip Van Winkle tale
that inspired a number of utopian
communities – one of the most
popular books of its day.
Nathaniel Hawthorne
*The Scarlet Letter; The House
of the Seven Gables*
Two classics by the Salem native.
Henry James *The Bostonians*
James's tale of a Boston feminist.
Stephen King *Cell*
Old-school, Boston-set zombie romp.
Henry Wadsworth Longfellow
*The Works of Henry
Wadsworth Longfellow*
Includes the famous poem
'Paul Revere's Ride'.
Robert Lowell *Life Studies;
For the Union Dead*
The poet's account of growing up
privileged in Boston – and hating it.
Norman Mailer
Tough Guys Don't Dance
Boston's ultimate cynic tells
another hard-edged tale.
Robert McCloskey
Make Way for Ducklings
The classic children's tale about
ducks in the Boston Public Garden.
Michael Patrick McDonald
All Souls
A bittersweet story of growing
up in South Boston's Irish ghetto.
Herman Melville *Moby-Dick*
The great American novel.
Melville's 19th-century search
for the great white whale.
Henry David Thoreau *Walden*
Thoreau's most famous work,
written while living in isolation
in a cabin for two years, two
months and two days.
John Updike *Roger's Version*
The writer's updated take on *The
Scarlet Letter*.
Dennis Lehane *Shutter Island*
A psychological thriller set on a
fictitious Boston Harbor island.

Non-fiction

Jack Beatty *The Rascal King:
The Life and Times of James
Michael Curley, 1874-1958*
Thoroughly researched biography
of the charismatic Boston mayor.
David Hackett Fischer
Paul Revere's Ride
Fine account of the legendary ride,
related as a historical narrative.
Noel Riley Fitch *Appetite for
Life: The Biography of Julia Child*
All about America's favourite TV
chef and Boston icon.
Barney Frank *Improper
Bostonians: Lesbian and Gay History
from the Puritans to Playland*
Comprehensive history of
homosexuality in Boston.
Sebastian Junger
A Death in Belmont
The author of *The Perfect Storm*
turns his attention closer to home
to explore whether a murder in the
1960s was by the Boston Strangler.
Doris Kearns Goodwin
*The Fitzgeralds and the Kennedys:
An American Saga*
America's answer to royalty.
J Anthony Lukas *Common
Ground: A Turbulent Decade in the
Lives of Three American Families*
The 1970s busing crisis, seen
through the eyes of an Irish-
American, a black and a white
middle-class family.
Dan McNichol & Andy Ryan
The Big Dig
The turbulent story of the biggest
highway project in US history.
Robert S Morse *25 Mountain
Bike Tours in Massachusetts:
From the Connecticut River
to the Atlantic Coast*
Guidelines and trips.
Douglass Shand-Tucci
*The Art of Scandal: The Life and
Times of Isabella Stewart Gardner*
Biography of Boston's famous
patron of the arts.
Dan Shaughnessy
The Curse of the Bambino
Entertaining look at the Red Sox
'curse' by local sports journo.

FILM

The Boondock Saints (1999)
A silly crime thriller with a cult
following about two brothers from
Southie who become vigilantes after
killing members of the Russian mob.

The Brink's Job (1978)
William Friedkin's film about the
infamous bank heist of 1950 (*see
p72* **Boston Illegal**).
A Civil Action (1998)
John Travolta stars in the real-life
tale of a town that was poisoned by
a chemical company, sued and lost.
The Crucible (1996)
Film version of the Pulitzer Prize-
winning play about the Salem
Witch Trials, with Winona Ryder.
The Departed (2006)
Adapted from the hong Kong thriller
Internal Affairs (Triad mole vs
undercover cop), Scorsese's Oscar
winner moves the action to South
Boston with Jack Nicholson,
Leonardo DiCaprio and Matt Damon.
Edge of Darkness (2010)
Mel Gibson is a cop investigating
the murder of his daughter in this
adaptation of a BBC TV series.
**The Friends of Eddie
Coyle** (1973)
A Robert Mitchum vehicle about
snitching and organized crime,
often touted by locals as the best
Boston movie ever.
Gone Baby Gone (2007)
Ben Affleck's foray into directing,
based on a Dennis Lehane story.
Good Will Hunting (1997)
Academy Award-winning film by
and about South Boston residents.
Filmed on location all over town,
particularly in Southie and
Cambridge, around MIT.
Legally Blonde (2001)
Bubbly West Coast blonde sets out
to win her blue-blooded fraternity
crush by attending Harvard Law
School – though the film wasn't
actually shot in Cambridge.
Love Story (1970)
Ali MacGraw and Ryan O'Neal star
in the classic weepie set in Harvard.
Mona Lisa Smile (2003)
Chick flick based on Wellesley
College's campus in the 1950s,
starring Julia Roberts.
Mystic River (2003)
Clint Eastwood directs this serious
drama starring Sean Penn – check
out his take on the Boston accent.
Next Stop Wonderland (1997)
Wonderful, low-budget romantic
comedy with nods toward Boston's
immigrant communities.
No Cure for Cancer (1992)
Concert film with local comedian
Denis Leary, who both typifies and
spoofs Boston's angry young Irish.

DIRECTORY

Prozac Nation (2008)
Christina Ricci acts out Elizabeth Wurtzel's famous novel about being stressed and depressed at Harvard.
The Thomas Crown Affair (1968)
Steve McQueen and Faye Dunaway star in the Boston-set original, about pulling off the perfect crime.
The Town (2010)
This Ben Affleck crime thriller focuses on Charlestown, alleged to be the US bank robbery capital.
21 (2008)
A highly stylized account of card counting in Las Vegas by MIT students (see p87 **Boston Illegal**).

MUSIC

Aerosmith *Toys in the Attic* (1975)
Essential album by the '70s rock band before they quit doing drugs.
Boston *Boston* (1976)
The city's namesake band had one of the best-selling albums of all time.
Buffalo Tom
Let Me Come Over (1992)
A seminal alternative rock band, one of the best of the era.
The Cars *Greatest Hits* (1978)
Popular new wave band from the late 1970s, fronted by Ric Ocasek.
The Dresden Dolls
The Dresden Dolls (2004)
Boston-based duo combining punk beats with Weimar-era cabaret style.
Dropkick Murphys
Do or Die (1998)

Irish-American working class punk anthems to shout along to.
Galaxie 500 *On Fire* (1989)
Second album from Dean Wareham's early band of Harvard peers, considered their defining moment.
Tom Lehrer *The Remains of Tom Lehrer* (2000)
Box set of snarky satire from Harvard University.
The Lemonheads *Car, Button, Cloth* (1996)
Funny, sad, wonderful songs by this quirky rock band, led by Boston-born singer Evan Dando.
Mighty Mighty Bosstones *More Noise & Other Disturbances* (1992)
Just watch the video for 'Where'd You Go?' and you'll know all you need to know about Boston.
Mission of Burma *Signals, Calls and Marches* (1981)
The album that made a name for Boston's indie godfathers.
Morphine *Cure for Pain* (1993)
The quirky Boston rock band with no guitar that was fronted by the late Mark Sandman.
Pernice Brothers *Overcome by Happiness* (1998)
Joe Pernice's first album with his brother Bob, featuring 'exquisitely sad' song 'Chicken Wire'.
Pixies *Doolittle* (1989)
Boston's own: on classics such as 'Monkey Gone to Heaven' these guys (and one girl) had it all – the rock, the quirks and the hooks.

Jonathan Richman & the Modern Lovers
Modern Lovers (1988)
Influential Boston-based proto-punk garage rock band.

WEBSITES

For the best of Boston's music-loving blogging community, see p211 **Sites & Sounds**. In addition, see p255 **Media** and see p259 **Tourist Information**.

www.boston.com
The website of the *Boston Globe*, the city's daily broadsheet.
www.bostonphoenix.com
This local weekly paper's site is great for what's happening, where.
www.bostonusa.com
The tourist office's site is packed with information about the city.
www.cityofboston.gov
The city's official website, with a section for visitors.
www.mass.gov
Includes extensive information about outdoor activities, culture and events.
www.mbta.com
Transport maps, bus schedules, ticket information and interactive route planners.
www.universalhub.com
Local website regurgitating blog comments and chiming in on mainstream media's inadequacies.

BOSTONIAN ACCENT & GLOSSARY

When a Boston native tells you to 'pahk the cah ovah by Hahvahd Yahd', you may wonder where all the r's have got to. They're not gone, they've just relocated – ask someone if they grew up in Southie, and they may well answer 'Yeah, I did.'

The Boston accent, so often mangled by Hollywood, sports a pedigree that goes back four centuries. Boston's first settlers, mostly Puritans from East Anglia, brought with them the slighted 'r' of 'yahd' and the broad 'a' of 'bahthroom.' Later waves of immigrants, particularly the Irish in the 19th century, infused the dialect with their own linguistic quirks. Today, the accent may be fading downtown, but thrives in Boston's older neighborhoods and the inner suburbs.

'Bawstin' English is renowned as one of the most difficult American accents for outsiders to understand. Add in some unique regional slang, a whacking number of place names with inscrutable pronunciation, and a tendency among locals to do the neat trick of mumbling while talking at top speed, and you may feel you've stumbled across a foreign language. Have no fear – a little practice and you'll be well on your way to comprehension. Just knowing how to pronounce 'Woburn' will set you apart from the garden-variety tourist.

Here's a brief guide to some of the odd place names, pronunciations and colloquialisms you'll hear about town:
Bang a U-y Make a U-turn
Big Dig The most expensive highway project in US history
Comm Ave Commonwealth Avenue
Frappe A milkshake – pronounced 'frap'
Hang a louey Take a left
Jimmies Chocolate sprinkles on top of ice-cream
JP Jamaica Plain
Khakhis What you use to unlock the 'cah' (car)
Mass Ave Massachusetts Avenue
Mem Drive Memorial Drive
Packie A liquor store (short for package store)
Quincy Pronounced 'Quinzy'
Shattered Very, very drunk
Southie South Boston
Spa Convenience store that sells food
The Pats The New England Patriots
The Pike The Massachusetts Turnpike
The Pit The centre of Harvard Square
The Pru The Prudential Tower
The Sox Boston's beloved baseball team, the Red Sox
Tonic Old Boston word for soft drink
Woburn Pronounced 'Woobuhn'

DIRECTORY

Content Index

INDEX

INDEX

Venue Index

INDEX

Advertisers' Index

Please refer to the relevant pages for contact details.

INDEX

Maps

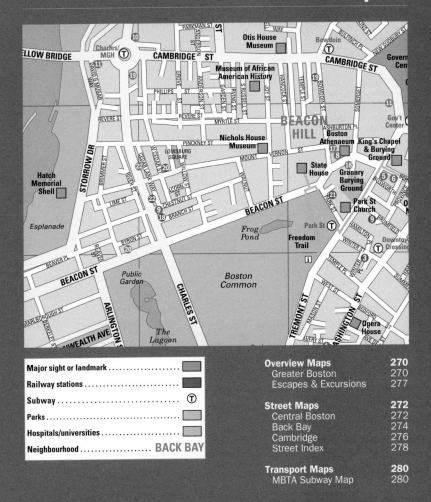

Major sight or landmark . . . .

Railway stations . . . .

Subway . . . . Ⓣ

Parks . . . .

Hospitals/universities . . . .

Neighbourhood . . . . **BACK BAY**

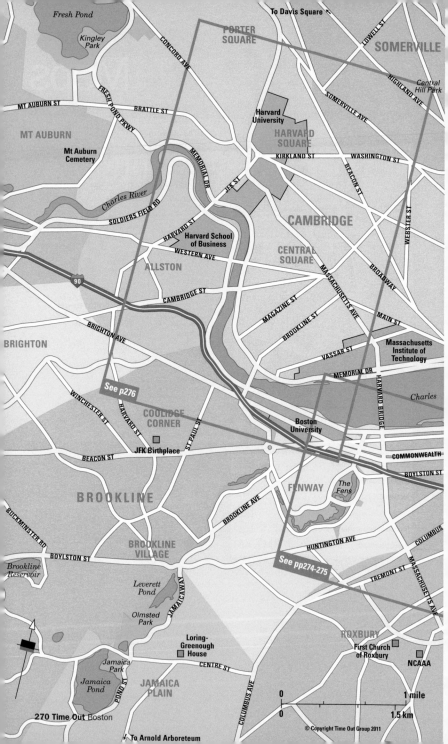

Fresh Pond

Kingley Park

To Davis Square

PORTER SQUARE

SOMERVILLE

LOWELL ST

HIGHLAND AVE

Central Hill Park

MT AUBURN ST

FRESH POND PKWY

BRATTLE ST

CONCORD AVE

Harvard University

SOMERVILLE AVE

MT AUBURN

Mt Auburn Cemetery

MEMORIAL DR

HARVARD SQUARE

KIRKLAND ST

WASHINGTON ST

BEACON ST

WEBSTER ST

Charles River

SOLDIERS FIELD RD

JFK ST

CAMBRIDGE

HARVARD ST

Harvard School of Business

WESTERN AVE

CENTRAL SQUARE

BROADWAY

ALLSTON

MASSACHUSETTS AVE

MAIN ST

90

CAMBRIDGE ST

MAGAZINE ST

BROOKLINE ST

Massachusetts Institute of Technology

BRIGHTON

BRIGHTON AVE

VASSAR ST

MEMORIAL DR

HARVARD BRIDGE

Charles

See p276

WINCHESTER ST

HARVARD ST

COOLIDGE CORNER

ST PAUL'S ST

Boston University

COMMONWEALTH

BEACON ST

JFK Birthplace

BOYLSTON ST

BROOKLINE

FENWAY

The Fens

See pp274-275

BROOKLINE AVE

HUNTINGTON AVE

COLUMBUS

Buckminster Rd

BOYLSTON ST

BROOKLINE VILLAGE

TREMONT ST

MASSACHUSETTS AVE

Brookline Reservoir

Leverett Pond

JAMAICAWAY

Olmsted Park

ROXBURY

Loring-Greenough House

First Church of Roxbury

NCAAA

Jamaica Park

CENTRE ST

COLUMBUS AVE

Jamaica Pond

POND ST

JAMAICA PLAIN

0   1 mile

0   1.5 km

270 Time Out Boston

To Arnold Arboreteum

© Copyright Time Out Group 2011

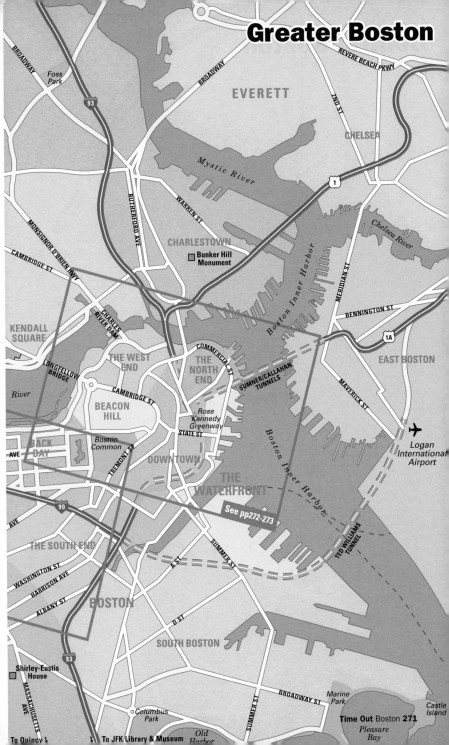

Greater Boston

BROADWAY

Foss Park

93

EVERETT

BROADWAY

REVERE BEACH PKWY

2ND ST

CHELSEA

Mystic River

1

Chelsea River

WARREN ST

CHARLESTOWN

Bunker Hill
Monument

MONSIGNOR O'BRIEN HWY

RUTHERFORD AVE

CAMBRIDGE ST

Boston Inner Harbor

MERIDIAN ST

BENNINGTON ST

1A

KENDALL
SQUARE

CHARLES
RIVER DAM

THE WEST
END

COMMERCIAL ST

EAST BOSTON

LONGFELLOW
BRIDGE

THE
NORTH
END

SUMNER/CALLAHAN
TUNNELS

MAVERICK ST

River

CAMBRIDGE ST

BEACON
HILL

Rose
Kennedy
Greenway

Logan
International
Airport

Boston
Common

STATE ST

AVE

BACK
BAY

TREMONT ST

DOWNTOWN

Boston Inner Harbor

THE
WATERFRONT

90

See pp272-273

TED WILLIAMS TUNNEL

THE SOUTH END

A ST

SUMMER ST

WASHINGTON ST

HARRISON AVE

ALBANY ST

BOSTON

D ST

AVE

93

SOUTH BOSTON

Shirley-Eustis
House

MASSACHUSETTS AVE

BROADWAY ST

Marine
Park

Castle
Island

Columbus
Park

SUMMER ST

Pleasure
Bay

To Quincy

To JFK Library & Museum

Old
Harbor

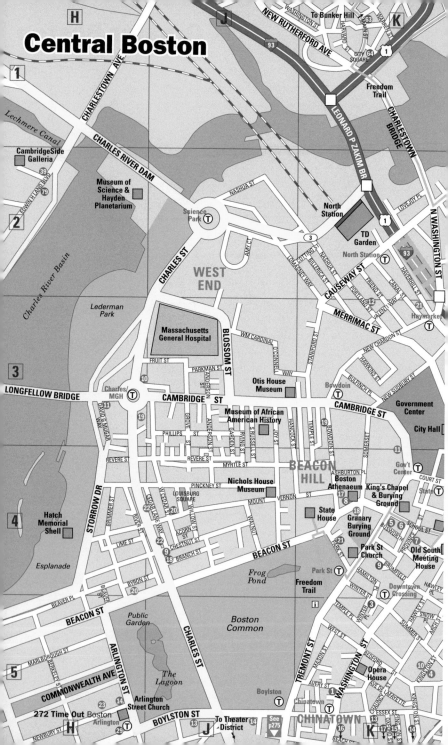

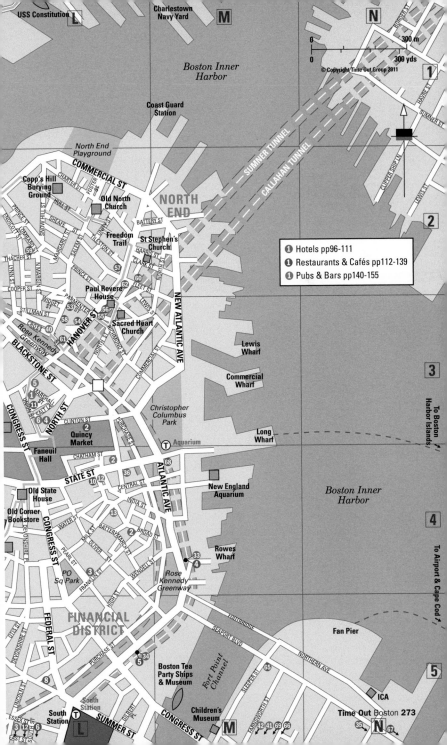

USS Constitution **L**

Charlestown Navy Yard **M**

N

Boston Inner Harbor

Coast Guard Station

0 — 300 m
0 — 300 yds
© Copyright Time Out Group 2011

1

SUMNER ST

CLIPPER SHIP LN

HAVRE ST

LEWIS ST

North End Playground

COMMERCIAL ST

CHARTER ST

FOSTER ST

HULL ST

Copp's Hill Burying Ground

Old North Church

SHEAFE ST

SALEM ST

TILLSTON ST

PRINCE ST

Freedom Trail

BATTERY ST

St Stephen's Church

NORTH END

SUMNER TUNNEL

CALLAHAN TUNNEL

2

ENDICOTT ST

COOPER ST

THACHER ST

LYNN ST

N MARGIN ST

STILLMAN ST

WIDGET ST

HANOVER ST

PARMENTER ST

HARRIS ST

CLARK ST

FLEET ST

NORTH ST

Harris ST

57
60
62
56 57
59
55
54
58

Paul Revere House

Sacred Heart Church

Rose Kennedy Greenway

CROSS ST

BLACKSTONE ST

40

NEW ATLANTIC AVE

❶ Hotels pp96-111
❶ Restaurants & Cafés pp112-139
❶ Pubs & Bars pp140-155

Lewis Wharf

Commercial Wharf

3

To Boston Harbor Islands

CONGRESS ST

NORTH ST

MARSHALL ST

UNION ST

5
1
6
2

CLINTON ST

Quincy Market

Faneuil Hall

CHATHAM ST

PURCHASE ST

Christopher Columbus Park

T Aquarium

Long Wharf

STATE ST

Old State House

Old Corner Bookstore

DEVONSHIRE ST

CONGRESS ST

2
36
10 12

CENTRAL ST

INDIA ST

13

ATLANTIC AVE

68

New England Aquarium

Boston Inner Harbor

4

WATER ST

MILK ST

BATTERYMARCH ST

OLIVER ST

BROAD ST

2
2

PEARL ST

PO Sq Park

3

FRANKLIN ST

HIGH ST

WENDELL ST

Rowes Wharf

33
4

Rose Kennedy Greenway

OTIS ST

DEVONSHIRE ST

FINANCIAL DISTRICT

8

FEDERAL ST

PURCHASE ST

5 34

NORTHERN AVE

SEAPORT BLVD

EVELYN MOAKLEY BRIDGE

Fan Pier

5

To Airport & Cape Cod

LINCOLN ST

ESSEX ST

South Station

T SUMNER ST **L**

GILBERT PL

Boston Tea Party Ships & Museum

Fort Point Channel

CONGRESS ST

Children's Museum **M**

FARNSWORTH ST

SLEEPER ST

65

42 41 69 66

ICA

35

N

67

3 12 1 6
EAST ST

Time Out Boston 273

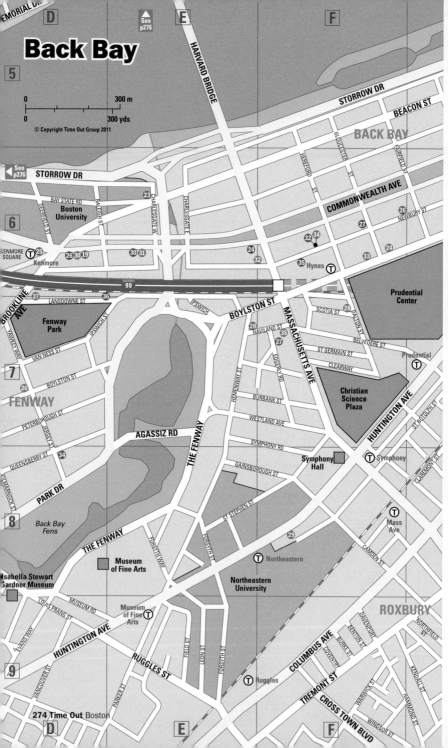

Back Bay

0   300 m
0   300 yds

D   **E**   **F**

See
p276

See
p276

STORROW DR

STORROW DR

BEACON ST

BACK BAY

COMMONWEALTH AVE

NEWBURY ST

Boston
University

BAY STATE RD

HARVARD BRIDGE

CHARLESGATE W

CHARLESGATE E

GLOUCESTER ST

HEREFORD ST

FAIRFIELD ST

KENMORE
SQUARE

Kenmore

LANSDOWNE ST

Hynes

Prudential
Center

BROOKLINE AVE

Fenway
Park

IPSWICH ST

VAN NESS ST

BOYLSTON ST

TAWNEY WAY

BOYLSTON ST

MASSACHUSETTS AVE

SCOTIA ST

DALTON ST

BELVEDERE ST

Prudential

FENWAY

PETERBOROUGH ST

JERSEY ST

HAVILAND ST

HEMENWAY ST

EDGERLY RD

ST GERMAIN ST

CLEARWAY

HUNTINGTON AVE

ST BOTOLPH ST

QUEENSBERRY ST

BURBANK ST

WESTLAND AVE

Christian
Science
Plaza

AGASSIZ RD

THE FENWAY

SYMPHONY RD

GAINSBOROUGH ST

Symphony
Hall

Symphony

CLAREMONT ST

PARK DR

Back Bay
Fens

TREMONTANCK ST

THE FENWAY

FORSYTH WAY

ST STEPHEN ST

Mass
Ave

Isabella Stewart
Gardner Museum

Museum
of Fine Arts

FORSYTH ST

Northeastern

Northeastern
University

ROXBURY

LOUIS PRANG ST

MUSEUM RD

Museum
of Fine
Arts

COLUMBUS AVE

DAVENPORT

BENTON S

BURKE S

NORTHFIELD

EVANS WAY

HUNTINGTON AVE

HEMENWAY ST

FORSYTH ST

COVENTRY

KENDALL ST

VANCOUVER ST

RUGGLES ST

PARKER ST

Ruggles

TREMONT ST

WARWICK ST

CROSS TOWN BLVD

WINDSOR ST

HAMMOND ST

D   **E**   **F**

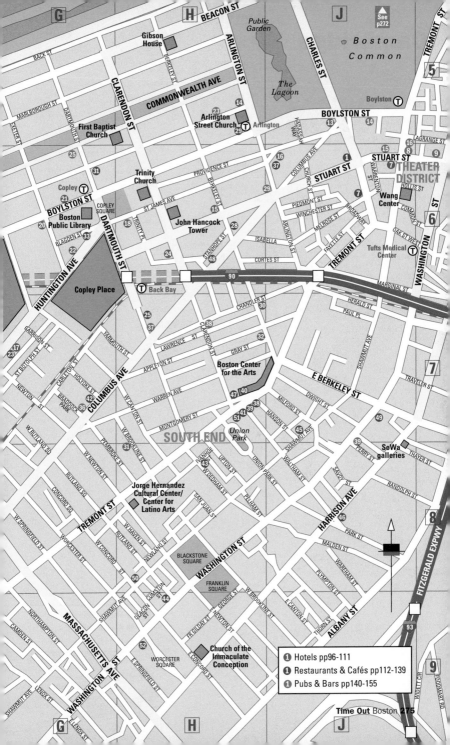

G **H** BEACON ST *Public Garden* **J** ▲ See p272

Boston Common

BACK ST

Gibson House

COMMONWEALTH AVE

The Lagoon

Boylston **T**

BOYLSTON ST

MARLBOROUGH ST

Arlington Street Church ②③ ①④
②⑨ Arlington **T** Arlington

⑬ ①④ ①⑥ LAGRANGE ST
⑧ ⑨

First Baptist Church

STUART ST
①⑤ ⑧ ⑨

②⑤ ①⑥ ⑦ **THEATER DISTRICT**

Copley **T** ③① Trinity Church ②⑨ ⑦

Wang Center

BOYLSTON ST
②①
Boston Public Library
②⓪ ③③ ①⑧

John Hancock Tower ②⑧

Tufts Medical Center **T**

②② ⑤

②⑥ ④⑧

Copley Place

T Back Bay

90

TREMONT ST

MARGINAL ST

CHANDLER ST
③⓪

HERALD ST
PAUL PL

②⑤
③⑦ ③⑧

LAWRENCE ST GRAY ST ③②

Boston Center for the Arts

E BERKELEY ST

TRAVELER S

④⑦ ④⓪

⑤① ④① ③⑨ ③⑧

SOUTHEND *Union Park* ④⑨

Jorge Hernández Cultural Center/ Center for Latino Arts

④⑤

③⑨ SoWa galleries

④③

COLUMBUS AVE

TREMONT ST

HARRISON AVE

⑧

BLACKSTONE SQUARE

④⑥

PARK ST

FITZGERALD EXPWY

⑤⓪

FRANKLIN SQUARE

93

MASSACHUSETTS AVE

⑤② ④④

WASHINGTON ST

ALBANY ST

Church of the Immaculate Conception

❶ Hotels pp96-111
❶ Restaurants & Cafés pp112-139
❶ Pubs & Bars pp140-155

G **H** **J** 9

Time Out Boston **275**

Cambridge

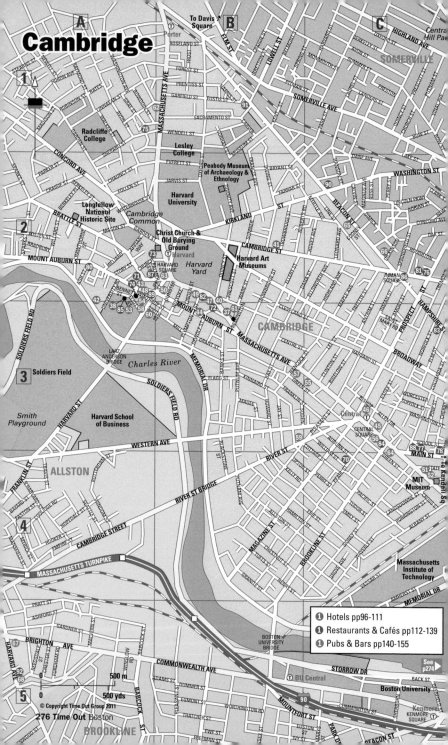

A
Porter ⊤
To Davis Square ⊤

B

C
HIGHLAND AVE
Central Hill Park

OXFORD ST

SOMERVILLE

WASHINGTON ST

1
STEARNS ST
HURON AVE
BATES
ROBINSON ST
CONCORD AVE
ROSELAND ST
FOREST ST
PRENTISS ST
GARFIELD ST
SACRAMENTO ST
WENDELL ST
MASSACHUSETTS AVE
62
75
Radcliffe College
Lesley College
Peabody Museum of Archaeology & Ethnology
Harvard University
BERKELEY ST
LOWELL ST
MONMOUTH ST
AVON ST
SUMMER ST
PITMAN ST
LANDERS ST
SOMERVILLE AVE
91
EUSTIS ST
BRYANT ST
DANE AVE
90
BEACON ST
LINCOLN PKWY
ADRIAN ST
CONCORD AVE

2
FOSTER ST
BRATTLE ST
BRADBURY
MOUNT AUBURN ST
PARKER ST
CRAIGIE ST
BERKELEY ST
HILLIARD ST
CHAUNCY ST
WILLARD ST
SPARKS ST
FAYERWEATHER ST
REED ST
CONCORD AVE
Longfellow National Historic Site
Cambridge Common
Christ Church & Old Burying Ground
WATERHOUSE ST
GARDEN ST
MASON ST
APPIAN WAY
FOLLEN ST
EVERETT ST
JARVIS ST
KIRKLAND
⊤ Harvard
73
80
71 74 43
97 63
Harvard Square
41
Harvard Art Museums
CAMBRIDGE ST
OAK ST
65
66
81 76
86
INMAN SQUARE
HAMPSHIRE ST
83

3
SOLDIERS FIELD RD
Soldiers Field
Smith Playground
HARVARD ST
42
38
85 53
58
60
Harvard Yard
82 47
49
40
72 37 61
44
MOUNT AUBURN ST
MASSACHUSETTS AVE
CLEVELAND ST
SAINT MARY RD
HARVARD ST
PROSPECT ST
BROADWAY
CAMBRIDGE
CENTRE ST
BIGELOW ST
LARZ ANDERSON BRIDGE
Charles River
SOLDIERS FIELD RD
MILL
GRANT ST
MEMORIAL DR
FLAGG ST
MAGEE
KINNAIRD
FRANKLIN ST
PLEASANT ST
AUBURN ST
57
35
GREEN ST
55
BISHOP
⊤ Central
46
45
CENTRAL SQUARE
56
84
WORCESTER ST
SUFFOLK ST
WASHINGTON ST
SCHOOL ST
MAIN ST
78

4
FRANKLIN ST
HARVARD ST
EASTON ST
HOOKER ST
EMPIRE
ALLSTON
Harvard School of Business
WESTERN AVE
CAMBRIDGE STREET
RIVER ST BRIDGE
RIVER ST
FRANKLIN ST
UPTON ST
PERRY ST
KELLY RD
PACIFIC ST
SIDNEY ST
HAMILTON ST
ERIE ST
MAGAZINE ST
BROOKLINE ST
TUFTS ST
CHESTNUT ST
HENRY ST
GRANITE ST
ALLSTON ST
EMILY ST
WAVERLY ST
TUDOR ST
PILGRIM ST
PUTNAM AVE
59
70
64
51
52
KENDALL ST
MIT Museum
STATE ST
MAIN ST

5
HARVARD AVE
67
92
68
BRIGHTON
AVE
PRATT ST
ASHFORD ST
GARDNER ST
CHESTER ST
BRAINERD RD
COMMONWEALTH AVE
ADAMS ST
DUMMER ST
EGMONT ST
THATCHER ST
BARBOCK ST
MASSACHUSETTS TURNPIKE
CAMBRIDGE ST
VASSAR ST
AMHERST ST
MEMORIAL DR
Massachusetts Institute of Technology
LANDSDOWNE ST
FORDINGTON ST
ALBANY ST
SOUDRON ST
PORTLAND ST
BOSTON UNIVERSITY BRIDGE
MOUNTFORT ST
STORROW DR
BACK ST
Boston University
90
BU Central ⊤
CUMMINGTON ST
BLANDFORD ST
⊤ Kenmore
KENMORE SQUARE

WESTERN AVE

0   500 m
0   500 yds

© Copyright Time Out Group 2011

276 Time Out Boston

BROOKLINE
EWE ST
FREEMAN ST
PARK ST
BEACON ST

❶ Hotels pp96-111
❶ Restaurants & Cafés pp112-139
❶ Pubs & Bars pp140-155

See ►
p274

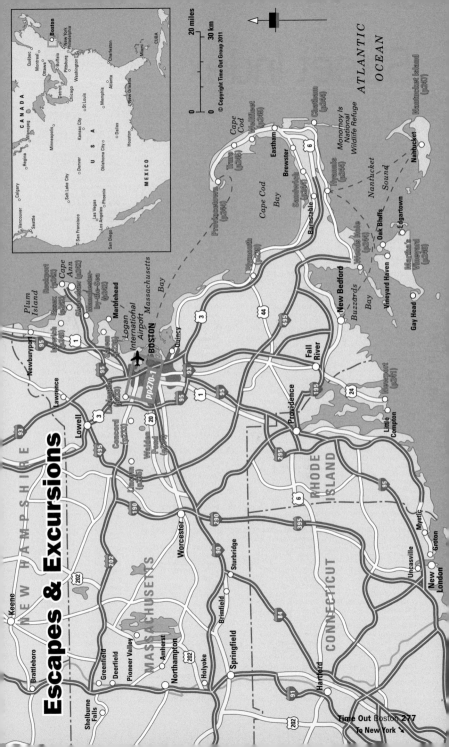

Escapes & Excursions

Street Index

STREET INDEX

MBTA Subway & Commuter Rail Map

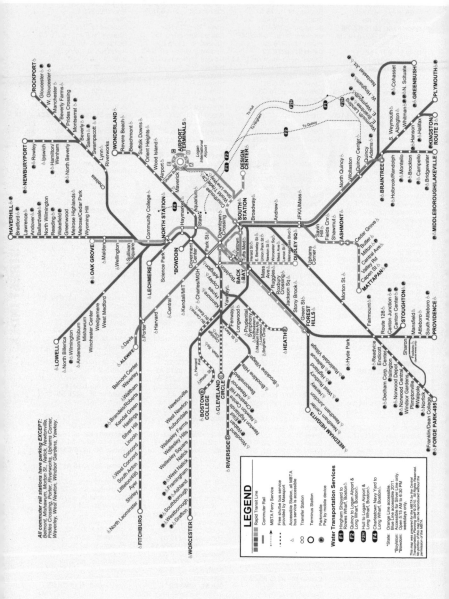